THE BUTTERFLY THIEF

Walter Marsh is a journalist and editor based in Tarntanya/Adelaide, and the author of *Young Rupert: the making of the Murdoch empire* (Scribe 2023). A former staff writer and editor at *The Adelaide Review* and *Rip It Up*, his writing has also appeared in *The Guardian*, *The Monthly*, *The Saturday Paper*, *Crikey*, *The Age*, and *InDaily*.

THE BUTTERFLY THIEF

Adventure, Fraud, Scotland Yard, and Australia's Greatest Museum Heist

Walter Marsh

SCRIBE

Melbourne | London | Minneapolis

A note for Aboriginal and Torres Strait Islander readers: this book contains the names of people who have passed away, along with references to colonial violence, historic museum practices, and outdated language.

Scribe Publications
18–20 Edward St, Brunswick, Victoria 3056, Australia
2 John St, Clerkenwell, London, WC1N 2ES, United Kingdom
3754 Pleasant Ave, Suite 223w, Minneapolis, Minnesota 55409, USA

Published by Scribe 2025

Typeset in 11/15 pt Minion Pro by the publishers

Cover images: portrait: *The Timaru Herald*/Aoraki Heritage Collection; butterfly: *Ornithoptera priamus poseidon*/The Trustees of the Natural History Museum, London/CC by 4.0

Printed and bound in the UK by CPI Group (UK) Ltd, Croydon CR0 4YY

Scribe is committed to the sustainable use of natural resources and the use of paper products made responsibly from those resources.

978 1 761381 47 8 (Australian edition)
978 1 964992 20 4 (US edition)
978 1 761386 36 7 (ebook)

Catalogue records for this book are available from the National Library of Australia and the British Library.

scribepublications.com.au
scribepublications.co.uk
scribepublications.com.com

Cherish the tender place in your nature which feels a pang when you pick up the little corpse, so happy two minutes ago. And when you have killed enough, stop.

Beware also of the snare which lurks under the intoxicating pleasure of collecting, and set a watch upon yourself lest you degenerate into a collector and cease to be a naturalist.

– A E Aitken, *A Naturalist on the Prowl*, 1905

CONTENTS

PROLOGUE

The Fake

The butterfly was already dead when the old man found it, lying in the snow 5,200 feet above sea level.[1] It didn't have a name then, as he bent down and scooped its lifeless body up from the ice — a tiny John Doe, light as a feather, barely visible to an untrained eye. But this encounter in the spring of 1922 wasn't his first brush with the short life cycle of an insect. It wasn't his first time on Barrington Tops either, a volcanic plateau perched high up in the Great Dividing Range of New South Wales. The man's name was Johnny Hopson, but to many he was known as the 'Father of the Tops' — this weathered fifty-five-year-old with a salt-and-pepper goatee knew every ridge, gulley, and track of the 'Land of the Mist' intimately from a lifetime corralling his family's cattle and planting orchards of oranges, apples, and pears down on the tablelands.[2]

It was no secret that the Tops were good butterfly country; if you picked your moment right, the mountain air would be thick with them, gathering at dusk in cloud-like clusters ripe for someone like Hopson to catch hundreds at a time with a sweep of their net, or simply pluck them from a bush with their fingers.[3] Or, in this case, a cold snap or unexpected snowfall might leave the white ground littered with delicate corpses, waiting in plain sight for a keen-eyed collector.[4] The butterflies were just the start of its riches, and once word began to spread of this 'Nature's Wonderland', those collectors swarmed like moths to a flame.

Hopson was there to guide the first scientific expedition in 1915, and then the successive waves of genteel academics, wet-eared university students, and avid amateurs who trudged up its misty slopes with their nets, killing jars, and ill-advised city shoes that fell apart on the rough, swampy terrain.[5]

In December 1921, Hopson rode up alongside Alec Burns, a blue-eyed boy from Melbourne who posed for a horseback happy snap along the way with Hopson and three other collectors. Burns was back again in January 1922, this time with the famous Athol Waterhouse, a seasoned entomologist from the Australian Museum with deep-set eyes, a brushy moustache, and a kindly manner. Waterhouse had literally written the book on Australian butterflies, and Hopson was always fascinated to hear how his own on-the-ground knowledge stacked up against the book-learning of the city scientists. They loved this 'salt-of-the-earth' philosopher in return, who would lead them up the mountain in his horse and cart, showing them new spots or reappearing at just the right moment to salvage an expedition's spirits and stomachs with a cartload of fruit, pies, and even fresh boots just as they began to resort to eating parrots, eels, and wombats.[6] After the 1922 trip, Waterhouse returned from the Tops so thrilled that he resolved to name one of his latest finds after Hopson.

Sometimes Hopson collected evidence, like a half-buried stone axe-head, that suggested this wasn't his land at all. That Barrington Tops had a deeper history before the scientists, before the colonial explorers and surveyors, the logging parties, the cattle rustlers, and the outlaw bushrangers lying low in the highlands. That, for countless generations, this was a place of sanctuary and ceremony for the Gringai people and their neighbours, where the butterflies and birds offered a way to read the seasons and to find water and sweet nectar.[7] That was before the settlers arrived with a new trick they pioneered called 'The Harmony', a nice word for the brutal practice of leaving arsenic-laced damper by campsites. Along with stories of a clifftop massacre — a flash of red coats, the sound of bugles — it gave the lowlands a reputation among survivors as a 'valley of death'.[8] On one expedition, Hopson reflected that, '[On] every trip he had a crank or two in the party; there was the butterfly crank, and the native relic crank.'[9]

Then, one day in June 1928, Johnny Hopson himself keeled over dead at the age of sixty. The story of his butterfly, however, didn't end there. Most of the 3,000-odd insects he'd collected were bequeathed to the Australian Museum in Sydney, but that little fellow from the snowfield had already passed into the hands and collection of Athol Waterhouse.[10] Finishing the work of other collectors, whether they were living or dead, friend or stranger, was nothing new for Waterhouse. He would never forget the days he spent with Hopson — 'the delight in the invigorating atmosphere, the wonder at the country passed through, the teeming insect life of the Tops and the enrichment of my collection', he once reflected — but he got down to business with clear eyes and an encyclopaedic knowledge of Australian lepidoptera.[11]

He soon set about identifying the body, and while lesser entomologists might mistake it for another variety of the silky hairstreak, *Pseudalmenus chlorinda*, found in the highlands of Tasmania, Victoria, and New South Wales, Waterhouse knew better. As he looked closer at its wings, he saw bright-red markings on the silky white underside, markings that told him this was something different, something new. Years earlier, another collector had found something similar near Hanging Rock, on the lands of the Wurundjeri, Dja Dja Wurrung and Taungurung peoples. But those specimens were lost, and on another trip to Barrington Tops in 1925 even Waterhouse found this rare breed eluded him. Hopson's butterfly would become a 'holotype', the first specimen of a species or subspecies to be documented by science, to be held for posterity as an essential reference point for future study.

Later generations of entomologists would give it a much cooler nickname — the flame hairstreak — but in 1928 Waterhouse dubbed it *Pseudalmenus chlorinda barringtonensis,* keeping to the Latin naming conventions dreamed up by the legendary Swedish naturalist Carl Linnaeus nearly two centuries earlier. It's an old joke among scientists that this long tradition dated back to the Garden of Eden; that when God presented Adam with 'all the wild animals and all the birds of the air' and tasked him with naming them, he created not only the first man, but the first taxonomist.[12] Of course, by the 20th century, the Book of Genesis had been thoroughly displaced by Charles Darwin's *The Origin of Species*, but Linnaeus retained a messianic status, the father of modern taxonomy whose apostles had spread their mission across the nations of Europe and their growing colonial empires, bestowing Latin names on everything that moved. As president of the Linnean Society of New South Wales, Waterhouse was himself an avid disciple—as a boy, his schoolyard nickname had been 'Aqua', for the Latin translation of his surname, *aqua domus*.[13]

It wasn't for lack of affection that Waterhouse didn't name *P. barringtonensis* after its collector—by the time of his death, Hopson already had several insects named after him, including a silvery sedge-skipper that Waterhouse himself dubbed *Hesperilla crypsargyra hopsoni* in 1927.[14] So, almost by default, Hopson's butterfly became the namesake of the fifth Viscount Barrington of Ardglas and Limerick, an obscure English aristocrat with the most tangential connection to this ancient, faraway continent, but whose name would remain on Australian maps long after the last viscount died without an heir.

Within just a few years of its naming, *P. barringtonensis* and the other 50,000 butterflies gathered over the course of Waterhouse's long life would join the rest of Hopson's collection in a new home. After a perfect storm of personal tragedy and professional crisis gave Waterhouse a new perspective on his own limited lifespan, he began a long and painstaking process of donating his collection to the Australian Museum, where he served as president and honorary entomologist. Stowed away among its seemingly endless drawers and cabinets, Australia's first and oldest museum offered a haven where *P. barringtonensis* would be preserved and protected long after Waterhouse followed Johnny Hopson and his butterflies off the mortal coil. At least, that was the plan.

One day in 2016, an email pinged into the inbox of Dr Michael F Braby with an unexpected attachment. It's a strange quirk of modern life that of the many thousands of emails a person will receive each year, most of us are resigned to the fact that a decent chunk of them will contain spam and scams. Some of them are obvious, arriving with dramatic tales of faraway princes and lost fortunes. Others are bait for the greedy, or prey on our fears. But this email had come from a reputable, familiar source—a collections manager at the Australian Museum, which since Waterhouse's day had grown into a leviathan of colonial sandstone and modern glass and concrete looking out over Sydney's Hyde Park and the skyscrapers beyond it.

Attached to the email was a photograph of a butterfly. Not just any butterfly: this was supposed to be the holotype of *Pseudalmenus chlorinda barringtonensis*, the same one that Hopson had retrieved from the snow over ninety years earlier. Like the millions of other dead birds, mammals, fish, and invertebrates in the museum's stores, it had a call number and a little label with an old, handwritten note, '30 Oct 1922'.

This wasn't the first time that Braby had encountered Waterhouse's handiwork; the cheerful, bearded entomologist is an associate professor at the Australian National University, a Fulbright scholar, and a researcher with over one hundred peer-reviewed articles bearing his name who has spent decades picking up the trail of his predecessors.

'You kind of wish you'd met these people,' Braby told me in 2024. '[Waterhouse] published over about a forty-five-year period from 1897, so I have all these papers, and I've read nearly all of them.'[15]

Often, this work is in service of the important but outwardly opaque process of taxonomic revision. Like Waterhouse before him, researchers such as Braby do the detective work of spotting the tiny differences between species and subspecies of the animal kingdom. Being able to tell whether two seemingly similar populations are siblings, or distant cousins, can hold the secret to migration patterns, reveal histories of divergent evolution and changes in the environment, and offer a glimpse of the future. A case of mistaken identity could mean these changes might go unnoticed—as a retired herpetologist once told me in dead seriousness, 'Bad taxonomy *kills*.'

'Nature is very complex, but the scientific process is to try and break that down and give some order to all that chaos, and names are a way of doing that,' Braby explained. 'It's a universal language that all scientists use around the world, whereas a common name can vary between regions, between places.'

Where the naturalists of Carl Linnaeus's era used the naked eye, and then candle-lit microscopes, to understand the chaos, present-day entomologists such as Braby can use genetic sequencing, or cutting-edge scanners that first smother the specimen in an atom-thick coating of pure gold, to spot differences that even Waterhouse himself might have missed. Sometimes, the number of hairs on an insect's hind-leg could make all the difference — a literal case of splitting hairs.

'First thing, you work through the science, and then you work out the names, and underpinning those names are the type specimens,' Braby explained. 'You should always look at types in museums.'[16]

Since Waterhouse's time, butterflies have come to play a key role in environmental research — they are known as 'flagships', the proverbial canaries in the coalmine whose fluctuations help shed light on a bigger, often unseen picture.[17]

'Insects generally have a bad reputation,' Braby said. 'The ones that come to attention are often the ones that cause human health issues, crop loss, economic and biosecurity issues. There are some champions, some *really good* ones, but from a conservation perspective, the insects always miss out. They don't really hit the radar.'

Butterflies, on the other hand, are colourful and conspicuous, and, thanks to generations of collectors and scientists, have been almost comprehensively named and studied. For Braby, *Pseudalmenus chlorinda* and its six variants were of 'high conservation interest' — it was a species with a deep evolutionary history, whose reliance on old-growth ecosystems and a precise combination of food and host plants made it particularly vulnerable to rapid environmental upheaval.[18] The Australian continent had seen plenty of upheaval since 1922, but when Braby opened up the image file, it sent him down a rabbit hole.

The photograph showed a butterfly pinned into place, with four black-brown wings and a creamy underbelly with streaks of black and orange. To the naked eye, this might have all seemed normal; but as Braby zoomed in on his computer screen, he grew increasingly puzzled. The label was correct, but there was something off about the markings. Waterhouse had noted that *P. barringtonensis* was the brightest and largest of its cousins, with distinctive orange-red bands on its dorsal hindwings and forewings that set it apart from the rest of *P. chlorinda* — the markings that put the 'flame' in 'flame hairstreak'. But to Braby, it seemed that those tell-tale streaks had been set out, not by millions of years of evolution and adaptation, but by a very thin paintbrush.

'I realised that there was something wrong with the specimen,' Braby said, with a tone of surprise that hadn't dimmed in the years since his discovery.[19] 'It'd been touched up. I'd never come across that before.'

Museum collections are curious, complicated things, and, like many people, I can't help but be drawn to them. In between jobs at struggling magazines that make up the bulk of my résumé, I've put my history degree to work in a variety of them over the years, from old colonial manors to venerable state institutions. In many cases, the grand halls and galleries full of school groups and tourists are just the public face of a deep network of locked storerooms and underground bunkers teeming with shelves and crates and jars and drawers. There are doors bearing intriguing titles such as 'spirits room', industrial freezers and humidity-controlled chambers, and kilometres of archival records in wheel-mounted stacks, navigable via huge digital databases, or, just as often, enormous old logbooks whose leather binding is gradually turning to dust.

In the final scene of *Raiders of the Lost Ark*, we watch as the Ark of the Covenant, rescued from Nazis by the gallant archaeologist Indiana Jones, is nailed into a wooden crate and filed away in a cavernous warehouse full of similar, mysteriously nondescript boxes. Real museums aren't so different, with thousands if not millions of objects and creatures hidden away where most members of the public will never see them, kept under lock and key, and floating in formalin — its signature scent hits you like a wall as soon as you cross the threshold, like you're walking into a sepia-tinted photograph.

Many of their contents are already extinct, some are well on their way, and others are relics that, despite Indiana Jones's opinion, perhaps never belonged in a museum to begin with. Under the post-Enlightenment tradition of museology that emerged in the 18th and 19th centuries, collection managers and researchers work to preserve and expand these collections for posterity, with the lofty goal of increasing humanity's knowledge and understanding of the planet.

'Collections are on a different trajectory to human life,' Braby explained. 'Human life might be seventy or eighty years, but a collection will last *hundreds* and *hundreds* of years — so you have to take a very long-term view.'

Ken Walker, a tall and affable entomologist at Melbourne Museum, once put it poignantly: 'I call them "postcards to the past",' he told me.[20] I first met Walker a few months after first speaking to Braby, on a research trip to Melbourne where I'd spent long days poring over documents in a sterile white corner of the modern museum's archive, watched over by a cardboard cut-out of a Roman legionary from a past exhibition. One afternoon, a friendly archivist whisked me halfway across the building to meet Walker, who took me behind a heavy locked door to see the collections he has studied and looked after for decades.

Walker was right; to glimpse rows of insects that have been in a museum collection for over 140 years offers a unique perspective of time and history. Some overseas collections house specimens that were collected from the moment of first contact between British naturalists on the HMS *Endeavour* and the southern continent now called Australia. Safe in their little drawers, they are silent witnesses that have outlasted empires and survived wars and air raids.

'They give us an insight into a world that is no longer here,' Walker told me. 'Many of our collections allow us to travel to countries that we are no longer permitted to travel to, or to habitats that are no longer extant.'

In the light of those histories, researchers today work in conversation with the past, present, and future all at once. The collector can't predict how a researcher in one hundred years' time might use what they've found, or even what tools or technology they'll have to do it with. So it's vital that each generation undertake their work with a light touch, preserving the integrity of the collection even if they don't fully know what use it will serve. In some cases, Braby has used collections from the 19th century to study species whose survival is now threatened.

'Because we had collections going back over one hundred years, we could actually work out where the species occurred in the 1800s,' he said. 'You think, "Golly, well, it's pretty different now—the area's been cleared, so those populations are no longer extant." But because we have historical records, that actually gives us a window into the past.

'They really underpin our knowledge of biodiversity—they are the foundations, the pillars, if you like. So once you start compromising that ... yeah, it's not good.'

At first, Braby assumed that the original *P. barringtonensis* specimen had been accidentally lost or compromised by some other researcher before him. Perhaps, in a moment of panic, they had dolled up and swapped in a substitute to placate their guilt.

'It does happen; specimens get destroyed, get damaged, and they might have just said, "I'll just get another one and we'll just make it look like *barringtonensis* by painting it,"' Braby explained.

But the scientific community had, over the decades, developed protocols for just this type of situation. Holotypes were so important that under Article 75 of the International Code of Zoological Nomenclature, provisions exist for the worst-case scenario of an original being destroyed or lost. In that instance, a back-up specimen of the same species—a 'paratype'—might be promoted to the rank of 'neotype'. But it wouldn't happen without a paper trail, and it certainly wouldn't carry the same old label as the lost holotype.

'There's a very formal process of how you replace a holotype,' Braby said. 'But it can't be done lightly.'

Clearly, this knock-off told a different story. He had emailed the Australian Museum within minutes of noticing the painted streaks, and the museum workers who had taken the photograph were flabbergasted. The broader issue of theft from zoos, galleries, and museums is not entirely unheard of, of course. In 2003, Independent Commission Against Corruption officers raided a house in regional New South Wales to find a menagerie of stuffed animals, including several lions, a gorilla, and a baby giraffe. In 2011, a promising young flautist faced court accused of having robbed priceless birds of paradise from a branch of the British Natural History Museum in Tring, a small market town in Hertfordshire. In 2023, a curator at the British Museum in London was sacked after a European collector noticed a series of ancient Roman cameos and coins listed on eBay.

Countermeasures are employed — locations are kept secret, alarms installed, staff movements logged — yet, time and again, the task of maintaining control over such enormous collections has proved practically Sisyphean. But the fake holotype that Dr Braby was sent in 2016 hinted at something entirely unique: more elaborate and under the radar than a smashed glass cabinet, and cannier than an inside job — this implied stealth, attention to detail, and a deep understanding of the world of entomology. And, it must be said, a certain artistic flair.

Braby didn't know it at the time, but Hopson's original specimen was still out there somewhere, hiding under a different label, a different collector's name, and a different origin story, along with a small piece of yellow paper. These yellow labels appear on thousands of specimen pins across Australia's biggest museum collections, as a last-ditch measure that had been dreamed up by a group of entomologists in post-war Australia who gathered in the aftermath of a scandal — a scandal they knew could threaten the integrity of all the precious data bundled up in those tidy rows of pinned wings, thoraxes, and antennae. These yellow labels would outlive them all to offer a warning to future researchers — people such as Braby — of the enormous mess they'd been forced to reckon with. The warning declared that these specimens had passed through a 'Theft Collection' bearing the name of another collector — someone that Athol Waterhouse had once considered a friend.

Like most Australian entomologists who learned their trade in the second half of the 20th century, Braby had heard talk of a case seventy years earlier that had rocked the world of science — and that might have accounted for the painted imposter. I'm no scientist, but while I was briefly working at the South Australian Museum, it took all of two days for a colleague to tell me the same story, with the dangerous suggestion that there might be a book in it.

In April 2024, in the depths of the Melbourne Museum, Walker showed me one of those yellow labels for the first time. It was a postcard to a very specific point in the past, and in the months that followed I would see hundreds more of them in specimen drawers around the country, their little yellow corners peeking out from underneath butterflies of every size and colour imaginable. These yellow tabs told the story of a case that plagued Australia's oldest and most respected natural-history museums, and saw scientists and police around the world join forces in a desperate effort to rescue thousands of dead butterflies and bring their abductor to justice. Braby hadn't just stumbled on a case of a single fake holotype that had gone apparently unnoticed for decades — it was a long-lost clue to one of the largest, most systematic, and baffling thefts in the records of natural history. This was the story of the butterfly thief.

PART I

So beauty lures the full-grown child,
With hue as bright, and wing as wild;
A chase of idle hopes and fears,
Begun in folly, closed in tears.

– Lord Byron, *The Giaour*

CHAPTER ONE

The Flight

On Tuesday 18 November 1975, Aviateca flight TG-AGA took off from Flores Santa International Airport, swooping up over the blue-green waters of Lago de Petén Itzá and into what airline officials would later concede to be *'al mal tiempo y poca visibilidad'* — bad weather and poor visibility.[1] The wet season had outstayed its welcome, with heavy rain and floods across the district, but even on a clear day, a seat-rattling, jaw clenching ride was not out of character for Guatemala's national carrier. The recent history of Guatemalan aviation had been riddled with accidents: combusting engines, emergency landings, wreckages strewn across hillsides, and groups of American tourists and history buffs who never returned from the moss-covered Mayan ruins on their bucket list. It was enough for one American journalist, in a travel column published in the *Chicago Tribune* just one week later, to quip that shortly after take-off, 'you wonder when the plane's one and only steward is going to pass out the parachutes'.[2]

Flight TG-AGA was bound for a small airstrip near the Mayan city of Uaxactún, an overgrown metropolis of weather-worn ziggurats, carved hieroglyphs, and ancient observatories that in centuries past had been a rival to its southern neighbour, Tikal. It had lain hidden for over 1,000 years until May 1916, when an American archaeologist from the Carnegie Institution for Science named Sylvanus Griswold Morley broke its 'majestic solitude' with the help of local *chicleros* — the hardened men who ventured into the jungle to tap liquid latex from sapodilla trees.[3] The short-statured, moustached Pennsylvanian barely survived the trip, set upon by Guatemalan troops who mistook his expedition for a band of left-wing rebels, and opened fire on them.[4]

By a stroke of luck, Morley made it back to British-controlled Honduras alive, but excavations at Uaxactún wouldn't begin until after the war — Morley was too busy moonlighting as a spy for the United States Office of Naval Intelligence, controversially using his archaeology as cover to study German movements from the Caratasca Lagoon to the bays of the Yucatán peninsula. By the 1970s, however, Uaxactún remained a more obscure, challenging destination than the tourist magnet of Tikal.

Aviateca TG-AGA would never reach the lost city, and while few details of the crash ever became public, it soon emerged that the plane came to ruin in densely jungled mountains a few kilometres outside El Caoba. It was a remote and inaccessible spot, with no roads and limited infrastructure, but as authorities worked to reach the crash site, an examination of the flight manifest revealed one passenger who stood out from the other Guatemalan locals on board: a Canadian citizen, a long way from home.

The man was no stranger to perilous flights to faraway outposts. He had caught dozens, perhaps even hundreds, of them over the course of his life, often in planes no different from the old pre-war Douglas DC-3s that airlines such as Aviateca still kept in the air. There had been the descent into the jungle of New Guinea, crowded into a Douglas C-47 with dozens of American and Australian army and airforce men, the air growing stuffier and sweatier as the engines roared and the treetops rushed up to meet them.[5] Twenty years later, in an isolated settlement in Canada's far north-west, he had visions of crashing into the water sealed into a metal coffin as he prepared to fly out in the only seat available: a small cavity in the float of a seaplane.[6] It was a bumpy ride, with one hand gripped tightly around a loop of string that held the hatch shut, and the other holding a paperback thriller that he read by a single slit of light.

The striped fuselage and silver hull of TG-AGA was badly burned by the time rescuers reached it. So were most of its passengers, and with their passports destroyed in the fire the only way to identify the Canadian was by the signet ring he wore on his finger — an old family crest of a proud lion and three bull heads.[7] When the Associated Press first broke the news to English-speaking outlets, there were few details to hand: just that fifteen of the twenty-two passengers had died, with seven survivors taken to Guatemala City hospital in a critical condition. Of the dozen newspapers around the world that ran a version of the report, just a handful from Florida to Saskatchewan included the small detail about the older man with Canadian citizenship.[8] Most of the specifics were lost in translation — the man's age, the spelling of his surname — but those who had kept an eye on the annals of 20th-century mountaineering and natural history might have recognised the name 'Colin Wiatt', still blazing a trail of adventure and discovery when most of his peers were settling into retirement.

But this was not out of character for a man who had lived a larger life than most. A man who had made headlines in nearly every territory he set foot in, rubbed shoulders with European royals, and bunkered down in Inuit igloos and Sámi huts above the Arctic Circle. Someone who didn't need a plane ticket to feel the rush of flight — he had spent his youth performing gravity-defying aerial feats that broke records and stunned onlookers. Some might have considered him a dilettante, a fraud, a thief, but even his harshest critics had to concede that he was excellent company — and had impeccable style. Of course, the brief, economic wording of the Associated Press report reflected none of this. In fact, it only raised more questions: by the time it went to print, the airline still hadn't clarified one important detail. It remained to be seen whether the Canadian 'Colin Wiatt' was among the survivors or the dead.[9]

CHAPTER TWO

The Fluke

When Dick Pescott later fronted members of the Australian press, he would describe the events of Monday 13 January 1947 as a 'merest fluke'.[1] It was an embarrassing admission for any director of a state museum to make, and for weeks he had been dreading the inevitable moment some reporter caught wind of the story unfolding beneath the National Museum of Victoria. The truth was, Pescott liked order — he liked it so much that museum staff would later swap stories about the tape measure he carried to make sure the men on his team had good, sensible haircuts.[2] The forty-two-year-old stood over six feet tall, with broad shoulders, long ears, and his own immaculately combed black hair greying at the temples — perhaps a little greyer since the day he took charge of the museum in late 1944, when Australia and much of the world was still embroiled in war. But even in those wearying years of chaos and deprivation, leaving things to chance was not part of the job description.

From the outside, the National Museum of Victoria didn't look like a typical crime scene. Entering from Swanston Street, the cascading stone steps and giant Corinthian columns brought a self-conscious echo of the Athenian Parthenon to this urban Australian streetscape. Set against the newsstands, the office workers, and the distant rattle of tramlines, it was the kind of architectural shorthand that told the visitor one thing:

this is a temple of knowledge and culture, home to not only the state's museum, but its public library and art gallery too. But although mid-century Melbourne was a long way from the marble ruins of Ancient Greece, behind the classical facade it too was already crumbling. Shortly after Pescott's appointment, he was troubled to learn that pieces of plaster and metal had started to come loose from the ceiling into the main zoological hall, just missing the displays and visitors. He fired off a memo, noting with understandable alarm that 'One of the metal pieces (forwarded herewith) is quite capable, in my opinion, of inflicting very serious injuries.'[3]

Visitors to the museum would usually slip in via the less grandiose back entrance on Russell Street, where between the falling debris they were met by 2,500 pairs of glass eyes staring petrified from fake mountains crowded with stuffed fur, feathers, horns, and hides from every corner of the globe. Standing tall, and somewhat incongruously over the articulated dolphin skeletons and moth-eaten lions of the main zoological hall was a twelve-metre–tall totem pole carved out of red cedar by the Haida people of Skidegate village in the Queen Charlotte Islands of British Columbia — a towering reminder of how the lines between natural science, colonisation, and human culture often became blurred in a Western museum.

Years earlier, a famous taxidermist from the Californian Academy of Science had likened the museum, and many of its Australian contemporaries, to a 'morgue'; outdated and overcrowded, full of 'blank showcases and [an] over-abundance of skeletons'.[4] He saw little educational value in any of it, with the exception of the zoological hall's biggest drawcard: the enormous body of Phar Lap, which had been the world's most famous racehorse right up until he was mysteriously poisoned in the middle of a triumphant tour of North America in 1932. After his unsolved death, Phar Lap's muscular, arsenic-laced frame had been mounted with state-of-the-art precision by the Californian's peers in New York, before being placed on display in Melbourne. Here, the dead champion became a macabre expression of a uniquely Australian sort of national pride — the horse had been born in New Zealand.

Equine murder mysteries aside, the subject of Pescott's attention on

13 January lay beneath the zoological hall, in a part of the museum that an ordinary visitor might never know existed. The Californian may have compared the ground floor to a morgue, but the opinion among staff of the museum's lower levels was hardly any sunnier; past a sign that read 'strictly no admittance', through a heavy iron door and down a narrow set of stairs, lay a damp, dark labyrinth of a basement that generations of museum workers knew simply as 'the dungeons'.[5]

If upstairs felt bleak, in the dungeons one could barely move for all the storeboxes and wooden cabinets. Behind the door designated 'Entomologist's Room' sat row upon row of them, in a space so tight that only one person at a time could comfortably work inside — any visitors had to sit cross-legged on the floor. Some cabinets were near-new, the varnish still gleaming, while others were more scuffed and well travelled, crafted an ocean away for an 18th-century French aristocrat; according to museum lore, Count Francis de la Porte Castelnau had commissioned a group of African labourers to house his insect collection, and it was generally agreed they did an admirable job despite never having laid eyes on glass-topped entomological cases.

Fixing the sad state of the entomologist's room quickly joined Pescott's growing to-do list: he noted after his first visit that, '[the] whole room is dull and dingy, and unattractive to workers'.[6] He ordered a fresh coat of paint for its dirty walls and dark ceiling as an urgent priority, but paint couldn't work miracles — it was said that if you left a piece of white paper on the single workbench overnight, by morning it would be covered in a 'grey ghost' of dust.

It was far more colourful inside the cabinets. Each one contained dozens of shallow specimen drawers, just deep enough to house thousands upon thousands of shimmering butterflies, dull little moths, and de la Porte Castelnau's prized range of hulking green beetles the size and colour of a Granny Smith apple.[7] Some, like the *Morpho* genus of butterfly from South America, were so famous for their metallic-blue colours that in bygone decades their wings would be sliced up and embedded into ladies' brooches, the light shifting and refracting with every swish and twirl.

For some collectors, it was all about the spectacle. In museum circles, men such as de la Porte Castelnau were often dismissed as 'stamp collectors', driven to collect by aesthetics, vanity, or obsession — their endgame was less about advancing scientific knowledge than assembling a dazzling *Wunderkammer* they could smugly show off at dinner parties. The era of imperial expansion that de la Porte Castelnau lived through was also a boom time for wealthy stamp collectors, and natural history museums around the world were full of their prized collections. But as long as they kept accurate labels, that was fine — their 'stamps' were still a valuable dataset that museum entomologists could put to work once acquired via generous bequest, or in a fire sale by a cash-strapped estate.

But of all the cabinets in the entomologist's room, it was the Lyell Collection that had become its new crowning glory. The reclusive George Lyell was no stamp collector, and although he had grown more reserved in recent years, his name and reputation was almost legendary. Up in the zoological hall, Pescott and his staff had been showcasing a snapshot of Lyell's butterflies and moths sixty cases at a time. These cases were a small taste of its 51,000 specimens — an entomological motherlode so vast that this exhibit was just one leg in a long 'relay' race that had been running since 1 April 1946.[8] The museum had planned to rotate thirty cases of the butterflies every few weeks, but even at this ambitious turnover rate it would take decades to show the entire collection. When the first cases went on display in April, Pescott circulated a folksy origin story to Melbourne's newspaper editors:

> In 1888, a young Victorian lad, George Lyell, collected his first butterfly at Albert Park, Victoria. He then set out to collect butterflies and moths seriously, and to amass the most comprehensive collection of Australian butterflies and moths ever known.[9]

Pescott would soon receive more publicity than he ever could have wanted. In the half-century since the 'lad' George Lyell had caught his first butterfly, a caper white that he fatefully brought into the museum for identification, he had indeed built an enormous collection, spanning 6,166 species and 534 types.[10] Its closest rival was that of Athol Waterhouse's — who wasn't a rival at all, but one of Lyell's oldest friends and closest collaborators, going back half a century.

In many ways, collections such as Lyell's and Waterhouse's represented the end goal of the museum's well-established community of amateur collectors and weekend scientists — an army reserve of eccentric men and a handful of women who were accommodated, encouraged, and given extraordinary access in the hope that they might one day donate their collections. As Pescott would later reflect, such instances were 'proof that a little encouragement to boyish enthusiasm may eventually prove of great value to science'.[11] But while few disputed the value of the Lyell Collection, it seemed no one truly imagined it could be the target of a daring heist. By the afternoon of 13 January 1947, this would prove painfully naive.

By 8.45 am, Alec Burns had arrived at Russell Street, ready to begin his first official day of work in the new year.[12] The eager young collector who had once ventured up to Barrington Tops with Johnny Hopson and Athol Waterhouse was now a forty-seven-year-old scientist with a doughy face and thinning hair. Burns had taken over as the museum's curator of entomology shortly after Pescott's arrival, and although initially only a temporary posting — he had just completed a stint in the security section of Australia's wartime intelligence corps — it represented a kind of homecoming. He had made regular visits to Russell Street as a boy, but unlike many other children who would race through the museum's halls, pressing their fingers and faces upon every glass surface within reach, the young Alec Burns arrived bearing specimens of his own. The boy's collection, which he had caught while exploring the forests and creeks of his neighbourhood, prompted Frank Spry, the museum's first entomologist, to remark that the 'youngster has the makings of a good naturalist', and soon Spry was bringing him along on field trips into the Dandenong Ranges.[13]

Burns was still in his teens when Spry saw him elected to the Field Naturalists Club of Victoria — a long-running fraternity of amateur and professional scientists with close ties to the museum that went back decades — and by the time he arrived back at Russell Street in 1944,

Burns had been all around the world, with stints at the British Natural History Museum and the Royal Botanic Gardens in Kew.[14] For nearly two centuries, these imperial strongholds of science had sought to collect and categorise the entire natural world, and for any serious naturalist they represented an essential place of pilgrimage.[15]

The National Museum of Victoria didn't open to the public until midday on Mondays, and in these quiet hours the first thing on Burns's agenda was the Lyell Collection, now well overdue for its latest rotation. No one had touched the Lyell drawers, either up in the zoological hall or down below, in weeks. Burns had last checked in on them in late November before dashing off for a two-week collecting trip to New South Wales; now, with the help of an attendant named Bill Newcombe, he set to work preparing a new cross-section of the collection to run back upstairs.[16] The pair went down to the dungeons and slid out a drawer containing a suite of birdwing butterflies of the *Troides* genus that they planned to bring out for the next leg of the Lyell relay.[17]

But straightaway something seemed amiss — there appeared to be three empty spaces in the tray. At first, this wasn't any cause for alarm; when the Lyell Collection was incorporated into the museum's existing collections, care had been taken to leave empty spaces for future additions.[18] Burns asked Newcombe if he noticed anything out of place. When Newcombe said he was unsure, they began pulling out drawer after drawer, finding gap after gap until they came to the bright-blue *Papilio ulysses,* one of the biggest and most famous breeds of butterfly in the region. This would settle the matter beyond doubt; Burns and Newcombe both knew that the drawer had been full of large, handsome specimens, each as big as the palm of their hand — its electric-blue wings fringed with black.

Instead, Burns and Newcombe saw two big, butterfly-sized gaps in an otherwise packed tray of tessellating wings, legs, and thoraxes.[19] Now with a growing sense of urgency, they continued to check cabinet after cabinet until much of the cramped little room had been upturned. As far as Burns could see, the scale of missing specimens couldn't be an accident; he was certain that someone had deliberately and precisely removed hundreds of specimens. What started as a few gaps in a drawer, discovered by chance, was fast snowballing into what would become perhaps the greatest crisis the museum had faced in its ninety-three-year history.

When Pescott was named director back in 1944, he had arrived at a rusted-on institution that seemed to want nothing to do with this government-appointed blow-in. Shortly after Pescott's appointment, Burns's predecessor, John Clark, had led a small exodus; a fiery working-class Scot, Clark had often waved the threat of resignation throughout his eighteen years as curator of entomology, with a long list of grievances against the museum hierarchy. By 1941, things had deteriorated to the point that when Clark noticed some labelling errors in a mammals exhibit, he opted to report it directly to the Public Services Commissioner rather than gently flag it with his colleagues.[20] When the news broke that Pescott would be parachuted in from the Department of Agriculture, Clark finally made good on his threats, preferring to live and die in virtual poverty in an act of passive-aggressive self-immolation — he had already sent his children to an orphanage after his second wife took her life in 1943.[21]

Then there was George Mack, the curator of ornithology, who lodged an official appeal against Pescott's appointment under the *Discharged Servicemen's Preference Act 1943*.[22] Mack had been the former director and board of trustees' pick for the job, and in parliament the Victorian premier and opposition leader almost came to blows over claims that the government had steamrolled the board's independence. ('Come outside,' the premier said defiantly.)[23] With the systematic pettiness of a scientist, Mack had included in his complaint a spreadsheet breaking down the new director's myriad shortcomings: compared to his own twenty-three years of museum experience, he placed a pointed 'nil' in Pescott's column.[24]

Despite the resistance, Pescott soon demonstrated the benefits of occasionally hiring a new broom to clean house — and the National Museum of Victoria sorely needed sweeping. Some problems were obvious, such as the large wooden ladder that Pescott noticed leaning against the external wall of the art gallery, linking the museum and lending library.

'This ladder, which is readily accessible to an experienced burglar, leads directly onto the roof of the buildings from which entrance to the Museum or Art Gallery could easily be made,' he wrote incredulously in August 1944, urging its removal.[25]

After receiving several reports that the museum's exterior doors had repeatedly been left unlocked overnight, Pescott was forced to issue a memorandum spelling out that it was Newcombe's duty to lock up all doors and downstairs gates each evening as, unbelievably, 'no definite arrangement appear[ed] to exist'.[26] Then, one morning in November, it was discovered that someone had used a 'jemmy' to break two locks and force open a display case in the Australian zoological section.[27] Nothing appeared missing, but it highlighted the fact that every day, for hours at a time, the zoological hall, balconies, and Australian collection were left without any floor attendant on duty — apart from one man minding the back door on Russell Street.

'This arrangement sooner or later must result in serious damage or loss occurring to the National Museum's collections,' Pescott wrote ominously before once again tapping Newcombe to cover the gaps in the roster.[28]

Then there was that heavy iron door at the top of the stairs leading from the public galleries down to the dungeons — who knew how long it had been broken for?

'I consider it most desirable that this upper door should function in the same manner,' Pescott wrote understatedly.[29]

As Pescott was quickly learning, however, it was a battle to get even these most basic problems addressed. Four months after he flagged the shrapnel and plaster falling from the ceiling in November 1944, a colleague asked Pescott if the problem had been addressed. Pescott responded with a frustrated, handwritten, 'NO!'[30] Like his predecessors, he struggled to make the case for better staffing, even as the lack of manpower placed the security and integrity of the collections in jeopardy. As it turned out, the basement wasn't just dank and depressing; some of its most irreplaceable ethnological collections had been left in a 'most disgraceful condition', plagued by pests after their collection manager took a post in the army's military-history unit for two years, knowingly leaving them to rot.[31]

'Some specimens had so deteriorated that they had to be destroyed,' Pescott complained.[32] In November 1945, he found himself forced to make an uncomfortable trade-off as he lobbied against the museum taking out insurance against 'thefts, malicious and accidental damage', arguing that the money would be better spent on additional attendants.[33] It was only in July 1946, just months before Burns's discovery, that Pescott finally won authorisation to build a strongroom 'large enough to house all the type specimens, and valuable and rare collections'.[34] But it was too little, too late. The fluke wasn't that someone had managed to breach the museum's security and make hundreds of butterflies disappear — it was that museum staff had noticed the theft at all.

'It was only by chance we discovered the robbery in Melbourne so quickly,' Pescott would later tell a colleague.[35] 'It could easily have been much longer'.

On Tuesday 21 January, a wizened eighty-year-old with a snow-white beard and bushy black eyebrows walked in from Russell Street with grim purpose. George Lyell was hardly recognisable as the young man who had walked through those same doors half a century earlier bearing a single butterfly — and the fact he was still alive was in some ways remarkable. It had been fourteen years since a near-death experience had forced the then-sixty-six-year-old to undergo emergency surgery to remove his prostate, an ordeal that moved him to pledge his collection to the museum while he was still alive.

'I always had it in mind to leave the collection to the nation,' he told a reporter from his hospital bed. 'But when I became ill four months ago it occurred to me that it would be better to do it now instead of passing it on in my will. I can perhaps help in its re-arrangement.'[36]

Lyell did more than help. Once he was out of hospital, he dedicated much of his retirement to dismantling the museum's entire lepidoptera collection and rebuilding it around his own.[37] Spread across 250 glass-topped trays and sixty storeboxes, the Lyell Collection contained everything from tiny creatures barely the size of a fingernail to thumping great moths whose wingspans measured nearly a foot wide. Lyell and the museum expected it to take a few years, but this soon proved wildly optimistic; in the end, this mammoth task took him well over a decade, with nine years spent on the 30,000 moths alone.

But now, who knew how much of it remained? Since the revelation of 13 January, Burns had marked at least 600 butterflies as missing. While he and Pescott had only worked with the collection for a little over two years, no one knew the museum's butterflies better than the man who had spent over a decade amalgamating its existing collection with his own private hoard. Three days after Burns and Newcombe's initial report, Pescott bit the bullet and summoned George Lyell himself.

It was a chastening call to make, given all the care that Pescott had taken to rebuild the museum's relationship with Lyell after the disruption of the war years. Lyell had been so focused on the job that during one visit to the museum in 1942 he had been 'astonished' to find John Clark picking out types to join the other treasures being packed up and sent away to the country.[38] Since the outbreak of World War II, museums around Australia had feared sabotage by 'enemy sympathisers', and once Japan entered the conflict a secret operation was ordered to evacuate over 180 cabinets, strongboxes, and metal drums worth of rare books and priceless zoological, mineralogical, and ethnographic objects to a series of remote safehouses.[39]

Having briefly considered commandeering the empty country manors of Australia's squattocracy, it was decided that the collections would be placed under lock and key in the rural gaols and courthouses of Ballarat, Bendigo, and Learmonth. These big stone buildings fitted the brief of being both fire- and blast-resistant, and safely removed from city and coastal areas, but their handy proximity to guards and police also meant that placing these rare and irreplaceable objects next door to a rogue's gallery of convicted criminals would, somewhat counter-intuitively, keep them most safe from potential theft.[40]

Lyell wasn't impressed. It wasn't the first time his work had been overshadowed by war, and he couldn't see the point in disrupting his work for something so frivolous.

'Surely the *basement* of the Museum is an infinitely safer place than any possible new location you can find in the suburbs,' he complained to Pescott's predecessor as soon as he got home. 'You will be dislocating the work, and running very great risk of damages in transit and in my opinion all to no purpose.'[41]

By November 1943, the initial spike of fear had subsided, and the collections were duly transferred by the truckload back to Russell Street, where Lyell finally completed the job in 1945. Although not quite on par with the gaols when it came to security, the dungeons were, in theory, a safe place for Lyell's collection and the other prizes of the museum's collections. After all, it was just across the road from the city's main police station on Russell Street, and despite the broken door it was supposed to be accessible only to staff, honorary scientists, or visiting students — people with very good reasons to be there.[42]

However, as he saw the reality of Burns's findings for himself, even Lyell would have to concede that the basement wasn't so infallible after all. With red pencil in hand, the old man began a detailed stocktake, poring over each drawer and comparing its contents with his own meticulous records. Lyell wasn't the only visitor to the National Museum that day; Pescott had already put in a call to the Central Investigation Branch of the Victorian Police, and as Lyell set to work, a detective named JJ Ryan and a fingerprint expert pressed Burns, Pescott, and Newcombe's fingers and palms onto pads of black ink.[43] As their fingerprints dried, Lyell's tally grew bigger and bigger, and by the end of his count, Lyell had dramatically revised Burns's initial estimate: the list of the missing had now risen to 825 specimens.[44]

This was, by any reckoning, a disaster, and that afternoon Pescott picked up the phone again. Over 500 miles away, in another Greek-revival building — this one overlooking Hyde Park in Sydney, with enough mounted animal skeletons of its own to make a visiting Californian despair — Arthur Walkom, the director of the Australian Museum, was about to receive a very worrying phone call. Eight hundred miles to the west, among the sleepy sandstone institutions in Adelaide, South Australia, Herbert Hale at the South Australian Museum would get a similar call. It wouldn't be long before Pescott's counterparts made a series of cascading discoveries of their own that seemed to confirm that whatever had happened in the dungeons below Russell Street was not an isolated incident. Soon, there was scarcely a natural history museum in Australia that wasn't a crime scene.

Across the road at the Russell Street station, the police mulled over the details of the case. Initially, the museum's suspicions centred on a Sydney-based collector, someone who Burns had heard on the museum grapevine was suspected of pocketing types and specimens from the Macleay Museum at the University of Sydney—home to one of the country's oldest and most prestigious insect collections outside the state museums.[45]

'For that reason [he] has been forbidden entry to that Institution,' Burns later noted.[46]

But that was just the first lead. On 25 November 1946, after he had made his last check on the Lyell Collection down in the dungeons, Burns had ventured north for another two-week collecting trip to Blackheath in the Blue Mountains of New South Wales. The days of hiking up bush tracks beside Hopson and Waterhouse were long gone, but Burns had fine company: for the final weekend, between 7 and 10 December, he was joined by two other Australian entomologists, Leslie Mosse-Robinson and Charles Oke, and an English collector named Colin Wyatt.

After briefly returning to the museum on 13 December, Burns left again on 20 December for another three weeks in and around the Blue Mountains, netting a bumper haul of imperial hairstreaks, whitewater rockmasters, graphic flutterers, and eastern evening darners. On Boxing Day, he headed back up to Barrington Tops, where the following day he uncovered a curious-looking pupa under the bark of a wattle tree. Burns didn't know it yet, but come springtime it would reveal itself to be a flame hairstreak, *Pseudalmenus chlorinda barringtonensis,* the first known specimen to be collected since Hopson's holotype from 1922. When Burns discovered the pupa, that holotype was still presumed to be safe in the Australian Museum in Sydney. But by the time the pupa crept out of its cocoon the following spring, it was a different story entirely.[47]

It was on 5 January 1947, in the final week of his trip, that Burns paid Mosse-Robinson a visit at his home in Narara, on the central coast of New South Wales.[48] This time, Mosse-Robinson mentioned something that Burns would look back on with interest; apparently, when Oke and Burns had left the Blue Mountains for Melbourne on the morning of 10 December, Mosse-Robinson had instead travelled to Sydney that afternoon alongside the Englishman, Colin Wyatt. Before making his way home, Mosse-Robinson crashed for the night at Wyatt's flat in suburban Woollahra, where he noticed that his host appeared to be making hurried preparations to uproot his life in Australia and head back to England.[49] Among Wyatt's luggage were several wooden entomological cases, which Mosse-Robinson could see had been neatly packed up, ready to be shipped halfway around the world. He couldn't have known, however, that inside those cases lay an extraordinary collection of rare Australian butterflies — an *impossible* collection.

CHAPTER THREE

The Collector

On a good day, striking out from some cosy little hut or tent pitched at the foot of a great mountain, Colin William Fforde Wyatt felt like Sherlock Holmes giving chase to a 'hot scent'.[1] By his early twenties, he was already a worldly young man who seemed to bear many of the hallmarks of the classic gentleman adventurer. As one newspaper reporter would later write, this charismatic stranger with the arched eyebrows, cleft chin, and woolly waves of ginger hair seemed the very 'prototype of the Cambridge-educated be-moustached Englishman one is sure to meet at the North Pole, in a cannibal village, or at a ritzy hotel in St Moritz'.[2]

Much like Sir Arthur Conan Doyle's famous detective, that pipe-smoking paragon of Victorian-era scientific rationalism, Wyatt prided himself on being able to sniff out his quarry with little more than deductive reason, instinct, and his intuitive knowledge of plants, geography, and wildlife. From the vine-strewn jungle monasteries of Ceylon to the High Atlas of Morocco, to the ochre cliffs and pastel-coloured eucalypts of Australia, he could be dropped into a new location, sight unseen, and after a swift survey of the foliage and topography of the surrounding countryside, the game would be afoot. But, unlike Holmes, Wyatt wasn't chasing murderers or thieves: he was hunting butterflies.

'You study the flora and the fauna and, to some extent, the geology of the country, and then you know where to find your butterfly,' he would later tell a Canadian newspaper. 'I study the map look for a certain kind of outcrop and when I do, there I am sure to find the creature I want.'[3]

Wyatt started young — one of his earliest, clearest memories was of the day his father, James William Wyatt, an older man already in his fifties by the time Colin was born, presented the boy with a child-sized net and a handful of setting-boards, and showed him the basics of catching, pinning, and identification.[4] It was a precise craft, halfway between mortician and model-maker, that used steam and patience to lessen the effects of rigor mortis long enough to reset the subject into position with wings permanently outstretched. Colin was only six years old, but it wasn't long before he could be heard running around the house, calling out to his mother, Margaret, at the sight of a pair of marbled whites mating in the yard. Before long, his bedroom windowsill was lined with gauze-covered shoeboxes teeming with wriggling caterpillars.[5]

Even years later, Wyatt's fingers still trembled with excitement at the memory of the first butterfly he caught with a net.[6] He could picture the curve in the road above Bolzano, and remember the anxious minutes spent standing on the tips of his toes waiting for it to settle at the end of a branch. Then came the sublime rush when it fluttered into his net, before he slumped to the ground to take a deep breath of relief.

This self-styled Holmes didn't need a Watson to chronicle his adventures; he had his own personal canon of boy's own bug-hunting stories, and whether he was in the company of strangers or friends, it didn't take long for the anecdotes to flow. There was the episode in Lapland a few summers before the war, when Wyatt had his heart set on the rare, unflatteringly named dingy fritillary, or *Boloria improba.* He faced a dilemma: to date, its only European sighting had been on a single mountain outcropping, within the borders of a national park and protected by law.[7] Undeterred, Wyatt tracked down a geological map of the region, and soon noticed another almost identical formation some fifteen miles away on the northern shore of a great lake. This, he deduced, might be just the clue he needed.[8]

To Wyatt, the lakeside mountain seemed like a desolate part of the world — deathly quiet, littered with the bleached bones and antlers of dead reindeer, under an eerily low-hanging sun that reminded him of the apocalyptic wasteland of HG Wells's *The Time Machine*. The nights were so bright that he slept blindfolded, but he didn't mind the solitude when his sleuthing paid off: he left the mountain with a good set of dingy fritillaries and a swag of other alpine species on the side.[9]

A few years earlier, in the village of Le Vernet in France's Bès Valley, the young Wyatt had spied a brood of scarce swallowtail caterpillars disguised among the leaves of a wild sloe bush. To a casual bushwalker, their pale-green bodies might have acted as the perfect camouflage, but Wyatt was harder to fool. Having picked his little prizes off the leaves, he now faced a new problem: how to keep them alive until he got back to England. This, in turn, led to a run-in with a stocky and suspicious French farmer in the countryside outside Toulouse who had rumbled the sheepish-looking redhead trespassing on the wrong side of a wire fence.[10] Wyatt tried to explain, apologetically, that he was only hoping to snip a few cuttings of blackthorn to keep his rare grubs alive for a few more weeks.

'*Pour mes chenilles*,' Wyatt pleaded to no avail in fluent French, and as the man continued to rage, Wyatt eyed the distance back to freedom. Then, in a moment of bratty defiance, he snapped off a nearby branch and made a break for it, easily outrunning his accuser and vaulting the fence with enough blackthorn to smuggle his caterpillars back across the English Channel, alive. It was stories such as these that led one journalist from *The Bulletin* magazine to observe that, 'Mr Wyatt skims from country to country, from mountain to mountain, with some of the apparent inconsequence of his own butterflies.'[11]

There were times when even Wyatt himself was surprised by the places he could wander into unchallenged. Decades later, when he was pushing fifty and preparing to mount a seven-month journey across the north-west territories of Canada, he found that staff at a lonely Arctic airbase barely batted an eyelid when he stepped off a public bus and walked right in. The arrival of the 'atomic age' had brought a network of northern airfields and radar stations that the Americans called the Distant Early Warning Line; but despite all the Cold War secrecy, no one at the base even asked his name. For all they knew or cared, Wyatt later reflected, he might have been 'Comrade Blowemupski'.[12]

Perhaps his most thrilling tale, however, had occurred some years earlier, in the early 1930s, when Wyatt was still fresh out of Cambridge and spending another season holidaying with his parents in South Tyrol and the Dolomites. Way up in the high country, where the edges of Italy and Austria kiss, these contested borderlands had been an important trade route since antiquity. The Romans laid the first roads, and then the Hapsburgs — a royal line fond of butterflies, decorating their palaces and jewellery with them — ushered it into modernity with their fortresses and railways. This alpine corridor was home to patches of steep mountainside dotted with white-blooming edelweiss. Importantly, it was also the preferred habitat of the little fritillary, or *Melitaea asteria*, a tiny, intricate butterfly with a fuzzy brown body and wings marked with orange and amber spots, bordered with black like a pane of lead-light glass.

A few years after Wyatt's visit on the fritillary's trail, this region would become a preferred meeting place for Benito Mussolini and Adolf Hitler — respective namesakes of a Libyan moth, *Hypopta mussolinii*, and a Slovenian cave beetle, *Anophthalmus hitleri*. The pair met several times at Brenner Pass, notably in 1940 to firm up their 'Pact of Steel', where they spent hours in Hitler's armed train carriage, its blinds drawn to prevent reporters outside from observing their body language as they plotted to carve up Europe.[13] But Wyatt's high-country adventure occurred before the twin fascists had their mountain rendezvous, before the Anschluss, at a time when continental Europe was becoming an increasingly fraught place to be.

Wyatt certainly knew that change was coming; on another family holiday a year before his fritillary hunt, Wyatt had encountered an ominous notice placed some twenty feet from the Austrian-Italian border. Printed in both German and Italian, it carried a warning that anyone seen attempting to cross was liable to be shot. The Italians, Wyatt would later recall, 'were being very fussy'.[14]

Undaunted by the prospect of being picked off by rifle fire, Wyatt had set out from the Tyrolean village of Steinach to a region high above the

Brenner Pass, practically straddling the border. Realising his destination could only be accessed from the southern side, Wyatt took care to legally cross at the official checkpoint before hiking a mile and a half into Italian territory, climbing higher and higher until the railway below looked like a children's playset. It was perhaps no coincidence that butterfly hunting often went hand-in-glove with his other great passion, mountaineering, and at such high altitudes he felt a rush best summarised by one of his favourite poets, Lord Byron, in 1816:

> To climb the trackless mountain all unseen,
> With the wild flock that never needs a fold,
> Alone o'er steeps and foaming falls to lean,
> This is not solitude; 'tis but to hold
> Converse with Nature's charms, and view her stores unrolled

By the time of this Tyrolean adventure, Wyatt had already spent many long days crossing trackless mountains and chasing nature's charms across the Alps and Pyrenees, long enough to develop a rousing repertoire of Austrian and Norwegian mountain songs and a crisp yodelling technique he wasn't shy about sharing. He could dance too, mounting public performances of the region's handclapping, shoe-slapping folk dances in full Tyrolean attire. With his piano accordion and trilling vocal register, Wyatt had even serenaded the king and queen of Norway, the future king of England, Edward VIII, and listeners to the BBC back home.[15]

Along the way, he would find Italian blues such as the azure *Erebia pheretes* congregating in small puddles along the track—'mud-puddling' is a popular pastime among many species of butterfly, who crowd around the stagnant little pools like a bar at happy hour, extending their proboscises and going to town on the dirty, salty water.[16] As expected, it didn't take him long to spot his prized fritillary in the wild, fluttering over the edelweiss and utterly oblivious of the out-of-place Englishman, his net at the ready.

It was while Wyatt was observing the butterfly that the first Italian frontier guard made himself known. He had been watching Wyatt ascend the mountain path, but after a brief exchange it became clear he was not one of the Carabinieri's finest — Wyatt noticed that the man's binoculars case was empty, inexplicably stuffed with edelweiss. All the same, Wyatt began to deploy the same easy charm that, with the exception of the occasional run-in with an angry Frenchman, had opened doors and alleviated suspicion throughout his life. In no time at all, Wyatt had turned the soldier into an eager spectator who cheered along every new catch.[17]

Moments such as these brought Wyatt a 'quite ineffable thrill', a magical feeling that recalled Vladimir Nabokov's memoir *Speak, Memory.* In Nabokov — a famous lepidopterist who, Wyatt would add, was also a gifted writer — he saw a kindred spirit, someone who understood an important truth about lepidoptery: whatever scientific justification they might invoke to dress up the hours, days, and years dedicated to tracking and catching insects, there was something deep, timeless, and at times inexplicable driving most collectors. As Nabokov wrote:

> This is ecstasy, and behind the ecstasy is something else, which is hard to explain. It is like a momentary vacuum into which rushes all that I love. A sense of oneness with sun and stone. A thrill of gratitude to whom it may concern — to the contrapuntal genius of human fate or to tender ghosts humoring a lucky mortal.[18]

Perhaps this sense of ecstasy explained why, after cheerfully bidding the Italian soldier farewell, Wyatt made a rash decision as he tramped down the mountain. He had reached a point some 1,000 feet above the railway station when he spied a shortcut through the woods, and decided to take it. He veered off the track, through the trees, and before long walked straight into the path of two more Italian troopers. This pair were far less accommodating, and soon Wyatt found himself sat down in front of their commandant — his eyes gravitating to the man's immaculately polished riding boots, in stark contrast to his own hot, dirty, and unkempt appearance.

Wyatt received an earful of furious and indecipherable Italian — for all his linguistic talents, honed while studying modern languages at

Cambridge, Italian was one of the few European languages that Wyatt didn't have a handle on. The commandant was unmoved by Wyatt's attempts to present his British passport, with the ink still fresh from the entry stamp earlier that morning. The butterfly-catching gear was also treated like a suspicious weapon as the Italians unfolded Wyatt's strange accessories. Suddenly, a few scraps of Romance languages floated up from the depths of his university days, just enough for Wyatt to string together a variation of '*rete!*' — the Latin for 'net' — and '*farfarlle*' — Italian for 'butterfly'.

As it happened, the guards weren't entirely wrong to be suspicious. Colin Wyatt wasn't the first Englishman to be caught out in a foreign territory with a curious set of equipment, professing to be nothing more than an innocent bug-catcher out of his depth.

'I was hunting butterflies, and it was always a good introduction with which to go to anyone who was watching me with suspicion,' wrote Lord Robert Baden-Powell in his 1915 memoir *My Adventures as a Spy*. 'Quite frankly, with my sketch-book in hand, I would ask innocently whether he had seen such-and-such a butterfly in the neighbourhood, as I was anxious to catch one.'[19]

Baden-Powell was famous for being many things — an outdoorsman, artist, storyteller, and founder of the international Boy Scouts movement — but entomologist was not one of them. Rarely pictured without his neat moustache, khakis, and broad-brimmed Stetson campaign hat, Baden-Powell had modelled the philosophies of his scouts on a heady blend of Rudyard Kipling's fictional boy spy, Kimball O'Hara, and his own storied military career in espionage and reconnaissance. In *My Adventures as a Spy*, Baden-Powell disclosed a series of astonishing — and almost certainly embellished — tales, ranging from his early days as a lieutenant cartographer in Kandahar, to scouting the Zulu in South Africa.

'We are as a nation considered by the others to be abnormally stupid,' Baden-Powell reflected, which was an attitude that he considered could be readily exploited. 'The exceedingly stupid Englishmen who wandered about foreign countries sketching cathedrals, or catching butterflies, or fishing for trout, were merely laughed at as harmless lunatics.'[20]

This cartoonish image was deployed by Conan Doyle himself in his 1902 novel *The Hound of the Baskervilles* when Watson encounters one of the Baskervilles' neighbours: a friendly, outwardly unthreatening naturalist who claims to have the most complete butterfly collection in south-west England:

> A small fly or moth had fluttered across our path and in an instant, Stapleton was rushing with extraordinary energy and speed in pursuit of it … my acquaintance never paused for an instant, bounding from tuft to tuft behind it, his green net waving in the air. His gray clothes and jerky, zigzag, irregular progress made him not unlike some huge moth himself.[21]

For Baden-Powell, it was an exceedingly useful stereotype, one that could explain away all kinds of suspicious behaviour. On one mission into southern Croatia, he armed himself with a sketchbook of half-finished drawings of red admirals and painted ladies; if caught, he could open his rucksack for inspection, confident that most officials would be utterly stumped by the scribblings of a field entomologist. Little did they know that Baden-Powell had devised a system for concealing intelligence in these diagrams — such as a fortress traced into the outlines of a moth's head, or enemy topography concealed in the patterns on an ivy leaf.

'Ninety-nine out of a hundred did not know one butterfly from another — any more than I do — so one was on fairly safe ground in that way, and they thoroughly sympathised with the mad Englishman who was hunting these insects,' he wrote.[22]

For true collectors such as Athol Waterhouse, the kinds of misconceptions that Baden-Powell both exploited and reinforced were a source of frustration. He complained in his 1932 book *What Butterfly Is That?* that 'the comic paper caricature of the butterfly hunter rushing madly after his prey is about as false as the popular belief that a butterfly is killed by transfixing it with a pin'. Many more, he added, were the result of 'patiently watching and cautious stalking than the most vigorous sprinting'.[23]

Waterhouse himself was a patient, practised killer; the genial, twinkly-eyed gentleman scientist's preferred method was to let a butterfly settle into a desirable position in his net before delivering a quick and painless coup de grâce by pinching the thorax between his forefinger and thumb.

'This breaks the nerve chain in the body,' Waterhouse explained. Other collectors preferred to use a 'killing bottle' rather than get their hands dirty—usually a glass jar with small amounts of cyanide, or some other poison. But for Waterhouse there was no substitute for the personal touch. 'A little practice is required to avoid damage, but one soon becomes very expert,' he added.

Even Conan Doyle understood how a love of lepidoptera could prove a visually striking symbol for deeper pathologies—a potent mix of fragility, beauty, metamorphosis, and death that in subsequent decades could be seen in John Fowles's 1963 novel *The Collector* and Thomas Harris's *The Silence of the Lambs* in 1988. In *The Hound of the Baskervilles'* denouement, Conan Doyle delights in subverting his earlier caricature of Stapleton the bug-catcher when he is unmasked by Wyatt's idol, Sherlock Holmes, as an imposter and as the mastermind behind the fraud and murder plot at the heart of the novel. As Watson recounted:

> All my unspoken instincts, my vague suspicions, suddenly took shape and centred upon the naturalist. In that impassive colourless man, with his straw hat and his butterfly-net, I seemed to see something terrible—a creature of infinite patience and craft, with a smiling face and a murderous heart.

That other literary hero of Colin Wyatt, Vladimir Nabokov, also knew that few betrayals stung like a fellow collector's. In *Speak, Memory,* Nabokov recalls how the family footman, who had once caught a swallowtail for the budding young entomologist, would later inform on the family to the tsar's secret police. Following the October Revolution, the same onetime butterfly collector brought a posse of Bolsheviks to the Nabokovs' front door to loot their family treasure.

Years later, Athol Waterhouse himself would gain a painful,

firsthand lesson in how the seemingly benign appearance of a fellow butterfly hunter might also mask duplicity and betrayal. To Waterhouse, someone like this could only be described in a few curt words: 'the cunning devil'.[24]

Luckily for Wyatt, as he sat detained by the Carabinieri, *My Adventures as a Spy* was never translated into Italian, while a local edition of Conan Doyle's *Il mastino dei Baskerville* wouldn't hit the shelves until 1950. But Wyatt's ties to the overlapping worlds of entomology and espionage would eventually grow closer than even he could appreciate at the time.

Years later, while reading a war memoir by a British officer named Julian Amery, Wyatt encountered a name that sounded familiar.[25] For years, he had been on friendly terms with a number of German collectors and benefactors, most notably the brothers Wilhelm and Frederick Brandt. The younger brother, Fred, had spent the 1930s travelling through Lapland and the Middle East, living in small mountain villages, falling in with the nomadic tribes near Chābahār Bay, or simply strapping his collecting gear to a camel and camping out alone in the open air.

It was enough for one British official to later speculate that 'perhaps the authorities thought the tattered, poverty-stricken European chaser of butterflies was semi-mad', but the rare and lucrative specimens that Fred caught and sent back to Wilhelm in Finland were worth it.[26] Wyatt became one of many collectors across Germany, Switzerland, Australia, Czechoslovakia, and Italy to exchange specimens with the Brandts, who soon earned a reputation in entomological circles for capturing new, previously unseen species — Fred even had a new genus of Persian moth, *Brandtina*, named after him.[27]

Then, a few years after the war, Wyatt saw Brandt namedropped in Amery's memoir, *Sons of the Eagle*. Amery had been based in Albania, tasked with recruiting German conscripts to kill their superiors, desert, and take up with the local guerilla forces, when in May 1944 he met a prime candidate: a German corporal named Fred Hermann Brandt.[28] Communicating through broken Italian and hand gestures, Brandt spun a tale that sounded straight out of Baden-Powell's old playbook; an entomologist by profession, Brandt claimed to have been forced into the German army as a translator, but now hoped to jump ship before Hitler lost the war.[29] Amery wasn't totally convinced by the 'White Russian adventurer'.

'The profession of entomologist is notoriously linked with that of espionage; and I could not help thinking that Brandt was more than just an interpreter-corporal,' Amery would later write.[30]

This proved correct when, a few days later, Brandt fronted up to the Englishman with another frank admission: up until that point, his whole story had been a ruse.[31] He had, in fact, been sent to win over the British officers, undermine their work, then arrest or kill *them* at the right moment.

The full story reads like a strange spy novel, teased out across lengthy interrogations in a prison camp in the Italian port of Bari, and then in England.[32] Brandt told his captors how, in 1938, word of his Middle Eastern exploits had led the curator of the Leningrad Museum to offer him a job. Before he could take it up, however, the outbreak of the Russo-Finnish war in November 1939 saw him stranded in Estonia with his new wife. This wasn't new; the Brandt brothers and their siblings were in fact born in St Petersburg, into a family of German Balts who for years had bounced from one Eastern European state to another, buffeted by communist revolutions and fascist takeovers that saw them settled and naturalised in a new home one year, and rendered stateless the next.

After slipping through German immigration with a false address, Fred tried to find another museum job, only to encounter blank stares from Posen to Berlin. His luck finally changed in Łódź, an industrial city in German-occupied Poland with its own zoological museum. It was a two-bit institution with a few stuffed animals and a laboratory, but he eventually talked the local authorities into appointing him curator. But there was a catch; first, Brandt was forced to prove his Aryan bona fides, naturalise as a German, and join the SS. Then, in mid-November, he was approached by a plump, balding, middle-aged man with a limp from an old war wound. He was the Leiter, a local official who had read Brandt's file and knew all about his travels in the Middle East. The Leiter also added that he was part of Hitler's High Command of the

Wehrmacht — and wanted to recruit Brandt to the Abwehr, Germany's military intelligence apparatus.

It was impossible to refuse. Brandt knew he was living on borrowed time in Łódź — he had lied about having a professorship to get the job, and now better-qualified scientists with real degrees were breathing down his neck. But he was also moved by his 'lust for adventure' and the possibility of returning to the mountains and its butterflies — even if it led him into a war zone. He agreed, and after being taken to Berlin to pledge loyalty to the Führer, swear to the strictest secrecy under penalty of death, and pick out a codename — he chose 'Armada', inspired by a group of butterflies he helped name — Brandt was given his first mission in March 1941.

He would be paired with another recruit, a thirty-five-year-old doctor, and sent into present-day Pakistan to parlay with Haji Mirzali Khan Wazir, the Faqir of Ipi, who had already declared war against the British in 1936. The doctor — a dark-blond, blue-eyed Hamburg native with a scar over his right eye — was already an expert in leprosy, which would provide the pair with a perfect, altruistic cover story. The doctor would offer to help rid the country of leprosy, while secretly trying to foment rebellion against the British. Brandt, meanwhile, would serve as assistant and Persian interpreter, while posing as a fellow doctor with an interest in entomology.

After attending a fourteen-day crash course at a 'sabotage school' outside Berlin, the duo made for the Afghan border in June. Once in Kabul, they spent weeks keeping up appearances, rubbing shoulders with Japanese, Turkish, Russian, and Italian officials at a series of parties and receptions. For the first time in his life, Brandt donned a stiff shirt and evening suit, and even struck up a strange rapport with the Italian minister's wife, a Russian-speaking 'Tartar Princess'. Whenever the opportunity arose, he ditched the suit, the parties, and the princess to disappear into the mountains chasing butterflies.

Brandt and the doctor finally set out for Waziristan in July, swapping their European clothing for desert robes as they trekked at dusk and hid by day. Then, one night, Brandt heard gunfire and shouting. He reached for the pistol stashed in his turban, but he and the doctor were both hit before the Afghan soldiers who had opened fire seized their bribe money, watches, clothes, and cameras. Brandt would later learn they had been set up and sold out, and that the soldiers ordered to bring them in had been warned the doctor would fight to the death rather than be captured.[33] That's what happened; forced to flag down a truck to take them back to Kabul, the doctor, who had been shot through the lung and stomach, bled out in Brandt's arms on the drive. After three months in a Kabul hospital recovering under armed guard, Brandt returned to Germany in November 1941 before being redeployed in March 1944 to the Shalë valley in north-west Albania, where his fateful rendezvous with the British awaited him.

Years later, a British newspaper would seize upon the wild story of 'The Crafty Butterfly Corporal'—'a master agent of the Nazis, one of the most incredible men in the murky wartime history of espionage and treachery.' Playing up the high drama of Brandt's deception, it cast the captured spy as a 'striking figure' with a 'shock of flaming red hair and luxuriant RAF-type handle-bar moustache' who claimed to have 'sent butterflies to the British Museum'—only to be exposed as a 'human spider spinning a web to enmesh all the British agents and bring their Albanian plans to ruin.'[34] It's worth noting that by the time the story was published in 1957, the British press had already had plenty of practice in writing dishy stories about a slippery red-headed butterfly collector being brought to heel.

Back in 1945, however, Brandt's British interrogators weren't quite as impressed. Across a long and recently unsealed paper trail, they tried to make sense of the stateless entomologist's convoluted and inconsistent testimony. Brandt's earlier lies had forced him to change his story between Italy and England, leaving his captors reluctant to believe a man who was, in the most charitable reading of his own life story, a liar, fraud, and opportunist with little concept of national loyalty.

'Only after many months is the final story obtained at Camp 020, and, thanks to his lying at Bari, his credibility is in doubt,' reads one comment in a 133-page secret dossier compiled between 1944 and 1947.[35]

Unsurprisingly, at the end of the war the British opted not to set Brandt loose in the mountains as he'd hoped, but instead sent the 'butterfly corporal' to a concentration camp in West Germany. Brandt had made his bed, one officer wrote, and now had to lie in it. But of all Brandt's shifting stories, a sincere love of butterflies was the one, unerring constant, and near the end of the 133-page report, in an itemised list documenting the over 200 personal effects in his possession at the time of surrender, were two important entries:

1 butterfly net
1 specimen bag

Back before the war, during his own interrogation in Italy, Colin Wyatt had also spread out his butterfly net and specimen case in front of the Carabinieri. Just as he began to envision spending the night in a cell in Bolzano — not to mention enduring the indignity of having to call on his parents at Steinach to bail him out — the commandant's remonstrations abated long enough for him to reveal his haul of newly caught fritillaries. Wyatt would later describe how, in a display that might have pleased Lord Baden-Powell, the commandant reacted with disgust, waving him away with a gesture that seemed to suggest he wanted to wash his hands of the strange young man and his butterflies. The two soldiers could hardly contain their amusement as they marched 'the mad *Inglese*' back outside and over the Austrian border.[36]

When Wyatt eventually gave his account of the Italian interrogation in his own 1955 memoir, *Going Wild: the autobiography of a bug-hunter*, he would reflect almost wistfully that, 'fortunately or unfortunately', this run-in at the Italian border amounted to the peak of his 'exciting' brushes with authority and the law — getting arrested by the Italian army was 'the best I could achieve'.

At the time of publication, of course, that wasn't quite true. This comical close shave was one of many instances when Wyatt caught the eye of authorities, and within a decade he would also rack up a sizeable secret dossier of his own as anonymous paper-pushers tried to decide whether this globetrotting Englishman was a loose-lipped security threat, a 'Fifth Columnist', or, just as inscrutably, a modern artist. It's the kind of small, salient, almost Nabokovian act of literary misdirection that might make one wonder about the rest of Wyatt's stories too.

Colin Wyatt was not a Nazi or Soviet spy, but neither was he quite the Holmesian sleuth or romantic Byronic hero he sometimes invoked. Wyatt's true nature was complicated by the fact that, like his onetime associate Fred Brandt, he was at times an unreliable narrator of his own astonishing adventures. But, like Brandt, one fact was beyond dispute: he did indeed love butterflies, and would go to great lengths, risk life and liberty, and say or do almost anything to get his hands on them. Wyatt was, in a word, a collector.

CHAPTER FOUR

The Confidants

By the time Athol Waterhouse had caught his first butterfly, collecting was already second nature to him — and seashells were the gateway drug. He was hardly the first; in 18th-century Europe, as collectors combed beaches to fill their curiosity cabinets, the Swiss philosopher Jean-Jacques Rousseau would dub the craze '*conchyliomanie*', or shell-mania. Waterhouse's mother, Janie, had caught the bug as a girl, scouring the beaches of Victorian-era Sydney and eagerly snapping up the rare and beautiful specimens brought ashore by sailors fresh from working the so-called South Seas trade.[1] Money was no obstacle for the daughter of a coal tycoon turned politician, and before long she had assembled a complete series of the gorgeous, delicate spiral of the paper nautilus, *Argonauta argo*, and the rare orange-and-brown shell of the tiger cowry, *Cypraea tigris*.[2] By the 1880s, Athol and his brothers would join her, rising early to visit Sydney's beaches, from Little Manly to Pussy Cat Bay, at low tide.[3]

The cowries were among the most prized, and for a time these 'gems of the sea' were perhaps the single most collected natural object in human history. Glossy, porcelain-smooth, and perfectly rounded, found in island lagoons and warm tidal pools from the Malabar Coast to the Persian Gulf, the *Cypraeidea* family of sea snails protect themselves by secreting layer after layer of calcium carbonate over their soft bodies, keeping this pearlescent armour buffed to a sheen. Over millennia, cowries have been found everywhere from Bronze Age graves to Ancient Egypt to the Han Dynasty, while one species — *Cyprae moneta*, more commonly called the 'money cowrie' — became a kind of currency, particularly in West Africa, where the shell had come to denote status, wealth, and divine favour.

Arab traders first brought money cowries to North Africa in the 10th century, but it was with the arrival of Dutch and English merchants in the 16th century that their collection and trade exploded with macabre utility: the shells were blood money. The shells would be harvested by the millions in the Maldives before criss-crossing the Indian and Atlantic oceans as ballast in ships' hulls, or as currency to purchase the ships' primary cargo — enslaved people. In West Africa today, observed the African American scholar Saidiya Hartman, stockpiles of 'blood cowries' once belonging to kings and traders lie buried in 'underground banks' in the savannah, after European colonisers, having leveraged the cowrie to wrest control of the continent's commerce, power, and people, moved to outlaw their trade as an inflationary relic of a brutal practice.[4]

But these legacies were far from the minds of Janie Waterhouse and her sons as they explored the Triassic coastline of Sydney, eventually gathering one hundred rare cowries, some of which hadn't been seen in Sydney waters before (or since).[5] Before long, the teenage Gustavus Athol Waterhouse — who went by his middle name to avoid confusion with his father, Gustavus John — had a prize-winning shell collection of his own and the beginnings of a butterfly collection that would one day become an all-consuming passion. But while Janie Waterhouse's shell-mania had successfully hooked her son on a lifelong natural history habit, there was one other person who would form perhaps the biggest influence on Athol Waterhouse's love of lepidoptera.

Waterhouse was still a nineteen-year-old university student when, one day in January 1897, the name George Lyell came up in conversation with the librarian at the Australian Museum. Waterhouse was no stranger to the museum — while studying at the elite boys-only Sydney Grammar right next door, the boy with the Latin nickname would spend countless lunch hours exploring its galleries on College Street.[6] That very same day, perhaps as soon as he got home, he dashed off a letter to Lyell's address that contained a gentle invitation: 'In speaking to Mr Rainbow today he mentioned you were anxious to exchange butterflies, so I therefore take the liberty of writing to you to see if you are willing to do so.'[7]

It was a fateful slip of paper. Lyell was twelve years Waterhouse's senior when he opened that envelope, but was still a fresh-faced and gently handsome young man, seen in one old photograph sporting a dapper quiff of brown hair and a bowtie. It didn't take long for the pair to begin exchanging boxes of specimens—the tentative first steps in a partnership that would span over half a century and create the greatest shared body of work that Australian lepidoptery had yet known.

In 1902, Waterhouse married a warm, funny, and beautiful reverend's daughter named Beatrice, and within a few years they began to lay down roots on a long, wild block in Killara on Sydney's North Shore. High above sea level and largely unspoiled by the urban sprawl leeching out from metropolitan Sydney, the end of their new backyard blurred into a forest of native eucalypts and wattles, carpeted with wildflowers and humming with insects, birds, lizards, and marsupials. It was hardly a coincidence that some of the region's best butterfly spots lay within walking distance, and Athol and Beatrice stocked their garden with the preferred foodplants of his favourite butterfly species to complement the already busy traffic of blue triangles, swallowtails, skippers, pencilled blues, and painted ladies that would wander in from the neighbouring scrub.[8]

Lyell, meanwhile, was based in Gisborne, a small town thirty-three miles outside Melbourne that was home to Cherry & Sons Co., a family firm once known for manufacturing wood-and-brass butter churners. Ever since Lyell had joined as a partner in 1890, it had also developed a convenient sideline in entomological cabinets and 'Natural History Requisites of every description', a set-up he soon formalised by marrying Fanny Ould, the widowed niece of his boss, Edward Cherry. It was an unconventional pairing—the twenty-seven-year-old already well on his way to becoming one of Victoria's foremost lepidopterists, and the widow eighteen years his senior—but it seemed to suit the Lyells.[9]

Living and working more than 540 miles apart, Waterhouse and Lyell were forced to conduct their collaboration largely via letters, written in between George's working hours at Cherry & Sons and Athol's day job as an assayer at the Royal Mint. It is this cache of handwritten notes and letters that opens a window into their partnership as it flourished on and off the page for over fifty years. Slipped in between the serious taxonomical jargon are sweet and fleeting glimpses of the intimate friendship that grew between the two men and their families, like dried flowers pressed between the pages of a book.[10]

They capture the thrill of winter giving way to a new butterfly season ('Hurrah! *O. genoveva* larvae in Sydney at last!'); the excitement of another bountiful trip to Barrington Tops ('should get plenty of material & perhaps something quite new'); the frustration of Waterhouse's health getting in the way of collecting ('I have slightly injured my heart ... I have to be careful, no climbing trees or hills'); and the shock of a fellow collector's sudden death ('He had seemed such a fine big strong fellow').[11] They reveal the Easters spent together in Killara, and the scent and colour of grape hyacinths, nerine, and lily of the valley blooming in the garden from bulbs that Lyell had sent to Mrs Waterhouse's delight. (While George and Athol bonded over butterflies, it seems that he and Beatrice shared a love of flowers.) In December 1913, Waterhouse told Lyell of his joy when Beatrice gave birth to twin sons.

'You know that we have always wished to have a son, though until the beginning of this year that blessing seemed to me to be impossible,' he wrote of the 'two fine little fellows whom I hope are destined to play no mean part in the world'.[12]

He also told Lyell of the loneliness he felt when the house was briefly empty, without Beatrice, the children, or even any butterflies on the wing. Over the years, their homes, company, and correspondence would become a place of comfort, vulnerability, respite, and mutual understanding against an occasionally maddening outside world — and any outsider that might threaten their work.

A little under a decade after that first letter, Waterhouse and Lyell embarked on their greatest joint endeavour. It had been half a century since someone had last attempted a major, comprehensive survey of Australian butterflies, when Alexander Walker Scott, a Cambridge-educated lawyer and former chairman of the Australian Museum, published his three-volume *Australian Lepidoptera and Their Transformations* in 1864. To bridge the gap, Waterhouse and Lyell set out on a years-long survey of the 15,000 specimens of their own collections, plus a further 6,000 in museums across every Australian capital and half-a-dozen more private collections. The book took them eight long years to complete, as the pair navigated 'oceans of work' on either side of the border.

'Of course we are a little at a disadvantage being so far apart,' Waterhouse reflected in March 1914, when the final manuscript was out of their hands, 'but I think we have managed to get together a very good looking specimen of printing.'[13]

When it was finally published on 25 July 1914, just days before the outbreak of World War I, *The Butterflies of Australia* was a grand tome running to over 230 pages with 888 illustrated specimens. In its opening pages, the pair drew a clear distinction between their work and that of so-called stamp collectors, writing that they had 'no concern with those collections in which butterflies are regarded as mere curiosities or ornaments.'[14]

But alongside the sober scientific language are echoes of the pair's pen-pal rapport — and moments of curmudgeonly perfectionism — that found their way to the page. Not even a legend like Johann Fabricius, trained by Carl Linnaeus himself, was immune from Waterhouse and Lyell's expert eyes; back in 1775, the famous Danish entomologist had been tasked with describing the hundreds of specimens brought back to England aboard the HMS *Endeavour* by the naturalists Joseph Banks and Daniel Solander years earlier.

'The name has been applied in error,' they wrote of Fabricius's *Mycalesis perseus*. 'This is only one of several instances in which names given to Australian insects have been applied by early entomologists to allied species from other countries and the error repeated by later reviewers.'[15]

But this was the beauty of science — it was constantly evolving, with the evidence preserved in hundred-year-old collections used to answer fresh questions and reopen taxonomical cold cases.

The book's publication cemented Waterhouse's reputation as Australia's leading entomologist; since he had begun corresponding with Lyell as a teenager, Janie Waterhouse's firstborn had bloomed from a teenage collector to a widely respected middle-aged scientist, prominent in all the major scientific circles, from the Linnean Society to the Royal Zoological Society, and by 1919 was an honorary entomologist at the Australian Museum. Waterhouse also had a reputation for generosity with young and established amateur collectors alike, from the stream of letters full of taxonomic questions and clarifications that filed through the letterbox at Killara, to the children of friends and neighbours who he would patiently spend hours with in his rambling garden and take out on field trips to the Hawkesbury River and the Blue Mountains.[16]

But in his letters to Lyell, Waterhouse felt safe enough to reveal another, sometimes less flattering side of himself: a fastidious, secretive perfectionist who was often exasperated and disappointed when other collectors failed to match up to his own encyclopaedic knowledge and scientific rigour — which they almost always did.

'He is a man of no personality, spasmodically energetic but unmethodical, immensely enthusiastic but pernickety,' Waterhouse wrote of one collector.[17] '[He] had not the slightest idea which was which,' he wrote of another.[18] Later, in August 1928, Waterhouse offered a withering assessment of their peers as he sought Lyell's counsel on the cusp of a major decision. 'I am in rather a different position to any other entomologist,' he wrote. 'I have a fine collection, well housed, a distinctly good library & a great deal of gear, whereas most of the others have little more than a killing bottle & a pair of forceps.'

Two years earlier, the closure of the Royal Mint had sent Waterhouse into a happy early retirement, the kind of retirement that, just shy of his fiftieth birthday, would allow him to fully devote many good years to his butterflies. Little did he know that he was about to enter the most turbulent chapter of his life to date.

Dr Robin Tillyard was a gifted scientist, but an odd duck. Even his hunched appearance, with his deep-set eyes behind round Windsor spectacles, evoked a strange, tall, and slender flightless bird. Like Waterhouse, Tillyard had begun collecting early, and by his teens was netting painted ladies, clouded yellows, and Queen of Spain fritillaries from Dover to the Isle of Wight — an escape, perhaps, from an apparently unhappy home life in Norwich. After studying maths and theology at Cambridge, Tillyard ended up in Australia, where he taught at Waterhouse's old secondary school, Sydney Grammar, until the insects that lay beyond the classroom inspired him to throw it all away and pursue the passion of his youth.[19]

'For a European naturalist, especially a young one, first acquaintance with the Australian bush is a most vivid and exhilarating experience,' Tillyard's son-in-law later remarked of this mid-career pivot, which Tillyard pursued with such fervour that within a few years he had won a job as chief of the biology department at the Cawthron Institute in Nelson, New Zealand. Under Tillyard's leadership, the institute went to battle against an invasive species of woolly apple aphid taking hold across New Zealand, unleashing a special parasitoid to take it down. The plan's early success made waves around the world — it was the kind of applied entomology that Tillyard viewed as instrumental to the future of the British Empire.

'We run the serious risk of being judged a race unfit to occupy these great areas, to the exclusion of other races, if we are going to allow them to "go under" in the grip of noxious weeds,' Tillyard had told the Royal Society of Arts in London in early 1926.[20]

It was this reputation that convinced the Council for Scientific and Industrial Research, a federal body charged with coordinating applied science across Australia, to lure him to Canberra to run its entomology division in 1928. At his best, Tillyard could be pleasant, generous, and funny, but the CSIR executive was quickly learning what Waterhouse and Lyell already knew; *The Butterflies of Australia* had highlighted several of Tillyard's specimens, but the pair found him to be 'a brilliant but most erratic scientist of very uncertain temper'.[21]

In 1928, Waterhouse was sounded out by the CSIR's chairman, who offered him a job as curator and librarian — with the quiet understanding that he might help smooth out any problems with Tillyard.[22] Despite their misgivings, both Waterhouse and Lyell agreed that he might be the only man who could act as a 'counterweight' to Tillyard. However, it didn't last. By November 1928, Waterhouse had mounting concerns that he refused to put on paper to anyone but his confidant, Lyell.

'All together I am in a very curious and at times in a very awkward position,' he told Lyell in January 1929,[23] before adding in April that, 'R.J.T. is almost impossible and it is becoming very wearisome trying to steer him correctly.'[24]

There was one other aspect of Tillyard's personality that may have frustrated these men of science: he believed in ghosts. For years, Tillyard had been a leading proponent of 'psychical research', championing spirit mediums who many would argue had already been exposed as frauds. Public interest in spiritualism and psychic matters had exploded after World War I, with millions of dead leaving countless more grieving loved ones to seek comfort and meaning in unexpected places. Encouraged by high-profile advocates such as Sir Arthur Conan Doyle — who had abandoned the scientific rationality of his famous detective, following the death of his eldest son, Kingsley, during the Spanish Flu pandemic — ideas that were once confined to incense-filled tents in funfairs were now splashed across front pages.

In an era of paradigm-shattering new discoveries such as the theory of evolution, radio, X-rays, and microbiology, Tillyard was one of many men of science in the 19th and 20th centuries drawn to new and challenging ideas. But one man's Galileo was another's charlatan, and many concepts were embraced — Lamarckism, eugenics, N-rays — that to modern eyes, and indeed many of their contemporaries, seemed either pseudoscientific nonsense, snake oil, or naked racism.

With his scientific bona fides and membership of prestigious groups such as the Royal Society in London, Tillyard was embraced by those who sought to prove the existence of a hidden world just beyond ordinary perception. By 1926, he had become an associate of Harry Price, founder of the National Laboratory of Psychical Research, who worked with Tillyard on numerous case studies ranging from the Romanian 'Devil Girl', Eleanora Zugun — who exhibited signs of stigmata and telekinesis — to Tillyard's own favourite subject, Stella

Cranshaw, a nurse turned reluctant spirit medium.

'It is a sad commentary on human nature that, even at the present day, when the reality of some at least of these phenomena has surely been put beyond the shadow of a doubt,' Tillyard wrote in *Nature* journal in July 1926, 'no scientific man can take up the study of psychical research without "losing caste" and undergoing either secret or more or less open persecution from his fellows.'[25]

In 1928, shortly after securing his CSIR position, Tillyard embarked on a tour of Europe and North America, where a handful of visits to American and European entomologists were soon overshadowed by an extended stay with his old Boston acquaintances Dr Le Roi Goddard Crandon and his young wife, Mina. By 1928, Mina Crandon's reputation for channelling the dead had already brought her fame and notoriety, thanks in no small part to the escape artist Harry Houdini. Houdini had become a renowned debunker of fraudulent mediums, and after five séances with the Crandons in 1924, he published a twenty-five-page illustrated pamphlet demystifying many aspects of Crandon's performance, calling it 'the "slickest" ruse I have ever detected, and it has converted all skeptics'.[26] Tillyard, however, remained a zealous believer.

Word of his paranormal adventures in Boston must have reached Australia—or perhaps George Lyell was a psychic too. On 17 August 1928, as he counselled Waterhouse regarding the job offer from the CSIR, Lyell offered a suggestion: to make it a condition that any papers to be published by Tillyard would have to be run past Waterhouse first: 'Your steadying influence would keep his soaring imagination within bound and prevent his hasty theories going into print on the spur of the moment.'[27]

The very next day, Tillyard published another *Nature* article, this time triumphantly sharing his latest experiments with the Crandons as 'Evidence of Survival of a Human Personality'.[28] It had taken some convincing to persuade *Nature*'s editor to run what Tillyard hoped would be a watershed account. Instead, the editor prefaced the article with a two-page editorial rejecting much of Tillyard's hypotheses as 'flights of phantasy'.[29] Across the four séances he had attended with Mina in May 1928, Tillyard had at least made one brief concession to his day job as an entomologist, presenting Crandon with a fossilised invertebrate and inviting one of the spirits she channelled to 'produce the corresponding living insect'. This, sadly, proved beyond her powers.[30]

In January 1937, two years after the CSIR executive forced his painful, protracted, but utterly inevitable exit from the organisation, Tillyard was travelling in heavy rain on the Hume Highway between Canberra and Sydney. His twenty-one-year-old daughter, Hope, was behind the wheel when, somewhere near Goulburn, the car slipped and overturned, and sent Tillyard headfirst through the windscreen. Hope and her friend in the back seat suffered only minor injuries, but Tillyard's feet had been caught on the dashboard, leaving his body trapped at the waist in broken glass. It was only after administering a powerful dose of morphine that paramedics were able to move him out of the wreck and rush him to a nearby hospital, where he died two days later.

When he heard the news, Tillyard's old partner in psychical research, Harry Price, raced to consult his old papers. Shortly after the Crandon séances in 1928, Tillyard had sent Price an airmailed letter, which Price had carried in his jacket pocket during a visit to a French medium named Jeanne Laplace in Paris. Price later claimed that 'Madame Laplace' held the blue envelope flat between her palms and began speaking in a stream-of-consciousness, telling Price that the letter had come from a 'doctor and scientist' who 'has not a long life to live' and would 'die through a railroad or automobile accident'. On his return to London, Price eagerly had Tillyard corroborate the lion's share of the fifty-three statements he had dictated from Laplace verbatim. But as for the vague predictions of his death by car or rail at some distant, indeterminant date, all Tillyard could say was, 'These things never come true!'[31]

Precognition aside, such accidents weren't that uncommon; in 1914, Tillyard himself had been thrown headfirst from a morning express service in Sydney, suffering permanent back injuries that left him five inches shorter.[32] Even Waterhouse had narrowly survived a horrific train accident in 1916 that left the carriage 'splintered into matchwood', and another car accident in 1928.[33] Nevertheless, Price was convinced he had snatched a bittersweet victory from the tragedy of his old friend's death, describing the Tillyard case as one of the 'best examples of prevision or fulfilled predictions'.[34]

Waterhouse, on the other hand, remained haunted by how his former colleague's career and life had gone off the rails — Tillyard had suffered a nervous breakdown shortly after the CSIR began to cut ties with him, leaving him a diminished figure long before the accident. Years after the crash, Waterhouse would ponder whether he could have done something differently to temper Tillyard's eccentricities, and perhaps even change his fate.

'I often wonder what would have happened if I had stayed on with CSIR,' he wrote to another colleague in 1940. 'He then might have been alive today.'[35]

Back in 1929, as the CSIR's Tillyard situation continued to spiral, Waterhouse was looking for an exit. Fate soon handed him a tragic one, spelled out in a solemn note to Lyell in August. His father, Gustavus Sr, had collapsed in the bath after suffering a stroke, before quietly slipping away during the night at seventy-nine years of age.

'Mother is bearing up splendidly, but has become very weak with very little desire to live,' Waterhouse told Lyell of his mother, who was now closer to the end of her life than the shell-collecting days of her youth. It was around the time of his father's death, and the rapidly souring state of the CSIR's entomology unit, that Waterhouse began to consider his own legacy. Later that month, he wrote another letter to Lyell.

'I have tentatively approached the Australian Museum with the offer of my butterfly collection,' he wrote to Lyell on 24 August.[36]

Years earlier, Lyell and Waterhouse had made a 'mutual agreement' that should either of them die, the type specimens described in *The Butterflies of Australia* would pass on to 'the survivor' — a joint Waterhouse-Lyell collection that would stand the test of time. Perhaps Waterhouse expected the older Lyell to pre-decease him, but with mortality on his mind, it seems he didn't want to wait for the pact to run its course.

'It would be a pity if eventually they are divided & housed in two different museums,' Waterhouse had told Lyell in August 1928, when he was first contemplating the CSIR offer. A year later, he had grown more decisive, but still wanted Lyell's blessing before sending his share in the Waterhouse-Lyell collection to the safety of the museum in Sydney.

In the end, Lyell opted against pooling their collections together in Sydney, and, following his own health scare, decided instead to deposit his butterflies and moths closer to home at the National Museum of Victoria. It was a rare moment of disagreement across the pair's decades of correspondence, but we only know Waterhouse's side of the conversation, carefully kept by Lyell at Gisborne and eventually bequeathed to the museum with all the other letters that Waterhouse sent him. Despite the closeness of his friendship, and his own scholarly commitment to record-keeping, Waterhouse destroyed 'some thousands of letters' sent by his friend.[37]

But the butterflies weren't all that Waterhouse planned to hand over to the Australian Museum that year. He would also donate his late father's collection of Pacific Island artefacts — a set of clubs, bowls, and model canoes — gathered during his own career as a merchant plying tobacco, timber, livestock, and coal in the same South Seas trade that had once delivered rare shells to his wife. In fact, the Waterhouse family had a long history in the Pacific, with Athol's great-grandfather having served as superintendent of the Methodist missions in the region — an experience so defining that in his last moments, the Reverend John Waterhouse reportedly sat bolt upright in bed and with his final breath yelled, 'Missionaries! Missionaries! Missionaries!'[38]

There was also the matter of Athol's mother's shells, the first and oldest of the Waterhouse family collections, that had played such a formative role in his own life as a scientist. A few years after Janie Waterhouse's own death in 1935, an Australian Museum conchologist reflected that, much like the G.A. Waterhouse Collection, the suite of shells she had gathered with her young sons, and meticulously catalogued and labelled, could never be recreated. Time and humanity had caught up with the once-abundant, unexpectedly powerful cowries:

> Today, many of the cowries Mrs Waterhouse so carefully collected then are no longer found alive in those spots, owing possibly to the contamination of the waters and an increased population.[39]

Collections such as the Waterhouses' offered a safeguard against the passage of time and the precarity of life out in the wild. But, as Athol's donations showed, they also made natural history deeply personal. They told the story of the collector's life in labels, a permanent record of where they went, who they knew, and what they found, to be witnessed by generations of scientists to come, just as Waterhouse and Lyell could retrace the travels of Joseph Banks through Johann Fabricius's pinned paper trail.

To hand over his family collections to a state museum was a gift to future scientists, but it was also a lasting tribute to his parents — a kind of life after death more tangible than anything some American psychic could summon into a Boston living room. It also meant that the wanton destruction of those legacies was a particularly unthinkable transgression. While he was making his pitch to his old friend George Lyell, Waterhouse argued that the Australian Museum was the safest, most obvious, place for their types, along with the rest of the Waterhouse collections:

> Of the State Museums, the Australian Museum is the largest and best endowed, and will always have at least one entomologist there, which may not be the case with the other Museums. In addition, the fact that I am a Trustee and could, as well as working at the collection, help to form the policy of the Museum, is of importance.[40]

In just a few years, this would prove to be one promise that Waterhouse could not keep, even if he wanted to.

CHAPTER FIVE

The Cadet

At thirty-six years of age, with wavy brown hair and a round, proud face, Nancy Bannatyne Adams was an unfailingly stoic fixture in the insects and arachnids division of the Australian Museum. While any museum department in the world can usually be found to harbour its share of institutional gripes and esoteric beefs, her colleagues noted that Adams was 'loyal and conscientious', 'never complained', and was 'always cheerful'.[1]

'Her character might be described by the word "fine", which was her invariable reply when asked how she felt,' reflected Anthony Musgrave, the museum's fifty-one-year-old entomologist of his long-time assistant.[2] Of course, whether it's a sigh of resignation or a curt refusal to elaborate further, that short syllable can encompass a world of meaning—especially when uttered by a young woman to her male superior.

Back in 1929, Adams had joined the small staff of the entomology unit as a teenager, and for a time the precocious school-leaver with the £78-a-year temporary assistant job was one of only two women on the museum's scientific staff. By January 1947, however, Adams was a museum lifer, and an essential part of the institution's day-to-day operations. While at first she had had been relegated to the precise but repetitive task of mounting and labelling the thousands of new specimens that arrived each year, it wasn't long before Adams joined her older male colleagues in handling the more specialised work of registering and cataloguing them too.

Adams proved a voracious learner inside and outside the museum's walls, continuing to study at the University of Sydney, the Sydney Technical College, and the Royal Art Society, where she became a student of Antonio Dattilo Rubbo — a dapper, goateed bohemian from Naples whose better-known disciples included modernists such as Grace Cossington Smith, Frank Hinder, and Roy de Maistre.[3] Adams, though, preferred to faithfully illustrate the thousands of specimens that came across her desk, with her work appearing in numerous scientific papers written by her colleagues and other celebrated scientists, along with articles she wrote herself for *The Australian Museum Magazine*. She would also help Musgrave overhaul and revise numerous collections and modernise public exhibits in the College Street galleries. Despite these accomplishments, along with performing a range of other duties beyond her pay grade while Musgrave was out in the field or attending conferences, for nearly two decades Adams had remained in the role of general assistant, although technically still classified an entry-level cadet.[4]

While promising male cadets could dream of charting a well-trodden path to assistant, curator, and possibly even director roles — Musgrave himself had started as a cadet in 1910 — Adams wasn't the first person to find that illustration was one of few professional pathways open to Australia's women naturalists. Back in the 1860s, it was Alexander Walker Scott's daughters, Harriet and Helena, who prepared the hand-coloured, life-size illustrations for the multi-volume *Australian Lepidoptera and Their Transformations* while also helping their father in the field. While Scott actively acknowledged his daughters' contributions, being a woman in Victorian-era entomology could still have its frustrations, which once drove Harriet to complain that, 'clearly I ought to have been Harry Scott instead of Hattie Scott'.[5]

Whatever Nancy Adams might have felt about her place beneath the museum's glass ceiling, there was one day in January 1947 where she became the single most important person in the building. It had all started years earlier, when Dr Athol Waterhouse made the decision to hand over his collection in the wake of his father's death. It would be an enormous undertaking; by 1930, the collection that Waterhouse had started as a teenager numbered around 50,000 specimens, making it easily the single biggest donation ever to pass through the entomology department. The G.A. Waterhouse Collection spanned the continent, featuring 333 recorded Australian species from Geraldton to Cairns, with his own prized specimens bolstered by trades with all the other prominent Australian collectors, such as Dodd, Elgner, Goldfinch, and Turner.

It fell to Adams to help Waterhouse get the job done, and for years they worked side by side to transfer his enormous collection into the museum's College Street premises. Given Waterhouse's perfectionism when it came to the important work of labelling and data, his seemingly matter-of-fact acknowledgement of Adams's contribution in the museum's 1933 annual report — he said she 'rendered very able assistance in the work of registration, her work being always carried out in a very capable and efficient manner' — was high praise.[6] They made a start in May 1930, but it would take Adams and Waterhouse years to complete; like the Lyell Collection in Victoria, it meant comprehensively reconfiguring the museum's existing lepidoptera collection.

'The monetary value of this huge collection is estimated at some three or four thousand pounds, but its value to entomologists is so great as to be difficult to estimate,' wrote Anthony Musgrave in October 1930. 'Suffice to say it that it would now be impossible to form one so complete and so rich in types as this which our public-spirited benefactor has presented to the state.'[7]

Unlike Waterhouse, Lyell, or even Nancy Adams, butterflies weren't exactly in the wheelhouse of Arthur Walkom, the director of the Australian Museum. A boyish-looking fifty-seven-year-old, the paleobotanist did at least have some experience in piecing together a trail of evidence — he'd built his career on the long-dead plants that lived and died hundreds of millions of years earlier, leaving impressions in layers of rock and sediment. On 21 January 1947, as his Victorian counterpart, Dick Pescott, filled him in on the growing crisis over in Melbourne, it seemed that his fossils would have to wait. Pescott explained that someone had cleaned out the Lyell Collection, and that, given the scale and sophistication of the theft, it wasn't out of the question that other museums might have been hit too. Walkom knew that an immediate check of the Australian Museum's holdings, with particular reference to the G.A. Waterhouse Collection, had to be made at once.

When it came to insects, Walkom would ordinarily defer to Musgrave. But Musgrave wasn't in the office — he was out on a field trip to Barrington Tops, collecting specimens and filming material for a planned documentary alongside Lindsay Hopson, son of the late 'Father of the Tops' who had accompanied a much younger Musgrave on that first scientific expedition to Barrington Tops in 1915.[8] While Pescott and Burns had brought Lyell in almost immediately, Walkom was hesitant to contact Athol Waterhouse himself; Waterhouse's health had started to catch up with him a few months after he and Adams began their work in Sydney, forcing him to withdraw from some of his honorary activities on doctor's advice and to relinquish the museum presidency. Then, in July 1943, Athol Waterhouse's lifetime of collecting, from the shores of Sydney to the heights of Barrington Tops, was dealt a devastating blow.

'You will be disappointed to learn that three weeks ago I had a slight stroke,' Waterhouse wrote to Lyell from a wheelchair, having been bedridden until a just few days earlier.[9]

As he sat in the sun on the balcony of the house in Killara, Waterhouse physically struggled to break the news to his old friend, laboriously tracing out each spidery letter with his left hand:

> I am hoping to get the use of my right hand soon. So far I can move everything more or less normally on the right arm down to the wrist. The right leg is almost normal. Today I walked a few steps with the nurse holding one.

Even after this debilitating episode, occurring just a decade after the stroke that killed his father, Waterhouse hadn't lost sight of what was most important: the butterflies. His letter to Lyell was accompanied by two specimens from New South Wales that he hoped Lyell could pin and mount—there was only so much he could do with them in his present state.

'I hope that I will be able to set again,' read the sobering note from the almost helpless old man.[10]

Waterhouse suffered more tragedy in October, when news arrived from the frontlines of World War II, where his and Beatrice's twin sons—the 'two fine little fellows' whose destiny he had hopefully pondered in letters to Lyell in 1913—were both serving. Lieutenant Stretton Gustavus John Waterhouse had been working as a clerk before he enlisted in July 1940, and in August 1943 set off from Cairns to New Guinea to join a fresh Australian offensive against Japan led by the American general Douglas MacArthur. Stretton was killed on 22 September, just shy of the twins' thirtieth birthday.[11]

By June 1944, Waterhouse had lost his mother, his father, and a son, and while he could at least dress himself, he still couldn't pick up a pin. He and Beatrice had even been forced to farewell Killara—the well-established gardens, orchards, and family home, filled with memories of childhoods, wedding receptions, and decades of butterfly collecting, had become too much to manage. By the time they moved to a serviced apartment in Potts Point, the abundant remnant bushland that once surrounded them had already begun to be swallowed up by residential development, along with the butterfly populations that had captured Waterhouse's imagination.

Back in 1900, the Sydney azure, *Ogyris ianthis*, was the first species Waterhouse named and described, based on specimens he had caught while circling a hilltop gumtree near Como railway station, not far from his future home in Killara.[12] When the museum acquired his collection, it was generally agreed that the five drawers of stunning metallic-blue *Ogyris* formed the 'piece de resistance', but within just a few decades, Waterhouse had watched as this prime spot near the station was cleared to make way for another house.[13] The world that Waterhouse knew had changed, and for all his promises of being a hands-on guardian of the Australian Museum's entomology collection, at sixty-seven years of age he was forced once again into retirement — this time, a real one.

Walkom knew he couldn't rely on the former president in this time-sensitive situation. But he knew just who to ask. It was Nancy Adams, the dutiful, underpaid assistant who had spent the previous seventeen years re-pinning and mounting nearly every insect to enter the building, who was perfectly placed to mount an immediate audit. Unsurprisingly, it didn't take her long to confirm Pescott and Walkom's initial fears: there were indeed specimens missing, but given that the perpetrator seemed to have worked with precision, picking and choosing just a few specimens from each species and locality, it was anyone's guess as to how many of the tens of thousands of insects had been affected.

Like in Melbourne, it would require practically a complete count of the entire collection before they had the full picture. Adams had already spent a week drafting her list of missing specimens by the time Musgrave finally returned from Barrington Tops; when they completed their tally, it had reached an extraordinarily high 1,600 — nearly double the number that Lyell had settled on in Melbourne.[14] Burns's fluke discovery was proving to be the worst stroke of bad luck to have befallen either museum in their history — and it wasn't over yet.

When Waterhouse and Lyell published *The Butterflies of Australia* in 1914, they included a brief passage warning the reader of the 'three foes of the collection': mould, other parasites, and liquified grease from the decomposing bodies of fattier breeds.[15] To keep these problems at bay, the pair recommended constant vigilance and regular checks, and, if necessary, a carefully administered dose of poisons, such as formalin or thymol. But in all their years of collecting, exchange, collaboration, and gossip, it hadn't occurred to them that a fourth threat might be a rogue collector.

In Sydney, on 24 January 1947, Walkom wrote an urgent letter to a colleague at the Imperial Institute of Entomology in London named Dr John Evans: 'Inquiries indicated that only one man had had constant access to the collection during the last year or two.'[16]

CHAPTER SIX

The Golden Age

Colin Wyatt seemed to come alive at high altitudes, and in later years he came to suspect this had something to do his first brush with death.[1] He had felt at home among the mountains from a young age — his father, James, had made sure of that, strapping his three-year-old son into a pair of skis when Colin had barely mastered putting one foot in front of the other. In an old family photo album, little Colin can be seen in dark ski goggles, broad-brimmed hat, and his hands snug in over-sized mittens as he looks back at the camera as if seeking approval. Looming large in the background is a set of snow-capped mountains, the kind of breathtaking alpine vista that most people could only hope to see on a postcard.

Everything seemed picturesque, until the day young Colin came down with a cold. It was a bad one, soon snowballing into bronchial pneumonia that knocked him off his feet and left him running high, fevered temperatures. The doctors ordered him to spend days at a time confined to an oxygen tent — a harrowing experience even if, in the moment, Colin seemed more concerned with the clutch of oak-eggar caterpillars he'd been raising in one of his shoeboxes.[2] His mother was repulsed by the hairy, four-inch-long fingers, but took care of them out of fear for Colin's mental state. Later, Margaret and the nurse were forced to crawl on hands and knees when the caterpillars escaped their cardboard prison and threatened to breach the sterility of the oxygen tent.[3] Colin watched on with amusement as they patiently scooped up each rogue grub with tablespoons, as though playing a bizarre game of lacrosse.[4]

Despite his confinement, Colin's health continued to falter. Nothing seemed to help the boy breathe again, until one day his mother resolved to uproot the family to the Swiss Alps, defying the advice of the doctors in England who were convinced that this would be the death of him. But Margaret was unyielding, and Colin would fondly remember the butterflies — clouded yellow and mourning cloak — that were still on the wing when they arrived in Switzerland in October 1919. As he looked out and down from their rented chalet, he could see across the valleys, past the yellowing autumn foliage to the crisp, white glaciers in the distance.[5]

The Wyatts weren't the first family to head for the hills in search of health and wellbeing — Switzerland was home to many quaint little sanatoriums that had sprouted up in the previous century during waves of tuberculosis and other modern plagues. The Wyatts based themselves at Gstaad, a small German-speaking town that in a few years' time would become a popular destination among artists, émigrés, and wealthy elites seeking sanctuary and respite in the thinner, cleaner Swiss air.

F Scott Fitzgerald was to borrow the town for his final novel, *Tender Is the Night,* inspired by the time he took his own daughter, Scottie, to its ski fields in December 1930. In the book, Fitzgerald's protagonist, Dick Diver, recalls Gstaad's 'crisp green rinks' and 'pale-blue skies', but the reality of their holiday was stormier: Fitzgerald had taken Scottie to Gstaad to take their minds off a harrowing visit to the Prangins Clinic in lakeside Nyon, where Zelda Fitzgerald had been confined since her latest mental-health crisis — according to her husband, Zelda had come 'within an ace of losing her mind'.[6] But she was still sinking by Christmas, and the family reunion ended in smashed tree ornaments and tears.[7]

Fitzgerald's friend Ernest Hemingway would also visit Gstaad, drafting *A Farewell to Arms* in one of the town's hotels. A black-and-white photograph from the period shows Hemingway grinning under his moustache and ski goggles, hands on hips and feet in skis, in a disarmingly playful holiday snap. Hemingway would send the photo to his publishers, with a dark joke written on the other side that he hoped might reassure them should they hear rumours of an author drinking himself to death.[8]

For the Wyatts, the change in scenery seemed to work wonders. Before long, Colin was up and about, and soon he'd snared an unusually pale female clouded yellow as pure and white as the snow around them. By Christmas, he was well enough for his father to take him out on a 1,500-foot descent — while back at the chalet, another cardboard box slowly filled with live specimens.[9] As the days grew longer, Colin was thrilled to see more butterflies creep out of hiding, ranging from sunbaking tortoiseshells to the rare and stunning Camberwell beauty — a species that was famously elusive back home in Britain.[10]

The Wyatts kept coming back to the chalet year after year, long after Colin's illness became a bad memory. The truth was that neither James nor Margaret Wyatt would have minded an excuse to spend their winters in the Alps. James William Wyatt's own childhood had come with its own breathtaking views, in a lakeside estate in North Wales on the doorstep of Yr Wyddfa, the highest point in Snowdonia. It was a picturesque seat for a lesser branch of a dynasty once famous for its royal architects and iconoclasts — as one distant relative reflected, the Wyatt family's fortunes had 'marched with the rise of Britain as the world's leading industrial and political power' before the 'inherited genius' once seen across the family tree 'sank with Britain's decline'.[11]

The Wyatt touch could be seen from Windsor Castle to Calcutta's government house, from the Rothschild mausoleum to the Roman-inspired Pantheon in London. The Wyatt who gave Windsor Castle a makeover had been commissioned by King George IV, who also pressured him to change his surname to 'Wyatville', purportedly to distinguish him from the glut of other architectural Wyatts.[12] The Wyatt who created the Pantheon at the age of twenty-three was perhaps the most famous of them all, a precocious gothic revivalist named James Wyatt (1746–1813) who was as controversial as he was prolific. At one point considered to be 'the First Architect of the Kingdom' by King George III, Wyatt's so-called restorations of already-iconic churches and palaces were often so transformative that his fiercest critics dubbed him 'Wyatt the Destroyer', 'a monster of architectural depravity', and even a plagiarist.[13] But it did little to dent his popularity, as his immense personal charm and gentlemanly manners papered over his tendency to over-promise, under-deliver, and, occasionally, see his creations catch fire or collapse.[14] As one newspaper satirist wrote:

> I know the foolish kingdom all runs riot,
> Calling Aloud for Wyat, Wyat, Wyat[15]

James William Wyatt shared the name of his famous first cousin once removed, but perhaps unsurprisingly for a boy raised in the shadow of Wales's greatest mountain, he preferred adventure to architecture, even as he dutifully trained as a civil engineer. With a lean frame, a long stride, and a penchant for Tyrolean lederhosen, Wyatt would spend his youth clambering up peaks from the Eastern Alps to the Dolomites, chasing butterflies and later collecting specimens of alpine plants for the Royal Botanic Gardens at Kew as he went.

He became a well-known personality in the rarefied ranks of the London Alpine Club, while his young wife, Margaret—from well-connected stock herself as the daughter and granddaughter of conservative MPs—was among the first to join the Ladies' Alpine Club upon its formation in 1907.[16] They had been rock-climbing together since their honeymoon, and for many years Margaret was always by James's side on the ski fields or, when the weather was good, hiking up a mountain.

The tales of James Wyatt's youthful exploits would capture his young son's imagination, supplemented by the giants of alpine literature such as Edward Whymper, who wrote about his historic conquest of the Matterhorn in *Scrambles Amongst the Alps*, and Alfred F Mummery, who perished in an avalanche while trying to reach the summit of Nanga Parbat in the western Himalayas.

Within a few years of Colin's bout of pneumonia, those winter stays grew longer as the Wyatts made Europe a second home in springtime too. They briefly enrolled Colin at the Institut Le Rosey, a famously expensive Swiss boarding school partially based in Gstaad, where he started to receive the kind of elite education favoured by royalty, the rich, and powerful, and, later, the children of rock stars.[17] One fine spring, James also took his son to Digne, a small town in France's Basse Alps, to continue his education in that other important field: butterfly hunting.[18] Sitting high on a plateau 1,955 feet above sea level, the area surrounding the town had a reputation as one of the richest collecting grounds in Europe — on a good day in August, this Mecca for European entomologists might have over one hundred species on the wing.[19] Years later, Colin would reflect that Digne might be the one place in the world where the sight of a net-carrying butterfly collector walking down the street was the subject of reverence, not ridicule. In fact, Wyatt found that a traveller could hardly move without being propositioned by an enterprising local promising to lead them to the best collecting spots.[20]

There were times when James Wyatt's passion for butterflies seemed to overpower all sense of reason or decorum. Colin would later recount the story of his father sunbathing naked in a seemingly deserted forest clearing when a passing purple emperor caught his eye. With nothing but his net, he gave chase, skipping through trees and rocks in pursuit until it sent him leaping over a ledge and into the path of three German women, also sunning themselves with less privacy than they expected. Appreciating the awkward optics of the scene — his son would later compare it to a Renaissance painting of the 'Rape of the Sabines' — James Wyatt sped giddily back into the forest to retrieve his clothing before the trio could raise any alarm about the tall naked man with a net who had burst into their suntanning session.[21]

Colin was delighted by his father's exploits, and as he grew older would find himself pining for the 'golden age' of European mountaineering and exploration that his father had known — before the explosion of leisure-travelling turned once-challenging high-wire acts into well-trodden tourist traps, complete with fresh roads, railways, hotels, and modern conveniences that even gin-soaked Jazz Age novelists could enjoy.[22]

The late Alfred F Mummery also resented the 'vulgarization' of the Swiss Alps, with its 'cheap trippers and their trumpery fashions'.[23]

In his 1895 book, *My Climbs in the Alps and Caucasus,* first published in the same year as his death and one of the 'classics' that Wyatt drew inspiration from, Mummery reflected that:

> A true mountaineer is a wanderer … a man who loves to be where no human being has been before, who delights in gripping rocks that have previously never felt the touch of human fingers, or in hewing his way up ice-filled gullies whose grim shadows have been sacred to the mists and avalanches since 'Earth rose out of the chaos'.[24]

As he soaked up these words and stories, it seemed unlikely that any son of James and Margaret Wyatt would ever be satisfied with travelling along the beaten path. By nature, or nurture, Colin Wyatt was a wanderer.

As he came of age, Colin also did his share to keep the famous Wyatt name in the spotlight. The flying start that his father had granted him as a three-year-old had paid off handsomely, and by his late teens Colin was making headlines as a prodigious champion skier, scooping tournaments around the mountains of Europe. It was an era when the sporting rivalries of Britain's elite made international news, when the young, rich, and athletic descended on slopes and ski resorts like they were 'Gods of Beauty of Vitality', with their exploits reported in gossip columns and breathless cables syndicated around the globe.[25] Among these 'angelic' young ladies and 'stout fellows', the trailblazing Wyatt captured imaginations and inspired many column inches.

'In the all-British world, Colin Wyatt shines as a star of great magnitude,' read one report in *The Sketch* in January 1931, describing 'a magnificent figure perched on a commanding boulder, arrayed in an azure pull-over'.[26] A fortnight later, *The Bystander* declared, 'The best ski jumper among Englishmen is undoubtedly Mr Colin Wyatt, an undergraduate who has performed amazing feats in this direction both this year and last year.'[27]

He was only nineteen years old when he came first at an inter-varsity event at St Moritz in December 1928 — according to one report, he 'rush[ed] down the mountainside at express train speed' — to lead Cambridge to a romping victory over Oxford.[28] The wins kept coming, and with Wyatt as team captain, Cambridge blitzed Oxford again the following winter.[29] A few weeks later, he led the British University Ski Club to victory over their Swiss rivals, the Swiss University Ski Club, at another annual grudge match in Mürren. The next year, he was one of two British skiers to compete against over one hundred of the world's best in the European ski championships.[30]

A photographer from *The Times* once captured Wyatt mid-descent, the faces of spectators frozen in amazement as he sped down the white slopes to complete the three-mile run.[31] He posed for more triumphant photographs with his teammates still strapped into their skis, in an image that recalls Hemingway's proof-of-life snapshot at Gstaad two years earlier — though still a teenager, Wyatt's beaming young face is already sporting the moustache that would not leave his lip for the next four-and-a-half decades of his life. ('He also wears side-whiskers,' noted *The Daily Express* in 1931.[32])

For all his thrilling exploits, however, there were soon signs that even the most high-flying wunderkind can have a short shelf life — and it wasn't long before Colin Wyatt came crashing back to earth. By January 1933, some commentators had reported that Wyatt was 'not at his best this year'.[33] '[He] seems to have lost the knack,' declared *The Tatler* after his latest season was derailed by a 'painful smash'.[34] 'Experts say he takes off too soon, but his last nasty crash has probably got something to do with it.'

While the limits of his earlier stardom were becoming apparent, Wyatt was harbouring bigger aspirations than enjoying a few years of sporting glory before settling into a respectable white-collar profession. Despite keeping up the appearance of yet another debonair member of London high society — regularly pictured in the social pages of *The Tatler* and *The Bystander* in a crisp tuxedo and bowtie, beside other darlings of the scene — Wyatt spent the early 1930s leading a colourful second life.

'Did you know the Cambridge ex-ski-Captain is a considerable artist, and wanders about Central Europe, easel in ruck-sack?' one gossip columnist for *The Sketch* later wrote of the skiing ace.[35] 'He is a climber — peaks, not parties — and an artist of promise,' added another from *The Tatler*.[36]

Despite his father's misgivings, Wyatt had left Cambridge before his final exams, and had spent the next few years following his paintbrush across Britain and Europe. There were stints at the Académie Delécluse in Paris, the Slade School of Art, the Grosvenor School of Modern Art, and a debut one-man show in the London headquarters of the Alpine Club. The exhibition ran for twelve days in November 1931, but was not exactly an overnight success; one reviewer from the *Daily Telegraph* found his paintings of striking mountain scenes a little overbearing and 'over-sweetened', preferring works that reflected a 'rather quieter mood'.[37] This included his more subtle watercolour studies of street corners and 'old domestic and ecclesiastical architecture' — a subject that might have pleased his long-dead relative Wyatt the Destroyer.

Wyatt's early output suggested an artist who was easily influenced and still finding his own voice and style — a talent in search of inspiration. He could paint highly realistic oil portraits of weathered-looking mountain guides, craft shiny chrome sculptures that looked like hood ornaments on a luxury car, or carve crisp linocut prints that bore the clear influence of his time at Grosvenor and its lead instructors, Claude Flight and Iain Macnab. Flight and Macnab finessed an expressive style of linocut printing full of clean lines and blocks of black and pastel-coloured shape and movement, a style that inspired many of their students — including Australians such as Dorrit Black, Ethel Spowers, and Eveline Syme

Although the crisp colours of Wyatt's prints were less intense than his oil paintings, a handful of works from 1932 betray a keen eye for drama and the balletic shapes he cut through the mountain air — *The Jumper* sees four cap-wearing skiers look up in amazement as another man soars above them headfirst, tracing an impossibly high arc against a pale-yellow sky.

It was of a style that was being readily embraced by advertising agencies and tourism bureaus around the world, for better or for worse.

To one critic from *The Scotsman,* Wyatt's work 'aim[ed] at a simplicity of shapes rather too reminiscent of posterwork', which 'empt[ied] scenes of the most fascinating and picturesque nature'.[38] While he struggled to match the heights of his peers and mentors — in an exhibition of the so-called Grubb Group of artists, one critic from the *Yorkshire Post* thought Wyatt was overshadowed by the likes of Flight and Macnab — he showed a nose for combining his various talents into paid side-hustles.[39] In 1931, he painted a series of alpine murals for a novel indoor ski school for Lillywhite's, a sporting-goods store in Piccadilly Circus. Set in an old dance hall in the Criterion Buildings, this 'Little Switzerland' came complete with artificial 'snow slopes' cooked up from eight tons of washing soda and acid.[40] 'Why Collide with the Alps? Learn Your Ski-ing in London,' read one headline in the *Illustrated Sporting and Dramatic News*, above a photograph of Wyatt executing an indoor *geländesprung* manoeuvre, tucking his knees mid-air over the fake snow.[41] But while the 'man-made mountains' of Piccadilly might have attested to Wyatt's artistic abilities, he continued to crave the real thing.

In September 1935, Wyatt and another member of the Alpine Ski Club spent ten days touring the Zillertal Alps, not far from the Tyrolean villages he had frequented with his parents — and the site of his earlier brush with the Italian army.[42] It was, at first, another glorious alpine adventure; setting out from Mayrhofen, they found that the trails and huts were blessedly free of the crowds of tourists found during peak season. They happily filled their hats and bellies with freshly picked raspberries and strawberries as they made their ascent, and after tackling the almost two-mile summit of Wollbachjoch were treated to spectacular vistas from the eastern Tyrolean Alps to the Dolomites. But there were clouds gathering, in every sense. As they climbed up the glacier, they encountered a young peasant boy trying to make his way to Germany, while avoiding the 'ever-watchful Carabinieri' down in the valley of Venezia Tridentia. Life in the valley, the boy explained, was increasingly an 'intolerable situation'.[43]

He wasn't the only one. Later, they cautiously approached another mountain hut after noticing an Italian flag flying overhead. There were no Carabinieri inside, but over breakfast the hutkeeper and her son told them how South Tyrol was in a 'sorry state'.[44] Once, parties such as Wyatt and his friends could regularly be seen enjoying the mountain trails, but these days young men were being barred from venturing up from the valleys at all, in case they fled over the mountains for Austria, just like the peasant boy. If they did manage to escape, Wyatt was told, it was the families they left behind who would be made an example of.

Wyatt had also seen how Europe's slide towards rearmament and war could manifest itself on its ski fields. At one jump meet in Oslo, a miserly snowfall saw a troop of idle Norwegian soldiers deployed to cart between 200 and 300 tons of snow to the run — apparently a common sight as the nations of Europe built up more battalions than, for the moment, they knew what to do with.[45] In the end, a burst of rain turned the transplanted snow into hard, slippery ice upon which Wyatt broke his collarbone, forcing him to be carried away in an army ambulance to get a small piece of metal set into his shoulder.

The golden age of European mountaineering that his father had known was long gone, but these incidents offered more evidence that the era of inter-war peace and relative freedom that Wyatt had come of age in was also slipping away. Europe might be closing its borders and bracing for war, but there were other mountains, other wildernesses, other adventures calling to him from the other side of the world. Places where a talented young man like him — a little bruised and battered, but still thriving fifteen years after his childhood doctors had predicted the worst — might still be able to experience a golden age of his own.

Of course, Colin Wyatt would answer that call.

CHAPTER SEVEN

The Wanderer

With his head cocked, hair swept back, and a pencil moustache neatly trimmed above his pursed top lip, the rakish young man in the portrait could be mistaken for a matinee idol such as Errol Flynn, Laurence Olivier, or perhaps Clarke Gable. Newspaper caricatures are not typically a flattering medium — a genre of buckteeth, bat ears, and bobbleheads — and usually the pages of a gossip rag such as *Table Talk* were no exception. And yet, when this edition hit Melbourne's newsstands in May 1937, there was no arguing that the twenty-eight-year-old Colin Wyatt came off rather well in black and white. In between the serialised whodunnits, hosiery advertisements, and coverage of the upcoming royal coronation that padded its page count, this brief, gushing profile — 'London Artist Mountaineers in New Zealand' — captured the soft glow of minor celebrity Wyatt had generated across his first grand tour across Australia and New Zealand.[1] The man in the caricature was the kind of dashing, well-connected interloper you might happily invite to your dinner party, to visit your holiday house, or to inspect your prized insect collection.

It was the call of the mountains — or rather, a request from the New Zealand Alpine Club and Ski Council — that had brought Wyatt to the Southern Hemisphere, sailing into Wellington in July 1936. Stepping off the SS *Arkaroa,* he was initially unimpressed with the Victorian-era architecture and seemingly idyllic rolling green hills of New Zealand's capital. Instead, he saw a landscape cleared of native vegetation to be replaced by mediocre wooden buildings, all of it plagued by the introduced ragwort weed that ran rampant despite the efforts of Dr Robin Tillyard at the Cawthron Institute a decade earlier.[2] In 1925, Tillyard had been so confident when his staff unleashed a swarm of specially bred British cinnabar moths to keep the ragwort in check. By the time Wyatt arrived, however, he was told that the local bird population had quickly made a meal of this novel new bug.[3]

But Wyatt wasn't there to look at weeds; despite his misgivings about the 'blatantly commercial' developments that had transformed the great mountains of Europe, he had crossed the equator ostensibly to help New Zealand's nascent ski-tourism industry find its feet.[4]

'In the carefree days of 1936, an unusual bird of passage arrived in New Zealand, not exactly unheralded, but at the invitation of our Ski Council,' reflected GG Lockwood, a Christchurch lawyer and member of the Alpine Club and Ski Council.[5]

Wyatt would be paying his own way, but the official invitation also presented him with an opportunity—a chance to channel the adventurous spirit of his father's youth and to explore challenging, less-trammelled country. Wyatt's ulterior motive soon became clear to Lockwood.

'Our objective was to have him instruct us in jumping, racing and tests,' Lockwood later recalled, 'his was to cram in as much touring and climbing as time and weather permitted.'[6]

With talent, panache, and the latest gear from Europe, Wyatt quickly made an impression with the locals, who could only watch as he 'plough[ed] steadily up at impossible angles on his latest tie-on plush skins'.[7] One reporter was moved to describe his style at length:

> His much-envied clothes are in character with Chalet life; he looks so White Horse Inn, especially in plus four style pants worn with navy socks with white and yellow daisies on 'em and in his Swiss quilted jacket.[8]

Wyatt soon backed the style with substance during a record-breaking appearance in late August at the New Zealand Ski Championships. He was one of forty competitors to make the early-morning trek up to Ruapehu, a 9,100-foot active volcano in the middle of New Zealand's North Island, only to be told to sit tight when mist came rolling over the course. The land, waters, and wildlife of Ruapehu were considered sacred, or tapu, by the Ngāti Tūwharetoa and Ngāti Rangi iwi, its Māori custodians who assiduously avoided scaling its peak and held grave misgivings about its new identity as a winter resort. Years later, Wyatt said he could understand why Māori regarded the mountains as sacred, living things — the mountains could be 'weird and uncanny', and fraught with danger for the visitors who flocked there despite the seismic rumblings of the still-active volcano, the dense, unnavigable scrub of its lower reaches, and weather that could go from fine and sunny to impenetrable fog within half an hour.[9]

That mist had engulfed several parties of climbers and students over the years, with some never seen again. There was a party of six lost tourists in 1913 who managed to crawl back to safety by retracing sulphur streams in the snow — with the exception of one of their group last seen going over a waterfall, survived only by his hat and coat later seen floating in a nearby stream.[10] In 1931, a pack of fourteen university students were caught by the mist, and it took a one-hundred-man search party to track them down — all except for their most accomplished mountaineer, whose tracks were found leading off the edge of a cliff.[11] Years later, a small plane with thirteen passengers aboard crashed into the side of the mountain just 500 feet from its peak, with rescuers only finding the wrecked fuselage when the snow and fog cleared a week later.[12]

'It was dangerous to move; a false step, a slip, might send one to the bottom of a crevasse, beyond human reach, to be held in nature's refrigerator till earth and sea give up their dead,' recalled one traveller who had braved the region during mist.[13]

Wyatt could feel the earth vibrating ominously under his feet when he arrived on the mountain, but seemed to brush off any sense of danger.[14] When the official tournament was put on ice, he was one of a handful of competitors to buck the official caution and strap on their skis regardless, and while the Australians took part in an 'unofficial' race, Wyatt took to the slalom course for a practice run. To the amazement of onlookers, he promptly set a New Zealand record with a 'spectacular leap' of over seventy feet before shooting down the slopes at sixty miles per hour.[15] Back at the safety of Chateau Tongariro—a postcard-perfect establishment painted in blocks of red, blue, and yellow to mimic the sulphur, rock, and water of the mountains—Wyatt offered his verdict to the local press, predicting it might soon become the preferred destination for British skiers looking overseas to hit the slopes.

'The natural facilities available at the Chateau Tongariro and in the South Island must result in skiing becoming a featured winter sport in New Zealand,' he told one newspaper.[16]

Wyatt had made such a memorable impression on the local ski community that when the Ruapehu Ski Club hosted its annual ski ball and fancy-dress parade at Chateau Tongariro in September, one entrant named Mrs Arthur Fair stood out among the other entrants decked out as recognisable characters and celebrities such as Mae West and Popeye the Sailor, as well as racist caricatures such as 'Hindu lady', 'Chinese Mandarin', and 'Negro washer-woman'.

'The elaborate beauty of many costumes, which had been brought to the Chateau specially for the occasion, vied with the amusing ingenuity of others which had been hastily devised on the spot,' read one newspaper report.[17]

Mrs Fair was, presumably, in the latter camp, but nevertheless impressed the judges enough to take home the 'most original' prize for her costume: a drag impression of 'the English skier Colin Wyatt', who the judges noted was 'dressed to sartorial perfection'.[18]

The real Colin Wyatt achieved another milestone soon after his stay at Tongariro, when in September 1936 he spent several weeks exploring Kā Tiritiri o te Moana, the enormous dividing range that runs down the western side of the South Island, with its largest peak, Aoraki, standing at over 3,000 feet. To most 20th-century explorers, Aoraki was known as Mount Cook, named after an English captain who never set foot anywhere near it, while the range itself was simply dubbed the Southern Alps.

According to Māori histories, the range had first been crossed a few hundred years earlier by a Kāti Wairaki woman named Raureka, who set out from her home at Lake Kaniere to cross the mountains. Her journey linked the people of the east and west coasts, and opened up a vital trade route for the sacred pounamu (greenstone) found in the rivers out west. The pounamu trade had since grown so valuable that later, while passing back through the North Island, Wyatt would notice a small island upon Lake Rotokākahi that was home to a Māori burial ground. Like Ruapehu, the site was considered tapu by its iwi, the Tūhourangi and Ngāti Tūmatawera, but Wyatt was told that the threat of white men with spades arriving to rob the site for pounamu and other treasures coveted by the international ethnology market had forced the government to issue an official decree restricting access.[19]

Back on the South Island, Wilczek Peak was the westernmost point of a rocky ridge fanning out from Élie de Beaumont, a 10,200-foot massif north of Aoraki, a dozen miles inland. Looking down to the Tasman Glacier, Wilczek wasn't without danger either. It had been named in 1884 by Austrian zoologist Joseph von Lendenfeld; along with his wife, Anna, he had made several daring climbs across the glacier in the 1880s before going on to name and chart much of the Mount Kosciuszko range in Australia. In 1883, von Lendenfeld inked a set of sketches from his ascent of the nearby Höchstetter Dome, featuring hair-raising scenes of serrated cliffs of ice and tiny figures inching across cracks in the mountain that resembled a hungry, gaping maw. The drawings included an ominous skull over two pickaxes arranged like crossbones, above the Latin credo, *NUNQUAM REGREDIMUR*— 'Never turn back'.[20]

A few years before Wyatt's trip, in January 1930, a small party of young women and a student guide had been found dead on the glacier. The climber who discovered them had only left half an hour after the girls, but sometimes that was all it took in these mountains. When a party was sent to retrieve their bodies, they reported being lashed by lightning and hail, their ice-axes 'crackling with electricity' and one man's pocket exploding when lightning ignited the matchbox he was carrying.[21] The official cause of the girls' deaths was exposure, but it was later theorised that their wet clothes might have turned them into walking lightning conductors.

Wyatt's companion on the 1936 trip was a junior guide named Mick Bowie, a thirty-five-year-old ex-shepherd and former ship's greaser with a deep, dark suntan from years in the glaring snow. He was popular with student groups passing through the area, which made it all the more heartbreaking when tragedy struck; Bowie had been part of the rescue party in 1930, and narrowly survived a near-death experience of his own on the same route a few months later, after falling through a hole in the snow and landing in the freezing water several feet below.[22]

Wyatt relished the company of outdoorsy men such as Bowie, who were often 'staunch anti-socialists', less likely to barrage him with questions about British life and the growing tensions in Europe — 'perpetual squabbles', he called them — that he had travelled south to escape.[23]

He preferred geography to geopolitics, and in early September the pair climbed the Tasman glacier under clear skies, retracing the hoofprints of the Alpine chamois, a species of feral goat that had arrived in New Zealand in 1907 as a gift from Austrian emperor Franz Josef and had since multiplied across the island. Before long, Wyatt and Bowie arrived at Malte Brun hut, a corrugated-iron structure that Bowie knew well — one of his first tasks after arriving on the mountain had been to lug up all those sheets of metal and wood on foot. But it was barely visible when they arrived, covered in snow that had broken through a window and filled the inside with a thick white carpet. Once they'd each shovelled their share of snow, the pair retraced von Lendenfeld's steps up Höchstetter Dome before skiing back downwards in some of the best runs of Wyatt's life to date.[24]

A few days later, they set their sights on Wilczek. It was still dark when they struck out from the hut by lantern-light, making zig zag patterns as they hauled themselves up the glacier. They left their skis behind at the second icefall, a twenty-foot-tall wall of frozen green water that gave way to a blast of morning sun on the peak of Élie de Beaumont. Then the real challenge began. The narrow path to Wilczek was an undulating ridge of rock as thin and sharp as a knife — Wyatt thought it looked like the bow of a great ship, upturned against the big blue above. The wind was mercifully still, but for long stretches Wyatt and Bowie had to straddle the crest rather than risk teetering over the 3,000-foot drop of sheer ice on either side. They reached the peak at midday — or, at least, they thought they did. High up on the craggy range, it was hard to tell exactly which part of the crest they had covered was really the highest point. As Wyatt looked out at the clouds below them, he couldn't think of another moment when he felt more isolated, perched so high up above the world below.[25]

By 1936, Wyatt had begun to experiment with photography, so, along their ascent, he paused to take a few black-and-white panoramas of Bowie hauling himself up the mountain, and at Wilczek he captured a coveted vantage point that had never been seen before. In mountaineering circles, the thrill of being the first to scale a challenging peak was a literal high, akin to a butterfly collector snaffling a rare, hitherto unrecorded species. A year later, a rival climber would bemoan that 'the peak had lost its virginal purity and its glory had been somewhat dimmed' since Wyatt and Bowie's conquest of it.[26]

Their luck ran out a few days after making their descent, when a fresh blizzard returned to blanket the hut in snow once more. In what Wyatt later described as the 'blackest period' of his trip, he and Bowie found themselves stranded, rising each morning well before dawn to check if the weather had cleared.[27] Having already exhausted the hut's supply of paperback westerns, they repeated this hopeless ritual for five days straight, until the sixth night, when the clouds cleared enough for them to see stars in the night sky. It wasn't the only time they were snowed in on the trip; despite covering impressive distances, Wyatt remained disappointed that the 'exceedingly erratic and uncertain' weather had stopped him short of scaling the likes of Aoraki and Mount Tasman.[28] All the same, when he and Bowie finally took off their skis, looking scruffy and bearded as they scrambled across the last snowy ridge, there was no question they had achieved something remarkable.

'Colin climbed the last hitherto unconquered 10,000-footer,' reported a columnist for *The Tatler* back in England, before wryly adding, 'and, I trust, left his antique blue sweater as a cairn.'[29]

Wyatt's months in New Zealand would leave a deeper impression, eventually achieving a cult status in certain corners of New Zealand's skiing community—who likened him to a 'Pied Piper' for ski-mountaineering.[30]

'Those who met him will remember many pleasant hours of song and story in the company of this most accomplished and incorrigible wanderer,' Lockwood concluded, referring to Wyatt's habit of producing an accordion to serenade his companions just as he had the royals of Europe.[31] 'Here is a stranger who, in a few weeks, does more pioneer work in ski-mountaineering than has been done by all of us in as many years,' read one report in the following year's *Australian and New Zealand Ski Yearbook*.[32]

Over sixty years later, a fellow mountaineer named John Harding would credit Wyatt's 'tour de force' of New Zealand in 1936 as bringing about the 'birth of ski mountaineering' in the country.[33] 'Their double traverse of the Main Divide set standards by which all subsequent NZ ski tours have been judged,' Harding wrote in the *Alpine Journal*.[34]

But to the broader community, Wyatt remained a 'little-known and enigmatic character' whose impact was largely under-recognised. There was, Harding added, a simple reason for his relative obscurity: 'old prejudices die hard'. Harding was referring to the often-uneasy place that 'ski-mountaineering' held in the alpine community, regarded by some as an unholy chimera of two distinct disciplines. But Wyatt didn't care for such arbitrary rules or boundaries—not if it allowed him to cover more ground, and reach greater heights, than the traditionalists who would only climb during the summer months. Regardless of what other people thought, he would leave New Zealand having achieved precisely what he had set out do: to recapture 'the same quiet ecstasy' that his father's generation had enjoyed across the mountains of Europe.[35]

But the trip was not over yet.

By the time he finally set foot in Australia, Wyatt's reputation had preceded him. 'British Champion Arrives' declared *The Sydney Morning*

Herald on 14 December, two days after he disembarked from the SS *Awatea*, feeling a little foolish as he shuffled through customs lugging three ski sets and an ice axe into the warm sunshine of a Sydney summer, the air purple with jacaranda blossoms.[36] The small news item, barely a dozen lines long, brought news of his recent exploits across the Tasman, but also invoked the Wyatt dynasty in terms that an Australian readership could appreciate: Test cricket.

'Mr Wyatt, who is related to the English test cricketer, R.E.S. Wyatt, won the title at St Moritz, Switzerland, this year,' the article read, referring to another distant member of the dynasty who had been embroiled in the controversial 'bodyline' saga that dogged the English team's 1932–33 Ashes tour.

While the mountains of Europe remained his first love, Wyatt had been fascinated during boyhood geography lessons by references to the 'Blue Mountains', which inspired fanciful visions of an almost lunar landscape of blue peaks and kangaroos.[37] But he had another good reason to visit: Colin had spent his entire life following in his father's footsteps, from the slopes of Switzerland to the butterfly fields of France, and, on some level, Australia was no different.

One of the many tales of adventure that James William Wyatt spun for his son was the time he himself had travelled to Australia as a twenty-two-year-old civil engineer in the early 1880s. James had an uncle who had already emigrated to run cattle in the Darling Downs, in Queensland, and soon after his arrival had caught word of a government expedition due to leave from Roma on 14 January 1881. Led by the former engineer-in-chief of Victoria, Robert Watson, the half-dozen members of the Trans-Continental Survey Party would set out to test the feasibility of a new railway to open up the colonial frontier for settlers, traders, and pastoralists. The adventurous young James Wyatt could hardly resist.[38]

He joined the exhausting four-month trek, navigating rough high country, crossing crocodile-filled rivers, and living off salted rations supplemented by the occasional boiled crow. Along the way, the young engineer made himself useful by transcribing copies of Watson's field notes, gathering geological samples, and trying to avoid clashing with the party's volatile guide, Frank Hann. Watson considered Hann 'one of the most accomplished bushmen in the colonies', but he also had a 'perfect curse' of a temper and a mutinous personality that to Watson seemed 'totally different in all respects' from the 'young gentleman' Wyatt, thirteen years Hann's junior.[39]

The tension between them exploded on 19 April, when an argument over water saw Hann 'completely [lose] it so far as to challenge Mr Wyatt to see who was master'.[40] When Wyatt refused to be goaded into a fight, Hann struck him in the face 'two or three times' in what Watson described as a 'most unjustifiable' attack', which Wyatt nonetheless received with 'with a great deal of forbearance'.[41] When the party finally rolled into Point Parker in the Gulf of Carpentaria in May, Wyatt, Watson, and several others were spent — sick with fever and 'completely prostrated'. 'The end had been attained, the motive was gone, and a temporary collapse ensued,' Watson would later report.[42]

Colin Wyatt would later explain that it was these eye-opening travels in Australia that gave his father a vivid appreciation of the study of nature, even though the ordeal had left him in such poor health — to say nothing of his experience with men such as Hann — that he had been advised to leave the tropics for good.[43] It was this bruising taste of Australia's colonial frontier that would send James William Wyatt back to Europe, to live out the adventurous alpine life that would, in time, inspire his son to travel all the way back to Australia and New Zealand fifty-five years later, seeking his own taste of the wild.

On that Saturday morning in December 1936, Colin Wyatt was met at Circular Quay by an old friend from Cambridge who whisked him away to a house right on the waterfront of Sydney Harbour. As Wyatt's senses became attuned to the scents and colours of this new landscape, his well-trained eye began to pick out a host of new and unfamiliar butterflies in the air — most likely blue triangles — fluttering black and blue against the lilac of the jacarandas.[44]

If he had arrived a week earlier, Wyatt might have bumped into Athol and Beatrice Waterhouse on the waterfront, fresh off the SS *Aorangi* after a six-month tour of the museums and collecting grounds of England, and no doubt craving the familiar sight of the garden at Killara and its own abundant blue triangles still on the wing. Wyatt, however, was just getting his first taste of Australia's butterflies—and the beginning of an obsession that would set both collectors on a collision course.

Wyatt's first trip to Australia would last just six months, but within a few short years he would be back. Like his father before him, Colin Wyatt had become the latest in a long line of Englishmen to sail into waters off the east coast of this southern continent seeking adventure, fortune, or freedom, only to find the course of their lives transformed by the wildlife they encountered.

CHAPTER EIGHT

The Flycatchers

'Insects in general were plentifull, Butterflies especially,' marvelled twenty-eight-year-old Joseph Banks as he scribbled in his journal on 29 May 1770. '[The] air was for the space of 3 or 4 acres crowded with them to a wonderfull degree: the eye could not be turnd in any direction without seeing milions & yet every branch & twig was almost coverd with those that sat still.'[1]

Banks was a tall, handsome Oxford dropout and gossip-baiting lothario whose family estates in Lincolnshire, Staffordshire, Derbyshire, and Sussex had given him a virtually blank cheque to pursue his dream career as the archetypal British gentleman naturalist. He'd been a terrible student at Eton and Oxford, more interested in hitting the sporting field and the mattress than his Greek and Latin readings.[2] The only exception was the natural world, which he found so fascinating that on one occasion the young Banks was dragged from a roadside hedge after being mistaken for a highwayman on the run.[3] Hauled before a magistrate, Banks explained that he was not a thief, but a wealthy, amateur collector—as if it was beyond the realm of possibility that one could be both.

A month earlier, in April 1770, Banks had looked out from the HMS *Endeavour* as it anchored at a rocky cove lined with eucalypts and encrusted shell middens, evidence of the generations of Gweagal people who had feasted on bream, snapper, and cockle on its shores for thousands of years. The Gweagal called it Kamay, on the east coast of a landmass that Europeans were calling 'New Holland', and it was also home to birds, animals, plants, and butterflies, most of which had never been seen by European eyes. Naturally, Banks and his shipmates raised their guns and fetched their nets.

'The trees over our heads abounded very much with Loryquets and Cocatoos,' Banks had written on the first day of May, before adding, 'of which we shot several'.[4]

Banks also caught a butterfly at Kamay, a dull orange fellow later dubbed *Heteronympha merope* by Johann Fabricius, its four perfect black circles across its wings like little brown eyes open wide with surprise or accusation.[5] They collected so many specimens that week that when their captain, Lieutenant James Cook, was drafting his map of the region, he marked the cove 'Botany Bay' in their honour.

A few weeks later, further up the coast on the lands of the Gooreng Gooreng people, Banks encountered those crowded acres of butterflies.[6] The trees were practically blanketed with them, idly waiting for Banks and his shipmates to bat them from the leaves with their sailor's caps. On one gumleaf, Banks found a shiny, silver chrysalis, which he brought back on board; the next day, it opened up to reveal a butterfly 'of a velvet black changeable to blue'.[7]

Back in England, Banks had bought his way on board the *Endeavour* in 1868 as it embarked on a Royal Society mission to observe the transit of Venus. While many rich young English bachelors aspired to sow their oats on a 'Grand Tour' through the brothels and cultural centres of Europe, Banks preferred to join Cook as the ship's resident naturalist, along with an eight-man team of illustrators, scientists, and servants, all paid for out of Banks's pocket. Cook dubbed them 'the Gentlemen', and perhaps the most important of them was Daniel Solander, a thirty-five-year-old Swedish naturalist who Banks had poached from the British Museum.[8]

Another apostle of the already-legendary Carl Linnaeus, Solander had joined the museum just a few years after the death of its de facto founder, Sir Hans Sloane. Sloane was an Irish-born physician who had tended to England's rich and powerful before taking a job with Christopher Monck — the second Duke of Albemarle and chancellor of the University of Cambridge, who was serving out his twilight years as the governor of Jamaica. Across his two years in Jamaica, Sloane collected hundreds of animal and plant specimens, enlisting the countless enslaved West Africans out in the field, upon whose forced labour the British colony was built. As a man of medicine, Sloane was viscerally familiar with the violence, what he called 'very exquisite Torments', inflicted upon enslaved workers. But he was not bothered by the plight of those he regarded as 'a very perverse Generation of People', and before long he married into Jamaica's wealthy slave-owning plantocracy himself.[9]

Sloane used his now-deep pockets to buy out other collectors and continue to expand his own collection, which by the end of his life included a deep library of 50,000 printed volumes, 12,000 boxes of dried seeds and fruits from around the known world, and over 330 massive folios of pressed plants, with each page crammed with so many specimens that the white paper was barely visible.[10] He had also acquired a grab bag of Egyptian, Roman, and Greek antiquities, and many thousands of preserved organic animal specimens. With no clear delineation between his collecting appetites, these books, bones, shells, and stones became the foundation for Britain's most important cultural institutions upon Sloane's death. His will instructed that they be sold to the Crown, so that his 'musaem or collection of rarities' would be preserved in order that it 'may be, from time to time visited and seen by all persons desirous of seeing and viewing the same'.[11]

But Sloane was not a trained scientist, and his volumes of handwritten foolscap catalogues were, at times, a mess. In 1763, Solander had been sent to London by Linnaeus to help catalogue the thousands of un-processed insects, amphibians, birds, and fossils held by the fledgling institution.[12] This is, most likely, where Solander first crossed paths with the 'young rich gentleman' Joseph Banks, who had obtained his reader's ticket to the British Museum at the age of twenty-one.[13] In a letter to his mentor Linnaeus, written shortly after the *Endeavour*'s departure in August 1768, Solander revealed that he could hardly believe his luck:

> I hope when we return to Europe our ship will surely be the richest in Natural Curiosities, for Mr Banks spares himself no expense, and he is a man who can lay out 8 or 10 0000 pounds Sterling a year.[14]

The *Endeavour* sailed from London to Rio de Janeiro, with Banks and his gentlemen bringing their own library, a greyhound, and enough bottles, boxes, baskets, and butterfly nets to capture a cross-section of every new place they visited.[15] The ship sailed on to Tahiti, where, in June 1769, Cook, Banks, Solander, and the crew watched as Venus passed overhead. It was at this point that Cook, having completed his official mission, tore open the sealed envelope from the British Admiralty that revealed the *Endeavour*'s other, secret orders: to find and survey new lands in the south 'that have not hitherto been discover'd by any Europeans and take Possession for His Majesty'.[16] From Tahiti, the crew set off for the islands that the Dutch explorer Abel Tasman had dubbed New Zealand — it was already Aotearoa to its existing Māori population — joined by a Tahitian priest named Tupaia, whom Banks would keep 'as a curiosity, as well as some of my neighbours do lions and tygers'.[17] But they met a frosty reception on the North Island, where the resident Māori did their best to stare down the new arrivals on the banks of the Tūranganui River.

'They were made to understand that we must kill them if they snatchd any thing from us,' Banks wrote in his journal on 9 October 1769, after a tense day — the 'most disagreable day [his] life has yet seen' — that saw Banks fire his own musket at the back of a Māori chief.[18] It was loaded with small shot, but the man and several others were later killed by the English party. Banks would draw his gun again after encountering the custom of Mokomokai, a Māori rite in which the tattooed heads of enemies or loved ones were carefully preserved after death. When their party met a man with several Mokomokai in his possession, Banks tried to acquire one for himself, only for the man to baulk at relinquishing the head. Banks 'enforc'd [his] threats by shewing Him a musequet on which he chose to part with the head rather than the price he had got'.[19] The price was a 'pair of old Drawers of very white linnen', in another demonstration of the

Englishmen's somewhat self-serving notion of fair trade, backed by force if necessary.

Banks continued to collect once they arrived at Kamay, and it wasn't just plant and animal life that caught his eye. As their landing party came ashore, they saw two Gweagal men looking out at the approaching boats. At first, Cook thought the men were beckoning them over, but he was sorely mistaken. They raised their spears, and within a few moments it became clear that 'in all appearance [they] resolvd to dispute our landing to the utmost'.[20] Cook fired upon the men, hitting one of them before the pair retreated into the bush. Once the coast was clear, Banks and the crew made landfall and soon found an emptied shelter with spears up to six feet long, some with tips barbed with fish bones.

'We therefore threw into the house to them some beads, ribbands, cloths etc. as presents and went away,' Banks wrote. He did not leave empty-handed: 'We however thought it no improper measure to take away with us all the lances which we could find about the houses, amounting in number to forty or fifty.'[21]

The spears arrived in England in July 1771, when the *Endeavour* returned to England a little lighter on men — a wave of mosquito-born malaria had killed many of the crew, including most of Banks's gentlemen — but laden with cargo. From the moment that Banks stepped off the boat, he began spreading word of their success: he and Solander returned with over 30,000 botanical specimens, plus hundreds more animal specimens, many of which had never been seen in Europe before.[22] One visitor to Banks's London home shortly after his return called it 'a perfect museum', with each room housing 'an inestimable treasure'.[23]

Banks's time in the Southern Hemisphere, and that staggering payload, won him instant fame. Carl Linnaeus dubbed him 'immortal' and 'unequalled', and within two months he had an audience with King George III.[24] Shortly afterwards, Banks burnished his own public image by commissioning two portraits, each carefully curated to project the image of a heroic young globetrotter. The first showed Banks standing tall, looking learned and cultured, his shoulders wrapped in a golden Māori cloak, standing in front of wooden spears and other fruits of his collecting. In the second, he was seated at a desk loaded with papers, quill at the ready, and a globe waiting to be spun to Banks's next destination. Both images would inspire their share of young British naturalists eager to emulate the life of adventure, science, and exoticism that Banks seemed to radiate — along with his voracious collecting.

There was also pragmatism to Banks's brand management: a year after the *Endeavour*'s return, his rapid rise and occasionally scandalous public standing — the tales of his sexual exploits across the Pacific compounded his rumoured abandonment of a young woman he had promised to marry before setting sail on the *Endeavour* — made him ripe for satire by cartoonist Matthias Darly. Titled *The Fly Catching Macaroni*, Darly caricatured Banks as a dandy with the ears of a donkey, astride two globes while waving after a pair of butterflies with racquet-like nets. 'I rove from Pole to Pole, you ask me why, I tell you Truth, to catch a … Fly,' the caption read.

But no cartoon could stop Banks's ascent. Leaving it to taxonomists such as Fabricius to slog through the paperwork of naming and cataloguing the 600 entomological specimens he and Solander had brought back, Banks leveraged his new fame to expand his collecting interests, which now included influential positions at the top of British science and culture. In 1778, Banks was elected president of the Royal Society, despite the Oxford dropout having only an honorary degree — leading some to compare him unfavourably to his predecessors such as Sir Isaac Newton, against whom Banks was like 'a flea upon a lion's hide'.[25] Within ten years, he was also a trustee of the British Museum, practically ran the Royal Botanic Gardens at Kew, was an adviser to the Admiralty and the East India Company, and was a member of the Board of Agriculture.[26]

Banks positioned himself as a key voice in the growing British Empire, and when options were being canvassed for a new penal colony, Banks's verdict took root. His testimony that there should be 'little Probability of any Opposition from the Natives' in New South Wales, whom he 'did not think there were above Fifty in all the Neighbourhood, and had Reason to believe the Country was very thinly peopled', helped inform the legal fiction of *terra nullius* that underpinned British settlement of the lands where he, Solander, and their gentlemen had caught butterflies and birds years earlier.[27]

As ever more British expeditions fanned out across the globe, the *Endeavour*'s success cemented natural science as an essential piece of the growing empire, rather than as an incidental activity carried out by rich amateurs such as Sloane. Banks would become a cheerleader for new expeditions into Africa and North America, assembling a network of collectors across the empire's growing reach, ranging from Linnean naturalists to doctors, gardeners, civil servants, military men, and East India Company employees. Before William Bligh famously suffered a mutiny in the South Pacific, one of his biggest supporters was Banks, who had encouraged Bligh's ill-fated HMS *Bounty* voyage, which had sought to introduce the breadfruit plant from Tahiti to the Caribbean as an alternative food crop for enslaved workers. Before setting out on the *Bounty*, Bligh agreed to collect for Banks along the way.

Another such collector was Henry Smeathman, a Yorkshire-born naturalist who spent the 1770s and 1780s travelling and working across Africa and the West Indies, rubbing shoulders and occasionally working with the merchants who made sites such as the Banana Islands, off the coast of Sierra Leone, a hub for the trans-Atlantic slave trade. He was sponsored from afar by Banks and a group of half-a-dozen cashed-up London collectors — wealthy stamp collectors who paid Smeathman a subscription fee in exchange for any botanical or zoological specimens he collected along the way. Smeathman would often send his cargo, from the Goliath beetle to the giant African swallowtail, back to England via slave ships, and in one letter he joked to Banks that his exposure to buying and selling human beings left him almost tempted to move sideways to become a 'dealer in souls as well as a merchant of butterflies and nettles'.[28]

At the same time, the growing importance of entomological science was becoming apparent across the colonised world, with Smeathman at one point lured to Grenada by the £20,000 bounty paid to anyone who could rid its sugar plantations of an out-of-control ant — a precursor to the kind of applied entomology practised by scientists such as Dr Robin Tillyard.[29] A love of nature wasn't all that Smeathman shared with Banks, and in their letters Smeathman jokes about being a 'flycatcher' in more ways than one, who 'married' several local girls as young as twelve.[30] For his efforts, Banks named a genus of plant, *Smeathmannia*, after him.[31]

Banks's network of collectors maintained his influence out across the empire, while he benefitted from the reverse flow of specimens, profit, and new observations back to him in London. This accumulation of knowledge and nature would become a fundamental tool of colonisation and a secret to Britain's success, with the unspoken mantra of this 'Banksian Learned Empire' and its far-flung emissaries parodied in verse by one pseudonymous wit:

> Go to the fields, and gain a nation's Thanks
> Catch Grasshoppers and Butterflies for Banks[32]

Banks's patron, the king, even made him a Knight of the Order of the Bath in 1795, prompting another cartoon satirising his remarkable ascent. Twenty-three years after *The Fly Catching Macaroni*, James Gillray portrayed the scowling, jowly, gout-ridden fifty-two-year-old as a human-headed 'South Sea Caterpillar' in the midst of metamorphosising into a 'Bath Butterfly', who had 'first crawl'd into notice from among the Weeds & Mud on the Banks of the South Sea & being afterwards placed in a Warm Situation by the Royal Society, was changed by the heat of the Sun into its present form.'[33]

'The first cabinet I saw was that of Sir Joseph Banks, in which are housed the first butterflies caught in New Zealand and Australia,' Athol Waterhouse told a meeting of the Australian and New Zealand Association for the Advancement of Science in January 1937, clearly still awed by his experience a few months earlier.[34] When Athol Waterhouse and George Lyell published *The Butterflies of Australia* in 1914, they made sure to devote its first sentences to the story of Banks and his exploits from Kamay to the Endeavour River, where he captured the 'first butterflies recorded from Australia'.[35] Over twenty years later, on a visit to England in 1936, Waterhouse finally made his own long-awaited pilgrimage to London's Natural History Museum.

An imposing neo-gothic stronghold in South Kensington, the museum was one of several national cultural institutions to be spun off from the original British Museum of Banks and Solander's era. Colloquially known as the 'Waterhouse building' after its designer, a Liverpudlian architect unrelated to Athol's branch, the museum had been envisioned as a 'cathedral to nature', its walls decorated in head-spinning detail with gargoyles, terracotta tiles, and stained-glass windows paying tribute to the living and extinct creatures collected and studied inside its walls. When it opened in 1881, visitors were greeted by a statue of Adam, the first taxonomist, who overlooked its dead menageries from his vantage point above the main entrance.

'I was deeply impressed with this truly great Institution and amazed at the immense number of butterflies contained in the cabinets,' Waterhouse recalled. 'I was delighted with the welcome accorded me by Mr N Riley, the Keeper of the Department of Entomology, who gave me a key that would open any of the cabinets and another that would unlock any of the bookcases.'[36]

With the keys to this little kingdom in his hands, Waterhouse made a beeline to the cabinet containing the Banks collection, which he was pleased to find were 'in a good state of preservation' 165 years after the *Endeavour*'s landing at Kamay.[37] In classic form, Waterhouse did, however, identify what he felt were 'many startling discrepancies' across the work of Fabricius and subsequent entomologists. But, having now viewed more Australian butterfly species than any living soul, he returned home more resolved than ever to bring as many specimens and types of Australian butterflies into the one place.

'It was such an enormous help when in London to find that they had gathered together so many types of the Australian butterflies,' he wrote to Lyell in November 1936 as he sailed back to Australia.[38]

Seeing Banks's Australian collection up close renewed Waterhouse's long-held dream that perhaps in another 165 years' time, future generations of researchers wouldn't have to cross the globe to see a comprehensive snapshot of their country's butterflies.[39] To Waterhouse, there was no safer place than the Australian Museum, a natural successor to the romanticised lineage of Western scientific enquiry and collecting culture that Joseph Banks had brought ashore in April 1770. Baked into the museum's foundations, however, was another one of Banks's legacies: a history of gunpowder and theft.

CHAPTER NINE

The Scoundrels

'Oh, my God, I am dead,' he said in surprise as the wound in his side bled out among the gumtrees of Minjerribah in the winter of 1831.[1] The dying man with the Lancashire accent and shotgun in hand was a collector named Thomas Holmes, Australia's first museum employee, but by no means its longest-serving one. He had been appointed by the governor of New South Wales just two years earlier, and the museum in question was little more than an old shed near Sydney's Hyde Park. If, by some happy accident, a member of the public were to stumble upon it, they would find Holmes politely sitting for five hours a day, waiting to show off its modest zoological collection.[2]

Back in 1827, a dispatch had arrived from London carrying a suggestion from Earl Bathurst, the secretary of state for the colonies. Bathurst told Governor James Darling that the creation of a 'Publick Museum at New South Wales' would be 'very desirable', featuring 'many rare and curious specimens of Natural History'.[3] But, Bathurst added, 'one of the first steps towards ensuring its success seems to be the sending out some proper person to assist in collecting and arranging such specimens'.

Bathurst left most of the details to Darling and his colonial secretary, Alexander Macleay — a late-career bureaucrat from a prominent Scottish landholding family who had also served on the council of the Royal

Society and as secretary of the London Linnean Society before sailing to the colony.[4] Macleay brought with him an enormous entomological collection of his own, having taken advantage of the Napoleonic Wars to scoop up practically every major collection that came up for auction in England — free from the rival bids of deep-pocketed European collectors shut out by the conflict — including several insects collected by Henry Smeathman.[5] As the colonial secretary, Macleay had bigger problems to deal with in the dysfunctional penal settlement, and so the responsibility of running the 'Publick Museum' fell to Holmes, a carpenter and joiner by trade who was perhaps better suited to building a museum's display cases than filling them.

Two years after his appointment, on 23 August 1831, Holmes and a convict named Samuel Saunders were trudging through the scrubland of Minjerribah on Quandamooka Country, renamed Stradbroke Island and Moreton Bay by their countrymen, when he spotted a cockatoo he thought might make a good addition to the shed gallery back in Sydney. Just as Bathurst had ordered, Holmes raised his rifle, pulled the trigger, and watched as a bundle of feathers tumbled down from the canopy. The convict Saunders would later claim that what happened next was a freak accident, as Holmes set out to retrieve his latest catch, and for just a moment set down his gun. Holmes leaned the shaft against his right-hand side, where, according to Saunders, it accidentally discharged at point-blank range into the collector's flank.[6] It remains unclear whether the cockatoo, won at such a high price, ever made it to a museum display, but Holmes was tragically right about the effect of the blast: the wound was fatal.

The museum sat idle for over a year, until a twenty-year-old man named John Roach sailed into the colony in May 1833.[7] With his initials tattooed on his forearm, Roach was already a thief, one of many convicts packed into the prison ship *Aurora* and banished out of sight and mind by the mother country. But there was also something that made Roach unique, both on the prison ship and in his new home: prior to being sentenced to seven years and transportation for stealing a coat, Roach had been employed in London as a taxidermist, and before long the new arrival had been taken under Macleay's wing and assigned to the fledgling museum.[8] With an 'expert' taxidermist now on staff to collect new specimens and mount the bird skins left unfinished by the late Thomas Holmes, it was soon decided to rename the former shed collection — previously referred to as the 'Colonial Museum' or 'Sydney Museum' — as the 'Australian Museum'.[9]

Roach's biggest break came in March 1836, when he became a last-minute addition to the colony's next inland expedition. The party would be led by the surveyor-general, Major Thomas Livingston Mitchell, a balding, middle-aged cartographer and veteran of the Napoleonic Wars who had served the empire in Portugal before heading south. Mitchell's latest trip would see him trace the course of the Barkaa River — renamed the Darling by Mitchell's rival Charles Sturt, in tribute to the now-ex-governor — as it dovetailed with the Murray. For months, Mitchell had been lobbying the governor to appoint a naturalist to accompany him on the journey.

Continuing the work of the late Sir Joseph Banks, science and natural history played a key role in Mitchell's expeditions into the interior and their place in the public imagination. As they left, an anonymous poet in the *Sydney Gazette and New South Wales Advertiser* captured in just a few stanzas how these expeditions would begin the transformation of the raw and wild unknown into something more orderly, understood, and readily controllable:

> What is thine aim in leaving human faces,
> And busy, stirring life?
> To follow nature in her wildest traces,
> Of harmony, or strife
> [...]
> To watch the thronging stars — earth's changing bosom,
> Her life restoring waters;—
> To claim for science many a lovely blossom,
> The Forest's unknown daughter[10]

But there was a problem: a vacancy had been open since Mitchell's last expedition the previous year, after a colonial botanist named Richard

Cunningham, a new arrival from the Royal Botanical Gardens in Kew, had disappeared after wandering off to collect plant specimens near the Bogan River. In March 1836, just a few days before the party was due to set out, it was finally confirmed that 'the man from the museum, and a collector of plants' would join Mitchell's twenty-five-man convoy of convicts and a wary handful of ex-soldiers and government men to keep them in line.

The plant collector joining Roach was a short, scarred, and tattooed thirty-nine-year-old named John Richardson, who by 1836 was on his third or even fourth chance at freedom.[11] In England, he had worked in a plant nursery before being sentenced to transportation for larceny at the age of nineteen. Four years later, in 1821, he was pardoned by the new governor of New South Wales, Lachlan Macquarie, and sent back to England on the *Dromedary* to care for a fresh shipment of 'Plants & Seeds of Australia' earmarked for the royal collection. The clean slate didn't last, and a year later he was back in Sydney after being rung up on a housebreaking charge and sentenced to death or transportation for housebreaking. For a few years, Richardson seemed to turn things around—he got married, started a family, and even earned his ticket of leave after working as an overseer in the government gardens. However, by the time he set out with Roach in March 1836, his wife had died, his children had been sent to a school for orphans, and his ticket of leave had been revoked following allegations of embezzlement and drunkenness.

But even a down-and-out recidivist like Richardson drew less attention than his younger companion, Roach, who quickly made an enemy of Mitchell's assistant, Granville Chetwynd Stapylton. Stapylton was no convict, born into a military family with a viscount for a grandfather, and over the eight-month journey he came to hate Roach with a special passion, peppering his journals with bitter asides about the 'mutinous behaviour' of the 'scoundrel Bird Stuffer':[12]

> This damned bird skinner has been spoiled in Sydney by Mr Macleay, and is quite the sort of free and easy vagabond with a flash shooting jacket that I feel especial pleasure in taking down a peg.[13]

In truth, there were few in the party whom Stapylton didn't loathe — he thought the English convict was 'the most offensive animal in the creation', and even grew increasingly resentful of Mitchell.[14] But he reserved his greatest animosity for the young man who, he said, turned the expedition into eight months of 'actual purgatory'.[15] Roach, for his part, seemed to delight in antagonising the deputy, kicking Stapylton's dog, and performing withering impressions for the entertainment of the other men. Roach would also casually share ammunition for duck hunting, despite express orders to preserve their small arsenal — after all, by September 1836, the group had already spent plenty of gunpowder.[16] Worst of all, Roach did all this with the apparent impunity of being 'Mr McLeays [sic] Protegee'.[17]

'I cannot describe the antipathy I entertain towards this vagabond — my turn shall come yet,' Stapylton wrote vengefully in October, as he fantasised about Roach meeting an accidental death.[18]

'It is my intention to forward him to Sydney in handcuffs by the first opportunity,' Stapylton wrote.[19]

But by the time the expedition returned to Sydney in November, and the full story of their journey came to light, Roach's indiscretions would be overshadowed by bigger, darker revelations about what had taken place up the river.

'I was a little behind that morning with Roach the bird-stuffer, when the Natives came on the camping ground,' the convict gardener John Richardson, one of several members of Mitchell's party called to testify in the expedition's aftermath, told the Executive Council on 16 December 1836. 'They were in great numbers, more than we had seen before; Major Mitchell sent word for us to join the party immediately.'[20]

Richardson, Roach, and the rest of their group woke up beside the river on the morning of 27 May 1836. The group was slightly smaller — Mitchell had ordered Stapylton and eight other men to stay behind at a depot camp with the bulk of the livestock and supplies — which may have added to the growing unease around the campsite. Since the expedition had set out two months earlier, they had repeatedly encountered parties of Barkindji men and other First Nations groups who made no secret of their resistance to this latest colonial incursion.

Over sixty years had passed since Cook, Banks, and the *Endeavour* crew had first touched down on the east coast, and word had undoubtedly spread up the river about what a caravan of horses, cattle, and gun-toting, red-shirted white men could mean for the lands and peoples they encountered. More vivid still was the memory of Mitchell's previous expedition a year earlier, with members of his party killing at least six people — including a Barkindji woman and child.[21] By the time Mitchell had set off for his latest trip, it had also emerged that the lost botanist Cunningham had seemingly been killed by a group of locals who had taken him into their camp, only to misinterpret his strange behaviour as a threat.[22]

As the men followed Mitchell and his party out from Lake Benanee and onto the lands of the Kureinji people, he grew increasingly apprehensive of what he called the 'lynx-eyed vigilance of the savages'.[23] One night, Mitchell had a flare shot into the air to ward the group away from the campsite, and on another, he sent a handful of his party after them bearing carbines, with orders not to shoot without Mitchell's whistle command. If it seemed that their pursuers would not take the hint, Mitchell was just as determined to ignore the clear signals that he and his party were not welcome. He would later insist that conflict seemed inevitable, in what he claimed was 'a war which not my party, but these savages, had virtually commenced'.[24] But this was a selective view of the chronology of colonisation, for which Mitchell was in every sense a part of an advancing, armed frontline.

Richardson later told the Executive Council that in the days after they left Stapylton's makeshift depot, the party had observed well over one hundred Aboriginal men gathering nearby, in what was taken to be an attempt at intimidation — and clearly a successful one. It also became clear that a handful of Mitchell's party had been recognised from the surveyor-general's last bloody expedition up the river a year earlier, adding to the tension. On 27 May, after setting out at 8.00 am, Richardson and Roach gathered to hear Mitchell's plan: the surveyor-general decided to mount an ambush, ordering half his party to double back to quietly outflank their unwanted chaperones while Mitchell, Richardson, Roach, and the others drew them out.

Before their departure, Mitchell had made sure that every man on the expedition was well armed, with eighteen carbine guns — specially chosen by Mitchell for their similarity to those used by the mounted police — plus eighteen pistols and six muskets among their supplies. Like the rest of Mitchell's men, Roach was issued a uniform and a pistol, officially designated as a 'fowling piece'.[25] But as the group travelled up the river on 27 May, the gun may have been put to a different use as they neared a hill that Mitchell would later give the euphemistic name of Mount Dispersion.

'I saw no spears thrown by the Natives,' Richardson said, explaining how, after a convict in the rear party opened fire, both groups started shooting as the Barkindji fled into the fast-flowing river, where many were either shot, drowned, or both — including a chief, identifiable by his distinctive possum-skin cloak. Mitchell would later tell Macleay that although he had not given the order to shoot, his men were soon 'pursuing and shooting as many as they could'. According to Richardson, every man in Mitchell's party — presumably including Roach — crowded along the bank of the river, continuing to fire even as some of their targets clambered up the opposite side to escape.

'I do not think the firing lasted altogether above four or five minutes,' Richardson said. 'I fired three rounds myself.'[26]

Another member of Mitchell's group, a former soldier, also testified that he fired 'several shots, as did most of the party with us'.[27] But as with many frontier encounters, finding the truth even among eyewitness accounts was fraught; the camp's medical officer, who was stationed with the rear party, estimated that the company of Aboriginal men numbered between 200 and 300, and that the shooting lasted a quarter of an hour as they fled across a river that was one hundred feet wide. Few witnesses could offer a firm estimate of the casualties, which ranged from a conservative seven to over thirty. Mitchell's ambush — what he would call a 'collision' — hadn't gone quite to plan, but he had no regrets, telling his superiors that, 'Thus, in a very short time, the usual silence of the desert prevailed on the banks of the Murray, and we pursued our journey unmolested.'

> I still look back on that eventful day with entire satisfaction, and a sense of gratitude to God for such a deliverance from impending danger, in a cause in which I considered myself an humble instrument in His hands for the common benefit of the civilised and savage portions of our race.[28]

Despite outrage in some quarters of the colony, Mitchell also had many defenders who echoed the lofty ideals of Banks's learned empire by framing Mitchell's expedition as having been conducted 'for the sake of scientific discoveries'.[29] It was for science, not merely the practical need to survey new lands and water supplies for pastoralists to build their fortunes on, that Mitchell had 'endured hardships of every descriptions, and deprived himself of the society of his family'. At the same time, the language used left no uncertainty that for many in colonial Australia, the science and the violence being deployed across the riverbanks, the mountains, and the mallee plains were both necessary parts of the same project.

'We cannot blush for the conduct of a Government which can thus immolate science and merit at the shrine of party feeling,' wrote Mitchell's supporters. 'Is there an instance in ancient or modern history, where the leader of a victorious army has been called to account for the enemies he has slain in battle?'

Mitchell would be officially reprimanded for his conduct, but continued to serve as surveyor-general before being elected to the Legislative Council.

Such 'collisions' would only grow more commonplace as expedition after expedition drew the colonial project further into unceded Aboriginal country across the continent. In June 1845, near the Gulf of Carpentaria, the behaviour towards Aboriginal women by members of an overland expedition led by the explorer Ludwig Leichhardt provoked a retaliatory night raid in which John Gilbert — an English naturalist from the London Zoological Society and Leichardt's deputy — was fatally speared. The cause of the attack was omitted from the marble memorial erected by public subscription in St James' Church, just opposite the future home of the Australian Museum. Instead, it bore the simple Latin inscription, '*Dulce et decorum est scientia mori*' ('It is sweet and fitting to die for science').

Decades later, in April 1881, a young James William Wyatt and the members of the Trans-Continental Survey Party would see first-hand the new reality that had taken root in the wake of explorers such as Banks, Mitchell, and Leichhardt. Wyatt seemed repulsed by the brutal and inhuman treatment meted out by white settlers, and noted in his journal that Aboriginal communities appeared to be hunted as if they were wild game.[30]

As the party made their own way towards the Gulf of Carpentaria, they encountered a squatter named Montague Curr, who boasted of having recently taken part in a mass killing in reprisal for the 'murder' of a stockman. But the more Curr told them, the more it became clear that the killing of the stockman was itself a reprisal attack after the man had invaded an Aboriginal camp armed with a revolver, driven its men away, and 'kept possession of the gins'.[31]

'Mr Curr told me that he and others had pursued the blacks and shot five; that the police were coming to give them a further "dressing" as that was the only thing they understood,' party leader Robert Watson would write in his field notes.

Watson reflected that such conduct by his white countrymen was 'simply disgraceful', but remained convinced nevertheless that 'there is no help for it except speedy and ostensible annihilation'.[32]

Back in 1836, John Roach would earn a £5 bonus for his participation in Major Mitchell's expedition and what would later be known as the Mount Dispersion massacre. While the details of Roach's actions on that morning by the river would be lost to history, both he and the Australian Museum would become beneficiaries of Mitchell's subsequently 'unmolested' run, when boxes containing the dozens of specimens collected on the trip were deposited at the Australian Museum shortly after their return. Roach's zealous collecting had, in fact, formed another bone of contention with Stapylton, who had hoped to gather some specimens of his own, but found that every new find, from 'a new Species of Opossum dark brown colour' to 'a grey Rabbit rat', were squirrelled away by Roach in the months after the Mount Dispersion episode:

> The scoundrel Bird Stuffer takes the greatest pains to conceal everything new from my sight. The collection for the Museum is already very extensive.[33]

When the Australian Museum printed its inaugural catalogue of 'Specimens of Natural History and Miscellaneous Curiosities' in 1837, the seventy-one-page list of butterflies, shells, fossils, birds, and marsupials would include many entries presented by Mitchell, including several 'New and Undescribed Animal[s]' fresh from the 1836 expedition.[34] Among the new additions were a handful of species such as a pink cockatoo, *Pyloctolophus leadbeateri*, and a hopping mouse, *Notomys mitchellii*, named in honour of Major Mitchell, along with towns, roads, a river, and a species of grass. It's an old cliché that history is written by the victors, but on the Australian frontier, it seemed that they also got to name the plants, animals, and landforms — a taxonomy of conquest.

One day in 1846, a steamship arrived at Sydney Harbour from Moreton Bay with a fresh consignment of animal specimens addressed to the Australian Museum. The cargo included a particularly interesting specimen for the museum's growing collections: the foetus of a dugong. When the ship docked, a man who presented himself as the curator of the museum came aboard and took possession of the special delivery, unflatteringly labelled 'sea pig'. But the sea pig never made it to the museum, where the real curator, a young Irishman named William Sheridan Wall, had been waiting in vain.[35] When it became clear that the package had gone missing, Wall set out for a certain curio shop on Hunter Street in the centre of the growing city.

The proprietor of the curio shop was a man in his thirties who, if you pulled up his sleeve, had a tell-tale 'J.R.' inked on his forearm. But Wall didn't need to see the tattoo to recognise John Roach, his predecessor as the Australian Museum's Collector and Preserver of Specimens. Roach had earned his ticket of leave shortly after returning from Mitchell's 1836 expedition, but within a few years had left the museum to set up the shop, which did a roaring trade with clientele across Europe hungry for new and exotic specimens from the Antipodes. It didn't take long to find the preserved dugong, or to identify the fake curator as Roach himself, who, it seemed, had taken advantage of his knowledge and experience — or the ignorance of the steamer's crew — to pass himself off as a museum worker.

Wall successfully retrieved the dugong from Hunter Street, and although the matter was referred to the colony's law officer, it is unclear whether the well-connected Roach was punished at all — or by what other underhanded means he might have stocked his Hunter Street shop. Roach continued to trade seemingly uninterrupted — a year later, he would draw attention once again after displaying a 'mysterious monster' in his shop window identified as the folkloric Australian creature the 'Bunyip'. According to one newspaper, the attraction 'excited the wonder of our unsuspecting town-folks and gullible country cousins', adding that this 'Munchausenic Wonder' was in fact a deformed foal that had been brought in by a horse doctor and sold to the apparently 'credulous' — or perhaps indifferent — John Roach.[36]

But Roach's inglorious career as a collector of 'rare and curious specimens' would not be the last time someone blurred the lines between collection and theft at the bleeding edge of the British Empire. The uncomfortable truth was that, from gentleman naturalists and explorers such as Sir Joseph Banks to convict scoundrels such as John Roach or John Richardson, the study of natural history in Australia, and that storied lineage of collectors, was often led by British men with sticky fingers who undertook their celebrated work while participating in the biggest act of 'collection' imaginable: the colonisation of a continent.

CHAPTER TEN

The Honeymoon

The young woman lay dozing in the snow, curled up in a ball in her knitted Fair Isle jumper, her feet tucked and crossed in hiking boots. Lying with her back to the afternoon sun, her face was soft, eyes shut, hands forming a pillow beneath her head, one on top of the other as if in prayer. The sun was low in the sky, or perhaps she was simply very high up—it cast a shadow in front of her like a reflection on a mirror lake. As he studied this moment of calm and quiet through the viewfinder of his camera, Colin Wyatt lined up the woman's little body in the frame, adjusting the focus, the aperture, taking care to capture the interplay of light, shadow, and shape just as he would with one of his paintings or sketches. Then he brought his finger down on the trigger, the shutter closing with a satisfying metallic *click*.

Since Colin had first come to Australia in the summer of 1936 and taken in the jacarandas and swallowtails of Sydney Harbour, he had gradually come to appreciate the bush that lay beyond it—from its distinct scent to its 'brittle, dancing light'.[1] When winter fell, the landscape would reveal an entirely different character from the dark monotony of Europe's fir tree forests. Instead, he would marvel at how the silvery trunks of hundred-foot eucalypts could catch the eye like towering lighthouses, revealing a vivid palette of soft lilac, sienna, salmon pink, pale yellow, blue, and gold.

It was, in other words, the perfect setting for taking an intimate, unguarded portrait. The photograph of that sleepy moment in the snow wasn't the first one he had taken of the woman, who looked twenty-one or twenty-two years old with a doll's face, a high-set forehead, and a crown of curls. It wouldn't be the last, either; on that same trip, he captured another candid moment down off the mountain, crouched in front of their tent hooking a billy can off the campfire with the end of a long, thick tree branch. Another shot, perhaps taken with a self-timer, the camera perched on the snow, had them both in matching white ski jackets — an ensemble that made Wyatt feel like 'the White Knight' of legend, with his compass and barometer slung around his neck, and a large bowie knife on his belt. In the photograph, the pair almost blended into the snow as they sat knees up, skis off, taking in the views of Kosciuszko National Park rolled out before them.[2]

Wyatt had her smile for the camera on the beach in Hawaii as they made their way through Canada, San Francisco, the Pacific, and New Zealand on a whistlestop tour, having set off from England in June 1939. They sailed into Sydney on a clear day the following September, and although she was born Mary Scott Barrett, the only daughter of a well-connected British army colonel based in Surrey, when she stepped off the SS *Mariposa* into Sydney Harbour, Mary answered to a new name: Mrs Colin Wyatt.

Wyatt had covered a lot of ground since leaving Australia in 1937. On his way back to England, he stopped over in Columbo, the capital of Ceylon — present-day Sri Lanka — where the twenty-eight-year-old was struck by a sense of peace and harmony. As he breathed in its air, ripe with the scent of frangipani and jasmine, he felt it all seemed primed to help someone tap into a deeper level of consciousness.[3] Fittingly, he would spend the trip visiting quiet Buddhist temples and ruined cities bordered by forests and littered with petals, where ancient statues of smiling Buddhas were slowly being reclaimed by jungle. The deep greens all around him contrasted with the blue and green butterflies on the wing and the saffron-robed monks deep in meditation.[4] In Europe, he would later reflect, this kind of site might have been picked over by antiquarians, perhaps even excavated and shipped away as curiosities bound for a drafty museum.[5]

In the forest, he found something rich and timeless, a sense of living spirituality that had lasted for centuries. He caught a northbound train from Ceylon, the verdant jungle scenery out his carriage window giving way to the drier landscapes of India, with monkeys swinging from trees as the temperature climbed. He spent a few days in Agra before moving on to Peshawar, having hatched a plan to head into Afghanistan to chase specimens of a rare butterfly in the Hindu Kush mountains — most likely it was *Parnassius autocrator*, which had been first described by the Russian lepidopterist Andrey Avinoff before his exile to America, and rarely seen since. But Wyatt's plans were foiled, as Afghan and British authorities handballed the Englishman back and forth until he had to concede that his prize would no longer be on the wing by the time he reached Kabul. He was disappointed to abandon what was an ambitious, expensive undertaking, for which he had secured financial backing from a German entomologist he had been corresponding with for some time.

But, as Wyatt later reflected, this was probably for the best — it would eventually emerge that the British had grown suspicious following reports that Germany had begun sending out spies under the cover story once favoured by Lord Robert Baden-Powell: the wandering bug-hunter.[6] It was only years later, when he read about Fred Brandt's exploits in Albania, that he fully appreciated the risk he had run on the trip. Back in 1937, he hired a car and drove up the Khyber Pass, as close as he could to Kabul, before returning to Peshawar for an express train to Bombay and a ship bound for England.

He didn't stay put for long. In 1938, he set out again for Lapland, a 'Land of the Midnight Sun' straddling Finland and Norway, where, in addition to capturing his dingy fritillary, Wyatt made a 314-mile trek by ski and reindeer sleigh to reach Europe's northernmost point. Along the way, he would adopt the heavy fur 'kolter' attire of the indigenous Sámi people, glimpse the shimmering golden curtains of an Aurora Borealis overhead, and pause to take photographs of ptarmigan tracks in the snow, the trees casting long, artful shadows on the white ground.[7]

He bunkered down in small huts, where at times Sámi men and women would huddle around a single stove and begin to sing in a sombre drone. As their song swelled in volume, Wyatt felt like he was being swept from 20th-century Europe to an ancient, timeless North.[8] On the final stretch, he travelled by ship to the island village of Skarsvåg, where he walked out onto a finger of rock one hundred feet above the ocean. Lashed by storm clouds and dark waves thundering against the cliff face, he pressed on until he found a small black signpost with the letter 'N' and an arrow pointing towards the North Pole.[9]

He also roamed the Albanian mountains, where, within a few years, Fred Brandt's career as a German spy would finally come unstuck. Near the village of Theth, Wyatt camped at an old Franciscan monastery, pitching a tent in a green meadow beside the chapel and cemetery to watch as the last rays of sun lit up the 5,000-foot-high ridges of the Zhapora mountain range in a shade of twinkling pink. As he drank coffee with the monks, the abbot explained in German that the valley's isolation — cut off from the world by twelve feet of snow each winter — made it practically a realm unto itself with its own laws.[10] These adventures would prove to be Wyatt's final taste of the Northern Hemisphere for the best part of seven years, as he decided to finally settle down — even if it meant uprooting himself to the other side of the world.

Europe, he would later claim, had grown too 'unsettled' — the looming geopolitical tensions meant people were tightening their belts, and his painting commissions had all but dried up. Recalling his blissful six months in Australia and the many friends he had made, Wyatt resolved to emigrate for a few years and to test the Australian market — and perhaps try his hand at cattle farming, just like his father's uncle had done in 19th-century Queensland.[11] But he wouldn't be going alone.

Given his many appearances in the gossip sheets of London society, it was little surprise that the engagement of the 'ace ski-jumper' Colin Wyatt arrived to great fanfare at the height of the ski season. 'Ski Champion Takes the Plunge,' declared the *Manchester Evening News*, while *The Sketch* and *The Sphere* ran a novel photoshoot that captured the young, stylish couple posing on another artificial mountain erected near Piccadilly Circus for the 1939 Indoor Skiing Championships.

'MR. COLIN WYATT, the famous ski-runner, artist and traveller, and his fiancé, MISS MARY SCOTT BARRETT, are here testing the snows of Earl's Court!' read *The Sketch,* beneath a photograph of the pair perched on the slope in immaculate winter-wear, Colin kitted out in his old Ski Club of Great Britain sweater, complete with the years 1931, 1933, and 1934 embroidered on his sleeve as a nod to past glories.[12]

In *The Sphere,* the pair were photographed gripping their skis, the tweny-nine-year-old Colin seen grinning at his young bride while Mary beamed a toothy smile as bright and white as the fake snow piled around them. Five months later, on Saturday 3 June 1939, Mary's father led her down the aisle at St Mary's Burgh Heath.[13] *The Tatler* might have described it simply as a 'country wedding', but for Surrey society it was an event to remember — the pews were dotted with other glamourous skiing champions who had come from far and wide to witness their friend Colin tricked out in a morning suit, while Mary clutched a prayer book under an old Brussels-lace veil that belonged to her new mother-in-law.[14]

'Having climbed several virgin peaks in New Zealand, this bridegroom thinks he is tired of Europe,' read *The Tatler*'s report.[15] '[So] after the traditional ten days on the Riviera they are going to settle in New South Wales.' This news, the columnist added, would come as a blow to the skiing community, as 'Colin Wyatt is liked as an original being.'

Within just a few months, Mary was halfway around the world, smiling again for the social pages, this time in Australia — the photographer from *The Sydney Morning Herald* had the new arrival sitting perched on the windowsill of their new flat, hands crossed in a neatly fitted dress. The Wyatts had only just moved to Woollahra, halfway between Sydney Harbour and Bondi Beach, and the leafy suburb would be their home for the duration of their marriage — even if, for long stretches of time, Colin would be taken far away from their Edgecliff Road address. When he was home, the 'champion British ski-jumper' and 'his pretty wife' were regularly namedropped in the gossip pages of *The Daily Telegraph* and *Truth,* lunching and dining among the 'well-knowns' and 'ultra-elegant' of Sydney's social set at trendy restaurants such as Prunier's, Romano's, and Prince's.[16]

'Too good a party to finish at 2 am, so Colin Wyatt dons his dashing cape, collects his attractive wife and gay crowd and sets off for Edgecliff home to entertain them with piano accordion until dawn-wards,' read one colourful sighting in the pages of *The Australian Women's Weekly*.[17]

Their emergence as a Sydney glamour couple to watch was tempered by some sobering developments, with the news arriving from England that Colin's father, James, had died at the age of eighty-two, not long after having fractured his leg in a 'severe accident'. Despite his injury and advancing age, the elder Wyatt had to the end refused to turn his back on the great outdoors that had sustained him all his life, from the brutal frontiers of colonial Queensland to the Alps of Europe. An elegiac tribute published in the *Alpine Journal* noted that the 'charming and genial' veteran mountaineer could still be seen out on the trails in his final years, practically dragging himself uphill with a stick in each hand.

'[As] late as 1937 he ascended the Gamskarkogel above Hofgastein, tackling the final rocks on hand and knee,' the obituary noted, while adding that his 'great mountaineering powers, topographical and botanical knowledge have descended in full measure to his artist son, our present member.'[18]

Fittingly, Colin and Mary would put James Wyatt's powers to good use in their new home; while his first visit had stopped just short of a full Australian winter, with his wife by his side Wyatt made up for lost time. He absorbed everything he could about the area's history, from the Kiandra Pioneer Ski Club — founded in 1861 to cater to Australian, American, and Chinese miners lured by the gold rush, making it even older than the first downhill ski club in Norway — to the alpine cattle runs that had followed the first colonial explorers into the mountains. He would take refuge in the old alpine huts originally built by those herdsmen years before, in a landscape he would later describe as 'the Wild West', perhaps unintentionally alluding to the history of violence and conquest shared by the American and Australian frontiers.

It was challenging, thrilling terrain, carrying ominous names such as 'The Perisher' and 'The Paralyser'. Alongside the old drovers' hideouts, Wyatt visited a hut built by the famous Australian Antarctic explorer Sir Douglas Mawson, who had subjected himself, his men, and his dogs to the rigours of the Australian alps to prepare for the polar extremes of his next history-making expedition. Colin and Mary saw up close how dangerous and disorienting these mountains could be — it wasn't unheard of for search parties to set off into the snow, only to find their target within half a mile of safety, lost and oblivious.

Mary herself wrote of one near miss for the *Alpine Yearbook*. After a run of bad weather, the Wyatts and five others had set out after breakfast to explore some paths in the sheltered Thredbo valley, enjoying a 1,000-foot run in a 'sharp little gully' before a Canadian in their party decided to peel off.

'By now the sun had gone in and we had the full force of the wind in our faces,' she wrote. 'Fog and snow had made the visibility very bad and by the time the top was reached we could no longer see the pair ahead.'[19]

Every skier on the mountain rallied into six search parties, who eventually returned before nightfall with a 'cold but cheerful Canadian and a story of extraordinary good luck'.

In Australia and New Zealand, Wyatt was far from the first to be intrigued by landscapes that felt untamed, even hostile, to interlopers like him. Echoing the colonial dogma of *terra nullius,* he would later compare the Antipodes to a block of granite being sized up by a sculptor whose chisel had barely begun to chip away at its edges.[20] Like the sculptor, Wyatt felt that these places triggered an innate urge to assert one's superiority over nature that could be seen across the history of exploration, ranging from his alpine heroes to Christopher Columbus and Francis Drake sailing around 'the New World'.[21]

Wyatt's fascination with Australia's lepidoptera, sparked on his first Sydney visit in the summer of 1936, would also flourish as he discovered a diversity of butterflies and moths more amazing than he had ever dreamed.[22] Up in the Blue Mountains, he learned about ancient granite caves whose clefts and crags were home to hibernating colonies of bogong moths, millions upon millions of whose dead bodies could form a layer on the cave floor up to four foot deep.[23] From sleeping moths to the sight of Mary catching a few winks in the snowfield, the mountains of Australia offered the Wyatts some tender moments of peace and discovery. But these were, in fact, just rare, peaceful lulls in the middle of a storm. In 1939, when the SS *Mariposa* briefly stopped in Auckland en route to Sydney, Wyatt spotted an old friend on the shore, waving a paper streamer bearing the ominous message, 'It looks like war!' By the time the ship had finished crossing the Tasman Sea on Monday 4 September, it was no longer a question of if or when.

At 8.45 the night before the Wyatts sailed into Sydney, prime minister Robert Menzies addressed the nation over the wireless, just half an hour after British prime minister Neville Chamberlain issued a similar broadcast from Downing Street: the British Empire was at war. On Tuesday, a small cocktail party had been slated to celebrate Wyatt's arrival at a friend's harbourside home. There is no record of it having gone ahead; if it did, it would certainly have been a muted affair. The Wyatt's honeymoon was over in every sense, and their new start in the Southern Hemisphere would be coloured by an almighty wake-up call sounding all the way from Europe. It would usher in six long, turbulent years in Australia that any marriage would be lucky to survive.

CHAPTER ELEVEN

The Camoufleurs

It was quiet and still at the crossroads — little more than two lonely houses, a timber yard, and a general store clustered at the intersection of two back roads.[1] A billboard advertisement for Kellogg's cornflakes ran down one side of the shop's outer walls, while 'Tea Revives You' read another — as if tea wasn't being rationed as much as everything else in wartime Australia.[2] They were scrappy-looking structures, much like all the other buildings on the outskirts of Bankstown, twenty-five kilometres from the centre of Sydney. It was hard to say whether they were run-down and neglected, or just shoddy to begin with. A short distance away, the old grandstand seemed to be caving in on itself, while the football oval — or perhaps it was an abandoned showground — was now just a smooth, windswept patch of deadened earth. Without the crumbling bleachers it would barely be noticeable, visible from the air as a faint round outline in the dead grass, like the traces of an old Roman fortress in an English paddock. There were times when the only living things seemed to be the cows, and even they appeared too lazy or depressed to move a muscle.

At certain times of the day, however, the whole quiet scene would spring to life. Like sets on a Hollywood backlot, the sides of the houses could be folded away at a moment's notice to reveal that they were little more than painted shells of plywood and cardboard over wooden frames. Inside each building, even within the dilapidated ruins of the grandstand, lay secret fuel stores and blast-proof hangars from which an RAAF plane might roll out from its hiding place, propellors whirring, and within seconds be ready for take-off. It was all fake — the entire little township, from the shop to the road, right down to the cows that grazed ineffectually in the distance. They were all made of papier-mâché.[3] Since the outbreak of World War II, the Bankstown aerodrome had become a launching pad for RAAF fighters poised to intercept an enemy attack on Sydney. But it was also an open-air laboratory for a special kind of warfare: the art of camouflage, conducted by a curious collective of leading artists, photographers, architects, and scientists who called themselves, simply, 'camoufleurs'.

'I had a most glorious flight the other day to take a whole set of photos,' wrote Colin Wyatt in a letter to his mother in July 1942.[4] According to Wyatt's fellow camoufleur, a young photographer named Max Dupain, these flights could be a sickening, stomach-churning affair: the photographer hooked into a harness, holding on for dear life as he gingerly pointed his lens down through the open bomb hatch of a spitfire or twin-engine reconnaissance plane that had taken off from the aerodrome.

As the pilot zipped back and around over the same coastline that Bankstown's namesake, Sir Joseph Banks, had collected butterflies and plants along 170 years earlier, camoufleurs such as Wyatt and Dupain would capture bird's-eye views of the fake towns and gunning posts covered in cement to resemble rocks and hidden radar stations, sometimes making a dozen passes at a time. The roar of the engines was so loud that it was impossible to hear the click of the shutter and the winding of the film roll as they captured this sublime, surreal perspective of the earth below them.[5]

'I gaze entranced at this utterly new spectacle of the earth beneath me: it moves slowly and changes as the plane roars through the sky,' Dupain would write in his diary.[6]

Back on solid ground, those photographs would be pulled apart to see if the camoufleurs' latest experiments had succeeded — that is, if they had made their subjects disappear. But if the experience ever got to

Wyatt's head or stomach, he didn't let on to his mother. It was all another adventure:

> We played around over the city & the harbour at 4000 ft which was very lovely. One could see right over the city, over Botany Bay, see the sweep of big beach south of it, & away to the hills by Bulli Pass, then we went over the edge of the Blue [Mountains] at 8000 ft.[7]

While Colin and Mary Wyatt were settling into their new life in Woollahra, a different kind of Sydney society was rapidly being organised across town. Its architect was professor William Dakin, a Sydney academic who, on face value, was an unlikely candidate to be leading any kind of military effort. Dakin was the professor of zoology at the University of Sydney and a trustee at the Australian Museum, but, as Colin Wyatt would later reflect, was no 'dry-as-dust' classroom academic.[8] To Dupain, he resembled a kind of tropical macaw, with a 'red plump generous face, with bushy eyebrows, high forehead, smallish eyes and huge jowels of fat that hang down over his colour'.[9]

Dakin's interests extended well beyond his expertise in marine biology, oceanography, and experimental zoology, which helped make him one of the Australian Broadcasting Commission's most popular radio presenters via the lively Sunday-night lectures he delivered in his crisp Liverpudlian accent. As one contemporary newspaper profile observed, Dakin 'like[d] to have his finger in every pie'.[10]

He was also well connected, with associates who included Dr Robin Tillyard — in 1934, Dakin and his wife had attended the Canberra wedding of the Tillyards' second daughter, Faith — and Eben Gowrie Waterhouse, Athol Waterhouse's younger brother and a renowned gardener and linguist, who, along with Dakin, attended an informal dinner club of current, former, and future chief justices and an ex-premier of New South Wales.[11]

Earlier, in 1938, the prospect of another European war had seemed to be all that anyone talked about. At the dinner club, Gowrie Waterhouse had given a speech recounting his astonishing tour of Europe in 1934, in which he was granted audiences with both Benito Mussolini and

Adolf Hitler — the latter just eleven days after the Nazis conducted the murderous purge known as the 'Night of the Long Knives'.[12] When Waterhouse met Hitler in a room in the Berlin headquarter of the Third Reich, the brown-shirted Führer seemed 'on the verge of a nervous breakdown', railing against the 'lies' of the foreign media and insisting, unconvincingly, that the recent 'counter-*putsch*' had been necessary to prevent civil war. It all seemed ominous.

'I felt him rather as a prophet, a visionary, a fanatic, than as a statesman,' Waterhouse would later reflect. 'He lacked the self-control and calm and poise of a Mussolini.'[13]

As the geopolitical temperature escalated, Dakin found his wandering focus increasingly drawn to the novel subject of camouflage. He wasn't the first to contemplate the secrets and subterfuge of the animal kingdom: decades earlier, the Boston painter turned amateur naturalist Abbott Handerson Thayer had drawn interest, and some ridicule, for his full-throated and at times anti-Darwinian arguments that camouflage dictated all animal colouration, from butterflies ('all tricked out in fine and powerful disguising-costumes') to flamingos ('how wonderfully such birds match or reproduce the colors of morning or evening skies').[14] Theodore Roosevelt had apparently dismissed Thayer's ideas as 'literally nonsensical', but many of his concepts were later embraced by Dakin.[15]

'It is common knowledge among naturalists that some of the most remarkable animal colourations, as well as shapes, enable defenceless creatures to escape observation by their enemies,' Dakin wrote, highlighting the white fur of Arctic animals, bark-coloured moths, and the stripes of a tiger or zebra.[16]

Military camouflage had evolved since Shakespeare's famous portrayal of the 'moving grove' of Birnham Wood in the climactic final siege of *Macbeth* — another favourite example that Dakin often invoked.[17] The last century had seen the British Empire pivot from wearing redcoats to khaki during its colonial wars of the late-19th century, and in World War I its experiments with disruptive 'dazzle' patterns saw warships painted in black-and-white stripes like a zebra or Moorish idol fish. But to Dakin, Australia's own camouflage efforts had been left to languish in peacetime. He wasn't alone: in April 1939, the Sydney arts impresario

Sydney Ure Smith visited the naval offices on Garden Island to sound out how the artistic community might be of service in the event of war. When he was rebuffed, Smith instead contacted Dakin and floated a plan: 'that a small group of interested Sydney gentlemen (chiefly artists) should be brought together for camouflage study with a view to giving aid in the event of hostilities.'[18]

By the late 1930s, Australia was home to a burgeoning modern art movement with an appetite for experimentation and iconoclasm, galvanised by the 1938 establishment of the Contemporary Art Society in Melbourne. While Victoria had the likes of Sidney Nolan, Arthur Boyd, and Albert Tucker leading the charge, Sydney soon mounted its own exhibition in 1940, featuring works from the abstractionist Frank Hinder, William Dobell, and Ellen D Rubbo — daughter-in-law of Hinder and Nancy Adams's Neapolitan painting teacher, Antonio Dattilo Rubbo. The group laid out a five-point manifesto, ranging from 'There can be no Art without Life' to, 'Vital art-work is controversial and displeasing to the majority.'[19]

At a second Sydney exhibition, held in 1941, that message bore a more explicitly anti-fascist bent: 'at a time when art is being vigorously and systematically suppressed over the whole face of Europe, [the exhibition] constitutes a challenge and an affirmation of our rights to freedom.'[20] While the movement explicitly pitted itself against Australia's conservative and censorious authorities, experimental camouflage would present a middle ground for even pacifists and conscientious objectors to contribute to a bigger fight. Or, as one camoufleur put it simply, it was preferable to die with a paintbrush in their hand rather than a rifle.[21]

Colin Wyatt had set his own designs on the city's art scene since arriving in Sydney. In October 1940, he made his presence felt after the artist Lionel Lindsay, part of the prominent Lindsay art dynasty and a friend of the Waterhouses, wrote to *The Sydney Morning Herald* savaging the Contemporary Art Society's first Sydney exhibition. Lindsay framed the entire modernist movement as a conspiracy by 'Jew dealers' in Paris to 'corrupt criticism, originate propaganda, and undermine accepted standards so that there should be ample merchandise to handle', and wrote off the local chapter as a derivative imitation of 'German degenerates' with a 'sad travesty' of a manifesto.[22] A few days after Lindsay's anti-Semitic screed, Wyatt weighed in with his own letter.

Citing his experience as a working artist who had spent years painting and studying in London, Paris, and Munich, and who had been exposed to exhibitions all across Europe for at least fifteen years, he rejected Lindsay's position regarding originality. These works, he argued, were far less derivative than the 'hackneyed symbols' found across Australia's art establishment. Wyatt took particular aim at the widely celebrated German-born Hans Heysen, whose distinctive gum-strewn landscapes he dismissed as a 'pleasant' but 'unoriginal' rendering of common scenes readily seen across Australia.[23]

Having put himself on the radar, Wyatt soon became a target for derision himself when two of his pieces were included in the Contemporary Art Society's second Sydney exhibition in September 1941. Appearing alongside works by Nolan, Dobell, James Gleeson, Herbert McLintock, Donald Friend, and his fellow Grosvenor alumnus Dorrit Black, Wyatt's submissions included a Salvador Dali–esque surrealist piece called *Vanity, Vanity, All Is Vanity.*[24] As early as 1935, his old Grosvenor mentor Iain Macnab had encouraged him to explore surrealism, and with this biblically titled tableau Wyatt departed starkly from the landscapes and skiing scenes of his earlier work. Its gothic dreamscape presented a tiger's skull with a severed human hand in its jaws, its fingers clutching a dart, which a brief description in *The Daily Telegraph* offered to decode for the reader:

> Hand and dart signify ambition towards certain aims. That ambition is useless, because death (tiger's skull) intervenes. Unfastened ladder in background represents futility of ambition.[25]

The show inspired a colourfully scathing review in *The Daily Mirror* from boxing promoter turned arts journalist Rex Rienits. Headlined 'Are These Things Art?', the article dismissed Gleeson's works as 'provocative', called Nolan's *Woman in Chair* a 'problem picture', and belittled Wyatt's canvas as 'another natty job', joking that anyone who paid the asking prices — twenty guineas, in Wyatt's case — should be able to use their new purchase to gain express admission to the local psychiatric hospital.[26] The *Daily Telegraph* was slightly kinder, writing that Wyatt's 'meaning may not be very obvious, but it is well designed', before warning that much of the exhibition 'will irritate and baffle'.[27]

These kinds of reactionary critiques and tabloid philistinism were like badges of honour for some modernists. Certainly, they were preferable to faint praise; later that month, Mary and Colin Wyatt were photographed once again by *The Sydney Morning Herald*, this time at a private viewing of Colin's first one-man exhibition in Australia — a more conventional set of landscapes shown at Macquarie Galleries.[28] The day before, however, the paper's art critic had published a lukewarm review, labelling Wyatt 'a sound technician' whose work betrayed 'an emptiness in most that would indicate the unique material he has had at his disposal has failed to stimulate his creative ability very deeply'.[29] Although already familiar with the futility of ambition, Colin Wyatt would not be quitting his day job anytime soon.

Within days of his and Mary's arrival, Colin had found work with the Department of Information, initially working as a censor before joining a dozen translators and broadcasters tasked with recording nightly short-wave radio programs that were transmitted around the world by the ABC. In his new role, Wyatt handled English and French broadcasts, but it wasn't the first time he had deployed his linguistic talents for the public broadcaster. During his first Australian trip, he had auditioned for the ABC on a lark, and had soon booked a £15-per-week contract touring his repertoire of European mountain folk songs around the country from March to April 1937. Although the Department of Information's publicly stated goal was 'to publicise Australia and to win her good neighbours on the air', Wyatt later described his work more bluntly: as propaganda.[30]

To Dakin and Ure Smith, artists such as Hinder, Dobell, and perhaps even Wyatt had an altogether different value. With Dakin as its chair, the Sydney Camouflage Group began to meet regularly, rallying its networks until the ranks of volunteer camoufleurs included prominent engineers, architects, and scientists, alongside a handful of artists from Hinder to Dupain, whose studio on Bond Street, Sydney, had become a hotbed for crisp commercial work alongside more experimental uses of light, shadow, and shape. The aims of the Camouflage Group were laid out in *The Art of Camouflage,* its self-published manifesto and how-to manual edited by Dakin and released later, in 1941. Featuring photographic studies of real fish and wooden ducks, it explained the four principles of modern camouflage: realistic painting; countershading or obliterative shading; disruptive colouration; and the removal of shadows.

Following one of their biggest meetings yet in September 1939, Dakin wrote to the defence minister to fill him in on the work of these 'prominent men'. At first, the minister was happy to humour the group's 'voluntary' efforts, but in November 1940, Dakin managed to get a meeting with the prime minister, Robert Menzies, alongside representatives from the navy, the army, and the Department of the Interior. He was joined by Daryl Lindsay, the curator at the National Gallery of Victoria and brother of Lionel, and Daniel Mahony, the director of the National Museum of Victoria and Dick Pescott's predecessor.

According to the Camouflage Group, the urgency of their work was being driven home by the camouflage techniques already being trialled by the other side.

'Nearly all [German] operational aerodromes and landing grounds on the Western Front have now been elaborately and effectively camouflaged,' read one report quoted in *The Art of Camouflage.* 'Collapsible churches, false canals, huts on trolleys and painted farmyard animals are being used in addition to ordinary netting and paint camouflage to make up a convincing pattern … any aerodrome, therefore, which is obviously an aerodrome is regarded with suspicion.'[31]

Dakin's dogged persistence paid off: in April 1941, the War Cabinet officially brought the Camouflage Group inside the tent, absorbing its activities into a Defence Central Camouflage Committee as part of the newly formed Department of Home Security. Professor Dakin was granted the official title of Technical Director of Camouflage for the Commonwealth government, while many of the group's camoufleurs were deployed as civilian officers for the Department of Home Security. Sub-committees would be established in each state and territory, while Dakin was handed control of a camouflage station at Middle Point on Sydney Harbour, and, under the auspices of the RAAF, allowed to test their initial experiments at the newly opened Bankstown aerodrome, where, before long, fake buildings, trees, and cows began to spring up.

'The outbreak of war was thus actually anticipated in so far as preparations for camouflage study were concerned,' Dakin later wrote, a little smugly.[32]

But now that war was upon them, it was clear that the handful of volunteers in the Sydney Camouflage Group couldn't cover it all. Before long, Dakin had recruited over one hundred artists and architects to the Department of Home Security, while some artists already enlisted as wartime labourers were brought over to work on Dakin's experiments — the artist William Dobell, who would controversially win the Archibald Prize in 1943 for his portrait of fellow artist and camoufleur Joshua Smith, was one of the men responsible for the fake cows that surrounded the fake town of the Bankstown aerodrome.[33] In a report for the Department of Home Security, Dakin laid out the ideal prerequisites for a camoufleur:

> A good camoufleur must above all things be a man of wide knowledge and good at improvisation. He must be keenly interested in the appearance of things — ranging from scenery to human and indeed, animal habits.[34]

It's unclear precisely when Colin Wyatt first fell in with Dakin's Camouflage Group — his personnel file in the National Archives of Australia notes simply that he was a 'Member of the Original Camoufleur Organisation'.[35] But given Dakin's criteria, it's little surprise that when Wyatt did formally join their ranks, the officer jotted down this brief assessment: 'Should make Good Camoufleur'.

CHAPTER TWELVE

The Decoys

Colin Wyatt woke to the sound of an aeroplane flying above his tent and mosquito net. It was around 2.00 am in Nadzab, a small New Guinea village 1,900 miles from Sydney, in a riverside clearing surrounded by green hills and forest. There was no such thing as a quiet night's sleep on this archipelago; as soon as the sun set, a disquieting choir of ghost-like birdsong would begin calling out to Wyatt from the nearby jungle.[1] But as his ears tuned into the hum of the aeroplane's engines, it dawned on him that they probably didn't belong to a friendly RAAF or American fighter plane. It had to be part of another Japanese raid, taking advantage of the Allies' patchy radar to sneak in undetected over the old colonial airfield.

The strip at Nadzab had been built by Lutheran missionaries prior to World War I before being abandoned and overrun by weeds, and, later, the Japanese. Then, on one fiery day in September 1943, a wave of American and Australian bombers and paratroopers seized the village in a surprise attack that blanketed the valley and its Japanese fortifications with fragmentation bombs and over 60,000 rounds of ammunition.[2] The sweeping operation had been ordered by the American general Douglas MacArthur, who, in the wake of Pearl Harbor, had taken control of virtually all Australia's military activities, from the fake buildings of Bankstown aerodrome to these islands in the north. This latest offensive,

Operation Postern, was an attempt to 'close the ring' around the port town of Lai, on the eastern edge of New Guinea. But, despite their success at pushing their enemy back, an atmosphere of death and danger still hung over the region.

At Lai, Wyatt had posed for a pair of photographs standing among the wreckage of a Japanese plane, its fuselage a tangled mass of shredded metal surrounded by tropical greenery. In Nadzab, Wyatt photographed his RAAF comrades mounting a game of cricket on a makeshift pitch within batting distance of the rows of little white crosses that marked the graves of the fallen. Later, on Goodenough Island, he witnessed an alarming incident when local villagers turned over a Japanese soldier who had been hiding out in a hillside village.

'Our men grabbed him and shot him on the spot,' Wyatt would later tell his superiors in a concerned memo.[3]

On this sleepless night in Nadzab, with the Japanese bomber looming ominously overhead, Wyatt opened his eyes to make out glimmers of light across the RAAF camp. He registered this detail with annoyance; ever since he had arrived in New Guinea, he had quickly learned that, despite all the official warnings and the extensive training materials and artfully designed posters that the Defence Central Camouflage Committee had provided, most of the RAAF outposts he visited would only plunge into true darkness when the red alert was sounded. But the red alert wasn't always effective — the previous afternoon, at sunset, another enemy plane had managed to shoot up the Nadzab airstrip, with the alarm only sounding once the raider had finished its pass and made its escape. That night, Wyatt had listened to the engines for a full minute before, finally, the alarm sounded and the sound of the engines above him faded away. They had gotten lucky this time, but whether the Japanese plane had bailed on a planned attack, or cut its night-time reconnaissance flight short, the fact that the immediate threat had passed did little to quell Wyatt's anxieties.

'There is no such thing as a "blackout" and lights blaze away all night,' he would later write in a frustrated five-page note sent to his superiors and Professor William Dakin on 1 March 1944, near the end of his time as a camoufleur.[4] 'In all cases, any destructive hits were made on something where a light had been left burning ... either these were lucky hits, or else their bombing accuracy on small defined targets is good.'[5]

When Wyatt had joined the Department of Home Security in April 1942, he had initially been charged with applying Dakin's teachings to disguise landing strips and radar stations up and down the New South Wales coast, periodically taking flight to inspect his handiwork from above. But in 1943, as MacArthur attempted to thin out Japan's presence across Australia's northernmost neighbours, he was soon transferred north.

Wyatt had flown out from Townsville in September 1943 in an old Douglas C-47, along with an assortment of Australian and American servicemen. Packed like sardines in a flying tin, the men grew briny with sweat as the temperature rose, the engines cut out, and the New Guinea jungle rose up to meet them.[6] He'd gained plenty of exposure to the humidity of northern Australia since becoming a camoufleur, but the tropical heat of New Guinea was something else again, hitting him like a hellish wave.[7]

Before he had left for New Guinea, Wyatt had been apprised of some new developments: after occupying a grey area in the broader military apparatus, the term 'camoufleurs' had been dropped in favour of the more official 'Camouflage Officer'. They now wore khaki uniforms similar to their military counterparts, with billowing, high-waisted trousers, pith helmets, and a badge bearing a newly designed emblem: a tiger holding a palm frond aloft in front of its face—a more rousing inversion of the bleak picture that Wyatt had painted in *Vanity, Vanity, All Is Vanity*.

Like his fellow officers, Wyatt had signed an undertaking that he would keep all information about his movements and work in the Camouflage Section secret. Almost immediately, however, he whipped out his paper and watercolours, and began documenting what he saw across New Guinea and the Trobriand Islands, ranging from village scenes to portraits of local girls holding fruit, to RAAF servicemen unloading barges.[8] Wyatt became a subject too, with his fellow camouflage officer and artist Robert Emerson Curtis sketching a scene of

Wyatt entertaining his comrades in the mess at Milne Bay, his foot raised as if tapping along to the tune wheezing out of the accordion across his lap.[9] Another scene on Goodenough Island showed Wyatt looking like a 19th-century explorer, standing with hand on hip and pith helmet on head as he looked out at a jeep and aeroplane made tiny by the massive, jungled mountain rising over them.[10]

But the artworks painted a quainter picture than the reality. In a preliminary report, Curtis wrote that the situation in New Guinea would demand camouflage at its 'most daring and brilliant form' to 'devise, deceive, bluff and mislead the enemy by every kind of cunning and employable trick'.[11] But, as Curtis noted, the assessment on the ground was bleak: 'the camoufleur in New Guinea will see great and unbelievable neglect and ignorance in matters of camouflage'.[12]

Dakin had idealistically pitched the Camouflage Group as an all-hands-on-deck collaboration that drew expertise and innovation from across the public sphere and military world for the greater good. But he was soon left 'aggrieved' and 'infuriated' by delays and friction with army officials. 'Money has been made available for a camouflage scheme but little has been done,' he told the press in December 1941. 'Why bring in men like myself to advise the Government in a voluntary capacity if that advice is not acted upon? Delay after delay makes one wonder what is going to happen.'[13]

Dakin's concerns were validated when, on the morning of 19 February 1942, over 200 Japanese planes mounted twin raids on Australia's northernmost city, Darwin. Their targets included an RAAF base and the city's oil reserves, both identified as priorities by the camoufleurs, who had questioned the design of the RAAF station the previous year. Dakin's pointed warning against delays proved brutally prescient: one of the ships hit by Japanese bombs was the *Zealandia*, a ship that had itself been covered in black-and-white 'dazzle' camouflage in World War I. It had been heading to Darwin with, of all things, a shipment of camouflage materials that ended up on the sea floor along with the rest of the ship.

Dakin later noted, with a grim sense of vindication, that among the bombed infrastructure was a fake squadron of flatpack plywood planes, designed by the camoufleurs and cheaply fabricated by a Sydney firm for airfields around the country.

'These decoys were regarded as jokes,' Dakin noted bitterly.[14] 'There is evidence from Darwin that the simple and cheap "flat" decoys — often laughed at by many officers — were well and truly attacked by the Japanese.'[15]

But it was small consolation; to Dakin, it seemed clear that Australia's military leaders viewed his work as a low priority and had 'no appreciation of what modern camouflage might accomplish in that area when it was most needed'. Even after Darwin's bombing, he was shocked to learn that a new fort was being constructed 'without any efforts to conceal the site or deceive as to intention'.[16]

From the beginning, the army had resisted the idea of taking advice from outside the military, let alone from the Camouflage Group's odd coalition of abstract artists and zoologists. By May 1942, the army insisted that only army officers would coordinate camouflage design across its operations, with its engineer-in-chief bristling at the 'almost unheard of' expectation that it defer to a 'Civilian Committee' back in Australia when coordinating frontline movements. Inside and outside the military, Dakin was also frustrated that camouflage was neither fully understood nor taken seriously.[17]

The image of Dakin's camoufleurs as a group of effete dilettantes — even some camoufleurs described themselves as 'camopansies' — with no business on the frontline clearly rankled Dakin, and soon he began to push back on the 'very definite idea prevailing that all Camoufleurs were artists'.[18] On paper, it's easy to see why some of their suggestions were scoffed at. 'How to make a dummy tree,' read one instruction. 'Take a real one, remove leaves, cover with machine cut net or with a little wire netting intertwined with hessian and fresh leaves occasionally'.[19]

By the time Wyatt arrived in New Guinea on 17 September, he found plenty of work; one commanding officer paid 'special tribute for the way he manhandled the job', while his personnel file noted that he was a 'good but rough draughtsman' with the 'capacity to get things done quickly', who might be 'more usefully employed [on] special missions'. Moreover, it concluded he was a 'very intelligent Camoufleur w/ particularly active and creative imagination'.[20] It was a far more resounding endorsement than that offered by the art critics back in Sydney, but even the best camoufleurs would find that as General MacArthur pushed the frontline further north, their work was increasingly sidelined.

'The feeling at present in this area is that things are moving so rapidly that camouflage is to all intents and purposes unnecessary,' Wyatt wrote in his dejected five-page memo, adding that there was a feeling among the RAAF that it was 'only a flea-bite' compared to the US forces, and had been relegated to do 'odd jobs' to keep them and their comparatively slow aircraft busy and out of the way.

'They strongly suspected that half the time there was nothing of any value at the receiving end of their bombs,' Wyatt wrote.[21]

It was a sentiment shared by Dupain, who undertook camouflage work across the islands at the same time, and thought the Americans seemed 'more keen to let the Japs have a good look' at their weapons and machinery, in the hope it might 'scare off' any attackers.[22]

Wyatt was also frustrated by the RAAF's relationship with locals. Years later, he would write about these encounters with the people of New Guinea and its surrounding islands with anthropological language typical of the time. He described the 'fuzzy-wuzzies' of New Guinea as 'primitive, darker-skinned' compared to the 'highly cultivated' Tahitians, while Trobriand Islanders seemed a 'stepping-stone' between the Polynesians and the Melanesians.[23] He was also titillated by the 'completely unmoral' sexual mores, while noting that the 'keynote' of the society was the 'bevy of maidens' in swinging grass skirts.[24]

All the same, he felt that his countrymen underestimated the islanders, failing to harness their deep understanding of the local environment while needlessly alienating them.

'The average R.A. completely under-rates their intelligence and just thinks of them as poor bloody niggers,' he wrote in his memo. As he outlined the incident of the executed prisoner on Goodenough Island, he added that the episode 'terribly upset the natives who had always been taught by us that killing was bad'. The result, he added, was that the villagers were unlikely to surrender any further Japanese soldiers that crossed their path.[25]

Dakin also noted the difficulties presented by the Pacific, later reflecting that 'our first men engaged in jungle warfare had little or no knowledge of bushcraft, jungle warfare, or the most elementary knowledge of fighting whilst in a concealed manner'.[26] One solution, and one of Dakin's proudest achievements, was the development of a product called Skin Tone Commando Cream, which addressed the problem that, in a largely white military, a 'pair of pink or even light brown' arms, legs, and faces became 'amazingly obvious' against the green jungle. Dakin enlisted the cosmetics giant Colgate-Palmolive, along with an 'actress who specialised in stagecraft', whose advice likely helped settle on a 'very dark brown' colour — inspired by the fact that, in an era where minstrel shows and painted-up Othellos were common, 'dark browns had already been used in theatrical work'.[27]

Here, Dakin's passion for evolutionary biology and camouflage intersected with another area of interest: he had been a proponent of eugenics for decades, and before World War I had mounted a lecture tour and even attempted to form a eugenics society. Even the biology textbooks he wrote touted the imperial significance of racial purity, and in 1935 he publicly backed a proposition by the Racial Hygiene Association to sterilise New South Wales's 'mentally and physically unfit persons'.[28]

'Eradication from the obvious physical defects could be carried out in one generation,' Dakin wrote.

In this light, Dakin's efforts to protect White Australia and its troops by encouraging them to channel the 'bushcraft' and skin tone of what he regarded as a less-developed race takes on an uncomfortable new meaning. Racial pseudoscience notwithstanding, the cream was still rejected by many soldiers, who complained of skin irritation, or, in some cases, thought the whole notion of camouflage was a show of cowardice — 'with some men, camouflage and concealment came for a time to be regarded as implying inaction,' Dakin noted. Set against these complex codes of military masculinity, it probably didn't help that Skin Tone Commando Cream was based on a 'make-up cream which girls had been using for colouring legs to resemble silk stockings'.[29]

By 1944, even Max Dupain had become convinced that camouflage had all but lost its relevance in the war effort, and sought to leave the Camouflage Section entirely. Soon after sending his five-page report, Wyatt was reluctantly reassigned to teach camouflage—after first spending a few days in a Townsville hospital with stomach pain.[30]

'I have long felt that Mr Wyatt's value to the service would be as an instructor rather than as a pioneer and ambassador in a new field,' Emerson Curtis noted in February, adding that Wyatt had previously agreed to move before changing his mind.

'I was astounded, therefore, to find on my return that he neither wished nor intended to proceed to Townsville without first enjoying some months in the cool south.'[31]

Within a few months, Wyatt had left the Camouflage Section, but by the time his March 1944 report reached Dakin there was little the professor could do except add it to his already long list of grievances. While Curtis noted that Wyatt's account betrayed 'a limited and definitely one-sided point of view', he also added, 'C.W. is very observant and I agree with much of what he says'.[32]

Wyatt's recall from the islands was part of a long, slow decline for the camoufleurs, whose numbers had been progressively cut by the Department of Home Security from 127 in February 1942 to just thirty-four men in July 1944. That month, Dakin wrote a 'distressed' memo complaining once again that the army would 'refuse to the bitter end to have anything to do with "civilians" no matter how much they know or can help'.[33] In just a few short years, Dakin's flawed dream of bringing science, art, and warfare together had, with poetic irony, faded into the background.

Wyatt would encounter more frustration back on the mainland when another solo exhibition opened at Macquarie Galleries in March 1944. Showcasing seventy watercolour snapshots of his travels as a camouflage officer, the show sold well, but received another, even cooler review from *The Sydney Morning Herald*'s art critic, who found the scenes so 'amateur' and 'timid' that they fell 'outside the realm of serious criticism'.[34] Despite his efforts, it seemed that neither Wyatt's older European landscapes, his attempts to blend in with the trendy surrealists, nor his raw depictions of Australia at war were making an impact in the local art world.

Even so, Wyatt managed to salvage some personal silver linings from his wartime service. Just as he used his invitation to New Zealand as an excuse to pursue his passion for ski-mountaineering, now, being set loose over the east coast of Australia, and later Darwin, Townsville, and the Pacific Islands gave him abundant opportunities to fall further in love with the region's butterflies.

From the outset, he made sure to steal a few moments each day to observe and collect.[35] Before his deployment to New Guinea, on an official visit to Kiama on the New South Wales coast, he had captured a rarely seen chequered sedge-skipper, and in January 1941, near Double Bay in Sydney, he had fatefully caught a small cabbage white butterfly.[36] This was a big deal; the cabbage white was an invasive species that had travelled over from Europe and Asia to ravage crops across the Atlantic from Canada to California, before arriving in New Zealand in 1930.[37] Within a decade, it was being recorded in great numbers around Victoria, but Wyatt's discovery was an important scientific breakthrough, marking the first of its kind to be caught in New South Wales.

Upon landing in New Guinea, the first thing Wyatt had done was to fetch his net as he encountered an eye-popping variety of insects from owl butterflies to bright-red dragonflies. Years later, Wyatt would recall with enthusiasm the 'gorgeous exotic butterflies' that seemed to be everywhere: blue emperors, green-spotted swallowtails, and white and scarlet delias. In tropical lagoons, he picked up the kind of stunning mottled cowrie shells he had once coveted as a child but, unlike Athol Waterhouse, could never get his hands on — one drawback of a childhood spent in the mountains rather than the coast. One day, as he cooled down in a creek, he spotted an enormous black swallowtail, followed by the green-and-gold colours of a birdwing. These 'Guinea golds' were soon fetching a high price among servicemen gathering exotic souvenirs to send home — a craze that took such a hold among the airmen that their commanding officer made it an offence to repurpose their life-saving mosquito nets into makeshift butterfly catchers.[38]

Early in his tour, Wyatt found two plump chrysalises dangling from the leaves of a tree, heavy in his hand and as big as his thumb. He left them in a box in his tent, and a fortnight later was delighted to find two fresh birdwings had emerged from their cocoons — a moment he would later describe as the 'biggest thrill' in all his years of bug-hunting.[39]

Even after all those years, in the middle of a war zone on the other side of the world, Colin was in many ways still the same little boy with shoeboxes in his bedroom. As he travelled the continent, juggling his various identities as a camoufleur, artist, skier, and husband, he would also work his way into another fraternity of curious eccentrics: Australia's butterfly collectors.

As he looked up at Colin Wyatt, perched twenty feet up a sheoak tree and clutching what appeared to be dazzling blue, red, and silver butterflies, Athol Waterhouse didn't yet know just how entwined their fates — let alone their butterfly collections — would soon become. The sixty-three-year-old's own tree-climbing days were behind him, but this young Englishman was half Waterhouse's age, and full of energy and enthusiasm for collecting that perhaps the older man recognised and appreciated. Perhaps he also felt some paternal regard for the younger man, just a few years older than his twin boys, who were already enlisted in the war effort. For that brief, fleeting moment, Waterhouse would even go so far as to describe Wyatt not merely as a fellow collector or companion, but as a friend.

Wyatt had been quick to make friends across Australia's butterfly-collecting community, having reached out to the Entomological Society of Victoria shortly after settling in Sydney. He soon began exchanging 'animated correspondence' and specimens with several prominent collectors, including John Cecil Le Souëf and Frances Erasmus 'Ras' Wilson, who he joined at meetings and on the occasional field trip while in Melbourne.

'Short of stature with a bristling uptrained red moustache, he was a charming companion with a fund of anecdotes on collecting butterflies in various parts of the world,' Le Souëf would later reflect, a first impression shared by many.[40]

Wyatt had first encountered Waterhouse around the same time, and in March 1941 Waterhouse wrote in *The Australian Museum Magazine* about Wyatt's foreboding discovery of the small cabbage white two months before.[41] Over several months, Waterhouse had also shown this charming new arrival some of his favourite collecting spots, from the suburbs of Sydney to Blackheath in the Blue Mountains.

But, if anything, that day roaming the scrub around Sydney's northern beaches was a vivid lesson that things aren't always as they appear—those red, blue, and silver butterflies in Wyatt's hands weren't butterflies at all. The pair had set out from Sydney in April 1941 on the trail of *Ogyris amaryllis,* a vivid-blue butterfly that had formed one of the crowning pieces of his original G.A. Waterhouse Collection.

To Waterhouse, the *Ogyris* was the most fascinating genus of butterflies—although found across mainland Australia, for years they remained a rarity in collections, thanks to their habit of fluttering high up in the treetops, out of reach of all but the most agile collectors. But there had been a recent breakthrough: the larvae of the *Ogyris* fed on a red-flowering mistletoe that crept parasitically on other trees. Once entomologists such as Waterhouse cracked this code, they were able to breed them in captivity in far greater numbers than could ever be netted in the wild. As Wyatt and Waterhouse discussed the quirks of *Ogyris,* Waterhouse shared the observation that some butterflies were drawn to bright colours—and that perhaps this might aid Wyatt's pursuit of his own free-range specimens.

'I mentioned this to my friend, Mr. C. W. Wyatt, and wondered if this blue butterfly would be attracted by blue colours,' Waterhouse wrote a few weeks later.[42]

Wyatt jumped at the task, and quickly produced a few scraps of 'brilliant blue, brilliant red and silver tin foil', which he began cutting into the outline of a butterfly. The next minute, he clambered up a tree where they had noticed the butterflies congregating, and fixed the fakes in place. Wyatt had tried the same spot a day earlier, but had only managed to catch a single, solitary specimen. But this time they seemed to flock to the bright-red foil—ignoring the blue and silver, but still lingering long enough for Wyatt to swing into action.

'They were definitely attracted by the red and settled within a few inches of it and so were easily caught,' Waterhouse wrote in another article, as he summarised the findings of their April adventure and another trip soon after.[43] When the final piece was published in the June 1941 edition of *The Australian Museum Magazine*, Waterhouse publicly resolved to undertake more experiments with the inventive young Mr Wyatt. Later, in his 1955 memoir, Wyatt would recall trying a similar trick in New Guinea to catch a blue emperor with the blue section of a Player's Navy Cut cigarette packet—this time, however, the *P. ulysses* refused to be fooled, and darted away before Wyatt could catch it.[44] By then, his days of friendly experimentation with Athol Waterhouse had long since passed, and the June 1941 magazine article would be the last time Waterhouse would offer such a glowing public account of his onetime companion and budding camoufleur. In fact, within just a few months of their day trip in April 1941, Waterhouse had decisively changed his tune on his friend Colin Wyatt.

'I soon found that he was not who he claimed to be,' Waterhouse would lament in September 1947.[45]

CHAPTER THIRTEEN

The Loot

Late on a Saturday night in January 1946, a member of the public reported something unusual as they walked down North Terrace, Adelaide's premier address. From the Public Library to the University of Adelaide, this row of prestigious sandstone institutions represented South Australia's intellectual and cultural heartland, watched over by statues of the dead British settlers whose pastoral and mining fortunes had bankrolled the colony's pursuit of knowledge and art. Chief among them was the east wing of the South Australian Museum, which opened out onto a grassy courtyard where a towering stone column stood sentinel-like over the lawn. Covered in Ancient Egyptian hieroglyphs, it was one of several built in the reign of Rameses II for the Great Temple of Herishef, where they had remained for over 3,000 years until a Swiss archaeologist excavated them in 1891. The columns were distributed around the world, from the British Museum in London to its counterparts in Boston, Manchester, and Adelaide, and on an ordinary night one might expect this exotic sight to command the attention of passers-by. On this Saturday evening, however, it was the museum's doors that caught their eye — they appeared to be swinging open in the summer breeze.[1]

It was almost midnight by the time the police arrived and confirmed that the heavy twin doors, which had been bolted firmly shut at five-thirty that afternoon, were now wide open. It seemed that someone had slid both sets of bolts loose, and then, with what must have taken an almighty effort, yanked the doors inwards to force open the triple Yale lock.[2] The only witnesses were the colony of European honey bees that lived in a glass-sided hive within the museum, its drones passing in and out through a vent in the window to the delight of children. But the bees definitely weren't talking. No one could figure out precisely when the break-out had happened, or how long the doors and the exhibits inside had lain wide open to passing foot traffic.

The museum had an anti-burglary system with a direct line to the City Watchhouse, and some 170 electrical triggers wired into its main doors and lower windows.[3] But, for most of the fifteen years since the alarms had been installed, their main function seemed to be providing government electricians with a near-constant stream of maintenance work. Despite their efforts, the museum averaged two false alarms a week, and on many evenings the whole system just stopped working. This, it seemed, was what had happened on 5 January.

Herbert Hale had been at the South Australian Museum since 1914, where he had started as a fresh-faced, dark-haired, and clean-shaven cadet still in his teens, and was now its veteran director, sporting a neat toothbrush moustache flecked with grey. Over the next few days, Hale ordered his staff to undertake a building-wide check of the collections — from the bronze, ivory, and wooden artworks of the ethnology collection to the forty-nine cabinets and 200 storeboxes of the entomology department. Although Hale would later admit that this must have been 'rather a cursory examination', initially it seemed that nothing was out of place.[4]

With the alarm out of action, it was entirely possible that someone had deliberately stuck around after the doors were closed to the public and the last attendant had locked up and headed home. Like the National Museum of Victoria, the east and north wings were a cluttered maze of crowded display cases and fading specimens; so much so that, before the war, the man from the Californian Academy of Science had also taken issue with Adelaide's 'natural history specimens constructed in bygone years by long discarded methods'.[5] On a busy day, visitors could barely move for all the display cases — the value of the plate glass alone, the Californian quipped, was enough to fund a much-needed facelift for the entire museum. Hale tended to agree: the enthusiasm of his predecessors had often outweighed their discretion, and the museum now had to cram a 'vast quantity' of material into its footprint.

'I must state that with the present lay-out and organisation of the Museum, it would not be an extremely difficult matter for anyone with ulterior purpose to conceal himself in the buildings at clearing time,' Hale would later admit.[6] 'The weak point, of course, is that any person determined to remain within the building after closing hours might find an opportunity of concealing himself in one or other of the galleries.'[7]

The alternative explanation was that a member of the public had somehow inadvertently found themselves locked inside after hours and, having missed the attendants making their final checks and being missed in turn, had heaved the doors open in a moment of panic or embarrassment, and slipped quietly into the night. As Hale also noted, there was also the 'unfortunate circumstance that one of the Attendants has become very deaf'.[8] Neither theory cast the museum's security in a particularly good light, but in lieu of more evidence, Hale and the board were content to remain blissfully, or perhaps wilfully, ignorant of what might have happened that night in 1946.

For just over a year, nothing more came of it, until 22 January 1947, when Hale received a phone call from Dick Pescott in Melbourne. Once Hale put down the phone, having heard all about the 825 missing specimens that George Lyell had finished identifying, he immediately ordered Herbert Womersley, the museum's entomologist, who had done the 1946 check, to look again.

This time, he was joined by Norman B Tindale, a towering figure with one good eye who would cast a long shadow over the museum — one that had little to do with height. 'Tinny' had started out as a cadet entomologist before his field work, which took him as far north as Groote Eylandt in the Gulf of Carpentaria, inspired him to reinvent himself as an ethnologist and anthropologist. He spent decades seeking out and studying First Nations communities around Australia, making notes, recording songs on wax cylinders and 16mm film, and collecting thousands of artefacts as he went.

In 1940, he published the first version of his most famous project, a map of 'tribal distributions' that set down on paper what Aboriginal communities had long known: the First Peoples of this southern continent were neither rootless nomads nor an homogenous group of 'natives', but comprised diverse neighbouring language groups with deep connections to Country who had developed complex systems of boundaries, trade, and cultural practices spanning the continent.[9] Despite this growing body of work, Tindale remained one of the few people on staff who knew the museum's butterfly collections intimately.

A week later, Hale wrote back to Pescott with the results of their search: 'This is the most amazing thing that has happened to me in my more than thirty years of Museum experience.'[10]

Despite Hale's tone of surprise, the threat of burglary had dogged the museums of Australia for years. A decade earlier, in a rare instance of the South Australian Museum's alarm system actually working, an alert to the watchhouse in July 1934 had prompted the caretaker to walk a lap of the building. At around 9.00 pm, he discovered a twenty-three-year-old man crouching beside the half-opened window of the taxidermist's basement workshop. The young man claimed to be simply sleeping rough, but when two plainclothes police officers emptied his pockets, they discovered a pair of leather gloves, two pairs of pliers, two chisels, a screwdriver, and a drill.[11] The following month, the thwarted cat burglar told the Adelaide Police Court that he was unemployed and broke, and had planned to make for the museum's second-floor coin collections — not realising, perhaps, that as early as November 1895, a predecessor of Hale named Dr Edward Charles Stirling had resolved to remove valuable gold from display after another young man named William Wyatt — with no discernible links to any architectural dynasties — forced open a window and stole gold nuggets from a glass cabinet.[12]

But break-ins were rare compared to the tried-and-true method of staying in and breaking out. One Saturday in August 1935, a cordon of forty police officers swarmed the purportedly 'burglar-proof' Australian Museum in Sydney after its mammologist heard a buzzing sound while working late.[13] It was a little after 6.00 pm, and, having called the police, he and the museum director raced to its source: a display of precious gems and minerals whose case had tripped an alarm when forced open. The pair moved quickly, striking matches to find their way through the dark until they came to the open case with three trays of alluvial gold worth £50 missing. There was more gold scattered on the floor, as though the intruder had spotted the flickering lights and left in a hurry.

The police arrived minutes later, slightly unnerved by the shadows cast by the mounted specimens of pythons and jungle predators as they scoured the galleries.[14] When an officer on the second floor noticed scuff marks on a grille leading to the elevator shaft, a very game constable climbed in and slid down the greasy steel cable inside, retracing a daring escape route that eventually led out through a window to Sydney Grammar next door.[15] It seemed clear that the perpetrator had thoroughly cased the building beforehand, timing the heist between the museum's 5.15 pm closing time and the watchman's first rounds at 8.00 pm.

'As it is impossible to break into the building without raising an alarm, the police are still convinced the man hid himself on the top floor,' read one newspaper report.[16]

A similar attempt had occurred a year earlier, when the mammologist was once again working late, and had once again heard something suspicious.[17] This time, the police were able to recover the gold and silver medals that had been taken from four broken cases, and to apprehend the perpetrator, who was found crouched among the zoological displays. (A *Daily Telegraph* report later included the irresistible embellishment that the 'intruder was found perched on the top of the cage of a stuffed lion').[18]

Half a century earlier, museums across Sydney and Melbourne were targeted by their first serial thief. On a Friday afternoon in August 1886, a young man calling himself CM Cook walked into a pawnshop on Elizabeth Street in Melbourne, and in a North American accent asked the owner if he bought old silver. It was Cook's bad luck that when he produced a hefty silver medal to show the pawnbroker, it was promptly handed to a plainclothes detective who had arrived earlier that day. The officer found another medal and a chunk of crudely melted silver on Cook's person, as the American spun a story about having been given the medal in Sydney. It would later emerge that Cook had already successfully told the same story to two other pawnbrokers across town.

While Cook toured the pawnshops of Melbourne, the staff at the National Museum of Victoria and the police on Russell Street were scrambling. That morning, an attendant had noticed that a case containing several gold, silver, and bronze medals that was normally screwed shut had been prised open overnight, along with a window.[19] In court, a museum attendant later testified that at four o'clock on the afternoon of the theft, he spoke to Cook shortly before he began shooing visitors out of the building before closing up.[20] Cook told the court that he had only recently arrived in Australia from California, had previously worked as a telegraph operator, but was now living in poverty while trying to support his young wife.[21] It also emerged, however, that CM Cook did not exist at all — the man's true identity was Donald McKenzie Forrest.

It was once the twin identities of Cook and Forrest became known that the Melbourne job was recognised as one in a multi-city spree. It emerged that a pawnshop on Oxford Street in Sydney had also bought a piece of jewellery from a man named CM Cook, while an investigation across the jewellers and pawnbrokers of Sydney revealed that Forrest had sold, under his own name, thirteen uncut diamonds to a well-known jewellery firm after telling them he just arrived from a diamond mine in South Africa.[22]

After facing court in Melbourne, Forrest caught a train to Sydney under police escort. Along the way, he told the detective — the same one who had arrested him at the Melbourne pawnshop — the full story. On 22 July, he had entered the Australian Museum on College Street at around 3.00 pm before hiding himself in a box of kangaroo skins once the coast was clear. He waited among the marsupial pelts for hours before re-emerging early in the morning to mount his smash-and-grab, having done the same to the Art Gallery of New South Wales two days earlier.

He also revealed that, while most of the items had been recovered, he had already sent a handful of jewels to England to be fenced. He insisted he was just a desperate man down on his luck, but the police became convinced that 'Cook' was in fact a wily career criminal who had arrived in Australia with a plan to systematically rob the country's public institutions.[23] The judge, however, thought that Forrest's crimes were 'an act of vandalism'.

While these thieves had their hearts set on gold and silver trinkets, some of the more valuable loot within the South Australian Museum was made of brass and ivory. On 21 November 1898, a shipment arrived at Port Adelaide, having been packed and sent that October by a London antiquarian named WD Webster. Arranged inside two crates designated as 'ethnographic specimens' lay half-a-dozen items, including a carved ivory tusk, the wide-eyed bronze head of a long-dead king, and a staff topped with a bird of prophecy, its wings outstretched.

'The following specimens were taken in Benin City. W. Coast Africa by the British troops in Feb. 1897,' read the notes from Webster, which added that the bronzes were believed to be around 400 years old.[24] Webster's sales pitch carried a note of urgency: he had already sold around £3,000 worth of Benin pieces to a prestigious client list that included museums in Oxford, Berlin, Vienna, Dresden, Edinburgh, Dublin, and Canterbury, and it would be 'impossible to get any later on'.[25]

'I may say that there is nothing left in Benin — what they were unable to bring away was destroyed,' Webster added.[26]

The shipment's recipient was Dr Edward Charles Stirling, the then-director of the South Australian Museum. Stirling had visited Webster on a trip to England in May 1897 with an eye to burnishing his museum's ethnological collection with rare objects from Webster's inventory. But there was a problem: the museum's funds were 'painfully low', so low that Stirling's staff could barely afford to print labels, let alone acquire sought-after treasures from around the empire. If the money couldn't be found, the items would have to be repacked, sent back to England, and sold to a better-financed collector or institution. It was an embarrassing prospect, and in a letter to the editor of the *South Australian Register*, Stirling made a public plea for some private citizen to purchase the cargo and, Stirling hoped, donate it to the museum. The alternative, Stirling suggested, would be a great loss:

> The passage from Mr Webster's letter referring to the disposition of the Benin specimens that have passed through his hands once more excites a regret that has been so often felt—viz., that collections gathered in English countries and dependencies have so often been allowed to pass from the countries to which they belong.[27]

When Stirling spoke of 'countries' and 'belonging', however, he didn't mean the city of Benin, the capital of Edo State in present-day Nigeria, or its people—he was referring to the British Empire that now laid claim to the territory. In the same breath, Stirling noted that Webster had provided the museum with many of its 'Australian' pieces—objects of craft, ceremony, and utility that had left the country of their makers and criss-crossed the globe in the same international artefacts trade that now dispersed the riches of Benin just eighteen months after the British breached the city's walls.

The story of how these works left Benin was later recounted in playfully lurid detail in July 1914 by Sir Henry Galway, the newly arrived governor of South Australia, who regaled an Adelaide audience with the 'thrilling exploits' of his soldiering days. In an era when vice-regal posts served as an imperial clearing house and golden handshake for fusty retired admirals or well-connected aristocrats, Galway had quickly charmed the locals by exhibiting the 'dash and courage of the soldier' and speaking with a refreshing 'freedom and happiness'.[28] This evening at the Public Library, just next door to the South Australian Museum, was no different, with Galway casting his mind back to a time before he gained a knighthood, married a baroness, changed his name from Gallway to the more respectable-sounding 'Galway', and played a key role in one of the British Empire's bloodiest conquests.

By 1914, Galway's account of the invasion of Benin City in February 1897 was a well-rehearsed one-man show. Complete with 'electric light illustrations', Galway explained how, as deputy commissioner and consul of Britain's Niger Coast Protectorate, he had sought to broker a free-trade treaty with Ovọnramwẹn Nọgbaisi, the Oba of Benin and heir to a long, uninterrupted line of monarchs dating back to the 11th century. With its strategic position along the Niger River and access to valuable commodities such as palm oil and rubber, Benin was prized as the European powers made their 19th-century 'scramble for Africa'. For years, the British Royal Niger Company had hoped to monopolise what Galway called 'one of the many blank spaces on the map known as Darkest Africa':

> The potential possibilities of those territories, of which Nigeria is the richest and most extensive, are incalculable. The very prosperity of our trade at home creates a demand for more markets — which lie in tropical Africa — and these potential markets are our own, we may do as we please with them.[29]

But, Galway said, it was 'very patent we could not attempt to open up the country by means of smiles and white umbrellas', and by the early 1890s the Oba had continued to hold out, asserting Benin's sovereignty and refusing to let the British in. Whereas earlier British attempts at a treaty with the Oba had failed, Galway travelled to Benin City in March 1892 with the aforementioned white umbrellas — and concealed revolvers for good measure. The young captain was forced to wait three days before finally gaining an audience with the Oba, who years later the governor would mock as 'his duskiness'.

Back in 1892, however, the captain was on the back foot, struggling to convey the terms of the boilerplate treaty document to the Oba's interpreters, a contract that would grant Queen Victoria's 'gracious favour and protection' in return for unrestricted free trade across the Oba's territories.[30] Through his interpreters, the Oba asked repeatedly if the document meant 'peace or war', receiving reassurances from Galway that theirs was a peaceful mission. (Clearly, his revolver remained hidden.) Galway would later claim that they came to an agreement, but even in his own account, there is little about the negotiations or the resulting document that sounds fair or binding — it was the captain himself who signed the treaty in the Oba's name.

The Oba did not consider Galway's piece of paper to hold any legitimacy, and over the coming years he continued to control trade, and even placed religious bans on some of the goods most coveted by the British. Within months of the document's signing, Galway and other British officials began plotting the Oba's removal, perhaps via a 'punitive expedition', using his disregard for Galway's dubious treaty as a legal pretext. In late 1896, James Phillips, a Cambridge-educated thirty-two-year-old serving as acting consul, wrote to the British prime minister complaining of the continuing obstacle that the Oba represented, and asked 'permission to visit Benin City in February next, to depose and remove the King of Benin and to establish a native council in his place'.[31]

Phillips never received a response, but in December 1896 he set out along the road from Gwato to Benin anyway with a small party of eight British men, supported by hundreds of African porters and workers. Phillips was resoundingly rebuffed, with the Oba's emissaries warning him that their king was in isolation and that the city was closed to outsiders during the sacred Igue festival. Any white man who attempted to enter, they told Phillips, would be killed. There were other factors that may have informed the Oba's reluctance to receive Phillips; by 1897, the British had driven a wave of regime changes across northern Africa, and even if Phillips was hiding his true intentions, they weren't hard to guess. Other neighbouring chiefs warned Phillips that he would be killed, but he pressed further down the road regardless. On 4 January 1897, a clash with the Oba's men saw Phillips killed, along with five British officers and two traders.

Galway found out what had happened, a week later, and promptly wired the Foreign Office to approve a retaliatory attack on the city. Within less than a month the British had assembled a force of 1,200 men deployed from as far as Cape Town, Malta, and England, with enough arms and provisions to lay siege to the city.[32] While the British would claim the Oba had forced their hand, the killing of Phillips provided a long-awaited cover story for a punitive exhibition that would achieve the very coup that Phillips had hoped for; like Major Mitchell accusing the

Barkindji of provoking the Mount Dispersion massacre, the justification of the Benin expedition relied on a selective reading of the timeline of colonial incursions and reprisals that recast a violent British invasion as a righteous act of self-defence. The remarkable speed with which a 1,200-strong invading force could be assembled was testament to just how well oiled the British 'punitive' machine had become.

The British forces were divided into three columns, armed with the latest in British war technologies, including Maxim machine guns, rocket tubes, seven-pounder mountain guns, 'gun cotton' nitrocellulose explosives, bolt-action rifles, and millions of bullets.[33] While British gunships approached the city from the river, Galway joined the first column of 500 men, who retraced Phillips's steps along the Gwato–Benin road, using their firepower to carve a path through to the city over five days of what Galway would describe as 'merry bush fighting'.

Galway's party arrived in Benin City on 18 February. Once inside, the captain — the only one of the invaders who had previously set foot in the city — led the way through to the Oba's compound. The Oba had fled, but the sight of many dead, some of whom had apparently been sacrificed by the Oba's priests to sway the outcome of the conflict, led the British troops to dub Benin the 'City of Blood'. For colonisers such as Galway, the macabre practice of 'fetish rule' was a perfect example of the civilising imperative of the British Empire — even as his troops laid waste to the city. Later, in Adelaide, Governor Galway would claim 'the enemy must have lost very heavily, but no reliable estimate can be given', before adding that they buried 'nearly 900' bodies in the aftermath. Soon after, Galway's countrymen razed the houses of the Oba's chiefs before a bigger blaze engulfed the entire compound. According to Galway, the city soon showed 'evident signs of the white man's rule: equity, justice, peace and security'. He also added, 'the place was a regular holocaust — and very little was saved'.[34]

What survived the fires soon left the country, with Galway noting 'that hundreds of bronze plaques of unique designs; castings of wonderful detail; and a very large number of carved tusks of considerable age' were soon discovered. Like other British visitors to the city, Galway had noticed such works during his treaty-signing mission, where altars and ancestral shrines seemed to feature in each house, and the Oba himself presided over a vast cache of carved and uncarved ivory tusks. In his November 1896 letter to the prime minister, even Phillips had flagged that 'sufficient ivory may be found in the King's house to pay the expenses in removing the King from his Stool'.[35] Photographs of the aftermath show British troops posing for the camera surrounded by bronze plaques and bundles of seized ivory tusks. Some even re-enacted the siege, donning blackface make-up decades before William Dakin's Skin Tone Commando Cream.

Over in Adelaide, Stirling eventually managed to find a local benefactor for Webster's wares: a rich merchant and former politician named David Murray, who would guarantee their eventual acquisition by the South Australian Museum. Later, in 1902, its Benin collection would grow to include an 'Ama', a bronze plaque depicting three figures — two collared chiefs and a priest bearing vessels aloft in their hands. The donor was Sir William Ingram, publisher of the *Illustrated London News,* which had sent its own correspondent, Henry Charles Seppings Wright, to Benin City just days after it was taken, selling many thousands of copies on the back of florid reports of the 'massacre' against Phillips and his men, along with on-the-ground reports of the horrifying scenes found inside the 'City of Blood'.

Importantly, Ingram was also Stirling's brother-in-law, and it was on another visit to England in 1901 that Stirling was handed a 'large bundle of ethnological specimens' from New Guinea and the Pacific Islands, along with a 'bronze plaque' that was 'obtained on the same expedition as the bronze mask presented to us by Mr David Murray'.[36] Ingram would also give the British Museum a number of Benin pieces — carved ivory tusks, altarpieces, and a life-like brass head created in the 16th century to commemorate the recently deceased Queen Mother Idia — and a range of boomerangs, message sticks, clubs, and spear throwers from Australia.

By 1899, stories had begun to circulate in the press that the 'great beauty' of the artworks had 'puzzle[d]' ethnologists, with one archaeologist at the British Museum publicly speculating that they were actually the work of 'some European bronze founders who settled there in the 16th century'.[37] Where Galway and his troops had used dubious legal documents and force to usurp Benin sovereignty over land and resources, the academics at the museum were now finishing the job by delegitimising Benin's connection to its cultural heritage as well.

The pieces from Webster and Ingram were presumably on display in May 1914 when a newspaper report of Galway's first tour of the museum's galleries noted that the new governor was 'naturally particularly interested in some exhibits from North-West Africa'.[38] Galway's support of the South Australian Museum throughout his term as governor would be recognised with the naming of a species of fish in his honour, and in December 1915, Galway presided over the grand opening of the museum's new east wing — the same imposing building that would later house its Benin pieces, whose doors were to be found wide open that night in January 1946.

At its grand opening in late 1915, a member of the museum's board of governors reflected on the clash of imperial powers that was currently raging around the world, where 'the vast heritage of the past' was threatened by the 'Teutonic barbarian knocking at the gate of Rome'.[39] Galway also spoke of the important role that museums played for the nation and the empire:

> The greatness of the nation must be measured not alone by its wealth and apparent power, but by the degree in which its people have learned together in the great world of books of art and of nature and of pure and ennobling joys.[40]

For all their grandiose language, such statements obscured the deeper role of the colonial museum. For years, antiquarians such as Webster and academics at the British Museum served as glorified fences while a broader network of natural history and ethological museums became places for Britain and other European powers to launder their reputations and their 'collected' spoils as they set about the dirty, extractive work of empire-building. Perhaps Governor Galway himself had put it more succinctly back at the Public Library a year earlier when describing the riches of Benin: 'A regular harvest of loot.'[41]

CHAPTER FOURTEEN

The Pride of the Empire

A little before eight o'clock on a Monday night in August 1903, a gravedigger, two police constables, and a government medical officer entered the West Terrace cemetery on the outskirts of Adelaide's square mile.[1] They passed by rows of ornate marble and granite headstones that bore the surnames of illustrious colonial families to reach a more modest gravesite, its headstone having been paid for as an act of charity. Soon after they started digging, their spades struck a pine coffin and a nameplate. It belonged to a Ngarrindjeri man named Poltpalingada Booboorowie, who on 4 July 1901 had died in an isolation ward at the Royal Adelaide Hospital.

With a thick beard and a penchant for dapper top hats, the seventy-year-old Poltpalingada had been a recognisable identity around a town and colony that was no older than he was. According to one newspaper profile, Poltpalingada gave the impression of being 'a chartered libertine with a sense of humour, frequently in trouble with the police and always a vagrant'.[2] But despite the merry performances he put on to win the loose change of passers-by, Poltpalingada was clear-eyed about the dispossession inflicted on his countrymen by the newcomers who cut down the trees, drove away the wallabies, killed the kangaroos, and asserted 'white fella justice' over land that did not belong to them.[3] Such protests were mocked in newspapers, and his headstone, purchased by the Adelaide Stock Exchange, announced both the English name that settlers gave Poltpalingada and the patronisingly racist regard they held him in: 'In memory of Tommy Walker, a dusky king, died July 4 1901.'[4]

The casket was virtually empty when the men opened it, and what remained was unrecognisable.[5] Over the next month, the group unearthed six other bodies under cover of darkness, each with a different cause of death. They were murder victims, suicide cases, and non-white men such as the 'Chinaman', Chun Ah Kiom, and a twenty-year-old African American named Emmett Harris. All of them were missing their skulls, and occasionally their fingers and toes too. And, like Poltpalingada, they had another thing in common: they had all passed through the care of Dr William Ramsay Smith, a hospital physician, chairman of the Central Board of Health, and the city's coroner.

The balding, moustached Scotsman had arrived in South Australia in 1896, but quickly became a polarising figure in Adelaide's medical fraternity—by the turn of the century, he had made enough enemies for someone to blow the whistle and complain to the attorney-general that the coroner had mutilated or mistreated many of the patients who crossed his mortuary table. The series of secret exhumations in 1903 had been ordered as part of a landmark public inquiry into Ramsay Smith's fitness to remain a public servant.

When the inquiry convened in September 1903, it aired evidence that was often confronting. The chief inspector of the Board of Health testified to once having transported a 'drayload' from the hospital to the coroner's office loaded with hundreds of jars and tins of body parts preserved in formalin.[6] A police constable named John Rea, who knew both Poltpalingada and Ramsay Smith, described being invited to the city morgue, just next to the West Terrace cemetery, to watch as his former colleague Ramsay Smith removed Poltpalingada's bones and placed them in a bag.[7] Before the trial, *The Chronicle* published an interview with an anonymous cemetery worker who claimed Poltpalingada's case was far from unique:

> We're used to that sort of thing, but we hold our tongues. When we are called into a hospital to conduct an interment we put the body in the

> coffin and screw it down, if we are told to. But sometimes the thing is all nicely done for us. We guess what sort of a 'body' is inside, but we take it away and ask no questions.

The paper also quoted a local doctor who claimed that 'very few natives who have died in Australia during the last 20 years have been buried whole', thanks to 'medical scientists [who] desired to secure specimens of the bones of a race which is gradually becoming extinct'.[8]

The inquiry heard from John Desmond, a veterinary surgeon at the hospital and a close associate of Ramsay Smith, for whom he had prepared numerous skulls. Desmond had also visited Kumerangk — a hallowed site on Ngarrindjeri Country renamed Hindmarsh Island by colonists — to remove as many as thirty Ngarrindjeri ancestors, enough to fill between eight and ten caseloads that he carted back to his Adelaide laboratory.[9]

While Poltpalingada's exhumation in August had been carried out with all the requisite paperwork and an official sign-off from the attorney-general, Desmond told the inquiry that he neither sought nor believed that he needed approval to disturb Aboriginal burial sites and bring them back to what his interrogators described as a 'chamber of horrors'.[10] Indeed, he had previously taken bones from 'black-fellows camps' in Victoria 'whenever [he] had the opportunity'.[11] Desmond's cavalier attitude to human remains was further revealed when the government counsel asked him to produce his wallet. When asked what it was made of, Desmond replied, 'human skin'.[12]

Dr Edward Angas Johnson, a member of the Royal College of Surgeons recently returned from England, also told the inquiry that skeletons of Aboriginal people were 'very much' of scientific interest.[13] These practices weren't just common, he said, but the greatest repository of human remains could be found at the Hunterian Museum at the Royal College of Surgeons in London, an organisation that counted the king of England among its fellows.

'This is the museum which has been described as the pride of the British empire?' the lawyer asked.[14]

'That is the one,' Johnson replied.

Years earlier, Johnson himself had removed thirteen buried ancestors from Blanchetown 'for scientific purposes', on behalf of the South Australian Museum and with the full knowledge and blessing of the government of the day.[15] Some of these ancestors, Johnson said, were sent 'all around the world' for scientific exchange, from a college in Cambridge to a baron in Russia. Johnson hadn't undertaken this work alone—he had been joined on the dig by no less than the museum's director, Dr Edward Charles Stirling.

South Australia's share in the loot of Benin was just one chapter in a decades-long acquisition drive that would come to define Stirling's tenure at the South Australian Museum. Known to most as Ted, Stirling had returned to Adelaide in 1881 as one of its brightest sons made good. Adelaide was still a small city with a shallow colonial history, but the Stirling family had already established deep ties ever since his late father, Edward Stirling Sr, had arrived in 1839, just three years after the city was established on Kaurna Country. As a spare son from an obscure Scottish landholding dynasty, the elder Edward's family wealth gave him the start-up capital to become a successful merchant, pastoralist, and politician in the new colony—in 1854, the Adelaide Hills township of Stirling, on Peramangk Country, would be named after them, while his sons, Ted and younger brother John Lancelot, would receive the best education the colony could offer at St Peter's College.

But while Ted soon proved to be academically brilliant, he could also appear shy and awkward—the kind of misfit who might attract cruel nicknames whispered across hallways and classrooms. When the Stirling family moved back to Europe to support the boys as they studied in England, Germany, and France, their mother, Harriett, hoped that London might draw her eldest out of his shell. In one surviving letter from 1866, she needled the seventeen-year-old Ted about attending a ball. 'I think you should take every opportunity of going into good society, it will do you good & shake off a little of your diffidence,' the letter read.[16]

By the time of his grand homecoming, Ted Stirling's London metamorphosis was complete. With a thick walrus moustache and dark curly hair he wore closely cropped or combed flat, the thirty-three-year-old was now a handsome Cambridge-educated fellow of the Royal College of Surgeons who had worked at a string of prominent London hospitals, and would now serve his home city as a surgeon at the Royal Adelaide Hospital with a teaching post at the new University of Adelaide. On paper, Ted Stirling seemed poised to bring new levels of respectability to a family already entrenched among the colony's elite establishment,

Given all the prestigious notches on Ted's belt, it must have been a comedown when he took on the chairmanship of the South Australian Museum in 1882. A quarter-century after it was established, the local museum was foundering, just as its counterparts in Sydney and Melbourne were coming to enjoy what Stirling called 'a European reputation'.[17] For years, the museum's collections had been crammed into the old Institute Building — later home to the Public Library, where Governor Galway gave his 1914 Benin speech — where they had become so badly damaged by pest infestations and neglect that its staff had been forced to dump the lion's share of specimens.

In another letter to the colony's newspapers, Stirling went public. 'The almost wholesale destruction that was quite unavoidable has left the collection deficient in a great number of specimens that ought to be in a museum,' he wrote. The museum would have to start virtually from scratch, he said, and Stirling's letter included another open call for members of the public to act as amateur collectors. The situation was so dire, Stirling explained, that even common species were in as much need of replacement as rare specimens — duplicates, after all, could be used as exchanges with interstate or overseas institutions.[18]

Within a few years, the call-out paid off handsomely. In 1888, a pastoralist in the Northern Territory sent in a spent cartridge box containing a small, blind marsupial mole wrapped in a kerosene-soaked rag.[19] The mole had decomposed beyond recognition by the time it had travelled the 1,000 miles to Adelaide, but soon Stirling was able to source better-quality specimens — often from 'the aboriginals' of central Australia, whom Stirling praised for their 'phenomenal powers of tracking'.[20]

When Stirling published his description and illustration of the marsupial mole, named *Notoryctes typhlops*, in *Nature* in 1891, the little blonde novelty caused a sensation in Britain — it was a prime example of convergent evolution, having independently developed many of the same characteristics as other mole species in far-flung locations around the world. *Nature* journal praised the mole as 'one of the most extraordinary discoveries in zoology made of late years', representing 'unquestionably a new and perfectly isolated form of Marsupial life'.[21] Stirling would eventually send type specimens of the mole to his alma mater in Cambridge, as well as a cast of a giant, wombat-like diprotodon.

These new discoveries helped make Stirling and the South Australian Museum famous in international zoological circles, but the novelty of Australian wildlife had begun to wane over a century since Joseph Banks and Daniel Solander's return on the *Endeavour*. In 1886, an English dealer grumbled that he would have difficulty selling the handful of Australian animals that Stirling had offered in exchange for a set of sought-after chimpanzee and gorilla skins and skeletons.[22] Soon, however, Stirling struck upon an area of collecting that combined his twin interests in anatomy and natural history, and was subject to growing demand around the world.

'We have about us in the Aboriginal races an almost exact counterpart of the most ancient men whose remains have come to light in recent years,' Stirling explained in an address delivered at the Town Hall, contrasting how, 'in the one case the primitive savage has developed into a race which can claim a Shakespeare or a Newton', while in the other 'he has remained practically unchanged through long ages and doomed to speedy extinction'.[23]

At the time, Stirling had just returned from his old haunts in Cambridge, where he had brought a special gift from Australia: a 'cast of the skull of King Rufus Billy', which his old lecturer Professor McAlister said was 'the most Neanderthaloid skull that he had seen'. Charles Darwin's theory of evolution, only relatively recently adopted by most museums and scientists, and the discovery in Europe of the fossilised remains of *Homo neanderthalensis* had sparked a renewed focus on human development and racial hierarchies. As early as 1884, Stirling had begun fielding requests from museums as far away as Berlin to exchange 'skulls of natives'.

By the end of the 19th century, Stirling had struck up correspondence with institutions ranging from the University Museum of Archaeology and Ethnology in Cambridge to the Smithsonian Institution in Washington, which in 1895 deemed a proposal to exchange ethnological specimens to be 'of mutual advantage'.[24] A few years later, in 1899, New York's American Museum of Natural History would also write to Stirling, seeking an exchange of 'types' that might address the fact it had 'no scientific collection from any tribe of Australia'.[25] Just as he had returned from London transformed, Stirling had in only a few years turned the once-ailing South Australian Museum into an institution with exactly the kind of international reputation he had once hoped for.

Stirling might have hoped to break new scientific ground by studying and trafficking Aboriginal bodies, but the practice of collecting and hoarding human beings had been entwined with British natural history museums since the very beginning. The collections that Sir Hans Sloane earmarked to form the British Museum extended beyond animal and plant specimens, with his handwritten catalogues including 760 entries listed under 'Humana'. Sloane had gathered enough human remains to fill a small parish cemetery, from the scalps and skulls of 'Indians' to 'a shoe made of human skin'.[26]

Years later, Joseph Banks's acquisition at gunpoint of a Māori Mokomokai would become one of many human remains sourced via his growing network of collectors across the empire. Meanwhile, back in Europe, Banks's blossoming social and professional network included notorious anatomists and body-snatchers such as the British surgeon John Hunter, whose London surgical school was periodically mobbed by protestors scandalised by its ties to an underground grave-robbing industry that fuelled the medical innovations he pioneered on the dissecting table. Banks had befriended Hunter before the *Endeavour* set sail, and he and Solander remained close with the surgeon in the years that followed.[27] Then there was Johann Friedrich Blumenbach at the

University of Göttingen, a pioneer in craniometry and emerging race science, and himself a prolific collector of skulls. in 1783, Blumenbach began corresponding with Banks, who would later ask his protégé William Bligh to 'collect Crania' for Blumenbach as he set out on the *Bounty*'s ill-fated voyage to Jamaica.[28]

Later, in January 1790, Banks asked Governor Arthur Phillip in the new colony of New South Wales to send him specimens. Phillip agreed, but the task was complicated by a smallpox epidemic that arrived with the British, ravaging the Aboriginal population while making their 'collection' impossible. ('You shall have heads when I can get any, but the Natives burn their dead,' Phillip told an impatient Banks.)[29] In 1802, Banks's collecting made the news when a customs officer in London noticed that a man's head, preserved in spirits, had arrived addressed to Joseph Banks: it was the fallen Bidjigal warrior Pemulwuy, who had waged a daring, organised, decade-long guerilla campaign against the colonists in Sydney—a far cry from the 'little resistance' that Banks had predicted years earlier. Upon his own death, Banks would bequeath half of his collection to join Sloane's at the British Museum, while the other half, including Pemulwuy, would go to Hunter, whose collection was eventually acquired by the Royal College of Surgeons to form the Hunterian Museum.

The practice of collecting human remains as a gentlemanly scientific pursuit was so widespread that when Sir Arthur Conan Doyle wrote *The Hound of the Baskervilles* in 1901, he also included an amateur scientist who wasted no time telling Sherlock Holmes that he would make 'an ornament to any anthropological museum'. 'I covet your skull,' the man said bluntly.[30]

From the early 1890s, Stirling and his colleagues at the South Australian Museum and the University of Adelaide pursued Banks's vision on a vaster scale. One of these colleagues, a respected surgeon named Dr Archibald Watson, had previously been arrested for piracy during his earlier career in the darker side of the South Seas trade, which, along with goods and seashells, also brought back young Pacific Islander men kidnapped or coerced into slave labour in the plantations of Queensland—a trade known as 'blackbirding'.[31]

In addition to their own excavations of disturbed burial grounds, Stirling and his contemporaries would draw on a Banksian network of amateur collectors that included colonial officials in far-flung parts of South Australia and the bordering Northern Territory and Western Australia. By the late-19th century, the Australian frontier was a long way from the east coast that Banks and Mitchell had explored, but it was hardly less violent, and often Stirling's collectors were also mounted police charged with brutally enforcing white rule.

South Australia was by no means unique; the Australian Museum in Sydney paid freelance collectors to build its own collection, circulating a pamphlet in 1887 titled *Hints for the Preservation of Natural Specimens of Natural History* that on page one declared, 'SKELETONS of Aborigines are most wanted, and for the benefit of collectors'.[32] Over in Victoria, anthropologists such as Walter Baldwin Spencer, an academic at the University of Melbourne, and later the director of the National Museum of Victoria, were enlisting the Field Naturalists Club — the same one that the former National Museum of Victoria entomologist Frank Spry had inducted George Lyell and Alec Burns into — to build the collections of their own institutions.[33]

Even Frank Hann, James William Wyatt's onetime travel companion, made contributions to the international trade in Aboriginal bodies. As a pastoralist and explorer, Hann had already developed a murderous reputation when, in 1909, he inspired outrage in the Perth broadsheets after describing a violent clash with four Aboriginal men while prospecting for gold on behalf of the Western Australian government.

'Had I shot the black with the red band I would have cut his head off and sent the skull to Mr Brockman, of Perth, who asked me to send him one, as a friend of his in London wanted one,' he told *The West Australian* in April.[34]

'I was very sorry that I could not send him the four, but later on I got him a splendid one,' Hann explained.

The interview revolted many readers, and prompted Brockman himself to write to the press to correct the record. Brockman had delivered an address to the Royal Anthropological Institute in London in 1907, and was subsequently asked by its secretary to procure an

'Aborigine' skull 'for scientific purposes'.[35] Brockman asked Hann to obtain one, and despite Hann's later attempts to 'mak[e] blood-curdling statements' for the purpose of giving reporters 'interesting copy', he had told Brockman that the skull 'was that of an old man who has been dead for some years'.[36] One way or another, his new nickname stuck: Headhunter Hann.

As Stirling would remark, with a cool scientific detachment that belied the active role that naturalists and museums had played in the previous 125 years of colonisation, death, and dispossession: 'It is, for natural history, unhappily inevitable that in a comparatively short time museums will be the only place where relics of the aborigines and examples of the many interesting forms of animal life can be seen.'[37]

Stirling's prominence in the thriving field of late-19th-century race science was further complicated by the fact that, in many ways, he was a walking personification of the murky ties between respectable British society, the bloodied origins of its wealth and influence, and the complex hierarchies of race and class upon which it was built. Before his father, Edward Sr, had arrived in the new colony of South Australia with enough money to make any questions about his past all but disappear, he had been born into slavery in Jamaica—the illegitimate son of an unknown enslaved woman and Archibald Stirling, a Scot who had spent twenty-five years in the Caribbean managing his family's plantations. Like many white men in the slave colony, Archibald fathered several children out of wedlock—in his case, at least six.[38] Archibald had brought his illegitimate son Edward back to the United Kingdom to be educated, but upon his return from the Caribbean soon married and produced a legitimate, and white, male heir. When the British parliament abolished slavery in 1833, he used part of the £12,500 he received in compensation for the family's freed 690 slaves to send Edward to a far-off colony with £1,000, a good surname, and, it seems, a tacit understanding that he would stay well away from his father's new family.[39]

While a painted portrait held in the Art Gallery of South Australia depicts Edward Stirling Sr as a typical Victorian gentleman with greying hair and sideburns, a long, straight nose, and sunken cheeks that appear to be a pale shade of pink, contemporaneous photographs of Edward — and oral traditions that his son's nickname around town was the racist slur 'The Nigger'— suggest there was no denying their mixed ancestry. On the one hand, the Stirlings' success shows that in colonial South Australia it was a kind of open secret that with enough money and connections you could hide in plain sight. But between the whitewashed portrait and Ted's nickname, it seems they must have held no illusions about their unique and precarious place in the racial hierarchies of the British Empire. Like his father, the only ancestry Dr Edward Charles Stirling would publicly identify with was his Scottish forebears, rather than those they enslaved.

Given the times he lived in, perhaps it's no surprise that the once 'diffident' young Ted leaned in to the persona of the Cambridge-educated gentleman scientist and doctor from venerable Scottish stock, even as his canny navigation of the elite worlds of academia, politics, medicine, and natural history museums saw him replicate many of the racial hierarchies that marked him, like his father, as 'other'. But perhaps his enthusiastic conformity to the archetype of the gentleman naturalist, the collector, also speaks to its power: that was the kind of man who could open doors, command respect and acclaim, and collect pretty much anything he wanted.

On Tuesday 13 September 1903, Stirling himself fronted the Ramsay Smith inquiry, which had already begun to scandalise Victorian-era Adelaide as the broader public began to grasp what was being done in the name of the museum and science. Johnson had already testified that Ramsay Smith had frequently consulted the museum's bone collections, and now Stirling himself confirmed that several skulls in the museum's collection had come from the hospital. When pressed about the legality of Ramsay Smith's actions, however, Stirling was able to confidently defend his colleague's conduct under the terms of the state's *Anatomy Act*.

'I fathered it,' Stirling said, explaining how he had helped draft the legislation during his single term in parliament twenty years earlier.[40]

As the inquiry wore on, a much bigger picture emerged: men such as Ramsay Smith and the skin wallet-carrying veterinarian John Desmond were not ghoulish rogues who had overstepped their authority, but cogs in a machine that had been running for centuries, that spanned the world and was plugged into many of the empire's most respectable institutions and museums.

In light of these revelations, and thanks in large part to Stirling's testimony, Ramsay Smith was ultimately and inevitably cleared of wrongdoing, with the inquiry finding that his treatment of patients such as Poltpalingada Booboorowie — whose remains Ramsay Smith sent to his old professor at the University of Glasgow — were carried out 'with either the consent or non-objection of the person in lawful possession of the body at the time'. In most instances, that person was the coroner Ramsay Smith himself. It did note, however, that Ramsay Smith had been 'indiscreet', and allowed his 'zeal in the cause of science to outrun his judgement'. It recommended he be stripped of his hospital role to mitigate the apparent conflict of interest as the living patients on his ward were transformed into British museum pieces.

Rather than end his collecting days, the inquiry only served to bolster Ramsay Smith's international reputation as an authority on Aboriginal physiology and culture — he even published a book of 'myths and legends', claiming sole authorship despite having appropriated its contents from the Ngarrindjeri inventor David Unaipon.[41] When Ramsay Smith died comfortably in his home at the age of seventy-eight, it was rumoured that no less than 180 skulls were found in his house. But that was nothing compared to the South Australian Museum; by the time Galway opened the new east wing in 1915, the end results of Stirling's decades of collecting were proudly on display. In his official history of the South Australian Museum's first century, Herbert Hale would later write that '800 aboriginal skulls grinned at the public from the wall cases near the front entrance'.[42]

As men such as Stirling and Ramsay Smith built careers and collections from disturbed burial mounds and the recently deceased, the welfare of living Aboriginal people seemed a distant consideration to them. In the aftermath of the Ramsay Smith inquiry, the Aborigines' Friends Association complained to the attorney-general that the widely reported revelations about Poltpalingada Booboorowie's treatment had created an 'uneasiness among the natives on the mission stations, and they are manifesting a disinclination to be sent to Adelaide Hospital in case of sickness'.[43]

After all, it was a hospital doctor who had admitted Poltpalingada to the isolation ward, supervised his treatment in the final days before his death, and then sent his remains halfway around the world while his too-light coffin went into the ground. For people whose country and way of life had already been seized, it seemed that not even death put an end to the theft.

When Stirling died in March 1919, seven years after retiring from the South Australian Museum's directorship, his impact on the institution and its collections was honoured with the renaming of the upper gallery of the east wing, the one displaying the museum's 'extensive ethnological collection'.[44] But the Stirling Gallery wasn't his only legacy; he might not have invented the practice of collecting Aboriginal ancestors, but Stirling helped make it a central priority for most modern Australian museums. He had been dead for a quarter of a century by the time Dick Pescott called upon his successor, Herbert Hale, on 22 January 1947, but the impact of his work endured.

In 1930, Norman Tindale and Hale himself had courted fame after excavating a rock shelter on Ngarrindjeri land, in an area known as Ngaut Ngaut but named Devon Downs by colonists. A major flood in 1917 had first exposed a gravesite along the riverbank, and when Hale and Tindale unearthed several infants' graves in their subsequent dig, the local press was ecstatic, declaring that that the 'Discovery by young S.A. Scientists will be world famous'.[45] In 1925, a Czech-born anthropologist from the Smithsonian named Dr Ales Hrdlicka visited the museum to study its skull collection. Hrdlicka, who was already building a reputation as a notorious eugenicist and grave-robber, suggested that Hale and Tindale make 'life-masks' of Aboriginal men and women so that 'permanent records of the features would be available for future investigators'.[46] Tindale and Hale started work on the project, even observing Hrdlicka's suggestion that they make their casts with the subject's 'eyes open, in order to ensure a life-like expression'. Tindale soon moved on to casting the dead.

Later, in the months of January and February 1947 alone, between letters about the rapidly escalating butterfly crisis, Dick Pescott would gratefully acknowledge the arrival of the remains of four Aboriginal ancestors into the National Museum of Victoria's collections. One, sent by a detective at the CIB at Footscray Police Station in Melbourne, had been found at Point Cook Aerodrome, while two more were from Deniliquin in New South Wales, sent in by a member of the public. In both instances, Pescott sent the same, grateful pro-forma response that he would send many times that year:

> Any tokens symbolic of the origin and culture of the aborigine such as stone, bone, and wooden implements are an aid towards a scientific study of this primitive race, and your assistance in this direction is deeply appreciated.[47]

A fourth would arrive from South Australia, where another successor of Stirling's, the professor of anatomy at the University of Adelaide, had completed a 'first rate' cast of a skull that had been uncovered along the Maribyrnong River, near the present-day suburb of Keilor on Melbourne's outskirts. For thousands of years, it had rested peacefully beneath fourteen feet of earth, until one day in November 1940 when it was disturbed by a workman's pickaxe and eventually brought to the museum. Earlier, in April 1946, days after circulating his media release about the Lyell Collection, Pescott also wrote a reference letter for a researcher from the University of Melbourne, confirming that the man, a specialist in paediatric dentistry, was 'recognised and authorised by this Museum to find and collect skeletal remains of the Australian aborigine'.[48] Such correspondence, quietly filed away with all Pescott's other outgoing mail, represented the banal reality that 175 years after Joseph Banks and Daniel Solander arrived with their muskets at Kamay and left with a clutch of spears, such collecting was business-as-usual for Australia's museums.

Even the family collections of Athol Waterhouse included several human beings among the rare shells and thousands of butterflies donated to the Australian Museum. One human head, clad in resin and inlaid with nautilus shell as part of a funerary rite, had been collected by Gustavus John Waterhouse from the Solomon Islands during his merchant career across the same island communities that his missionary grandfather had once sought to civilise, and that Blackbirders such as Archibald Watson had enslaved.[49] A second man's head, collected from the Sepik River in New Guinea, had been carefully covered with clay and inset with cowrie shells by the man's family, and later donated by Athol's younger brother Leslie — it would feature on the cover of *The Australian Museum Magazine* in 1949, which noted how such tributes 'are kept in the men's clubhouse where they become the abode of the spirits of the dead'.[50] The magazine didn't dwell on how or why such a sacred object had left a clubhouse in New Guinea to make its way to an Australian museum.

Whether they knew it or not, anyone who stepped through a museum's doors was entering more than a temple of knowledge and scientific discovery. The taxidermist from the Californian Academy of Science wasn't far off when he described Australia's museums as 'morgues'; they were also evidence lockers for a centuries-long process of extraction and theft, to which naturalists and collectors were both accessory and alibi, from Benin bronzes to Aboriginal ancestors to zoological collections whose earliest specimens were collected during colonial expeditions marked by barely concealed violence. Many might argue that there was nothing illegal about any of this 'collecting'. But by any fair reckoning of the past, the museums of Australia were all crime scenes long before their butterflies went missing.

'We find to our horror that our butterflies also have been badly ratted,' Herbert Hale wrote in a letter to Arthur Walkom on 29 January 1947.[51] It was the pair's first correspondence since Dick Pescott had called them both barely a week earlier to break the news of the National Museum of Victoria's 825 missing butterflies. But while Walkom waited for Nancy Adams to deliver the bleak findings of their audit of the Waterhouse

Collection, the verdict from Adelaide was already in: Tindale and Womersley had identified another 600 specimens that couldn't be accounted for.

As in Melbourne, there were only one or two missing from each drawer, which had been subtle enough for Womersley to have reasonably missed their absence during his earlier check in January 1946. But the connection between the January incident, the Melbourne theft, and this latest discovery was still little more than a guess—Hale and his staff had no sure way of knowing when or how the butterflies had disappeared. Before he had left to join the RAAF in February 1942, Tindale had made a final check of the lepidoptera collection, telling Hale that 'all was well'.[52] But that was half a decade ago, and had it not been for Burns's breakthrough in Melbourne, the theft may have gone unnoticed for months or years.

In a confidential report to the South Australian Museum board, Hale explained how, '[it] was at once apparent that our collections had been systematically raided, and that here too types and rare material had been abstracted'.

'Such a collection could have been made only by a very expert Lepidopterist, and there can be no suggestion of petty or unpremeditated theft,' he wrote.[53]

A little over a fortnight had passed since 13 January, and Pescott and his counterparts had to accept that, between their three museums, over 3,000 rare butterflies had been carefully and methodically slipped out of their drawers and taken out the door. It was, without rival, the most widespread, audacious, and well-targeted serial robbery in the wild and convoluted history of Australian museums. By the end of the month, the National Museum of Victoria had sent cables to every museum in Australia and New Zealand that hadn't already checked their collections. Across Christchurch, Wellington, Brisbane, Hobart, Launceston, and Perth, museum directors received the same urgent message:

> Confidential and not for publication. Extensive thefts from butterfly collections Melbourne, Sydney, Adelaide stop. Have you missed any stop. Please advise by cable.[54]

Meanwhile, in Melbourne, Pescott and Burns tried to piece together what had happened between 4 and 6 December 1946, in the brief window when Burns was still off collecting butterflies in New South Wales. They soon received a report from a museum attendant who recalled being on duty at the back entrance on Russell Street on or around 5 December 1946. For all the security problems that Pescott had flagged over the years, that door was the one place that was reliably staffed around the clock whenever the National Museum's doors were open.

'[The attendant] stopped a man who was carrying a bundle of boxes,' read Burns's note. 'The man said "these are insects" and "I was going downstairs with them".'[55]

Incredibly, the doorman apparently asked no further questions, sought any official identification, or asked to see inside the boxes. Burns also heard from Stanley Mitchell, a sixty-five-year-old retired metallurgist and a close associate of Walter Baldwin Spencer. Mitchell's amateur interest in Aboriginal culture had seen him serve as president of the Field Naturalists Club, establish the Anthropological Society of Victoria, and become an honorary mineralogist and ethnologist at the National Museum of Victoria. By 1945, he was also serving as treasurer on the National Museum's board of trustees. Mitchell told Burns that around 5 December he saw that the door was open to Burns's basement rooms beneath the zoological hall, but when he let himself in, he discovered that it wasn't Burns who was working in the dungeons.

'[He] saw a man there with drawers of butterflies,' Burns later noted. 'He spoke with the man, asking him if he could identify a "bug" for him.'

Mitchell apparently didn't recognise the stranger, but when he helpfully obliged and identified the insect for him, Mitchell assumed he must have permission to be rifling through the drawers and cabinets of the entomological collection, and apparently left him to it without querying who he was or why he was there. He did make one observation, however.

'Mr Mitchell said that the man spoke well and with a rather cultured accent,' Burns noted.[56]

A picture was soon forming of a well-spoken, scientifically literate man who seemed to know his way around the museum and its collections, and who could confidently talk his way out of any suspicions raised by his behaviour — a man who could be caught in another man's underground office, practically up to his elbows in butterflies, by no less than the museum's head bean-counter, and still manage to walk out the same door he'd been waved through earlier with an armful of boxes.

The more information that came to light, the more it appeared that the Lyell Collection, and perhaps its counterparts in Adelaide and Sydney, had been ransacked not in a daring after-hours burglary or by someone using an elaborate disguise, but in a cool and collected act of daylight robbery by someone who looked and sounded like they belonged there. But perhaps this wasn't surprising: from the very start, Australia's museums had been built on the exploits of generations of collectors who, for over a century, had gone where they pleased and taken what they wanted. Whoever he was, the butterfly thief fitted right in.

CHAPTER FIFTEEN

The Homecoming

According to Colin Wyatt, a butterfly collection meant much more than a scientific dataset, dried-out and sterile. There was the aesthetic angle, of course, but for Wyatt the greatest pleasure lay in the memories that each little insect evoked. In the final pages of his 1955 memoir, he described how, on a dreary winter afternoon, he could stave off boredom by sliding open his drawers and casting his mind back to the sunny collecting grounds in faraway countries from which he had returned triumphant with the perfect souvenir. As he ran his eyes over the glass-topped cases and took in the pinned bodies and handwritten labels, he could feel the warm air, smell the flowers, and remember the strange characters and unlikely adventures that had each led him to the moment of truth, when the wings of a butterfly met the fibres of his net.[1]

Perhaps, as he waxed nostalgic while typing up his manuscript, Wyatt also had in mind one memorable week in January 1947 that he had spent surrounded by butterflies as one winter's day blurred into another. It was bloody cold, Wyatt thought at the time, as a wave of frost, fog, and snow engulfed ports, canals, and roads across the British Isles. From north to south, low-temperature records that had sat unchallenged for decades were broken as meteorologists struggled to get their weather balloons into the sky.[2] In one corner of Surrey, the ghostly moan of an old malfunctioning air-raid siren rang out in the cold air; in another corner, a member of the public said the cold was worse than the war, telling a journalist that, 'We kept going through the blitz, and flying bombs, but this beats us.'[3]

Wyatt, of course, had spent those difficult years in Australia, and when he did finally return to England, he appeared oblivious to the hardships his countrymen had endured. Writing to an acquaintance back in Australia in late-January 1947, it seemed to him that city had hardly changed; everyone he met appeared cheerful and friendly, and the bombed-out corners of London he casually dismissed as 'just a few holes'.[4]

As the temperature dropped, Wyatt was warm and comfortably holed up in another part of Surrey, at his mother's new house in Farnham. Profiled by *Country Life* magazine in 1919 as one of its 'Lesser Country Houses of Today', Cobbetts was a charming red-brick manor, with a high-pitched roof and a sprawling garden of chestnut, oak, lime, and cypress trees, and beds of roses, peonies, and perennials.[5] As the rock garden, the waterlily pond, the summer house, and the tennis lawn turned to white, Wyatt had spent a week surveying the fruits of his seven years in Australia.[6]

Earlier that month, on 18 January, the SS *Perim* had floated up the Thames loaded with shipments of food and cotton, and, among its general cargo, four cases marked 'scientific specimens'. Despite a bent antenna or two, the thousands of butterflies inside had held up remarkably well as the steamer repeated the equator-crossing migration made by similar crates and boxes packed up by generations of naturalists ranging from Joseph Banks to Edward Charles Stirling. Wyatt had seen the four cases, along with a trunk and his Vauxhall motorcar, loaded aboard the *Perim* in Sydney back on 10 December, before following it by air a little after Christmas. He had arrived in England on 29 December, seven-and-a-half years after he and Mary left for Canada and, eventually, Australia. Three weeks later, on 24 January, he travelled into London to collect his things from the Royal Victoria Dock.

Back in Farnham, Wyatt had spent days carefully transferring the thousands of specimens of his prized Australian collection into a newly acquired fifty-five-drawer mahogany cabinet.[7] He'd picked it up

Above: Alec Burns (far left) and Johnny Hopson (second left) on 1921 expedition to Barrington Tops. *Courtesy Museums Victoria*

Left: Gustavus Athol Waterhouse, 1930. *GC Clutton, Courtesy Australian Museum*
Right: The undersides of fake flame hairstreak *(Pseudalmenus chlorinda barringtonensis)* holotype (left) and 1922 original (right). © *Dr Michael F Braby*

THREE BUTTERFLIES are missing from this tray, part of the George Lyell collection of 12,000 at the Melbourne Museum. It is believed they are among the 3000 butterfly specimens suspected of having been stolen from Melbourne, Sydney and Adelaide museums.

Above: Three gaps in a drawer spark an international search, February 1947. *Sun News-Pictorial, Courtesy State Library Victoria*

Left: Russell Street entrance to the National Museum of Victoria. *Courtesy University of Melbourne Archives*

Above: George Lyell, 1940. *Courtesy Gisborne and Mount Macedon Districts Historical Society*

Above: 'When and Where London Dances' — Colin Wyatt in *The Tatler* with fellow champion skier Nancy Berry, June 1935. © *Illustrated London News Ltd / Mary Evans Picture Library*

Left: An 'unusual bird of passage' arrives in New Zealand, July 1936. *The Timaru Herald, Courtesy Timaru District Libraries* **Right:** The ex-Cambridge champion in full flight in New Zealand. *Australia and New Zealand Ski Annual, Courtesy State Library Victoria*

MR. COLIN WYATT, *the famous ski-runner, artist and traveller, and his fiancée,* MISS MARY SCOTT BARRETT, *are here testing the snows of Earl's Court!*

Above: Colin Wyatt (left) beside his works *The Race* and *Slalom* at the Palser Gallery, London, October 1938. © *Illustrated London News Ltd / Mary Evans Picture Library*

Left: Colin Wyatt and Mary Scott Barrett announce their engagement across the society pages of London, January 1939. © *Illustrated London News Ltd / Mary Evans Picture Library*

Above: Wyatt entertains his fellow camoufleurs at Milne Bay, New Guinea. *Colin Wyatt, 1943*, by Robert Emerson Curtis (Aust. 1898–1996). *Australian War Memorial Collection. © Courtesy Josef Lebovic Gallery, Sydney*

Right: *Goodenough Air Strip, Camoufleur Colin Wyatt, 1943*, by Robert Emerson Curtis (Aust. 1898–1996). *Australian War Memorial Collection. © Courtesy Josef Lebovic Gallery, Sydney*

Left: 'Entomological Superman' and camoufleur Gervaise Purcell. *Gervaise Purcell Collection, Courtesy Australian War Memorial* **Centre:** Mary Wyatt makes the Sydney social pages within days of arrival. *Sydney Morning Herald, Courtesy State Library Victoria* **Right:** Wyatt as a desk-bound public servant, mid-divorce, October 1946. *Alec Iverson, Courtesy State Library of New South Wales*

Butterflies like these were among those stolen from Sydney Museum by Colin Wyatt.

TAILED EMPEROR, found from Sydney to Cape York. It is a large black, offset by grey and cream, with a touch of orange.

A MEMBER of the Blues family —Brown, yellow spots, an indigo tinge on the lower wings.

A SKIPPER found in North Queensland—brown with orange markings.

Above: 'Museum to Recover Stolen Butterflies', May 1947. *Sunday Telegraph, Courtesy State Library Victoria*

ARTIST ON TOP OF THE WORLD

COLIN WYATT, artist, linguist, photographer, mountaineer, and British ski jumping champion, is leaving Australia soon in pursuit of his ambition to paint and photograph snow and mountains, and to make a name as a painter of snow and ice.

Wyatt has been in Australia a few years with the RAAF and British Information Office. He has already photographed mountain tops in three continents. Some pictures he took on these occasions are shown in this series.

"I badly want to get to the Himalayas of India as soon as I can," says Mr. Wyatt. "Then I want to go to the South American Andes and finally to Mt. Kenya in Africa. I also would like to get to the glacier peaks in Dutch New Guinea, but to do it in reasonable time and comfort would mean parachuting down with all supplies and skis, and then walking out with periodic supply drops of extra food, and anything else wanted.

He first visited New Zealand in 1936, when the Government Tourist Bureau invited him for six months to advise on winter sports.

New Zealand has mountains and glaciers as fine as Europe, he says, also more severe ice conditions, a 10,000ft. peak in NZ being equal to 14,000ft. in Europe. Australia's Alps are good skiing country, rather like Norway, but cursed by the weather. Kosciusko could be a wonderful tourist attraction but present accommodation he says is antiquated, uncomfortable, restricted, and appallingly expensive.

Above: Wyatt triumphantly announces his return to Europe, January 1947. *PIX Magazine, Courtesy University of Adelaide Library*

Colin W. Wyatt, of Farnham, England, who was fined £100 at West Ham Police Court on May 21 in connection with the theft of 1,600 butterflies stolen from the South Australian and New South Wales Museums during the war when he was a camouflage officer in the RAAF.

Left: Wyatt appears in court, May 1947. *The Chronicle, Courtesy State Library Victoria*

ENTOMOLOGISTS from the Adelaide, Sydney and Melbourne Museums examining butterfly specimens which were stolen from Australian museums by a member of the R.A.F. The butterflies were returned to Adelaide last month. RIGHT: Parts of the old Roman wall and many relics of that age have been revealed during excavations in a bomb-devastated area of London, near the famous Guildhall. The picture shows the excavation work in progress.

Above: Norman B Tindale, Alec Burns, and Anthony Musgrave sort through thousands of recovered specimens at the South Australian Museum, September 1947. *The Chronicle, Courtesy State Library Victoria*

Above left: Dr John Evans shortly after becoming director of the Australian Museum, 1955. *Courtesy Jeremy Evans* **Above right:** Brigadier William Harry Evans inspects his butterflies. *Courtesy Jeremy Evans* **Right:** One of thousands of yellow labels in collections around Australia. *© Dr Michael F Braby*

Passed through
C. W. Wyatt Theft Coll.
1946–1947.

Above: 'Bug lovers' Free Masonry' — Colin Wyatt (second left) resurfaces at the Lepidopterists Society annual meeting at the Central Experimental Farm in Ottawa, July 1952. © *Edwards Photo, Courtesy Canadian National Collection*

Left: Aviateca TG-AGA on the runway at Tikal, Guatemala, years before its final flight. *Courtesy Zoggavia*

Below: The true 1922 *Pseudalmenus chlorinda barringtonensis* holotype alongside Wyatt's painted fake at the Australian Museum, September 2024. *Author's photograph*

second-hand for a song—in Australia, he reflected, old George Lyell and the Cherry & Sons workshop would charge double for this kind of workmanship. But, with a bit of luck, he hoped to fit the entire collection inside. The bulky selection of *Troides* took up the most space, but he had managed to fill an entire drawer with *Ulysses joesa,* and another with the blue *Ogyris*—the specialty of his onetime collecting partner Athol Waterhouse.

Along with his old Palearctic [Eurasian] collection—which had survived The Blitz intact, but was left 'in a hell of a jam'—these Australian specimens would form the centrepiece of a butterfly collection that now numbered around 40,000, well on its way to rivalling the likes of Waterhouse and Lyell back in Australia.[8]

With his butterflies nearly sorted, Wyatt hoped to skip over to Switzerland for a long-overdue rendezvous with the European ski fields—his first since that last season before the war, when his engagement to Mary was first announced.[9] But, this time, he'd be going alone, just as he'd flown back to England without her. Mary was supposed to be travelling over to England by ship, but, for all he knew, she could be in Sydney, Melbourne, Hong Kong, or battening down in another part of Surrey with her own family. It was a remarkable eighteen-month turnaround; for at least a few months following his return from New Guinea and the world of camouflage, he and Mary had been closer than ever. But by November 1946, there was no going back.

A pair of portraits taken by a photographer from *The Sun* newspaper in November 1946 capture a side of Colin Wyatt that, for all the memorable shots of him taken over the years, appears almost unique. Snapped in an office building in Martin Place, Sydney, there are no mountains or forest backdrops, no hiking boots or skis to be seen—just a deskbound public servant with vacant-looking eyes and a flat expression, his ski-suit swapped for a tie and rolled-up shirtsleeves. You can almost feel an exasperated sigh coming, with scissors and stacks of black-and-white photographs fanned out on the desk in front of him. He had another brush with *The Sun* two months earlier, when the Australian journalist

Mungo MacCallum also paid a visit to the British government's Central Department of Information, and described meeting the 'brisk Cambridge man' who had been tasked with 'tying the ties of Empire hand over fist'.[10]

Wyatt had joined the department as a visual publicity officer in September 1944, shortly after calling time on his career as a camoufleur. As Australia looked increasingly towards the United States of America in the post-war shake-out of Western power, Wyatt and his colleagues' work was part of a soft-touch propaganda campaign that sought to remind the former colony of Britain's industrial, military, and cultural relevance.

'The Americans could get stuff out in Jig-time by bomber, while our stuff took three times longer,' Wyatt told MacCallum, who published the encounter in his 'National Circus' column. 'But in the last year of the war we were level-pegging with them.'

At the department, Wyatt spent month after month circulating other people's photos — ranging from images of the latest English theatrical productions to men in white lab coats illustrating new medical breakthroughs — to newspapers around the country. He also sent out thousands of posters bound for Australia's shop windows and classrooms in a series titled 'Our Hearts of Empire'.[11] Despite the tedium of office life, the job did occasionally allow him to escape from the city; on junkets run by local publicity departments equally keen to promote Australia to the English, he was flown around the Great Barrier Reef and Whitsunday Islands, where he could admire and collect green-and-black spotted swallowtails and black-and-white crow butterflies as he went.

Back in Sydney, Colin wasn't the only Wyatt on the Central Department of Information's payroll. For much of the war, Mary Wyatt had kept busy with voluntary office-bearing roles with the Red Cross, making regular appearances in newspapers and women's magazines as she organised charity balls and fundraisers. At a Red, White and Blue Ball at Sydney Town Hall October 1943, she oversaw twenty-two debutantes, a stage festooned with massive Union Jack and other Allied flags, and overflowing flower arrangements of arum lilies, amaryllises, and roses put together by Janet Waterhouse, the wife of Athol Waterhouse's younger brother Eben Gowrie.

'Real party frocks shimmered and shone at the Red, White and Blue Ball in the Town Hall last Friday,' read one account in the women's letters section of *The Bulletin*. 'Some of them hadn't seen the light of the electrics for two or three years and seemed to rejoice in their second blooming.'[12] With her white crepe and paisley ensemble, it was Mary who *The Bulletin* named the 'most admired' among the 'large, young and bright party'.

By January 1945, however, she had also landed a job at Martin Place as an information officer alongside her husband. Whether it was a step up or a comedown from her earlier war work, when she was featured once again in *The Australian Women's Weekly* in February that year, Mary proudly showed off the department's library of 'all the latest magazines and books sent from England'.

'We hope to specialise in news of women's war-work and housing in England,' she told the reporter.[13]

This period, when Colin and Mary's work and home lives were more intensely entwined than at any other time in their marriage, was not to last. By January 1946, Mary had left their home at 25 Nelson Street, Woollahra, not far from that first flat where she had sat beaming for *The Sydney Morning Herald* in 1939.[14] Colin would later claim that the couple had argued about Mary's relationship with an unnamed man from the Royal Navy—the officer had since left Australia for Hong Kong, but it seemed they had seen enough of each other for Colin to grow jealous.

'She decided to go away,' he would later explain. 'I cannot remember the exact words but I tried in every way to make her remain.'[15]

At first, Mary seemed ambivalent about their future together, but that changed as the months passed and she travelled around New South Wales and then Victoria. There was an attempt at a reconciliation in March, when they met in Sydney on the neutral ground of a mutual acquaintance's house. But the reunion failed, and when they spoke again on the phone a few weeks later, Mary requested Colin's signature for a new passport so she could return to England. When the application form arrived in the post shortly afterwards, Colin sent her a letter dated 9 July 1946.

'Mary Darling,' he wrote, 'I have been hoping that you have been thinking over my plea to you to return home; I do so want you here & have everything ready for you.'

As for the passport, he wrote that he had no objection to Mary visiting her parents 'for a few months', provided it was just a visit before promptly returning home. He sent the application form with the letter, signed on the understanding that she would return to Woollahra.

'And now, darling, please be sensible & come home to Sydney where we can be happy together in our own home,' he wrote.[16]

But it was all in vain. Mary Wyatt would never return to Woollahra.

Given the many column inches devoted to the glamourous, well-connected couple since they'd arrived in Sydney in 1939, it was little surprise that when it all came to a head in the Supreme Court on Tuesday 19 November 1946, the case of *Wyatt v Wyatt* caught the eye of a *Daily Telegraph* court reporter. In the paper's gossipy 'Dramas of the Court' column, the once-dashing Colin Wyatt appeared a somewhat diminished figure — a 'slight, red-haired and red-moustached man' — as he gave a sworn deposition testifying to his failed marriage.[17]

Back in September, Colin had filed a petition with the Matrimonial Causes Court to 'decree a restitution of conjugal rights to your Petitioner from the said Mary Scott Wyatt'.[18] They had met again in Melbourne, but while Mary did return to Sydney, she never came back to Nelson Street. Two days after the petition was filed, on 1 October, a clerk from Wyatt's law firm — whose offices on Hunter Street were just a few doors from the site of John Roach's old curio shop a century earlier — tracked Mary down to serve her with the petition and a deadline. Mary signed the man's piece of paper, but as the deadline came and went, she continued to keep her distance.

As the judge looked over an evidence file that included a green slip of paper — a certified copy of their marriage certificate from Somerset House in London — and the lovelorn letter from July, Colin summarised the couple's time in Australia and testified to the 'affectionate' letters that Mary had sent him during his time away as a camoufleur.

‘Were you and your wife living happily till the end of the year?’ Wyatt’s lawyer asked.

‘Yes,’ he replied.

‘Between you and your wife, what happened towards the end of last year?’

‘She decided to go away. There were words between us about her going with another person, and she said she would go away. I tried to stop her; I cannot remember the exact words but I tried in every way to make her remain.’

When his lawyer asked if Mary had been upset when the unnamed man from the Royal Navy left for Hong Kong, and if she said she missed him, Wyatt replied, ‘Not in so many words, no’.

‘You sincerely want your wife back?’ the lawyer asked as he wrapped up his questions.

‘I do,’ Wyatt responded.[19]

One other witness was called, a surgeon in the Royal Australian Navy named Peter Blaxland. A bachelor with a similar taste for adventure as his friend Colin Wyatt, Blaxland had joined Colin and Mary on some of their ski adventures through Kosciuszko National Park, the ones that Colin had happily captured on film.[20] In court, Blaxland explained how he had since witnessed the Wyatts’ relationship go downhill in more ways than one.

‘[You] were a living for a time with Mr Wyatt in his flat, this year?’ the lawyer asked.

‘Yes, I was,’ Blaxland replied.

‘Do you know whether Mr and Mrs Wyatt have been living together this year?’

‘No, they have not, to my knowledge.’[21]

The judge found in favour of Colin’s petition, and ordered that Mary return home with ‘the petitioner’ within twenty-one days, ‘render unto him conjugal rights’, and subsequently file a certificate of her compliance at the court registry within four days of her return. Mary did none of this.

To modern eyes, a legal process compelling a woman to return to her husband’s house and bed reads like a jarring judicial invasion. But in a time before no-fault divorces, establishing a cause for dissolving a marriage, whether on the grounds of adultery or desertion, was a laborious, public, and unavoidable act of laundry-airing overseen by judges and lawyers. And, in the wake of World War II, business was booming; while the outbreak of war had seen a spike in marriages, its end drove the divorce rate to new heights, as couples who had spent months or years apart found there was no going back to the way things were.

Wyatt's fellow camoufleur Max Dupain went through the same process when his first wife, the photographer Olive Cotton, decided to leave him in 1942. In May that year, Dupain had sent Cotton, once his childhood friend and collaborator, a very similar letter proclaiming that 'life has never really been the same since you left' and begging her to come home.[22] Dupain had in fact already fallen in love with his future second wife, and had come to regard Cotton with a mix of pity and 'brotherly sorrow', but such letters, with their desperate language and notes of cautious hope, were necessary to establish for the court a chain of evidence that the husband had indeed tried everything.[23]

'I hate it all,' Dupain would reflect in his diary at the height of their divorce hearing. 'Privacy is one of the elements of freedom of living which we are supposed to be fighting for. Christ! What hypocrisy!'[24]

It was only when the absent wives rebuffed their attempts by letter, or ignored them entirely, that husbands such as Dupain or Wyatt could move to the next stage of the process. Today, the emotional theatre of such letters makes for compelling reading, but when even the most amicably parted couple had to go through these painful, public motions, they remain a tantalisingly unreliable source. Whether by design or desertion, Mary's voice is almost completely absent from the paper trail bundled together under the case file simply titled *Wyatt v Wyatt*.

One way or another, ending a marriage in 1940s New South Wales was a bruising, highly public exercise for all parties. For Dupain, the dual experiences of divorce and serving in the Camouflage Section left him with deep questions about modern life, writing in his wartime diary, 'How can a man's ideals survive in this world — how can he become anything but a cynic?'[25]

Given their parallel experiences, one wonders if Colin Wyatt was left feeling similarly disillusioned as 1946 wore on.

***

In later years, Mary's family back in England would rarely discuss her first husband and brief life in Australia. Within a few years, she had remarried, given birth to a daughter, and adopted a son, and her seven-year lost weekend as Mrs Colin Wyatt became a story best left in the Southern Hemisphere. She died under her new surname, Waterslow, much later, in 2006, but, according to one nephew, Mary occasionally alluded to the miserable time she had had living in Australia. While her husband was flying around the country making art and collecting butterflies, she had found the place to be 'hot, remote, and a cultural desert'. Whatever the truth of their split, Mary's only other contribution in Australian archives appeared just one day after the Supreme Court hearing, when she returned a favour and signed a Department of Immigration form declaring that:

> I, Mary Scott Wyatt, the wife of Colin William Fforde Wyatt of 25 Nelson Street Woollahra NSW Civil Servant do hereby consent to the grant of passport to in favour of my said husband enabling him to travel beyond Australia.[26]

Just a few months after begrudgingly giving consent for Mary to renew her own passport and visit her family, Colin had told the judge he too planned to leave the country, ostensibly as part of his work for the Central Department of Information. Wyatt claimed he planned to visit England for between six to twelve months before returning to Australia to live permanently.

But he spun a slightly different story in the pages of *Pix* magazine, which in January 1947 ran a three-page spread of his photographs and life story. Headlined 'Artist on Top of the World', the upbeat piece was a world away from *The Daily Telegraph*'s courthouse coverage, with snow-covered vistas ranging from the Swiss Alps to the 'knife-edge ridge' he and Mick Bowie had navigated on their way to the Wilczek Peak in 1936.[27] The article also added that this 'artist, linguist, photographer, mountaineer, and British ski jumping champion, is leaving Australia soon in pursuit of his ambition to paint and photograph snow and mountains, and to make a name as a painter of snow and ice'.

'I badly want to get to the Himalayas of India as soon as I can,' Wyatt told the magazine. 'Then I want to go to the South American Andes and finally to Mt. Kenya in Africa.'

It seemed that, despite the deflating reviews he had received from Australia's art critics, from his surrealist pivot to his wartime watercolours, Wyatt was not yet ready to put down his paintbrushes. With his passport approved, he quit his day job at Martin Place on 1 December and spent his last few weeks in Australia tying up loose ends. In the first week of December, he ventured back out to Blackheath, in the Blue Mountains, for one final weekend of butterfly collecting. This time, he would not be joined by Athol Waterhouse, but by Charles Oke, Leslie Mosse-Robinson, and Alec Burns from the National Museum of Victoria.

It was after this trip that Mosse-Robinson accompanied Wyatt back to his flat in Woollahra on 10 December, in a brief stopover before catching the train home to Narara. As Mosse-Robinson later reported to Burns, he had seen Wyatt's four cases of insects already packed up for their overseas journey. But this didn't fully convey the situation at 25 Nelson Street: Wyatt was packing up his entire life in Sydney, ready to leave behind his marital home and the now-concluded chapter it represented.

In his 1955 memoir, Wyatt would condense the life-altering decisions of these turbulent final months into one six-word sentence: 'In 1947 I returned to Europe.'[28] By the next paragraph, he wrote that the 'travel bug' had caught him once again as he left the country of his birth for another adventure like those he had before the war, before Australia and its camoufleurs, modern art movements, and entrancing butterflies. But if those six words understandably glossed over the messy details of his divorce, they also failed to fully convey just what happened next in January 1947.

On 28 January 1947, Wyatt wrote to his acquaintance back in Australia—the Victorian butterfly collector Frances Erasmus 'Ras'

Wilson. Showing no sign of stress or worry, this lively letter described the 'pleasant week' Wyatt had just spent rearranging his butterfly collection in his mother's study, and recounted his occasionally 'hair-raising' return to England.[29] While he had travelled to Australia by sea, on the cusp of a new life of domesticity and marital commitment, his homeward journey had been one of fittingly untethered adventure, hitching a ride in an airforce plane. He described flying through the Yangon region of Myanmar, and passing over the Shwedagon Pagoda, a dazzling gold-plated Buddhist temple said to be thousands of years old. Then the pilot performed a daring fly-by over the Dead Sea and the Jordan Valley, plunging down through rose-coloured sandstone gorges to the ancient carved city of Petra.

In a brief stopover in Cairo, Wyatt had lunch with some acquaintances before spending the afternoon visiting pyramids and recently excavated tombs. It was a memorable way to turn the page on an era that, for all its moments of wartime thrill-seeking and bountiful butterflies, had also brought him plenty of disappointment, frustration, public humiliation, and grief. As he took stock of his insects, Wyatt seemed uncertain but upbeat about his future; in his letter to Wilson, he concluded simply, 'Blowed if I know!!'

A few days later, in the late afternoon of Friday 31 January 1947, a group of uninvited guests came calling at Cobbetts. Standing on his mother's snow-covered doorstep were three men — two of them strangers, while the third was more familiar, a man Wyatt had known over a decade earlier, when he was still an ace ski jumper barely out of his teens. Wyatt hadn't seen him since before he'd left for Australia in 1939, but there was no chance he didn't recognise the keeper of entomology at the British Natural History Museum.

In a few moments, Wyatt would learn that the other two were police officers — one a local inspector from the Farnham CID, and the other a detective sergeant from New Scotland Yard. One of the officers had a search warrant ready in his pocket, but Wyatt didn't even ask to see it before welcoming the men in from the cold. Despite the appearance of happy ignorance he had feigned in his letter to Wilson just days before, it was almost as if he'd known that this day would come.

PART II

The habitations of all things which dwell,
Were burnt for beacons; cities were consum'd,
And men were gather'd round their blazing homes
To look once more into each other's face

– Lord Byron, *Darkness*

CHAPTER SIXTEEN

The Australian

The British winter of 1947 wasn't so much a cold snap as a shattering spell. As January wore on, local newspapers around the United Kingdom read like a daily catalogue of minor and major miseries: in Birmingham, buses skidded into each other on ice-slicked roads; in North Wales, fishermen used iron bars to free swans trapped in the ice; and in Shropshire, farmers circled their cars around the cracked surface of a pond, as police and the RAF worked in vain under headlights to recover a young boy and girl who had fallen through.[12] Facing a manpower shortage, the government resorted to deploying German prisoners of war — those who hadn't already been deported like the butterfly spy Fred Brandt — to shovel snow off roads from Somerset to Devon.[3] Fuel shortages meant that streets and homes were plunged into darkness; there were even times when Big Ben's clockface was one of the few lights visible in Westminster, even if the cold caused its famous chimes to drop a few notes from its nine o'clock melody.[4] If that wasn't enough of an affront to British national spirit, in Kent there were reports that people had resorted to emptying their hot-water bottles in a pitiful attempt to make tea.[5]

The snowstorm was looming like a threat on the morning of Wednesday 22 January when, over in South Kensington, in the New Spirit Building of the Natural History Museum, an applied entomologist named Dr John Evans received a message to stand by for an incoming call from Melbourne, Australia.[6] This was unusual; international calls were still expensive and rare enough that it must have been something important. Evans was perhaps the antithesis of the eccentric obsessives, dashing explorers, and vainglorious stamp collectors who loom large in the annals of natural history. Tall, handsome, with elfin ears and once-dark hair already showing signs of grey, Evans was modest and clean-cut, often seen clutching his tobacco pipe, happy to keep his head down paying his dues in whatever dull corners of the empire needed an entomologist.

As the day wore on, the forty-year-old had hours to ponder which figure from his past might be calling, and why. Throughout all the years he had spent in Australia, Evans had told himself that he was still, in his bones, an Englishman — albeit one born in colonial India. From Canberra to Melbourne, and Adelaide to Tasmania, he had done his best to keep a safe distance from the personalities and politics of the 'local scene', but it was only when he returned to England that it dawned on him just how much his adopted home had rubbed off on him.

'To my surprise,' he later reflected, 'I found that to a great extent I had become an Australian.'[7]

It wasn't just the decade and a half he had spent in the Antipodes that left Evans feeling like a foreigner in his own country. When he'd arrived back in London three years earlier, in April 1944, the whole city had a surreal quality — even Big Ben was blacked out overnight, while an armada of silver barrage balloons hung ominously over the skyline. In South Kensington, the statue of Adam, the first taxonomist who had watched over the Natural History Museum since it opened, was long gone, having been dislodged during The Blitz and shattered on the steps below. Within a few days, Evans had been handed an identity card, gas mask, tin helmet, and ration books, and heard for himself the nocturnal rumblings of falling German bombs and the British anti-aircraft guns that roared in response.[8]

During his younger years at boarding school, Evans had so hated all the militaristic rituals that by sixteen it was clear he would never follow his father and grandfather into the armed forces to wind up as a brigadier or general administering colonial rule in far-flung corners of the British Empire.[9] But as The Blitz dragged on, he found himself volunteering as an air-raid warden, spending every third night keeping himself awake in dread of the Luftwaffe's latest invention: a two-kilogram ordnance that fluttered harmlessly down to street level, waiting for some movement or disturbance on the ground to detonate its payload.[10] They called this monster the 'butterfly bomb', and as Evans grew familiar with the nightly routines of sirens and shelters, it felt like he'd been cast in some nightmarish play.

On off nights, he tried to sleep in a South Kensington boarding house, and by day put in bleary-eyed shifts across the road in a corner of the decade-old New Spirit Building, which had taken on the overflow from the museum's crowded entomology section. As he settled into his new role at the Imperial Institute of Entomology, he kept an ear out for air-raid warnings that would send him and his colleagues scrambling into one of the windowless storerooms, where they would wait out the alarm surrounded by shelves of preserved animals.

It was just one uncanny image in an era full of them; one day in the stairwell of the New Spirit Building, he was surprised to find a Camberwell beauty fluttering in a sunny spot by a window.[11] Evans was no expert in lepidoptera — he had chosen to specialise in cicadas years earlier — but even he knew one of England's most rare and striking butterflies when he saw it. It would be the first and last time he saw one alive and on the wing, and he never quite solved the mystery of how it ended up there — it was just a small, inexplicable moment of wonder that can occasionally surface among death and destruction.

Evans wasn't the only entomologist in his family, and when it came to butterflies, most people would bypass him entirely and go straight to the south-west basement of the Waterhouse building, which for years had been occupied — and then some — by the entomology department. Down in the underbelly of the Natural History Museum, one could reliably find John's ageing father, the retired brigadier William Harry Evans, surrounded by cabinets with an open tray in front of him. Having spent his career serving the empire from India to Somaliland to France, earning a companion of the orders of the Star of India and the Indian Empire along the way, the brigadier now ran out his final decades poring over half a million specimens of a single genus of butterfly: skippers, or *Hesperiidae*.

It was a fitting project for a man who, in the classically Banksian mode of globetrotting colonial naturalist, had spent every spare minute of leave collecting butterflies from Darjeeling to Malaya.[12] By the time his son joined him at the museum, the brigadier was as much a part of the furniture as the cabinetry: when Australian entomologists from Alec Burns to Athol Waterhouse made their pilgrimages to the museum, they would invariably fall under the brigadier's wing.[13]

The brigadier was so consumed by his museum work that he rarely left his desk, even as much of London was shut down or evacuated. The old soldier moved slower in these days, partially deaf and unable to walk more than half a mile, due to a long history of bad knees — one nasty fall while catching butterflies in the Burmese jungle had left him lying semi-paralysed on his back, and forced to crawl the two miles home.[14] One day at the museum, when the tell-tale whirr of a falling V-1 bomb outside on Cromwell Street sent the younger Evans diving below his laboratory bench, the brigadier remained at his desk, oblivious, as the bomb spiralled to the ground one hundred feet away. The blast tore through the bird and upper mammals galleries, shattering so much glass that for years afterwards museum staff had to take extra care while handling specimens in case splinters of glass shook loose from the fur. The brigadier was left sitting, stunned and further deafened, in front of an empty drawer that, moments earlier, had been full of skippers — the rush of air from the explosion had sent the tray-load of butterflies flying off their pins in every direction.[15]

John had rarely been as close to his father as during those months in South Kensington. The brigadier had also been born in India during his own father's colonial posting, and in due course sent his only son back to England at the age of two to be left in the care of a distant relation named Dorothy Dickens. 'Aunt' Dorothy was also a granddaughter of Charles Dickens, whose eldest son had married into the Evans family via the brigadier's aunt — a matter of some controversy, given the bride's publisher father had fallen out with the literary giant, who had refused to attend the nuptials.

The seaside town of Broadstairs had been a favourite retreat of Dorothy's late grandfather, and became a natural playground for the young John, who would fondly remember scouring the beach for cowrie shells, like Athol Waterhouse and countless others before him. John's fond memories of communing with nature were interrupted only by visits to his grandparents and other obscure aunts, and the occasional, miserable attempt at taking swimming lessons from a gruff neighbour who tried to make 'a man' out of the awkward, nature-loving, and decidedly sports-shy youngster.[16] It was another uncle, rather than the brigadier, who first took John to the Natural History Museum at the age of eight, to marvel at what the older man regarded as some of the finest architecture in the empire. John didn't care much for the building, but its contents emboldened the budding naturalist.

'My secret, which I have long wished to share, is the pleasure to be derived from small, obscure creatures, known only to a few, which have lived on earth for a very long time,' Evans would later reflect. 'They have also courted and sung songs and have been blissfully unaware of the coming of an ingenious animal, bringing death and destruction in its wake.'[17]

By the age of sixteen, Evans had escaped boarding school for Cambridge, to study zoology, botany, and geology — the brigadier thought Cambridge a 'less effeminate' choice than Oxford.[18] Eventually, Evans took the plunge to move to the Southern Hemisphere for an entry-level post in Australia at the newly established Council for Scientific and Industrial Research. He soon began to specialise in entomology, a fateful development that saw him sent across the Tasman Sea for a year-long study placement at the Cawthron Institute in Nelson, New Zealand, to learn from one of the most renowned entomologists that the British Empire had to offer.

Evans's new boss greeted him as he stepped off the boat in Wellington. A gangly older man, he soon become a sort of paternal figure for the young and green Dr Evans — perhaps even more influential than his often-distant father. The man's name was Dr Robin Tillyard, and it wouldn't be long before this new mentor took Evans to some strange and unexpected places.

***

'Go on, Walter,' Evans heard Dr Tillyard say from across the pitch-black room. 'You can pull my hair or bite me if you like.'[19]

Tillyard would later claim that he felt a tugging at his scalp and a spritz of cold water across his right hand before Walter replied in his gruff, manly voice, 'That's damn good', and whistled with satisfaction.

Walter Stinson had been a twenty-eight-year-old railway worker with a coarse voice and coarser sense of humour. Across three nights in Boston in May 1928, he entertained a small circle of strangers holding hands in the darkened parlour of his younger sister, Mina Crandon née Stinson, as he had done many times before. With the doors locked and the windows barred, John Evans listened alongside Tillyard and the Crandons as Walter swore, joked, and completed a set of scientific tests for his audience.

These peculiar feats were particularly remarkable given that the handsome young Walter Stinson had been crushed to death on the railroad back in 1911. All the same, for the past four years, his sister Mina had attracted international infamy as a spirit medium under the alias 'Margary', while the Crandon house at 10 Lime Street became the site of regular séances in which she channelled the dead and departed, spilled gooey ectoplasm out onto the table, and produced a dark, fleshy 'teleplasmic hand' from beneath her skirt. It made for some spooky, oddly erotic scenes, where 'Walter', the spirit of Crandon's long-lost brother, was often the star attraction.

Despite the theatricality, Tillyard considered these sessions serious experiments, and even when Mina's face was placed under a red light, 'Walter' kept on talking as Tillyard and Evans stared intently at her motionless lips and larynx. As the nights wore on, Evans occasionally became more participant than witness, with 'Walter' whistling 'God Save the King' at Evans's request, and even passing commentary on the young entomologist's love life.[20]

On the fourth evening, this time held at another house eight miles away, Evans dutifully stood guard outside a room containing only Tillyard, Crandon, and one other witness, as 'Walter' dutifully pressed his fingerprints into a cold packet of dental wax in another show of corporeality. Tillyard would later claim he could feel Walter's 'smooth, soft touch, slightly cool and dampish', brushing over his arm during the session.[21] Unlike Tillyard's new colleagues at the CSIR back in Australia, or his critics in England, the dead railway worker was receptive and encouraging to the embattled professor.

'You don't need to bother about the people in London who are squabbling about me,' said 'Walter' reassuringly.

Evans had been drawn into Tillyard's world of psychical research shortly after arriving in Nelson, when he was invited to have dinner at the Tillyard family home each Sunday. While Evans became acquainted with the professor's young, beautiful, and virtuously named daughters, Patience, Faith, Hope, and Honour, he also couldn't help but notice a wax impression of a hand perched on a table.

'Though it was never mentioned in my presence,' he would later recall, 'I supposed it was the cast of an ectoplasmic hand.'[22]

By the time Tillyard had brought him to the Crandons' front door in Boston in 1928, Evans had been enlisted as a reluctant and slightly bewildered paranormal research assistant. In Tillyard's widely disseminated account of the four séances they attended, Evans would be a recurring player as he helped his mentor with a series of convoluted tests and experiments.

Despite the public humiliation that followed the publication of Tillyard's 1928 *Nature* article, his protégé soon followed him when Tillyard moved to Canberra to take up his ill-fated post at the CSIR.[23] Evans still believed that Tillyard was a brilliant scientist, but even he could see that this mentor's feet weren't always firmly on the ground, and it wasn't long after arriving in Canberra in 1929 that he attended the farewell party for Athol Waterhouse.[24]

If Evans's loyalty and high regard for Tillyard had remained unwavering, despite all he had witnessed, there was another good reason: he had fallen in love with Tillyard's second daughter, Faith, and after a brief and dull interlude in Adelaide working at the university's Waite Agricultural Research Institute, he returned to Canberra in 1934 to seek her hand.

'Not only was she lovely to look at with an affectionate and compassionate nature, but she alone of Dr Tillyard's daughters shared his enthusiasm for natural history and his love of insects,' Evans would later reflect.[25]

To the apparent surprise of her parents, who thought Faith too much like her father to settle down with the staid and agreeable John Evans, she agreed to marry him in a quiet church ceremony in February 1934. Among the attendees was Professor William Dakin, future camoufleur and seemingly one of a handful of scientific luminaries that Faith's father had yet to alienate.[26] That day in Canberra must have been a rare moment of joy in an otherwise grim period for the family, with Tillyard's health suffering after his nervous breakdown, and the humiliation of his exit from the CSIR still smarting. The following year, the newlyweds moved further south to Hobart, where they would spend close to a decade raising a young family while John worked as government entomologist in the Tasmanian Department of Agriculture. Then, one day in 1942, Evans looked out over the Derwent River and realised that Hobart suddenly looked incredibly small and remote, overshadowed by the great Mount Wellington. It was, in many ways, the 'end of the world', and he began to pine for something bigger.

By the time he'd heard about the vacancy at the Imperial Institute of Entomology in London, Evans had spent over a third of his life in Australia and New Zealand, and there was hardly a museum, university, or scientific institution in the country he hadn't worked with. Despite himself, Evans had made a deep network of connections that were professional, personal, and familial, or a combination of all three.

As Evans sat by the phone on that bitterly cold day in January 1947, the mystery caller from Australia could have been anyone. An old colleague from the CSIR? Someone from the university in Adelaide? Maybe even Athol Waterhouse, who Evans knew remained on good terms with the brigadier? For a moment, perhaps, Evans might have dreaded another terrible message from his mother-in-law, like the news of Dr Tillyard's fatal accident on that rainy day in 1937.

It was a little after 2.00 pm, nearly midnight in Australia, when the call finally came through, carrying the voice of Evans's old friend

Dick Pescott across nine time zones. For years, Pescott and Evans were interstate colleagues, both applied entomologists working in government departments in Victoria and Tasmania, but since Evans's move to London, his old friend had risen to the directorship of the National Museum of Victoria. No doubt sounding a little tired after another long and stressful day, Pescott told Evans that museums in Melbourne and Sydney had both discovered 'big robberies' affecting their entomological collections, with over 800 specimens taken from the Lyell Collection and several hundreds more from Waterhouse's in Sydney.[27]

'All specimens taken are rarities,' Pescott explained, while adding that a detailed list would be forwarded by airmail the following day.

Pescott told Evans that they had also identified a suspect, who they believed had left Australia in a hurry three to four weeks earlier, having previously shipped a consignment of specimens that may or may not have already arrived in England. He asked his old friend to contact New Scotland Yard, warn British museum staff and local insect dealers to keep an eye out for a collection of Australian butterflies, and perhaps even intercept the shipment and stop it being opened.[28]

Evans reluctantly agreed, and over the coming months would become a semi-official fixer for the Australian museums — their man on the ground as the search that began in Melbourne continued to unfold on the other side of the world. But it wasn't just his time in Australia, and his ready familiarity with its scientific institutions and eccentric characters that made Dr John Evans the perfect man for the job.

When Pescott revealed the name of their chief suspect, Evans must have felt a pang of recognition — the same mix of shock, outrage, and dread shared by museum workers and entomologists around Australia and the world, as word of the thefts gradually fanned out in hushed phone calls and panicked telegrams like the thud of a falling rock setting off an avalanche. Like the rest of them, it turned out that Evans knew the Englishman Colin Wyatt too.

'He came to see me in Hobart with a letter of introduction from, I think, Waterhouse,' he wrote to Pescott, committing to paper a distant memory that now bore an ominous new meaning. 'And we had him out to dinner.'[29]

CHAPTER SEVENTEEN

The Confrontation

John Evans made a beeline to New Scotland Yard, where the first officer he spoke to didn't seem to know what to make of the man from the museum.[1] It was the first time that its Central Investigation Department had heard of a case of missing butterflies, and as Evans relayed what Dick Pescott had just told him over the phone, he could sense that the officer required some convincing as to why a raft of insects disappearing in some faraway corner of the empire was a problem for the Metropolitan Police. Eventually, Evans managed to break through, and the case was assigned to Detective Sergeant F Cameron, a seasoned officer who Evans quickly sized up as an 'educated and intelligent man'. But there would be no flash of sirens or handcuffs until Cameron had received more evidence from the Australians — something he could work with beyond hearsay from an English entomologist.

Back in Australia, it was a sign of the unique and brazen nature of the thefts that the list of suspects was always short. The day before contacting Evans in London, Pescott had taken care to avoid naming names when he first revealed the Melbourne situation to Arthur Walkom and Herbert Hale. Instead, he said only that the National Museum of Victoria's suspicions centred on two unnamed men, one in Melbourne and one in Sydney. The deliberate intrigue was enough for Walkom to shoot back a letter the next day.

'Could you let me have the names of the two people you mentioned on the telephone so that we can keep them in mind!' he wrote.[2]

The list had already halved by the time Walkom's letter arrived. The first suspect that Pescott had raised with the Russell Street police on Alec Burns's suggestion was a mysterious man named 'B Salkeld', whom Burns understood had recently been barred from the Macleay Museum and the collections of the late colonial secretary and patron of the bird-stuffer John Roach.[3] But Salkeld was quickly eliminated, and by the time Pescott picked up the phone to Evans, the search had been whittled down to one man, one name, and one address in southern England.

A net of circumstantial evidence had quickly been drawn around Colin William Fforde Wyatt. There was the entomologist Leslie Mosse-Robinson's account of Wyatt's curious behaviour and swift departure after their Blue Mountains collecting trip with Burns and Charles Oke in December. Shortly after making his discovery on 13 January, Burns had dashed off a letter to Mosse-Robinson asking for Wyatt's home address, to which Mosse-Robinson quickly offered a house in Farnham, Surrey, named Cobbetts. Mosse-Robinson also told Burns that he had received two airmail letters from Wyatt since they'd parted, filled with the usual kind of chatter — recommendations of English suppliers of entomological equipment, and some griping about the 'irksome' paperwork of post-war travel.[4] Even Burns had received an undated letter from Wyatt, written from Darwin as he made his way back to England in late December. Much like the 28 January letter to Ras Wilson, which Wilson also surrendered to Burns, it seemed that Wyatt fully intended to keep up appearances with his Australian associates — there was no sign in any of the letters that he planned or expected to cut ties with a community that would soon be 'electrified' by news of the thefts.

There was also Bill Newcombe, the National Museum of Victoria attendant with whom Burns had made the initial discovery on 13 January. It transpired that in early December, while Burns was still off collecting, Newcombe had encountered Wyatt on the museum's premises on two occasions.

'It was ascertained from Mr Newcombe that Colin Wyatt visited the Museum on two consecutive days — presumably the 4th and 5th

(Tuesday and Wednesday) of December, 1946,' read a confidential internal report written by Burns himself.

Wyatt was seen hanging around late on the Tuesday afternoon, with Newcombe later reporting that 'he had to be told that it was locking up time just before 5 pm'. 'He was there again the next morning,' the report added, without making it clear whether Newcombe saw Wyatt on the floor of the public galleries browsing the taxidermy, or down in the dungeons. At any rate, Burns and Pescott would soon learn from the attendant at the Russell Street door, and then from the museum's treasurer, Stanley Mitchell, that a man fitting Wyatt's description had been seen coming and going, rifling through the drawers of the entomological collection, and carrying large boxes he admitted contained insects.[5]

Meanwhile, in Sydney, the knowledgeable cadet Nancy Adams hadn't just identified gaps in the G.A. Waterhouse Collection with characteristic efficiency—she had also pointed Walkom to the most likely culprit almost immediately.

'Miss Adams informed me that the only person who had much free access to the Collection during the past few years was a Mr. Colin Wyatt, a lepidopterist who had evinced an interest in a new edition of Waterhouse's "What Butterfly Is That?"', Walkom would later report.[6]

It would emerge that neither Waterhouse nor his publisher, Angus & Robertson, had any idea about a new edition of the out-of-print 1932 book, let alone given it their blessing. Invoking the name of his old friend Athol Waterhouse seemed to be part of Wyatt's modus operandi—like Evans in Hobart, Pescott himself seemed to recall that when Wyatt first introduced himself at the National Museum of Victoria, he did so bearing a letter of introduction from Waterhouse himself.[7]

'I met Wyatt several times when he came to see the collection,' Anthony Musgrave would later tell a Sydney newspaper, still incredulous that such large and delicate specimens had been spirited away. 'It never occurred to me that he planned to steal the butterflies ... Wyatt was a very engaging fellow, with a sound knowledge of his butterflies.'[8]

When Walkom and Pescott spoke again on 23 January, it quickly became clear that both of their staff had independently come up with the same suspect. There were still other details to iron out, but Pescott and Russell Grimwade, the chair of the National Museum of Victoria, and Detective Ryan at Russell Street were concerned enough by the fast-moving situation — and by the possibility that the specimens in transit might slip through their fingers — that the order was given for Pescott to call his old friend Dr John Evans to enlist the help of British authorities.

By January 1947, the Evans family, including Faith and their two children, had settled down in an old house on an acre and a half of land in Chalfont St Giles.[9] It was surrounded by wild blackthorn hedges, and it took a four-mile walk and an eighteen-mile train ride just to get to work in South Kensington each day, but the quaint village atmosphere and sound of nightingales in the bluebell trees was usually worth the hassle. John Evans was there on the evening of 29 January, bumping around in the attic trying to get the frozen-over pipes working, when Detective Sergeant Cameron called with news.[10] Evans had called Cameron himself earlier that day after a cable from Pescott brought breaking news from Australia: since Walkom had spoken to the police on 25 January, a detective from the Sydney CIB had begun combing through shipping records to identify which London-bound ship had sailed out from Sydney with Wyatt's cargo.[11] Within two days, they'd cracked it; on the afternoon of 28 January, Pescott shared the news, even though the telegram service misspelled the name of the ship and the house:

> Goods left Sydney on PERIN tenth December STOP included were four cases scientific specimens STOP address given care Corbetts Farm Farnham, Surrey England[12]

Cameron had been away from his desk when Evans had first called, but when the detective returned the call that night, he explained to Evans that he too had received a similar cable from the police at Russell Street. This one brought the fresh revelation that the SS *Perim* had sailed into England on 18 January. The news left Evans stunned — while he and his Australian colleagues had been on tenterhooks for days, the missing specimens had been in England the whole time. But even this breakthrough wasn't enough evidence for Cameron, who continued to press Evans for more information from Australia, anything at all, that could put some meat on the bone they had pointed at this man Wyatt. All Evans could do was make an educated guess.

'I told him I imagined what had happened was that someone at your museums had discovered the theft by chance,' Evans wrote of his conversations with Cameron. 'That the collections were not available to the public and this man was the only person known to have had access to them since they were last examined.'[13]

Two key pieces of evidence were still in transit: Pescott had promised to send via airmail the full list of 825 specimens missing from the National Museum of Victoria, plus the Sydney list as soon as it was completed. But there was no sign of either, and, as things stood, Cameron said the case remained in a 'very delicate position'. If they went down to Surrey half-cocked, he explained, Wyatt might deny the accusations, insist that the butterflies were all his, or claim he didn't have them at all.[14] Both Cameron and Evans were hungry for new leads, and when Evans arrived at the museum the following morning to find an airmail from Walkom at the Australian Museum dated 24 January, he pounced on it.

'This is a sad tale you may hear from Pescott by telephone before this letter reaches you,' the letter read.

Walkom explained how in the two days since Pescott had delivered the news from Melbourne, his staff had discovered that Waterhouse's butterflies had also been targeted in their hundreds. Walkom told Evans he believed it was 'obviously the work of an Entomologist', based on the prevalence of 'rarities and a number of types' among the missing, and relayed Nancy Adams's confident belief that only one such man had been granted access to the Australian Museum's butterflies in the previous year.[15]

Evans immediately rang Cameron at New Scotland Yard, who told him that news of the SS *Perim*'s arrival had caused a jurisdictional mess; when it emerged that the butterflies had already been picked up from the dock on 24 January, the case was reassigned to the police department closest to the recipient's listed address in Surrey. The Farnham police had picked up the case, only for it to stall when a clerk from the local courthouse refused to issue a search warrant for Wyatt's mother's house, deeming the evidence from Australia 'inadequate'.[16] Cameron decided to press on without the cooperation of local law enforcement if he had to, and on the morning of 31 January arrived at the museum to collect the Walkom letter from Evans as evidence.

It was while Evans and Cameron were still discussing the case that another call came through to Norman Denbigh Riley in a neighbouring office. Fifty-six years old, with spectacles that magnified his eyes to bug-like proportions, Riley had joined the Natural History Museum at the age of twenty-one before working his way up to the post of keeper of entomology in 1932. By this time, the 5,500 insects and arachnids of Hans Sloane's original collection, to be later expanded by the likes of Daniel Solander and Joseph Banks, had ballooned to include over eight million specimens and 279,000 species.[17] That number had only grown since Riley's arrival, and for years he had been its genial custodian and a jokey repository of anecdotes and museum lore who was happy to share its collections with visiting researchers such as Athol Waterhouse.

Riley already knew all about Colin Wyatt and the missing butterflies — while Evans did the legwork, Pescott had taken care to keep the Natural History Museum's senior management apprised of the developing situation in Australia. But this latest call came from the headquarters of the Museums Association of Great Britain, whose secretary had just received an intriguing sheaf of documents posted from Melbourne with urgency. The detailed list of missing specimens that Pescott had promised to send to Evans days earlier had never materialised, swallowed up by the postal system somewhere between Melbourne and London. But now, in an overdue stroke of luck, it seemed that a back-up copy had found its way to England.[18] Riley immediately dispatched a messenger to the Museums Association to fetch the lists, and before Evans knew it, Cameron was busy making plans.

The detective was on the train to Farnham in a matter of hours — with the roads still covered by snow, rail was the only safe way to make the forty-mile journey, even for a New Scotland Yard detective in a hurry.[19] He wasn't travelling alone, either; Cameron may have had the long-awaited specimen list in his hand, but he was only too aware that the pages of Latin scientific names were a foreign language to him. When the detective had requested an expert to accompany him in case a technical question arose, Evans had been reticent to volunteer — he knew his own limitations when it came to butterflies, and, if he was being honest, didn't fancy adding another long, cold train ride to his day. But even Evans was surprised when Riley himself dropped everything to join Cameron in an unlikely double act: the detective and the entomologist, boarding a train on a dark and frigid afternoon, armed with a search warrant and a long list of missing butterflies. An inspector from the Farnham CID met them at the station, and the three men bundled into a car to make the final journey to Cobbetts.

The warrant stayed in Cameron's pocket as Colin Wyatt, thirty-seven years old, wearing the sun-kissed face of a man still fresh from seven years in Australia, appeared at the door. He didn't ask for any documentation or credentials as he welcomed the three Englishmen in from the cold, and just listened patiently as they got down to business. They told Wyatt they were making enquiries about the loss of some 1,600 butterfly specimens from a string of Australian museums, a search that had already led them to the four crates labelled 'scientific specimens' that had left Sydney the previous December. It was that same trail that had led them to the Royal Victoria Dock, where those crates had arrived in London a week earlier bearing the address of this exact property in Farnham.[20]

For a moment, Wyatt appeared cooperative.

'There are some of the cases,' he told the trio, pointing nonchalantly to a set of boxes sitting idly in the warm study where he had spent that pleasant week rearranging them.[21]

They had some miles on them, but they were without a doubt the same ones that Leslie Mosse-Robinson had seen at 25 Nelson Street in Woollahra, all packed up and ready for their journey a few days later — the same boxes that Pescott, Walkom, and the police in Sydney had tracked with bated breath halfway around the world. And there they were, just sitting in Margaret Wyatt's study, given up with little more than a shrug.

The police took careful note of every word that Wyatt said.

'Altogether there were some 8,000 of them,' he continued in a casual, matter-of-fact tone. Then he added, 'If your stolen specimens are there, you are welcome to them.'[22]

The trio looked over the study, Riley taking in the familiar sight of an entomologists' workspace. When he had first heard the news of the missing specimens, Riley had told Evans that it seemed unlikely that they would be bound for the private collectors' market. For one thing, the demand for exotic butterflies was experiencing a lull, and a quick, quiet sale would be practically impossible. But Riley also had a feeling that Wyatt might prefer to hold on to them as another prized collection for him to 'gloat over'.[23] Sure enough, here they were, in the process of being relocated to a new and well-appointed cabinet.

They continued to ask Wyatt questions, and despite the thousands of Australian butterflies right in front of them, he continued to profess innocence and ignorance. Later, Cameron would claim that this continued for many long, uncomfortable minutes, as Wyatt continued to dance around their questions, 'adamant' that the Australian thefts had nothing to do with him.[24]

Then, all of a sudden, Wyatt's tone shifted. Perhaps he realised that he wasn't standing among a Frenchman's blackthorn trees, with a getaway route just a sprint and a jump away. Nor was he being interrogated by the Carabinieri, where a case full of butterflies might help him wriggle off the hook after an unauthorised border crossing — if anything, the butterflies were now the most incriminating thing about him. Then there was Riley from the museum, one of the United Kingdom's leading entomologists, whom Wyatt hadn't seen in years.

After fifteen minutes, he buckled.

'I don't know what possessed me to take them,' Wyatt said solemnly. 'I was very worried over my domestic affairs at the time and could find relief from my worries only in my hobby. I'll give you every assistance in their return, but it will take some time. I have incorporated some of them in my collection.'[25]

After cautioning Wyatt for the second time, the officers began taking down a formal statement. From the warmth of his mother's country house, Wyatt cast his mind back to the true origins of his new

Australian collection — providing a much different story from the one he had presented in his cheerful letter to Ras Wilson a week earlier.

Wyatt first gave a truncated history of his seven years in Australia as he cut a long, winding, and incriminating path to the country's museums. He told the men how in 1941 he had joined the RAAF, and then from 1944 had worked with the British Central Department of Information. But in Wyatt's telling, it was in January 1946 that things began to fray, as he and his now-estranged wife experienced 'considerable marriage troubles'.

'We parted,' he said simply. 'I was driven to distraction over this matter, so I threw myself into my only hobby, namely, entomology. I have a collection of 40,000 butterflies. I paid frequent visits to the National Museum of Melbourne and the Australian Museum of Sydney.'

Wyatt told the men that he was 'envious' of the rare butterflies on display at each museum, gathered from 'remote parts of Australia where I could never obtain access':

> I'm afraid my state of mind at the time was such that I just didn't care what happened, so I took these butterflies from the collection and in a series of visits placed them in tins which I carried about in each pocket. These tins were cut away at the top end and I just slipped the butterflies in.[26]

He told the men that he could fit between fifty to one hundred normal-sized butterflies in each tin. A quick calculation would have revealed that Wyatt must have carried out these heists over multiple visits to each museum — perhaps even half a dozen each. At the time of Wyatt's questioning, neither Adams and Musgrave in Sydney, nor Tindale and Womersley in Adelaide, had completed their audits, so the museum directors and police in Australia had only given their British counterparts a rough estimate of 1,600 missing specimens. This was the number that the detectives had put to Wyatt, who unsurprisingly quoted their own figure back to them.

'Altogether I took about 1,600 specimens from the Museums,' he told them. 'I can't say how much from each.'

Wyatt said that after completing each quiet raid, his pockets bulging with tins of butterflies, he would spend his evenings happily arranging and classifying the new additions to his collection—a scene that to a veteran entomologist such as Riley must have seemed a strange parody, as if they were a swag of freshly caught specimens from a field trip rather than museum pieces that had already been carefully set, labelled, and catalogued.

'I found this to be the perfect way to keep my mind off my troubles', Wyatt said.

He also noted that, much like George Lyell and Athol Waterhouse, he had mixed the museum specimens in with the butterflies he had legitimately collected during his time in Australia—which he believed totalled 6,000—some through exchange, but 'the majority of which I had caught myself'. He told the men that on 1 December 1946 he resigned from the Department of Information, citing his 'matrimonial difficulties', and made for England.

'I wanted to get home before my wife, who was about to leave by ship,' he said. 'I packed up my whole collection of butterflies including those taken from the Museums and shipped them to this country per SS *Perim*.'

Having walked the two detectives and entomologist through a condensed twelve-month timeline of his disintegrating marriage, the series of thefts that followed, and his abrupt exit from Australia, Wyatt offered a moment of reflection, if not contrition: 'I realise now that I have been incredibly foolish and can only blame my state of mind at the time. I of course am ready to give every assistance to the return of the butterflies.'[27]

'Since I last wrote things have moved a bit,' John Evans wrote to Dick Pescott on 1 February, the day after Cameron and Norman Riley returned to London with Wyatt's signed statement. It had been a long day, and an eighty-mile round trip through the bitter cold—Evans couldn't help but sound a little awed by Riley, who hadn't arrived home until ten-thirty that night. There were still plenty of questions to be answered, and the four cases of specimens remained, for the moment, sitting in the study of Wyatt's mother's house in Farnham. But Cameron, the Farnham inspector, and Riley had managed to coax out as complete a confession as anyone could have hoped for.

Cameron was right to have insisted on Riley joining him, just as his earlier instinct that Wyatt might try to deny the charge had been proved correct. To the detective, it seemed that it was being confronted by the presence of Riley, one of England's pre-eminent entomologists, that had brought Wyatt's initial wall of denial crumbling down. Had the questioning been left only to Cameron and the inspector from Farnham, there was every chance that Wyatt would have stuck to his initial claims of innocence, comfortable in the knowledge that neither officer would have much luck reconciling Lyell's list with the contents of the crates.

But there was, perhaps, another reason why the arrival of Riley—who, for all his virtues, was no one's definition of an intimidating interrogator—had pressured Wyatt to confess so quickly. Wyatt may have blamed the Australian thefts on being temporarily 'driven to distraction', but he and Riley both knew that the older entomologist had something else up his sleeve, something that might have cast the entire Australian affair in a new and alarming light. While it wouldn't become public knowledge for decades, this exchange at Cobbetts wasn't the first time that Norman Riley had to talk to the young Colin Wyatt about a mysterious case of missing butterflies. Nor was it the first time that police officers had quietly attended Wyatt's home address asking questions.

Down in the south-west basement of the Natural History Museum, it was no secret that a cloud of suspicion had swirled over Colin William Fforde Wyatt for years. John Evans knew it too, and when Pescott called him on 24 January, it wasn't just his memories of a single dinner in Hobart that spurred him to action. It was written plainly in a follow-up letter he drafted to Pescott the very next day.

'The man you mention is well known here,' Evans wrote, 'and is debarred entry to the Department of Entomology at this Museum.'[28]

CHAPTER EIGHTEEN

The Dossier

'DO NOT TRUST LANDSCAPE PAINTER,' read the slip of paper unfolded in Athol Waterhouse's still-steady hands.[1] It was 14 January 1942, and while Waterhouse could not yet imagine all the ways that his life would be transformed over the next eighteen months, this cryptic yet urgent message made sure it was off to an ominous start.

It had all begun over two months earlier, when Waterhouse had penned a letter to Brigadier William Harry Evans in London on 4 November 1941. 'I wonder if Riley has ever heard of a Colin Wyatt,' Waterhouse had written, doing his very best to sound casual, as if this was just an ordinary letter between two old friends.[2]

Waterhouse and the brigadier had been corresponding for many years, in a transcontinental friendship forged across long days out in the field and while hunched over specimen drawers in museums in Adelaide, Sydney, and London. Waterhouse had already crossed paths with the brigadier's son, John, at the CSIR in Canberra when, in 1932, the newly retired brigadier and his wife had made a two-month stopover in Australia.[3] The Evanses were on their way to start their new life in London, but would first visit their only son, who, in the thirty-five years his parents had lived in India, could count on one hand the number of times he had stayed under their roof.[4]

But it seems that the brigadier spent as much time with Waterhouse as with his son on the trip. Nearly every day, the pair would meet to study the skippers held at the Australian Museum in Sydney, where Waterhouse and Nancy Adams were in the process of depositing his own collection, and the South Australian Museum, several suburbs away from John's work at the research institute in Adelaide.[5] The brigadier had brought with him many specimens from his own collection, and those two months left Waterhouse practically buzzing with the 'many new facts' that the pair uncovered together.

They had stayed in touch, and when Waterhouse wrote to the brigadier in November 1941, he would have known that his old friend's vantage point in the basement of the Natural History Museum — a nerve centre for British entomology and all the gossip that came with it — meant that if anyone could shed more light on Colin Wyatt, it was him. It had been five months since Waterhouse last wrote publicly about his 'friend' Colin Wyatt, in that glowing article in *The Australian Museum Magazine* recounting their field experiments outside Sydney. But whereas Waterhouse had once been charmed enough by the energetic Englishman to take him out collecting, by November he was harbouring serious doubts:

> He claims to have a wonderful Palearctic collection. I wonder if it is all talk. He is out here just at present. At first I thought that he had some sort of scientific knowledge, but of late I have come to the conclusion that he is only a hoarder of a long series of specimens. He seems to have travelled about Europe a good deal.[6]

He also noted one further detail: 'In addition he is a landscape painter.' Waterhouse might have begun to question Wyatt's scientific bona fides, but even he must have been surprised when the forcefully worded cable arrived from London, signed by no less than Norman Riley himself. Waterhouse studied the cable's wording, noting Riley's careful, coded use of 'landscape painter' rather than Wyatt's name. By the time that Waterhouse had written his letter, it wasn't just the limits of Wyatt's expertise that had given him pause. On one of their collecting trips, Wyatt had mentioned in passing that John Clark at the National

Museum of Victoria had given him a handful of specimens — something that Waterhouse later brought up in one of his letters to George Lyell in Gisborne.[7] Lyell promptly asked Clark about it on his next visit to the dungeons of the National Museum of Victoria, where the temperamental Scotsman was unequivocal: he had never heard of this man Colin Wyatt, and had certainly never handed him any butterflies.

Then there was the day when Waterhouse and Wyatt were out chasing butterflies near Blackheath in the Blue Mountains, and suddenly arrived at a bend in the road. Out of nowhere, Wyatt remarked that they were 'near the new aerodrome'.[8] Two years into World War II, and with both his sons enlisted, Waterhouse knew that this was sensitive information. Whether it was the ease with which Wyatt disclosed it, or the fact that he knew the aerodrome's location at all, Waterhouse was left unsettled.

If these questions had already been playing on Waterhouse's mind, this brief warning from Riley pushed him into action. Riley had concluded his telegram with a short and sharp promise to send a follow-up letter with more information — 'WRITING,' it said simply. But a letter could take weeks or months to arrive from London; in the meantime, Waterhouse called Professor William Dakin, a fellow Australian Museum trustee whose Camouflage Section now counted Wyatt among its camoufleurs. However, when Dakin wasn't to be found in his office, Waterhouse went straight to the army itself, where he laid out his concerns.

Waterhouse was advised to keep Dakin in the dark for the time being. But, at the same time, an anonymous staffer somewhere in Australia's wartime counter-espionage apparatus began typing up a report; over the next week, Waterhouse's tip-off launched a new wave of enquiries into Colin William Fforde Wyatt. When a Captain Newman of the Intelligence Section forwarded the report to the Sydney state branch of the Counter Intelligence Corps on 24 January — describing its origins merely as 'a source known to you' — Waterhouse's complaint became the latest entry in Dossier No. 13956, a growing pile of paperwork with Wyatt's name on the cover. In fact, the Wyatt file had been running for several years: its first entry had been written within days of him stepping off the SS *Mariposa* in 1939.

***

Mary Wyatt had been in Sydney for less than a week when she found two men waiting at the front door of her and Colin's new apartment in Potts Point. The Wyatts' flat in the Pomeroy complex on Macleay Street was just temporary, a pitstop until they found something a little more permanent. But, with its harbourside setting and stylish art-deco buildings sprouting up all around it, there were worse places to get a taste of modern, cosmopolitan Sydney. By the end of the month they would be settled in Woollahra, ready for the journalist and photographer from *The Sydney Morning Herald.* But as Mary opened the door on 9 September 1939, it seemed that the *Herald* would be thoroughly scooped by two constables from the Paddington police station, who had arrived with questions of their own for the Wyatts.

Mary was home alone that day, with Colin having landed his new job as a censor just days after the *Mariposa*'s arrival. When the constables asked to see their papers, she helpfully obliged, and watched on as the men flicked through the pages of Colin's well-travelled passport. The constables noted his age (thirty), his place of birth (London), and his occupation ('artist and painter'). More to the point, they also noted that his passport entitled Wyatt to visit all the countries of Europe, including French Morocco, the Spanish territories, and the Union of Soviet Socialist Republics — and clearly he had made good use of those privileges. Mary told the officers that she too had been born in London, that her father held a commissioned rank in the English army, and that she and her husband wouldn't be staying at the apartment for long. It was still unclear just where in Sydney they would end up, but she promised to lodge their new address with the bank as soon as they were settled.

'They have no children and, so far as can be ascertained, Wyatt is not a member of any Alien Club in Sydney nor has he any alien associates,' the constables' report noted.[9]

This would have been news to the vast international network of entomologists, athletes, mountaineers, and artists that Wyatt had associated with over the past decade. Equally, it seemed that no one in Australia had heard of or read the newspaper clippings of Wyatt's 1936 tour of New Zealand, in which he had spoken glowingly of how 'German people are kindness itself to visiting sportsmen'.[10]

'The treatment I received there seems so much to clash with what I read in the papers about the spirit of Germany,' Wyatt told a group of mountaineers at Taranaki in October 1936. 'I know of no kinder and more charitable people. Bad sportsmanship is just not in them.'[11]

When the constables' report was submitted, they concluded that, 'it is considered from a Police point of view that no further action is necessary'. A house call to check on the status of a newly arrived, well-travelled couple who happened to have landed on day one of a new world war wasn't exactly unusual. But it would be the first of many instances in which the Wyatt name was flagged by watchful authorities.

In June 1941, his name caught the attention of army security when a letter was intercepted from a Melbourne clerk named Arthur to his son, a stamp-collecting twenty-one-year-old also named Arthur. The younger Arthur had enlisted a year earlier, and while the young private was off serving in New Guinea, his father appeared to have crossed paths with Wyatt's mother, Margaret. She left such a strong impression that the elder Arthur had to recount it at length.

'The other P.G. (paying guest) is a Mrs. Wyatt who has lived almost entirely in Germany and Switzerland, and I strongly suspect has horribly pro-German ideas,' he wrote, citing as evidence the time she exclaimed, 'Oh, I was a Pacifist before the War.'

> She has one only son who is (she says) so very valuable he can't possibly serve in the Army, the Navy or the Air Force. So, when War was certain — he packed himself and his wife and every penny he possessed off to Australia where he bought a farm. He is a great linguist, and couldn't waste his talents on poor old England. He is broadcasting I understand from the B.B.C. in Sydney on Ski-ing in Norway and Sweden. It makes my blood boil every time she gets a letter from him saying how gay they are. They've plenty of money too …[12]

Arthur Sr could not know that, within less than a year, the very son he was writing to would be killed in transit between Rabaul and Port

Moresby, but given his outraged response to Mrs Wyatt's comments, he must have dreaded the possibility. A major in Southern Command security forwarded the letter for the army's files in case any 'any action [was] deemed necessary'.

A week later, another memo reported that, despite the Australian Broadcasting Commission having been granted official clearance to hire Wyatt in 1940, a radio station manager from Melbourne named Basil Kirke had been officially interviewed about Wyatt's character. Kirke had met Wyatt on his first Australian trip years earlier, and told the interviewing officer that he did not consider Wyatt to be 'the type of person who would be guilty of any disloyal or subversive sections'.

Ordinarily, this might seem a good thing, but Kirke clarified that, 'even if WYATT were given the most confidential and secret information under any circumstances that would permit him to use it against the country's war effort, he would have neither the grit nor the brains to do so'. The memo also noted that another ABC manager named Arthur Dibley seconded Kirke's unflattering opinion.[13] This wasn't the first time that Wyatt had left his ABC colleagues bemused; back in 1937, his eight-week radio tour brought reviews as polarised as his art career did. One of the kinder reviews actually came from Kirke himself, who reported that Wyatt 'offer[ed] little variety, but as a Yodeller and Accordeon player, is decidedly a feature'.[14] From Tasmania, however, the station manager reported to the ABC's Federal Controller of Music that while 'Mr Wyatt did all in his power to put the program over', he failed to resonate with listeners and that 'the season must generally be considered unsuccessful'.[15] It was worse in Perth, where the station manager dubbed him a failure.

'I thought him a very poor yodeller and his presentations particularly weak,' the note read.[16]

Wyatt failed to impress in Brisbane either, where it seemed that he had better places to be: 'Mr Wyatt appeared rather indifferent, and on one occasion arrived at the studio, barely in time to be put on the air.'[17]

These reports might have limited his career as a travelling folksinger, but, as neither uninspiring yodelling nor a lack of 'brains' or 'grit' were actionable risks for the Australian security services, the reports were filed away for months until Riley's warning prompted the authorities to take notice once more. On 24 January, a week after Waterhouse raised his suspicions, a new report was compiled that noted with concern Wyatt's 'flat [that] overlooks the harbour', the 'seven languages' he spoke, and the curious comment that his 'own nationality is unknown, apparently his appearance is that of a "red-haired Irishman"'. It also revealed that the authorities were paying close attention to the Wyatts' appearances in the social pages of Sydney's newspapers: 'Mr and Mrs WYATT seem to have established themselves in "society," that is, their names and photographs appear in the papers now and then.'

In a detail that might have delighted the likes of the Contemporary Art Society, the dossier also captures officials trying to make sense of Wyatt's artistic career in terms that betrayed a casual disdain for the movement: 'As an artist he is not much good; described as "pathetic" but this may mean very modern.'[18]

The same day, an order was given by the Intelligence Section for a month-long period of 'scrutiny' — opening and reading the Wyatts' local and overseas mail — to begin at once, citing Wyatt's 'considerable time in and around Central Europe', along with the possibility that he was 'engaged in subversive behaviours'.[19]

Despite the surveillance order, for months the only new addition to Dossier No. 13956 came from an anonymous informant who, in February, reported having met the Wyatts back in November 1939. They had met through an English acquaintance, a woman who was supposedly a cousin of Colin's; she initially had no recollection of the man she shared a surname with, before later conceding they must have met as children. In the tip-off, the informant reported that, among the general chatter about the war and English skiing, Mary revealed that her husband 'was on some important confidential work which she could not disclose and which took him off at all hours'. It was a revelation that perhaps says more about the stress placed upon Colin and Mary's marriage than the threat either posed to national security.

Then, one day in early June, word reached the Intelligence Section that Waterhouse had finally received the letter from Norman Riley that he had been waiting for. Written back on 12 January 1942, before Riley had sent his alarming cable, the single-page letter was far more colourful than anything compiled in the dossier to date.

'Evans has just shown me your letter of 4th November and particularly called attention to the paragraph about Colin Wyatt,' Riley wrote. 'This man has collector's mania and is not to be trusted with specimens.'[20]

In April 1930, nearly seventeen years before Alec Burns made his 'fluke' find in the dungeons of the National Museum of Victoria, Norman Riley had made a discovery of his own while checking the *Parnassius* collection at the Natural History Museum. According to Riley's contemporaneous report, the cabinets that housed the genus *Parnassius* sat just a few metres from his workbench, in full view of the spot where Riley spent nearly every hour of the working day. He was sure that no one had opened the drawers and started sifting through the rare butterflies almost right under his nose — and he certainly hadn't seen anyone linger long to extract over 250 of them.[21]

Narrowing the window of opportunity was easy; Riley knew that many of the missing specimens, which included thirty-one types or co-types, had only been added to the drawers in the first half of March 1930, shortly before his last thorough inspection. As far as he knew, only two outsiders with an interest in *Parnassius* had visited the collections that month. The first was a colonel who Riley was sure had only accessed the *Parnassius* under his supervision. The other was Colin Wyatt, the young Cambridge scholar and champion skier who Riley had personally shown around on Thursday 20 March.

Wyatt had had a bruising start to the year. After the highs of his wins at St Moritz in December, by January his triumphant season had come crashing down when a botched landing saw him tumble down the run in pain, with limbs and skis splayed in every direction — to spectators, it looked like one of the skis had almost taken his eye out.[22] Back home in England, with his vision mercifully intact, Wyatt called again at the museum on 22 and 29 March, this time examining *Parnassius* without the assistance of Riley or his colleague, and visited once more on the afternoon of Saturday 12 April.

Riley immediately reported the missing butterflies to the police, and two days later, on 19 April, he gave a detailed account of what was lost. Then, on 24 April, Riley received a curious visit from a retired officer — not Brigadier William Harry Evans, but a brigadier-general named Bertram Hewett Hunter Cooke. Cooke introduced himself as a personal acquaintance of both the young Colin Wyatt and his ageing father, James, and after the pair had words, Riley sent Cooke a letter that, with the permission of the chief inspector of the Metropolitan Police, outlined the unpleasant situation.

Two days later, on the morning of Saturday 26 April, a twenty-one-year-old man with strawberry-blond hair walked unannounced into the museum to visit Riley. It was Colin Wyatt himself, and as he and Riley discussed the *Parnassius* mystery, he offered to do whatever he could to help locate the missing butterflies. According to Riley's contemporaneous notes, Wyatt expressed his 'great regret' at the museum's plight, while also volunteering some information: he had seen a handful of other people during his visits to the collections who he thought might be involved. When Riley was able to swiftly eliminate on the spot each name that Wyatt gave, an unspoken implication hung in the air, growing bigger with every evasive comment, every attempt at helpfulness, until the elephant in the room was big as anything in the galleries upstairs.

'[I] pointed out to him the awkwardness of his position,' Riley would later recall.[23]

When Wyatt floated another friendly offer to make enquiries with other entomologists who he knew took an interest in *Parnassius*, Riley gently put his foot down. He dropped a thinly veiled ultimatum, telling Wyatt that, personally, he only cared about the recovery of the specimens, and should Wyatt or anyone else be able to arrange their safe return, the museum would in all likelihood drop any further action. It was at this point that Wyatt reportedly changed tack, telling Riley that he did, in fact, have possession of 'certain specimens' of the same species that had disappeared from the museum — specimens that Wyatt had by some coincidence been trying to sell. Riley called his bluff, explaining that, at any rate, all foreign museums and dealers had been tipped off to the theft and provided with descriptions of the missing specimens.

Whoever had the missing *Parnassius* specimens would find it near-impossible to move them.

It was an uncomfortable, polite, and perhaps unfailingly English confrontation, and Wyatt took his leave. Then, without any further discussion, something unexpected happened: the very next afternoon, on Sunday 27 April, someone walked into the main hall of the Natural History Museum and left a mysterious delivery with the attendant on duty — a cache of 279 *Parnassius* specimens. As Riley would later report, the butterflies were returned by 'a visitor who has not been identified'.

'I was not able to prove him the culprit [but] the fact that they came back after a long and very pointed discussion with him convinced me that he had them,' Riley concluded years later in his letter to Athol Waterhouse.[24]

In the letter, Riley explained that the *Parnassius* episode was one of several 'little incidents of a like nature' that had made him wary of the young Colin Wyatt. Francis Hemming, another respected amateur lepidopterist and passionate taxonomist, had also told Riley about an encounter with Wyatt at Mount Canigó in the Pyrenees, where he listened to the young man's long and apparently tall stories about catching the 'most remarkable species' in the area — species that Hemming 'knew did not and could not occur there'.

'It is a great pity because he is quite a pleasant fellow to talk to, and I think keen on European butterflies,' Riley told Waterhouse, 'but he is quite unreliable.'[25]

As Waterhouse read the letter, with its raft of allegations that were surely beyond anything he'd expected, he made what would later prove to be a fateful decision: he would keep it to himself. Perhaps, in a mix of naivety, secrecy, and hubris, he decided that he was the best person to keep a close eye on the Wyatt situation. Or maybe the memory of Robin Tillyard's tragic unravelling had left Waterhouse sensitive to the unforeseen consequences of an eccentric fellow collector being publicly brought down. One thing was clear: after the initial flurry of activity that followed his report to the army of Riley's cable to him in January 1942, Waterhouse's caution left Australian authorities at a loose end.

'Dr Waterhouse has the letter from the Chief Entomologist but it is understood that he does not wish to make a copy of it as it is libellous, etc., and he does not like the idea of a copy being in circulation,' wrote an unnamed captain from the Security Service in a 2 July memo.

The captain surmised from Waterhouse's account that the Riley letter contained limited actionable information, and without the original to refer to, he even passed on the incorrect observation that Riley 'did not suggest whether Collector's Mania or another motive was behind the suspected theft'. Nevertheless, the captain remained concerned:

> The serious aspect of the situation is that WYATT has been employed by the Camouflage Section of the Department of the Interior for some months past and that the nature of the particular work which he is doing give him complete access to matters than which there are none more highly confidential.
>
> During the past few months has visited areas and seen things the nature of which, if improperly disclosed, could lead to disastrous consequences.
>
> It is not suggested that the alleged incident at the British Museum brands WYATT as a Fifth Columnist, but it will be recalled that other matters, disclosed in previous submissions, go to show that he is an individual whom one cannot state unequivocally to be free of reasonable suspicion and suitable to be engaged upon some of the most highly confidential work in the country.
>
> The informant feels that this is a matter demanding urgent and searching inquiry.[26]

Another entry was added to the Wyatt dossier in August 1942, when the officers charged with reading his post highlighted four sentences in a 28 July letter sent from his home in Woollahra to his mother, Margaret. 'MEMBER OF SECURITY FORCES DISCLOSES INFORMATION,' read the note, before quoting Wyatt's account of catching a sleeper train to northern Australia 'for a job on an aerodrome', and then of his 'glorious flight' taking aerial photographs over Sydney Harbour, Botany Bay, and the Blue Mountains.[27]

One final entry arrived from another anonymous informant on 31

January 1943, who noted in a slightly paranoid tone that Wyatt claimed to be a painter, but hadn't painted any new pictures since arriving in Australia. Instead, the informant claimed, Wyatt began working at the censor's department, and was known to 'entertain quite a number of foreigners at rather hilarious cocktail parties'.[28] The report raised the familiar questions, 'Is he really an ENGLISHMAN?' and 'Where do his apparently reasonably large financial resources originate?' These were, ultimately, the wrong questions, and they provoked no further action — after all, the Paddington constables had sighted his passport back in September 1939, and the only new bombshells were that Wyatt had seemed too busy to paint, but could throw a hell of a party.

In the absence of more compelling evidence from Riley or Waterhouse, the official consensus appeared to be that even if Wyatt was a little eccentric, prone to self-aggrandising indiscretions, and subject to unverifiable hearsay from far-off entomologists, the risk he posed to Australia's national security was limited. Ironically, while staff at the National Museum of Victoria were busy evacuating its rarest specimens to gaols and courthouses to protect them from 'enemy sympathisers', Australia's shadowy security network was closing the book on Colin Wyatt and Dossier No. 13956, and the known threat to museum collections it contained, with a collective shrug.

Waterhouse, meanwhile, would soon be in no position to reconsider his initial discretion. In the middle of June 1943, he suffered the stroke that would leave him bedridden, unable to write, walk, or even pin butterflies, and would eventually force him and Beatrice to leave their beloved gardens at Killara. The famous Athol Waterhouse could no longer be a constant, vigilant presence at the Australian Museum, or the prolific pen pal who maintained networks of friendships with collectors around Australia and the world.

As far as the wider entomological community knew, in Waterhouse's absence and without any word to the contrary, Colin Wyatt still had the unwavering support of Australia's greatest living lepidopterist. After all, he had publicly and repeatedly vouched for his onetime friend in the pages of *The Australian Museum Magazine*. Riley's letter had left Waterhouse harbouring no illusions about Wyatt's character, but for years afterwards the Waterhouse name would continue to open doors and collection drawers for the charming Englishman. It would see him invited out to dinner with John and Faith Evans in Hobart, score him an introduction to Dick Pescott's office at the National Museum of Victoria, and gain a warm welcome at the Australian Museum in Sydney, whose trusting staff believed Wyatt's story about working on a new edition of his old collecting partner's out-of-print book. Wyatt had even presented a seemingly legitimate letter of introduction from Waterhouse himself.

All the while, filed somewhere among Waterhouse's papers, the final words of Riley's January warning lingered on the page with prophetic weight: 'I should encourage him in his landscape painting and hope he does not develop an interest in the Australian butterflies.'[29]

CHAPTER NINETEEN

The Evidence

'When the Scotland Yard men came I told them to have a good look through my collection,' Colin Wyatt said from a hotel in Switzerland. He had left England on 12 February, and as he spoke over the phone to a reporter from the *Daily Mail,* he innocently explained how, a fortnight earlier, he had obligingly shown New Scotland Yard his butterflies, some 2,000 of which were later packed up and taken back to London, as evidence, with his full cooperation. Around a sixth of his Australian collection, he told the reporter, were obtained through exchanges with other collectors, much like philatelists traded postage stamps.

'I think some of the butterflies have been through more than one hand,' he added. 'It's possible some of these mightn't have been obtained lawfully — you can never tell.'

Having all but implicated every other Australian collector he had ever crossed paths or exchanged specimens with, Wyatt continued to downplay his own connection to the sensational theft that was about to hit newspapers from Melbourne to London.

'Police told me their visit was quite definitely a pure formality,' he added, in a final flourish that would be printed unchallenged by the *Daily Mail* on 17 February 1947, and then republished and syndicated by dozens of newspapers around the world.[1] That may have been the official line when Detective Sergeant Cameron, Inspector Hall, and Norman

Riley first introduced themselves on that afternoon in Farnham, but the tenor of the discussion had undeniably shifted by the time they left with Wyatt's signed statement — his confession — in their hands. He was not a witness, but the prime suspect. The *only* suspect.

In London, John Evans could scarcely comprehend what he was reading. Of course, that wasn't just the *Daily Mail*'s fault; he could hardly see anything from his desk in the New Spirit Building, where continuing power shortages had driven museum administrators to ban the use of electric lights for all but a few daylight hours.[2] By mid-morning, the sky outside had grown so dark that Evans and his colleagues had to toil in a muddy twilight. It was below freezing too — the museum's central heating had been turned off since its boilers ran out of coal, leaving Evans looking like he was dressed for the outdoors all swaddled up in his greatcoat. He had spent the morning doing his best in the cold and dark to put the final touches on a five-page document he hoped might seal the case against Colin Wyatt, no matter what the papers were printing. At lunchtime, Evans stepped out into the London chill to airmail a copy of this new dossier to Dick Pescott in Melbourne. In the letter accompanying the report, he made a note to Pescott that 'all the papers are full of it today'.[3]

In Melbourne, Pescott was equally incredulous. There was, of course, the still-fresh revelation of Riley's lost 1942 warning. Later in February 1947, Pescott told Riley that, 'the thefts came as a big shock to us all over here, because none of us in Melbourne or Adelaide had received any warnings concerning the man in question'.[4] Even George Lyell, who must have been privy to some of Waterhouse's suspicions back in 1941, had declined to share them when Burns had told him about his plans to travel to the Blue Mountains with Wyatt, Charles Oke, and Leslie Mosse-Robinson. All Lyell had offered was a cryptic remark about Wyatt being 'enterprising to say the least of it'.[5]

Then there was the media coverage. Having managed to keep the growing butterfly crisis out of the papers for over a month, it was with a sense of inevitability that Pescott admitted to Evans that, 'the matter has at long last got into the hands of the Press, and the papers here are running pretty hot at the present time'.[6] It was a Melbourne-based correspondent for *The Times* who had initially broken the story, and Pescott would later be driven to ask Sir Keith Murdoch — a trustee of the Public Library and National Gallery who was also one of Australia's most powerful press barons — to find out how the story had leaked to the Australian and British media. But wherever *The Times* and the *Daily Mail* had first gotten wind of the story, the local papers had run with it, and as Pescott surveyed the headlines coming in from around Australia, it was already being embellished in ways he could only describe as 'an awful lot of rubbish'.

'Butterfly Chase Traverses World,' screamed the previous day's *Courier-Mail* in Brisbane, with a page-turning tale of how 'Detectives chased 3,000 stolen butterflies from Australian and New Zealand collections through all States, New Zealand, and America, until they "netted" them in England'.

'The detectives had no experience in chasing butterflies so they began by making enquiries from museums, private collectors and entomologists in Victoria,' read the report. 'They then extended their butterfly hunt to all States to New Zealand, and finally to England.'[7]

This seemed a dramatic way to describe an investigation that had, for the most part, consisted of Burns and Pescott writing letters and making phone calls to their museum colleagues. Some papers, such as *The Newcastle Sun*, had even reprinted quotes from Wyatt's surprised mother, Margaret, who had told the *Daily Mail* that, 'Colin went to Switzerland because he was feeling run down.'

'His father was an expert entomologist,' she said, 'I'm sure Colin will be glad to do all he can to help police.'[8]

Meanwhile, in Broken Hill, the *Barrier Daily Truth* spun a ripping yarn about 'The Long Arm of Scotland Yard' and the 'Amazing Case of Theft of Rare Butterflies'.[9]

'Scotland Yard, after months of inquiry, thus believes it has solved one of its strangest cases,' read the breathless report, which incorrectly claimed that the chase had begun a year earlier in 1946, when 'two Australian detectives, J Ryan and P Walsh, investigated and discovered that three thousand butterflies were missing, many of them unique.'

This was a flattering portrayal of Russell Street's contribution to date — at that moment, DS Cameron and his colleagues at New Scotland Yard were, in fact, growing increasingly frustrated that their counterparts in Melbourne had yet to send them a full report. But besides Wyatt's own interview, perhaps the most glaring example of how stretched the newspapers' facts had grown was the remark that detectives were 'puzzled because the collections were kept in locked cabinets and were almost constantly under observation by museum attendants'.[10]

Anyone with any real knowledge of the case, or of Australia's museums, knew that this was a very generous assessment of the security measures in place across Melbourne, Adelaide, and Sydney. Even discounting the missed warning from Riley five years earlier, the serial theft was a tragicomedy of malfunctioning alarms, broken doors, skeleton staffing, and shallow auditing of vast collections. As the directors and trustees across all three museums debated how best to respond to the missing butterflies, the inevitable prospect of a 'good deal of undesirable publicity as to the possibility of thefts from museums' loomed large in their thinking.[11]

Then there was the stickier, more intractable issue: the warm welcomes that Wyatt had received in Melbourne and Sydney — and, perhaps, the low profile he was able keep in Adelaide — were part of a longstanding convention of open access and collegial reciprocity that was baked into the museum system. On any given day, most museums saw a variety of amateur collectors, trustees, and honorary scientists come and go, taking and leaving specimens, often based on handshakes and informal agreements with select members of staff. Even Waterhouse had literally been handed the keys to the Natural History Museum's entire entomology collection on his 1936 visit. The bigger and more brazen Wyatt's thefts appeared, the more glaring and systemic the failures of the museums became.

The Australian Broadcasting Commission, meanwhile, faced its own embarrassing situation, with its *Country Hour* program replaying a talk recorded by Wyatt before his return to England entitled 'Butterfly Immigrants Overrun Nation'.

'There has been a lot of talk lately about immigration, how Australia needs immigrants, and what type of immigrants she needs,' Wyatt told listeners in late January, just days after Pescott began sounding the alarm. 'But probably very few people realise that since 1939, when they first landed in Melbourne, we are rapidly being overrun by hordes of most unwanted newcomers.'[12]

Wyatt was, of course, using a classic bait-and-switch to jokingly frame the arrival of the cabbage white in the xenophobic rhetoric that Australia, with its 'White Australia Policy' still in effect, knew all too well. Just a few weeks later, those words gained an unexpected new meaning.

Even in Adelaide, where it seemed Wyatt had never personally presented himself, his name still rang bells. In February, Herbert Hale conferred with sixty-four-year-old Sir Douglas Mawson. The famed explorer's Antarctic days were behind him, but he remained a trustee on the board of the South Australian Museum while also serving as its honorary curator of geology. Mawson couldn't have known that Wyatt had once bunkered down in his old mountain hut near Kosciuszko, but he had somehow heard about Wyatt's time in New Guinea as a camoufleur. Mawson also told Hale that his son-in-law, a Welsh zoologist based in Sydney, had reported that, 'Wyatt and his friends when in Sydney were busy making insect boxes for collections of butterflies.'[13] Another acquaintance had also crossed paths with Wyatt in the Pacific, where they saw him 'busily engaged in collecting butterflies', before later recognising him in the January issue of *Pix* magazine. Once again, Colin Wyatt seemed to have been on everyone's radar without ever drawing suspicion.

While none of the museums provided substantive detail to the newspapers, Pescott did, at least, provide a brief comment to Murdoch's *Sun News-Pictorial,* and allow a photographer to visit the National Museum of Victoria to take a shot of a young woman smiling alongside the gap-filled drawer of birdwings that Burns had identified in January. As the reporters tried to make sense of this strange case, Pescott told them it was difficult to place a monetary value on the butterflies, but gave a ballpark figure of £1,000.[14] He wasn't the only one who would struggle to convey the scale of Wyatt's transgressions.

***

The detectives at New Scotland Yard weren't happy about the press coverage either. DS Cameron arrived at the New Spirit Building shortly after Evans returned from his lunchtime mail run, and however confident he might have seemed after leaving Farnham on 31 January, Cameron appeared more apprehensive every time Evans saw him. Cameron had once seen no problem with Evans immediately writing to Pescott, Walkom, and Hale to break the news about Wyatt's signed statement, but he now warned him against discussing the 'confession' at all in his cables to Australia. Evans knew that the peculiarities of English law might produce some snags, but Cameron worried that, despite Wyatt having admitted to the theft, the signed piece of paper might not be enough evidence for the Crown to hang a prosecution on.

'I think it is because the police have to be careful in these matters in case in court they are accused with forcing confessions from people,' Evans told Pescott on 10 February.[15]

Evans had initially assumed that the butterflies themselves would provide plenty of physical evidence. On the morning of 13 February, with intense trepidation, the recovered boxes were opened at the Natural History Museum in front of Evans, his father, and a handful of additional museum staff to bear witness. Thanks to the snow-covered roads, it had taken another fortnight for Cameron to make the drive back to Farnham, by which time Wyatt himself, in another gesture of cooperation, had voluntarily set aside the specimens of dubious origin. In South Kensington, an initial count identified 2,700 specimens—far more than the estimated 1,600 Wyatt had admitted to taking, but a few hundred shy of the numbers that had eventually trickled in from Melbourne, Sydney, and Adelaide. Most of the specimens still had some form of labelling, but as Cameron handed them over to Evans, he noted that Wyatt appeared to have made changes.

Riley, Evans, and his father tried to make sense of the recovered butterflies, with Riley himself combing through *Papilionidae* and *Pieridae* genuses while the brigadier naturally took care of the skippers. But they soon grasped the scale of the task in front of them: all the red 'type' labels seemed to have been removed, and reconciling the contents of the boxes with the lists of names and numbers sent over from Melbourne, Sydney, and Adelaide wasn't so simple.

'The results are not very satisfying, for although there is not the slightest doubt that the material is stolen material, an exact correspondence between specimens and lists seems almost impossible to achieve,' Riley later explained to Walkom in Sydney. 'In some cases we have too many specimens, in others too few, and many of the labels seem to have been replaced by Wyatt's own handwritten and very poor labels.'[16]

John Evans even found a handful of specimens with labels from the Queensland Museum, despite its recently appointed director, George Mack — the ornithologist who had quit the National Museum of Victoria in outrage over Pescott's appointment — confirming that their collections appeared intact.

'It may be that Queensland was considered small fry compared with the southern capitals,' Mack told Walkom on 5 February.[17]

It would take the brigadier weeks to finish sorting through the recovered specimens, and in the meantime his son tried to find a solution to what Riley, Cameron, and all interested parties around the world agreed was the biggest legal issue: proving larceny. In the days before Wyatt's interview with the *Daily Mail* hit the newsstands, Evans had typed up a summary of their work to date in a new dossier of evidence against Wyatt, something that might hopefully make the case stick — even if they couldn't rely on the confession:

> I, John William Evans of Mill Field, Mill Lane, Chalfont, St Giles, am by profession an Applied Entomologist and employed by the Imperial Institute of Entomology. Between 1926 and 1944 I lived in Australia. I am on terms of friendship with the Directors of the Australian Museum, Sydney, the National Museum, Melbourne, and the South Australian Museum, Adelaide. I have visited and worked at all three Museums on several occasions. Although I am an Entomologist I have but little knowledge of butterflies, do not collect them and have no special interest in them. I have met Mr C Wyatt on one occasion when he called on me with a letter of introduction when I was living at Hobart, Tasmania.[18]

Over five pages, Evans rehashed the timeline of discovery and the international investigation that followed, while making a valiant effort to distil the basic tenets of entomology and taxonomy in terms that police officers, prosecutors, and judges alike might understand. More to the point, Evans sought to explain how the labels of data affixed to every pin, of every specimen, provided scientists with 'the name of the collector, the locality where the insect as caught, and the date it was caught'. This, Evans explained, could form a body of circumstantial evidence triangulated around Colin Wyatt; if each label contained an alibi for that specimen, the boxes that he now dubbed the 'Wyatt Collection' held hundreds if not thousands of opportunities to expose theft and fraud.

'Butterflies are not universally distributed; each kind has a certain range,' he wrote. 'Thus one sort may occur only on a remote island and another on top of a single mountain. A butterfly which bears a label showing it has come from a remote locality may not depend solely on the label to prove its place of origin as if it has a restricted distribution this will be well known to specialists.'[19]

To illustrate his point, Evans offered a hypothetical example of how prosecutors might catch Wyatt in a lie:

> This is a moth. On the label is written Dover, 12/35, Tasmania, J.W. Evans. If asked to prove that the moth is mine I could bring evidence to show that I was at Dover in December, 1935. If I had stolen it, but had really been to Dover, though was there in April and not December, anyone who knew about this insect would realise I was lying, as the moth only flies in December.[20]

When Evans hit the limits of his own knowledge of lepidoptera, he had something else up his sleeve: if these specimens were postcards to the past, he had spent years of his life developing the deep personal connections with the places and people of Australian entomology to decode them. He drew up a list of ten examples, beginning with a specimen of skipper collected in 1932 by Athol Waterhouse and his own father, 'the world authority' on the genus:

> In April 1932, Dr Waterhouse visited Adelaide for the purpose of studying, together with my father the Lower collection of butterflies at the South Australian Museum. While they were in South Australia they drove down to Port Noarlunga, which is about 30 miles south of Adelaide, to search for a rare skipper which they had reason to believe occurred there and which was to be found only in April. They caught several. My father is satisfied that the butterfly bearing the above label in the Wyatt collection must belong either to the Australian Museum or the South Australian Museum.[21]

He cited another example of a green birdwing, *Papilio priamus*, that had also been collected by Waterhouse, who, Evans explained, 'has been an invalid for several years, [and] long ago presented all his collection to this Museum.' Another specimen collected in Wyndham, Western Australia, in 1931 had been netted by an Australian collector named NJ Willings, whom Evans knew well — he also knew that Willings had died several years earlier.

Evans continued to rattle off names of former CSIR colleagues and deceased Australian dealers until he came to perhaps his most poignant example. It was an Australian blue — the precise species had yet to be determined, but its label was intact enough to make its provenance clear. It had been caught on Cradle Mountain in Tasmania, on 17 January 1917. This was long before Evans arrived in Australia, but the name on the label was one that he knew all too well.

'The late Dr R.J. Tillyard was my Father-in-law,' Evans wrote. 'He was living in Sydney in 1917 so that this specimen presumably comes from the Australian Museum.'

Dr Robin Tillyard, Evans's late mentor and the flawed patriarch who had dragged him halfway around the world searching for proof of life after death had given his protégé and son-in-law one last gift from beyond the grave.

These ten examples were merely the tip of the iceberg; as the full lists were compiled, any keen-eyed entomologist could find plenty of famous names and personal connections. There was *Papilio macleayanus*, a swallowtail named for the late colonial secretary Alexander Macleay;

Hesperilla crypsargyra hopsoni, the skipper Waterhouse had named after Johnny Hopson in 1927; *Delias ennia tindali*, named after Tindale at the South Australian Museum; and even *Papilio aegus beatrix*, named by Waterhouse in 1908 in an apparent tribute to his beloved wife, Beatrice.[22]

In his concluding remarks, Evans tried to drive home how much trouble this 'deliberate theft' had inflicted upon Australia's national collections; since its discovery, the case had wasted the time and money of people and institutions all around the world, left some specimens physically damaged, and would inevitably leave more in even worse shape by the time they had been sorted and returned to their rightful homes. Then there was the question of the scientific integrity of specimens whose labels had been removed or altered, and 'are as a result of this action, either rendered worthless, or almost so, by this act of deliberate vandalism'. He concluded:

> In the eyes of the general public the theft of butterflies may seem to be a trivial matter, not compared with say the theft of postage stamps which have a great commercial value and since they belong to national museums they are public property. Their alleged theft by a visitor to Australia from this country, who was received there as a serious student, was a most despicable action.[23]

It was a strong note to finish on, and after sending the pages to Pescott, he then spent two-and-a-half hours going over the statement with Cameron. Evans thought the labels would be enough to 'clinch the matter', but the detective still seemed unconvinced. As he explained, even if the labels identified them as being sourced from a museum, Wyatt could always insist that he had bought them from a dealer whose name he had forgotten.

'That would end that line of attack, as it's up to the police to show he is guilty and *not* up to him to prove his innocence,' Evans wrote in another letter to Pescott later that day, pressing the pen and paper against his knees as he thawed his feet over the fireplace at home:

> It's all becoming surprisingly complex. Part of the worry is because he is apparently wealthy and could bring a leading counsel to defend him, who would tear to pieces our evidence. In fact all the evidence I or anyone else could give would be secondhand evidence (that is hearsay). I could only say 'I have been told these butterflies have been stolen', I couldn't say I *know* how they have been stolen, or I would be caught up at once, as they could ask if I had ever seen them in our Aust. Museum, and if I said yes, then how did I know these were the identical specimens, etc.[24]

Evans had done his best to make the case that, in the museum world, there were few kinds of evidence more sacrosanct than specimen labels, and that, despite Wyatt's efforts to cover his tracks, those labels still held more than enough information to incriminate him. But, as Evans handed over his five-page brief, there was little more that he or the scientific community could do. It would be up to the British justice system to decide what came next.

CHAPTER TWENTY

The Plea

The wood-panelled walls of the West Ham Magistrates Court bore witness to almost every shade of human conflict over its eight decades of administering justice. There was the 'Forest-Gate murders' in 1919, when an ex-serviceman confessed to killing his aunt, her husband, and their two young daughters with an axe; a string of medical experts claimed the man suffered epilepsy and trauma from having been captured and tortured during the war, but he was sentenced to death by the jury. The winter of 1931 saw a twenty-eight-year-old piano-maker front the court on what was meant to be his wedding day, accused of stealing a cabinet filled with cash — not butterflies — from a pair of blind brothers.[1] One of the brothers had identified the cabinet for police by touch, and the piano-maker was sent to prison instead of to his honeymoon. Decades later, a twenty-two-year-old labourer was luckier when he attended court immediately after his wedding to enter a guilty plea for assault — feeling merciful, the presiding magistrate, AA Pereira, commuted his prison sentence to a fine as a wedding present.

Then there was the summer of 1965, when a dozen police officers formed a cordon around the courthouse's yellow-brick facade as hundreds of young girls jostled for a glimpse of a twenty-one-year-old Mick Jagger and his fellow Rolling Stones Bill Wyman and Brian Jones.[2] Inside, sixty lucky teenagers listened from the gallery as the trio were accused of 'insulting behaviour which might have caused a breach of the peace'—the rock stars had been caught relieving themselves on the wall of a service station that had refused them use of its lavatory after hours. When the hearing concluded, the police held back the crowds as the Stones slipped out into a chauffeur-driven Daimler, each of them £5 poorer but free to promote their new single, 'Satisfaction', released in England a month later.

Few cases could match the fanfare of 200 Stones fans, but the morning of 21 May 1947 came close, as newspaper reporters and photographers descended on the footpath outside for a case unlike anything heard at West Ham before or after. Inside the crowded public gallery sat John Evans, the brigadier, Norman Riley, and DS Cameron, and it was already shaping up to be a long day.

Evans had risen early at 5.45 that morning to make his usual trek from Chalfont St Giles to South Kensington before 9.00 am—his journey made a little easier since that brutal winter had finally given way to spring.[3] All packed up and ready in the main hall of the Natural History Museum was a cross-section of the so-called 'Wyatt Collection', carefully sorted into glass-topped museum boxes by the brigadier, ready for their big day in court. A large police car arrived soon after, along with Cameron and a detective from Farnham, who helped load several boxes into the boot ready for the ten-mile drive to the courthouse. Evans piled into the police car with Cameron, while behind them followed Riley and the brigadier, with yet more butterflies packed into Riley's car.

The West Ham Magistrates Court had been an arbitrary choice of venue; since the case had volleyed between the jurisdictions of New Scotland Yard and Farnham police, it was eventually decided that West Ham's proximity to the docks where the SS *Perim* had unloaded its cargo four months earlier made it the most appropriate place to hear the case of Australia's missing butterflies.

Evans and the others had brought the cases into the courtroom and placed them on the solicitors' table in front of the magistrate, AA Pereira—the same judge who a few years later would set free the brawling groom. Next to the magistrate sat Sir Charles McCann, a racehorse-loving importer-exporter who was now serving his second stint as agent-general for South Australia. McCann was the only Australian representative in the building, a development that struck Evans as disappointing, but perhaps not surprising. The agents-general of all affected states had promised to attend, but Tully from New South Wales and Martin from Victoria were no-shows, and even McCann seemed a reluctant participant.

'He looked very apologetic and sheepish and clearly was embarrassed being associated with something below his dignity and in being seen in such sordid surroundings,' Evans would later reflect. 'West Ham is more or less in the East End slums.'[4]

For weeks after the 31 January confrontation, both New Scotland Yard and the Australian authorities had mulled over their options for the Wyatt case. When Cameron visited Evans on 17 February, he asked Tully to cable Sydney to see if the museums might pool their resources to send an expert witness across to England. This would hopefully address what Cameron still felt was the greatest weakness of Evans's evidence brief—it lacked someone who could front the court and give a definitive answer to the question, 'Do you recognize these butterflies as coming from such and such a Museum and were they stolen?'[5]

In South Australia, Herbert Hale thought it obvious that extraditing Wyatt and his collections to Australia under escort was the best means of extracting justice. But both options were dealt a final blow when the cost of extradition—anywhere between £1,000 and £1,500—and even of sending a witness became evident. It seemed that the 'heavy cost' was more than any Australian state government was willing to stump up for a case of missing butterflies—Hale's own minister had even refused him permission to travel to Melbourne in February for a crisis conference with Pescott and Walkom, insisting that any deliberations could be held over the telephone.[6]

In the end, New Scotland Yard decided that an Australian witness wouldn't be necessary. It all came down to the Evanses, and on 14 March, Cameron and another officer spent six hours at the museum taking additional 'expert statements' from father and son, to be submitted to the director of public prosecutions.[7] By a small stroke of luck, the brigadier had managed to identify three specimens that had previously been recognisably photographed and published by Norman Tindale in Adelaide, and a type specimen of *Andaluma urumelia* that the brigadier could personally vouch for having seen.

'The detective in charge of the case told me that it was my evidence which had persuaded the Director of Public Prosecution to take up the case,' the brigadier would later reflect, with no small amount of pride.[8]

But as the hearing got underway, both Evans men would be forced to watch on in stunned silence.

From the opening address, it was clear something was afoot. Colin Wyatt was there, the champion skier and celebrity mountaineer now playing the role of defendant for the first time. As Evans and the rest of the gallery understood it, Wyatt had been summoned for the offence of 'unlawfully receiving 1,600 Australian butterfly specimens at the London Docks, West Ham, on January 24th, 1947, knowing them to have been stolen or unlawfully obtained'.[9]

England's Larceny Act of 1916 encompassed a rainbow of ill-gotten gains, from garden-variety house-breaking and extortion to some very specific forms of theft. There was larceny of cattle, larceny of dogs, killing animals with intent to steal their carcass, damaging 'tree, sapling or underwood growing', the 'abstracting of electricity', and even the theft of 'ores'.[10] But stealing butterflies that were already dead, from a state institution in another country, with ambiguous monetary value and no apparent intent to re-sell them, seemed to have slipped the mind of English lawmakers. And, as much as some in the museum world might regard the theft of type specimens as an unholy desecration, Section 24 of the Act quite specifically confined 'sacrilege' to the breaking in or out of a 'place of divine worship'—and a museum didn't count.

No sooner had the courtroom settled than the prosecutor, MJ Jardine, asked Pereira for the summons to be amended from 'unlawfully receiving' the butterflies, to merely having them in his possession. This was a small but important semantic distinction; under Section 33 of the Act, 'receiving' stolen goods—whether it was a mail bag, postal packet, or any 'chattel, or money, or valuable security'—was equivalent to the theft itself, and carried a maximum prison sentence of fourteen years. However, a person who received or had in his possession 'any property so stolen or obtained outside the United Kingdom' faced a maximum sentence of only seven years. Jardine's request was granted. With the charge now successfully downgraded, Wyatt immediately entered a plea: guilty.

Jardine stood up again and explained to the court that the charge was an unusual one — perhaps even unique. Evans listened as Jardine ran through a truncated account of the English investigation and how, on 31 January, Cameron and Riley had visited Wyatt's mother's house, asking questions about the missing specimens and the cases he had collected at the Royal Victoria Dock. Jardine explained how Wyatt pointed to the cases in the study, and then admitted to having taken them.

'I don't know what possessed me to take them,' Jardine quoted Wyatt, reading from a copy of the detectives' notes.[11]

Glossing over his initial denial, and subsequent false statements to the *Daily Mail*, Jardine noted Wyatt's offer to help return the specimens, before reading out the full 400-word signed statement that Cameron had transcribed. He continued to explain how, after the confrontation at Farnham, the police had taken a large section of Wyatt's collection away, which experts at the Natural History Museum had since examined and checked against the lists of missing butterflies from Australia. The experts, Jardine said, considered the 'Australian blues' to be the 'largest and finest collection of blues they had ever seen — in fact, they had never seen such a fine collection outside Australian Museums'.[12] Gathering such a collection, he explained, would have required Wyatt to mount a series of expeditions into some of Australia's most remote locations. But as he continued, Jardine seemed to consider the theft a mild inconvenience rather than an extraordinary betrayal:

> I have not mentioned money, nor do I think that money enters at all into the case. The collections are of course almost priceless, but the defendant is a collector and there is no reason to suppose that he intended to dispose of the collection in any way. The case has, of course, caused a great deal of worry to the authorities in Australia

> especially to the curators of these museums. It is granted that most of the missing specimens have been recovered, but they are not in such good condition as they were, when originally in these museums, as they have been handled and shipped, and that is not conducive to keeping specimens in the best possible condition.[13]

Then Jardine said something surprising. He told the court that, as far as was known, Wyatt had an 'exemplary character', and that he saw 'no useful purpose' in calling police officers or any witnesses to testify to it, unless the magistrate thought it necessary. Pereira agreed, saying he did not require any evidence to Wyatt's character — this, he said, was 'not in dispute'. As Jardine sat down, Evans considered it all a very poor showing. But the worst was yet to come: Jardine's limp performance would soon be outmatched by Wyatt's defence counsel, a fifty-year-old barrister named Gerald Howard who seemed to embody precisely the kind of 'leading counsel' that Cameron and Evans feared.

Like Wyatt, Howard came from privileged stock, an Oxford-educated former RAF flight lieutenant and son of a land-owning MP who, in a few years' time, he would succeed into parliament. He was an experienced prosecutor himself, having cut his teeth as counsel at the Old Bailey before a term as high sheriff of Cambridgeshire and Huntingdonshire. Howard had also helped prosecute some of post-war England's most high-profile trials, including the 'Cleft Chin Murder' of 1944, in which a Swedish-born US army deserter posing as a Chicago gangster went on a crime spree with an eighteen-year-old Welsh woman, culminating in the killing of a taxi driver.

Howard did, on occasion, turn defence, and a few months before the Wyatt trial had made the newspapers when representing sixty-six-year-old Thomas Ley, another Englishman who had tried to leave behind a colourful past in Australia.[14] Born in Bath before moving to Sydney as a child, Ley had climbed his way to parliament and a stint as New South Wales justice minister, earning the nickname 'Lemonade Ley' for his teetotalism. Ley could be a divisive figure, but his political fortunes were badly tarnished after the suspicious disappearance of a Labor Party rival who had previously accused Ley of attempted bribery. When another of

Ley's critics was later found dead at the base of cliffs in Coogee in 1928, he finally became political poison and drifted into obscurity.

A decade later, Lemonade Ley resurfaced in England, where in 1947 he was tried for murdering a bartender he mistakenly thought had taken up with his long-time mistress, Mrs Brooks. Her late husband had been a Sydney magistrate who, incidentally, Ley was also suspected of killing — Byron Brooks had supposedly died in a freak wasp attack during a family picnic attended by Ley.[15] Whatever murderous rumours dogged Ley in Australia, this latest case became a sensation in the English papers, who nicknamed Ley the 'Chalk Pit murderer' after the site in Surrey where Ley was accused of dumping the man's body.

It took the jury just fifty-five minutes to announce to a packed Old Bailey that Ley was guilty. He was sentenced to death, but just weeks before the Wyatt case, the former minister was given a last-minute reprieve and sent instead to Broadmoor Criminal Lunatic Asylum after being found to have displayed signs of 'delusional insanity' and paranoia at the time of the murder.[16] Ley would die at Broadmoor a few months later — a remarkable outcome given the decades-long trail of suspiciously strategic deaths that followed him around the world.

At West Ham, Howard already had Wyatt's plea deal in hand when he began to speak. He began by asking Pereira to bear with him, before launching into a lengthy monologue recounting Wyatt's history, 'in order that the Magistrate might consider whether there was anything which afforded some explanation'.[17] In essence, Howard sought to convince the court that Wyatt's offence amounted to a lesser misdemeanour, rather than a felony:

> The defendant was an only child. He was extremely delicate and owing to that fact he was never sent away in the ordinary way to school, with the result that he became a shy, self-centred, aloof, lonely little boy. From the age of eight he was encouraged by his father to take an interest in the collection of butterflies. Thereafter he did, and in fact he had collected some 40,000 specimens. When he grew up he was sent to Cambridge, where he became the captain of the ski-ing club, and was ski-jumping champion. In 1931 or thereabouts, in addition

> to collecting butterflies, he became interested in art and showed some considerable promise.[18]

By 1939, Howard explained, the 'lonely self-centred boy thought he had found for the first time perfect and absolute happiness' with his marriage to Mary. Later that year, the newlywed Wyatts emigrated to Australia, when suddenly war broke out.

'He obtained employment, first of all, with the Australian Censorship and afterwards when Japan became a menace thrusting herself nearer and nearer to Australia, and camouflage became important he was appointed to special officer for camouflage and this involved a good deal of flying with the RAAF, where he acquitted himself in a most praiseworthy manner and did extremely well,' Howard said.

At this point, Howard produced two letters by unnamed authors. He handed them to Pereira, and as the magistrate quietly read them, the silk explained how the letters made it clear that Australian authorities had 'formed a very high view of him and of his character and were ready to recommend him to this country as a person well worthy of employment'.

It was true that, over the years, Wyatt had accrued his share of glowing recommendations — such as the one clearing him for employment at the ABC, the endorsement of Professor William Dakin and the officers of the Camouflage Section, and even Waterhouse's letter of introduction. But Evans, Riley, and Cameron knew that there was also a good deal of official paperwork expressing very different opinions. Finally, Howard got to the business end of what he called 'these disastrous happenings'.

'With his flying duties he was away a considerable amount of time, sometimes for long periods together,' Howard said. 'Whether rightly or wrongly I am not prepared to say, but there is no doubt the defendant formed the opinion that his wife had, during his absences, been doing what a wife should not do, and for this reason they in fact parted and war, as happens in many cases, had broken up another marriage.'

> The man who had found such absolute and complete happiness in marriage became plunged in the most profound and desperate despair.

> He plunged back into his original passion for collecting butterflies to keep his mind from his trouble. He went to various museums in Australia and stole these butterflies. There is no doubt about that.
>
> No one can excuse his action and I do not seek to excuse him and the observations I am making are merely justified if they show some explanation for his conduct, and why this man, who had done no real wrong in the whole of his life, who had occupied a most respectable position in life, should suddenly commit an action of this kind.[19]

On paper, it was true that Wyatt had never before been formally accused, let alone convicted, of any crime. Riley's decision in 1930 to follow the advice of Wyatt's father's friend and quietly resolve the situation of the lost *Parnassius* might have ensured the quick and safe return of the specimens, but making the issue go away had allowed Wyatt to land in Australia with a clean record and reputation — a man who had done 'no real wrong'. Those in the courtroom had no idea that Wyatt's serial Australian thefts might not have been a once-off — or thrice-off — lapse of judgement, but part of a seventeen-year pattern of behaviour that was only now being held to account. Once again, a behind-closed-doors arrangement teed up through England's old boys' network had worked to help a privileged young man with his whole life ahead of him avoid any real consequences.

'The first thing that strikes me about this case, and Mr Jardine admits this, is that there is no monetary consideration in it at all,' Howard continued. 'He did not sell or attempt to sell, nor had the slightest intention of selling a single specimen. No one suggests he thought of selling them or making money from them, in any shape or form.'

He then quoted Jardine's comments that most of the missing butterflies had been safely recovered, and blamed any discrepancies between the numbers missing and those surrendered by Wyatt on the museums' own lists.

'I think I should explain that the slight difference is probably due to the fact that the lists sent over from Australia contained all the butterflies missing from the Museums,' Howard said. 'There may be some missing for other reasons, but the fact is that the whole of the butterflies which

Wyatt took, have been returned. This man has in fact returned to the authorities everything which he took.'

Howard concluded his remarks by saying it would be wrong for him to make any commentary on the question of punishment. He then proceeded, however, to argue that 'the interest of the public and of justice might well be served by some form of punishment which would not involve sending the defendant to prison'.

'He had suffered considerably from having to sit in the dock, in public gaze and admit that he had committed an act such as the one now described,' the lawyer said before resting his defence.[20]

From the public gallery, John Evans found it all rather galling. After all, he too had been a lonely, shy, awkward only child with a distant father obsessed with butterflies, and he had never systematically robbed three different museums over a twelve-month period, divorce or not.

'By the time he had finished we were all left with the impression that Wyatt was almost a hero,' Evans reflected after the trial. 'That this little slip was because his wife had gone astray and to soothe himself he threw himself into his childhood hobby of butterfly collection.'[21]

After all the hours that Evans, the brigadier, Riley, and Cameron had spent preparing evidence for the prosecution, let alone the days and weeks of near-constant correspondence with the museums back in Australia, the prosecutor, Jardine, had called no witnesses and submitted no evidence beyond the signed statement. On the solicitors' table, the cases of recovered butterflies they had so carefully sorted and arranged, that Evans had risen before dawn to help bring to the court, had sat completely untouched for the entirety of the hearing.

Having heard all the evidence and arguments that the prosecution was willing to tender, Pereira spoke. He told the court room that he had considered carefully the sole piece of evidence submitted — Wyatt's statement of 31 January — and the speeches given by Jardine and Howard, and had arrived at a decision. At the time that Wyatt 'committed the act' — the serial robberies by now condensed into a single indiscretion of taking possession of the stolen goods — Pereira concluded that he was 'not in the full possession of his faculties in the ordinary sense of the word'. The magistrate didn't call on any expert witnesses or cite any legal or psychiatric literature before making this diagnosis, which all but absolved Wyatt of responsibility for his months-long spree:

> I think you were suffering from distraction of the mind, which caused you to do something you would not have done in your ordinary senses. I have taken into consideration your admirable character, and all that your counsel has said about your feelings today, and I feel I can inflict a lesser punishment than prison. You will pay a fine of £100.[22]

It was all over. Jardine hadn't even asked Pereira to issue a costs order, and as Evans, the brigadier, and Riley let the verdict sink in, Wyatt was allowed to slip out a side door to avoid the media scrum, much like the Rolling Stones eighteen years later.[23] Having avoided prison, he now planned to be in Sweden by the end of the week, almost as if the trial had never happened at all. Like the explorer Major Mitchell, the scoundrel John Roach, and the over-zealous anatomist William Ramsay Smith before him, the admitted butterfly thief had been let off the hook. Those specimen cases remained unopened as Wyatt ducked out of the courtroom, but as far as the British justice system was concerned, the case was closed. It would be left to Evans, Riley, and the entomologists of Australia to clean up the mess.

CHAPTER TWENTY-ONE

The Superman

'According to Mr Musgrave, if this mythical collector G Purcell had existed he would have been an entomological Superman,' reported *The Sydney Morning Herald* in September 1947. 'The labels give the impression that one day he was netting rare specimens at Groote Eylandt, then after a brief interval was doing the same in remote parts of Victoria or South Australia.'[1]

Few insect collectors can claim to be household names, but Purcell was an unknown quantity even among the close-knit world of Australian entomology. He had no publications under his belt, no record of correspondence or exchanges with better-known collectors or museums, and not a single cameo appearance in any nature journal or periodical. Purcell was so obscure that when they first encountered his name, Anthony Musgrave, Alec Burns, and Norman Tindale — three of the most respected and well-connected entomologists in Australia's museums — assumed he was entirely fictitious.

Purcell did exist, but he was no Superman. Compared to the tens of thousands of specimens in the Lyell and Waterhouse collections, the five or six boxes of insects he collected held little consequence. For Gervaise Churchill Purcell, butterflies were little more than a wartime hobby before he returned home to Sydney and his day job as a commercial photographer. While Purcell moved on with his life, those boxes lay practically abandoned in a spare room, along with all his other papers, old cameras, and negatives, until one day many years later his granddaughter asked after them. Purcell had died in 1999, and it had been a long time since his grown-up son, Leigh, had last dug his father's old insects out of storage. When he finally did, he was disappointed to find little more than empty boxes.

'They'd all gone to dust,' a seventy-three-year-old Leigh Purcell later told me.[2]

Some years earlier, Purcell had tried and failed to source sachets of naphthalene to preserve the collection, but in the intervening years the fruits of his father's short collecting career had succumbed to one of Waterhouse and Lyell's 'three foes': the school of tiny predators whose voracious appetite has earned them the inglorious nickname of 'museum beetle'. With them, any material connection between the name 'G Purcell' and insect collecting disappeared. Almost.

For a brief period, there was another set of specimens — less than half-a-dozen insects, practically a rounding error — that also bore Purcell's name. These were the butterflies that Musgrave spoke of in *The Sydney Morning Herald*, and if you were to study their labels, you could retrace Purcell's seemingly remarkable movements around Australia in the final years of World War II. There was the rare moth captured in 1944 in Milingimbi, in the Northern Territory. Then there was the spinifex sand-skipper, brought home from the 'Iron Ranges' — a mysterious site in far-north Queensland that didn't appear on any maps. Later, Musgrave would learn that 'Iron Ranges' was a codename used by the Americans for a wartime outpost halfway between Cairns and Cape York.[3] Unlike the rest of the Purcell collection, these weren't relegated to a dusty corner to be gradually swallowed up by time and parasites; these specimens travelled halfway around the globe twice, even making their way to the hallowed halls of the British Natural History Museum to be studied by world-leading entomologists.

All of which was news to Leigh Purcell. But perhaps that wasn't a surprise; if his late father even knew about these errant specimens, he might have had good reason for not sharing the story with his son. It seemed that these butterflies had all been stolen from Australian museums, and that, at some point after their initial theft, their labels were removed or cut up, and the original collectors' names swapped out for the words 'G. Purcell'. Someone had tried, quite literally, to pin these stolen specimens on Purcell.

When Leigh was growing up, his father didn't talk much about his wartime service. A handsome young man with a wide smile, Gervaise had enlisted in February 1940, a few months shy of his twenty-first birthday. Then, in 1942, he was discharged to be redeployed to the Department of Home Security to serve in Professor William Dakin's Camouflage Section. When he did talk about it, there were a few recurring names that stuck with Leigh — Max Dupain, Frank Hinder, and Russell Roberts. But, when I asked if his father ever mentioned the name Colin Wyatt, Leigh drew a blank.

'No,' he said. 'The name doesn't mean anything to me.'[4]

The three middle-aged men grinned under the flashbulbs, dutifully pointing and gesturing at the eight full trays of butterflies laid out on the table in front of them. One held up a notebook as if checking off a list, another stared intently at a single butterfly he held up an inch from his one working eye, while the third took off his glasses to peer down a microscope. It was the morning of 20 August 1947, and as photographers and reporters from Adelaide's morning and afternoon newspapers gathered in a book-lined room of the South Australian Museum, it was unclear if Anthony Musgrave, Alec Burns, and Norman Tindale's smiles were a sign of relief, joy, or simply the bemused recognition that the international incident Burns had kicked off seven months earlier had, once again, strayed into farce.

There were no smiles to be found three months earlier, when John Evans's blow-by-blow account of his deflating day at the West Ham Magistrates Court arrived via airmail. Museum offices all around Australia were practically seething with outrage and indignation at the seemingly meagre £100 fine and the remarkable indifference shown by the English prosecutors, magistrate, and their own agents-general.

In Melbourne, Dick Pescott dismissed the defence's sad tale of domestic stress as 'all moonshine'; in Adelaide, Herbert Hale called it a 'masterpiece of lousiness'.[5] Like Pescott, Arthur Walkom felt that the 'sob stuff' that the magistrate had swallowed so uncritically didn't square with the reality: the three-city butterfly heist could only have been a carefully planned and executed scheme carried out over many, many months.[6]

Alec Burns agreed; he and his fellow collectors had been aware of the gradual collapse of Colin and Mary Wyatt's marriage, but the timeline didn't seem to match the twelve-month window between the suspected Adelaide break-out and the Melbourne thefts. Nor did it account for the 'cunning and intrigue' that the heist had required.

'Wyatt was removing specimens for months before his domestic troubles grew really serious,' Burns would write. 'I know of these troubles through a friend of mine in New South Wales, and who was a friend of Wyatt's, and one who had extended much sympathy and kindness to Wyatt.'[7] In a letter written to Le Souëf in August 1936, Wyatt had shown no sign of distress at all. Much like his note to Ras Wilson the following January, he told the Victorian collector he was 'over' the worst of his crumbling marriage, and was now having 'a hell of a lot of fun', even if the break up was sapping his funds.[8]

Then there was the impact of the thefts, which no one in the courtroom apart from DS Cameron, Norman Riley, and the two Evanses seemed to understand or appreciate.

'As for the "no damage was done", that is just ridiculous and would have been refuted if the scientific witnesses had been called,' Walkom wrote. 'They could have pointed out that the types were unrecognizable, that labels had been rewritten, and original data is lost or confused.'[9]

It was this problem of the rewritten labels and 'lost and confused' data that had brought Burns and Musgrave to the South Australian Museum on 20 August 1947. The butterflies were already waiting for them when they rolled into Adelaide the night before, having driven for thirteen hours straight to cover the 463-mile distance from Melbourne.[10] The three cases, each one containing nine storeboxes with 3,124 butterflies between them, had travelled even further, arriving in Adelaide aboard the SS *Stratheden* in late July. Their homeward journey to Australia had been settled at West Ham; by virtue of being the only agent-general who had bothered to attend, Sir Charles McCann, the embarrassed-looking representative from South Australia, would take responsibility for the shipping of the entirety of the recovered butterflies in one bulk lot.

After all the brigadier's efforts to prepare his sample of evidence for the magistrate, Cameron and the entomologists were left to take the unopened cases back out the way they came upon the hearing's conclusion. Despite Wyatt admitting to having possessed only 1,600 butterflies, he had since cooperated in surrendering a further 210 specimens after the trial, while also making a series of handwritten notes on a copy of the lists compiled by Riley and the staff of the Natural History Museum. Despite this assistance, it was still too big a job for the Englishmen.

'When we first recovered the specimens we tried to allocate them in accordance with your lists, to the three museums from which they had been stolen,' Riley explained. 'We had to abandon this idea, for we found that it was quite impossible to carry out.'[11]

Riley, Evans, and the brigadier did their best, but the labels were in such a state that eventually they had to concede it was essentially guesswork. McCann arranged for the packed cases to be shipped aboard the *Stratheden*, taking care to insure the precious cargo for £320. They would travel back to Australia inside Wyatt's own cases—another source of controversy at both ends of the journey.

'The store boxes containing the specimens, by the way, are Colin Wyatt's property,' Riley had clarified. 'I should have thought that under the circumstances Wyatt would hardly have the face to demand their return.'[12]

For Pescott and his colleagues, this detail only added to the disbelief that the prosecutor had made no attempt to seek a cost ruling against Wyatt. A tentative effort by the Australian museums to claim the proceeds of the £100 fine was rebuffed, leaving Pescott and Hale more than a little outraged that, in addition to the time and resources already sunk into the case, they might in the future be expected to bankroll the return of Wyatt's property.

But the boxes were, on balance, a low priority. As Tindale, Musgrave, and Burns got to work on their contents, they quickly realised that it would take much longer than the two or three days they had initially set aside. Tindale's secretary took shorthand notes as they unpacked each case, meticulously recording the number of specimens claimed by each museum in the event of any 'future litigation' should anyone question their work.

They began with *Papilionoidea,* and methodically sorted through every row of every box, pausing to compare specimens with illustrations or existing museum registers. As they combed through the collection, they were dismayed to find that all the registration labels made by the Australian Museum had been removed, forcing the men to identify Waterhouse's specimens from the style of black enamel-coated pins he had used almost exclusively.

They also noticed that while many specimens retained their original labels with the correct locality, day, and month, in many instances the year had been altered to coincide with Wyatt's collecting activities and travels in Australia. Others had the collector's name 'snipped off' and replaced with 'G. Purcell' or another pseudonym, 'J.B.' Like John Evans's evidence brief in London, there were times when the men were able to draw on firsthand experience — such as a 'glaring' falsified label on the 'G. Purcell' specimen collected from Groote Eylandt in the Gulf of Carpentaria. The location cited was, as Musgrave noted, 'about 150 miles from the Island, and only Mr Tindale has collected insects there, so far as is known.'[13]

Despite the chaos, Tindale did give Wyatt some small amount of credit, telling Hale that, 'fortunately he apparently did so with an eye to the preservation of the general data as to locality and month of capture.'[14] It seemed that even as he covered his tracks, Wyatt couldn't quite bring himself to completely erase all the data that would showcase how far and wide his collection reached. For Alec Burns, the entomologist who had known Wyatt best and seen him at work in the field, the state of the recovered specimens only added to the intrigue; the collector he knew didn't seem like someone suffering from 'distraction of the mind', nor someone 'not in the full possession of his faculties'.

'From what I personally know of his collecting activities he always labelled all specimens he caught, so it is only reasonable to believe that he would later attach the correct information to these butterflies,' Burns would later write in his report of the week:

> The altered dates on specimens would not be of any use at all unless Wyatt had a code book in which he inserted the correct information relating to each specimen concerned. Without this the scientific value of each specimen so dealt with would be absolutely nil.[15]

No code book was ever recovered, and as the trio unravelled Wyatt's handiwork, Burns only grew more frustrated. It wasn't just the divorce story that didn't add up; the explanation that Wyatt had offered to Cameron and Riley in his 'untrue and unreliable' statement—how he had smuggled the specimens through small tins hidden inside his jacket—seemed physically impossible.

'According to his statement this box would hold about 100 specimens, *and it could be carried in his pocket*,' Burns reported. 'A normal sized pocket box will hold up to 30 or so small butterflies and probably only one or two of the very large ones.'[16]

By the end of their nine days in Adelaide, Burns had set aside enough of these 'very large' specimens to fill a fourteen inch by ten inch double-sided storebox. This wasn't the only plot hole left unfilled by the official investigation. In his report of the trial, Evans touched on another by-product of the prosecution's striking incuriosity: Wyatt had pleaded guilty to possessing 1,600 butterflies, but the details of precisely when and how he had struck the Sydney and Adelaide museums remained an unknown. This was, at least partly, the fault of the local police.

'We still don't know how he got away with the Adelaide material as he had left Australia by the time the Museum was broken out of,' Evans had written after the trial.[17]

Hale was surprised by his confusion, having clearly stated in his earlier correspondence that, since Wyatt had never made himself known to anyone at the South Australian Museum as he had in Melbourne and Sydney, the January 1946 break-out was the most likely time of the theft.[18] However, as Cameron had promptly taken the original letter as evidence, Evans had no way to check the details when New Scotland Yard was later assured by the Adelaide CIB that Wyatt had already left the country when the museum's open doors were first reported. Hale was left bewildered that his own police had mixed up the dates.

'It was remarkable, because it was explained ad nauseum to the two detectives in charge of the case that this breaking out had occurred a year before Wyatt had left Australia and that, in our opinion, this was the only time at which the theft could have occurred,' Hale said to Evans.[19]

The Adelaide detectives had promised to contact Canberra and other cities to correlate Wyatt's movements with the dates, but it seemed that they made some basic errors — if they bothered to investigate at all. By the time that Burns, Musgrave, and Tindale called it a day in Adelaide, the injury that Wyatt had inflicted to their collections was compounded by the insulting response seen from almost every level of government, law enforcement, and the legal establishment that had touched the case in Australia and England.

'I deplore the apathy and lack of interest taken by the agent-generals for the States of Victoria and New South Wales,' Burns wrote in his final report. '[This] has clearly indicated that they do not understand the value of scientific material from either a personal or public point of view, and it is my opinion that they failed in their duty as overseas representatives of the two States concerned.'[20]

The three men had spent nine days at the South Australian Museum, and while they had done their best to set the collections in order, the recovered cache of butterflies remained riddled with gaps — at least seventy specimens were still unaccounted for — and big, unanswered questions. The code book that Burns had hopefully theorised about remained lost to them, if it ever existed at all.

'In the case of the Australian Museum several unique specimens are still missing,' Burns wrote. 'If these are not found in Adelaide they must be still in Wyatt's possession.'[21]

It seemed clear to all three of them that the matter should remain 'sub judice' until further study could be completed.

In the meantime, the trio arrived at the unanimous conclusion that in many cases, the museums 'should regard the *remainder of this material* as *suspect* and discard it from their research collections'. Practically, this meant that the scientific integrity of many specimens had been so undermined that they were useless for anything other than public display—tragically, a once-formidable set of biological data had been reduced to a nice stamp collection.

'It is our intention to relegate as many as possible of the lesser specimens to gallery display series, thus they will eventually be destroyed after they have become faded through exposure to light,' Tindale wrote in his report to Hale in September.[22]

Burns, Musgrave, and Tindale also had one further recommendation before they drew a line under their time in Adelaide.

'It has been proposed that an identifying label be placed on each specimen which has passed through the Wyatt collection, only in this way can future students of geographical distribution be placed on their guard against possible sources of error, since it would appear that Wyatt transposed and faked some of the labels on specimens,' Tindale's report read.

They suggested that 4,000 labels be printed, each bearing the same warning:

> Passed through
> C.W. Wyatt Theft Coll.
> 1946–47[23]

These new yellow labels were an eye-catching declaration that after Burns, Musgrave, and Tindale went their separate ways, the story of the butterfly heist would still be far from over. As Musgrave told *The Sydney Morning Herald* in its 6 September report, '[It] will take years before the full extent of this confusion is known, and it may never be completely cleared up.'[24]

As for the mythical G. Purcell, an answer arrived in September in the form of an anonymous letter sent to Alec Burns marked 'CONFIDENTIAL'. The letter provided Gervaise Purcell's full name, explaining that Purcell had been a camoufleur with the RAAF, stationed at Townsville at the same time as Colin Wyatt and the letter's author.

'Colin got Purcell interested in wogs [insects] and he started a collection, but was transferred to Darwin not many months after he started,' the letter read.[25]

Its author added that Purcell had 'no scientific knowledge and did not know technical names', and that although Wyatt had stayed in touch with Purcell after the Darwin move, his interest in entomology quickly waned. The next time the letter writer saw Purcell was in Sydney, near the end of the war, where he gathered that Purcell had all but abandoned butterfly collecting, stowing away his small private collection for posterity—or for the museum beetles.

The Purcell puzzle had been solved, but in their scramble to make sense of Wyatt's mess, the men at the museum had overlooked another collector with unfinished business of his own.

CHAPTER TWENTY-TWO

The Dirty Work

On 6 September 1947, Athol Waterhouse opened his Saturday-morning copy of *The Sydney Morning Herald*, where the seventy-year-old was dismayed to find his name on page two. In the same lengthy report on 'The Strange Case of the Stolen Butterflies' that had speculated about the identity of the 'entomological Superman' G. Purcell, the staff correspondent had also made frequent references to 'the cream of the great Waterhouse Collection in the Sydney Museum'.[1]

Arthur Walkom had initially told Waterhouse about the thefts back in February, but as the investigation dragged on, and dozens of letters and phone calls were exchanged between Sydney, Melbourne, Adelaide, and London, it seemed that Waterhouse was one major player who had been left — or, rather, cut — out of the loop. This was why, as he read the article closely, Waterhouse was astonished by several pointed revelations — such as the fact that Wyatt had not only invoked his name to gain access to his collections, but had also claimed to be writing an updated edition of Waterhouse's own 1932 book. Waterhouse might have been forced to slow down in the years since his stroke, but by the time he put down the newspaper, he was moved to pick up his pen almost immediately.

'In justice to myself, my friends, and the public, I wish to emphasise that the article on the stolen butterflies in Saturday's "Herald" was not seen by me until it appeared in print,' read the letter, published in *The Sydney Morning Herald* three days later. 'Strangely enough, I only knew that the butterflies had been returned to Australia a few days ago.'[2]

Waterhouse then gave readers an abridged account of the case from his distant and frustrated vantage point.

'I knew Wyatt when he first came to Australia and helped him by showing him my best collecting spots,' he wrote. 'In return he stole some specimens I had collected and given to the Australian Museum.'

Waterhouse said Wyatt 'could not be called a scientist', and sought to correct the record that he had never consented to a new edition of *What Butterfly Is That?* Nor could he believe that his publisher, with whom he had worked 'on the best of terms for 40 years', would have entertained any such arrangement without first consulting him. As for the stolen butterflies, Waterhouse insisted it would never have happened on his watch:

> Because of my serious illness in 1943 I was not able to see the collection for some years. Some of these specimens I collected over 50 years ago and would be recognised by me anywhere. Had it not been for my illness the specimens would never have been stolen, as I would have noticed any marked removals.[3]

But the pages of *The Sydney Morning Herald* weren't the only outlet for Waterhouse to vent his frustrations. In the days that followed, he also reached out to Nancy Adams with a request to bring a storebox of specimens out to him in Potts Point to see the damage for himself. Anthony Musgrave was less than thrilled by this development — the day before Waterhouse's letter was published, he had resolved to continue to sideline the old man.

'I feel that there is nothing to be gained by disturbing Dr Waterhouse (who is, from all accounts, mentally ill-fitted to undertake work of any kind), with the task of identifying any of the material not named by the British Museum,' Musgrave wrote in his report of those nine days in Adelaide.[4]

Now, though, for better or for worse, Waterhouse appeared still sharp enough to be a thorn in Musgrave's side. On 22 September, Musgrave worked up the courage to write to Waterhouse, offering a carefully worded summary of his trip to Adelaide and the mess that had awaited them inside the storeboxes from London.

'Your collection, is therefore, not as you know it,' Musgrave concluded poignantly, 'and to check through the registers will involve a great amount of time.'

Musgrave also added, somewhat defensively, that their 'task was not rendered any easier' by the fact that Waterhouse had contributed specimens to so many museums over the years that even his tell-tale black pins didn't necessarily mean a 'Waterhouse' butterfly belonged to the G.A. Waterhouse Collection.

'I trust the above will set your mind at ease for the present,' Musgrave concluded hopefully. 'Later you will see what a huge task confronts those who endeavour to restore order out of the chaos our friend Wyatt has created.'[5]

Waterhouse's mind was not, in fact, put at ease. On 3 October, Musgrave paid Waterhouse a visit, bringing with him the thirty-five foolscap pages of notes he had compiled in Adelaide. It must have been a nerve-wracking few hours, for, within days, Walkom was circulating to Pescott and Hale a set of terse annotations Waterhouse had made, highlighting errors in Burns, Musgrave, and Tindale's work.

'If this is a sample of what I may find when I see the specimens the memorandum will not be much use,' Waterhouse wrote.[6]

Neither Pescott nor Walkom were particularly thrilled to receive the memo attacking the 'three trained men [who] had a most difficult job to carry out'.

'I do not think that Waterhouse is at all fair in some of his statements of the dirty work that had to be carried out by the three entomologists in Adelaide,' Pescott wrote on 10 October.[7]

Pescott had no doubt that Waterhouse would identify several errors when he made his own close inspection of the specimens returned to each city. He was, after all, an authority almost without peer in Australian lepidoptery, who held a personal connection to many of the stolen specimens that neither Burns, Musgrave, nor Tindale could hold a candle to. But while he would never say it to his face, Waterhouse's critiques rankled Pescott for another very good reason:

> [To] cast a slur on the work of the three men as he did in that statement above is not appreciated in Melbourne and in very bad taste, particularly when we remember that Waterhouse was warned about Wyatt from England when he first came to Australia.[8]

Of all the systematic security failures across Australia's museums that had allowed these thefts to occur, at such an unprecedented and ultimately unknowable scale, Waterhouse's fateful decision remained perhaps the most frustrating.

There was, at least, one man alive who could empathise with Athol Waterhouse's growing despair; on 20 September, Waterhouse once again wrote to George Lyell, confiding in his old friend with a level of frankness unseen since the Tillyard years.

'Now I have seen some of the mess the cunning devil has made, some sort of a label will have to be used,' Waterhouse wrote.[9]

Waterhouse had initially resisted the idea of a yellow label tarnishing the museums' collections, but was now forced to concede that Burns, Musgrave, and Tindale's proposal wasn't a bad idea. All the same, their reluctance to include him in their deliberations nagged at him.

'I recognise they had a difficult job, but why was I not consulted?' he wrote. 'I probably know the collections of the Museums as well as the entomologist in charge.'[10]

In his absence, Waterhouse seemed staggered that the three best working entomologists that Australia's museums could offer up had fallen so short of his own high standards. Musgrave, Burns, and Tindale might have managed to locate many of Waterhouse's specimens, even without their original labels, but he was surprised that they couldn't differentiate specimens clearly set by Lyell from the work of another collector — taking it for granted, perhaps, that his own intimate knowledge of Lyell's handiwork had taken nearly fifty years.

'Enough of this,' Waterhouse added bitterly, 'I hate to deal with incompetents.'[11]

As Waterhouse combed through his old collection and the growing mountain of paperwork that had accrued since 13 January, he identified specimens that earlier audits hadn't even noticed were missing. Before they sent the three cases off on the SS *Stratheden*, Riley had prepared a detailed register of all the butterflies recovered from Wyatt's home. As Waterhouse studied the document, however, he spotted several species that didn't appear in the preliminary lists prepared by Nancy Adams and Anthony Musgrave. With Riley's list in hand, he tracked down additional instances where a rare specimen had been removed, with a more common species bearing a passing resemblance pinned in their place.

'There was no one here capable of recognising this substitution,' he told Lyell, before adding, 'Do not mention it to anyone as I do not want it to get to Musgrave's ears.'[12]

Despite everything, Waterhouse's secrecy proved a hard habit to break. Eventually, the museum had cabinets worth of specimens sent out to Waterhouse's home, where he continued to survey the wreckage as the year drew to a close. By March 1948, neither Walkom or Musgrave seemed quite sure how long the old man would keep at it; whatever energy Waterhouse could summon to write a pointed letter or scan a list of butterflies, it was common knowledge that since his stroke in 1943, Waterhouse had been plagued by a seemingly constant stream of health problems. Eventually, Lyell would admit to Waterhouse that he too had conspired to keep the state of the collections secret from his old friend, after Pescott and Walkom decided the 'bad news' might pose a risk to his health.

'Your uncertain health seems to have been the only possible excuse for keeping you in the dark so long,' Lyell wrote apologetically on 29 October.[13]

However well meaning their thinking, the entire affair left Waterhouse feeling aggrieved, betrayed, and powerless in his twilight years. He had dedicated his life to Australian butterflies, but through a twist of fate, betrayal, and his own tragic miscalculation, he now faced one final quest to undo the damage to his life's work — decades of meticulous effort thrown into chaos in just a few months. But Janie Waterhouse's firstborn son, the young beachcomber with the Latin nickname, whose once-nimble fingers and hunger for knowledge had sacrificed thousands of butterflies to the altar of science, was now a weary old man slowed by years of illness. He was in a race against time, and as the 1940s came to an end, even the great Gustavus Athol Waterhouse would have to face the bittersweet truth at the heart of collecting: collections are meant to outlive their collector.

The years finally caught up with Athol Waterhouse on 29 July 1950, when he died in Pymble at the age of seventy-three. The tributes flowed, as glowing in death as they had been in life.

'Waterhouse was in the widest and truest sense a very learned man,' read a tribute from the Linnean Society of New South Wales. 'He was a master of detail and his mental energy was tireless in seeking the truth. He knowledge, though profound, was unobtrusive, and his great learning intensified his natural humility.'[14]

Walkom's dealings with Waterhouse in those tense final years might have pushed the limits of Waterhouse's humility and 'unobtrusive' nature, but the director had a keen sense of what was lost. The Australian Museum had been Waterhouse's second home since boyhood, and of all his contributions to science, it remained his greatest beneficiary.

'By his death the Museum, as well as the scientific societies, lost one who had made a notable contribution to the advancement of natural history in Australia,' Walkom wrote in an official tribute.[15]

Less than a year later, on 10 May 1951, Dick Pescott received a letter from Gisborne. 'He has certainly surprised us the way he has improved,' read the note, written after George Lyell had experienced yet another health scare. 'How long it will last is hard to say.'[16]

Nine days later, Lyell died at home at the age of eighty-four. In the days that followed, as newspapers around Australia reported on the 'Death of Noted Naturalist', many also invoked the name of his old friend Athol Waterhouse and the remarkable work they did together — some even noted that thirty-six years after its publication, *The Butterflies of Australia* remained the standard text for Australian lepidoptery.[17] In the Melbourne *Herald*, a journalist also added that, after the months of disruption that began on 13 January 1947, the National Museum of Victoria had pressed on with its 'relay' of George Lyell's life's work: 'Although the museum has been exhibiting fresh cases in the main hall every fortnight for the past four years, it has not yet been through the whole collection.'[18]

Dick Pescott was more prosaic in his own statement: 'The Lyell Collection of Australian Lepidoptera will forever remain a monument to the industry, patience and ability of one of Australia's notable sons.'

Of course, the temporary display in the zoological hall wasn't the only lasting tribute. Spread across hundreds of drawers in museums around Australia, the thousands of labels bearing Waterhouse and Lyell's names would offer a continual reminder to future researchers of these two men, their lifelong partnership, and the staggering amount of butterflies swept up by their nets. It was a small but pointed postscript, however, that in the case of several hundred of these specimens, their own names would share equal billing with that of another collector, another former friend, printed on a tiny slip of yellow paper: 'C.W. Wyatt'.

Three years after Waterhouse and Lyell's deaths, the 'C.W. Wyatt Theft Collection' would once again become John Evans's problem. It wasn't long after Evans had sent the recovered specimens on their way back to Australia in June 1947 that he found himself itching to follow them. He had come to England to broaden his horizons, however mad it had seemed to uproot Faith and their young family from quiet Tasmania to bombed-out London. But by the end of 1947, he found himself stuck, and yearning to escape the Imperial Institute of Entomology.

'I am seeking another job,' Evans wrote to Arthur Walkom in December 1947, in a private note written from the family home in Chalfont St Giles. 'It's no good and I must get out.'[19]

First, Evans resolved to take a shot at Professor William Dakin's zoology chair at the University of Sydney when the sixty-four-year-old retired. In the meantime, however, Evans asked Walkom to let him know if anything came up. It would be another six years before a viable escape route finally presented itself, when in 1954 Evans received word that a position was being advertised in the Australian papers: director of the Australian Museum.

Evans jumped on the opportunity, even as he knew that Walkom's successor would have their work cut out for them. It wasn't just the unflattering revelations about the 1946 thefts; Evans knew that the museum had been languishing for years, underfunded and neglected by the government, with a workforce that was often difficult, lacking in scientific qualifications, and plagued by terrible morale.

Evans's application was successful, but, upon taking up his new position, he would find himself in a similar position to Pescott in Melbourne in 1944, and Edward Charles Stirling on his return from England in 1881. He deemed the museum's public galleries to be 'deplorable'—dull, dark, and outdated with a footprint that hadn't grown since 1909. Its collections, meanwhile, had ballooned in size, and behind closed doors every free corner of space—the 'temporary' storage sheds out the back, the cellars down below, and even the offices of curators—had taken on the overflow. Understaffed curators could barely find the time to do any actual research, and, when they did, had to rely on 'ancient' microscopes that could have passed for museum pieces themselves.[20]

Shortly after his arrival, the museum's entomology department had to contend with the loss of another key player when Nancy Adams died one night in January 1955, her final years having been plagued by the colon cancer that finally took her life at the age of forty-four. In *The Australian Museum Magazine*, now edited by the newly appointed Evans, her old boss Anthony Musgrave paid tribute to his 'loyal and conscientious colleague'. Her role had finally been reclassified a year after the butterfly case, her nineteen-year cadetship finally complete.[21]

The new director didn't shy away from College Street's many challenges. As he settled into Walkom's old office, Evans moved the desk to sit beneath the portrait of Alexander Macleay, the colonial secretary who, in 1836, had headed the Australian Museum's first management committee before fatefully sending his protégé John Roach up the river with Major Mitchell. Recognising the historic lineage he was now part of, Evans also had two additional portraits dug out of storage; before long, Macleay was flanked by two Wedgwood plaques of Joseph Banks and Daniel Solander.

'[It] seemed appropriate that the two first naturalists to set foot in Australia should be honoured in its oldest scientific institution,' Evans would later reflect.[22]

As a spiritual successor to Banks, Solander, Macleay, and all who came after them, Evans was now responsible for over 180 years of history and legacies that ran deeper, and were often far more troubled, than cramped sheds and tired exhibits. Set against that grand sweep of history, the yellow warning labels of the Wyatt Theft Collection were just one of the little timebombs waiting among the museum's bulging collections. But in this small area, at least, Evans could rest assured that it wasn't just the museums of Australia that would be haunted by the case of the stolen butterflies.

Pescott, Burns, and the police might have been frustrated by the initial press coverage back in April 1947, but the countless column inches around the world devoted to this novel heist would deliver a different kind of justice—even *Time* magazine had covered the trial, telling American readers of the crime of passion committed 'for the love of Lepidoptera.'[23]

'I don't want to give the impression that Wyatt has received no punishment,' Evans had written back in May 1947 in the hours after the trial at West Ham. 'The fine of course means nothing to him but he has had a very harrowing experience, the publicity in tonight's papers and there will be more tomorrow morning, will damn him for life, and I daresay it will be a long time before he returns to England.'[24]

PART III

Now fare ye well! enjoy your little hour;
Go, grasp the shadow of your vanished power;
Gloss o'er the failure of each fondest scheme;
Your strength a name, your bloated wealth a dream.
Gone is that Gold, the marvel of mankind,
And Pirates barter all that's left behind.

– Lord Byron, *The Curse of Minerva*

CHAPTER TWENTY-THREE

The Pilgrim

The young man seemed charming, cultured, and thoughtful as he greeted the English strangers, peering out through thick-rimmed glasses, his black hair closely cropped and his lean frame bundled up in maroon-and-yellow robes. The twenty-one-year-old had been born to humble circumstances, the son of a peasant farmer in a village along the disputed border between China and Tibet, and had just spent six long days travelling by foot, donkey, jeep, and finally an airforce plane as he made the 1,300-mile journey from Lhasa, the capital of Tibet, to a now-independent India.[1] But he wasn't like the hundreds of other pilgrims who had descended on New Delhi that week in November 1956 for a UNESCO-backed symposium on art, literature, and philosophy. When he stepped off the plane, the peasant's son was greeted with all the fanfare of a king, a god, or both, from the first prime minister of India, Jawaharlal Nehru, and his daughter, Indira Gandhi, to the reverential mass of supporters, thousands of them clad in yellow, waving welcome banners, and bearing flowered garlands.

He had been born Lhamo Tondrup, but his life and name had changed since the day a group of high priests from Lhasa had descended on his childhood home, convinced by a series of omens and visions that the then-two-year-old was in fact the reincarnation of the recently deceased thirteenth Dalai Lama.[2] Little Lhamo was now the fourteenth

Dalai Lama, the leader of Tibet, and for all intents and purposes a living deity — even if Tibet's 1950 invasion by the People's Liberation Army of the Chinese Communist Party would soon render him a 'god-king' in exile.

The three white Westerners certainly seemed in awe of him, having stood among the thousands of devotees that greeted the Dalai Lama off the plane, snapping photographs and filming every colourful moment for members of the Buddhist Society of London back home. The trio had already had quite an adventure, first travelling to Kathmandu in Nepal along with 300 conference delegates to the Fourth Congress of the World Fellowship of Buddhists. But now they had him all to themselves as a cabinet minister from the Indian government introduced each member of their small delegation by name.

The chief delegate was an older man with a pinstripe suit and patrician accent named Christmas Humphreys. The founder of the Buddhist Society of London, Humphreys was no peasant's son: he was a Supreme Court justice whose family had been a staple of London's courthouses for centuries. Humphreys had charted his own high-profile legal career that included war-crime trials in Tokyo, and hundreds of murder cases as chief prosecutor at the Old Bailey — even if his interest in Buddhism made him an outlier in the legal fraternity. In Humphrey's later years, the British press would be amused by the 'judge whose religion wouldn't let him harm a fly'.[3]

'To Buddhists all life is sacred,' he later explained to one British paper. 'Extremists even refuse to wear shoes in case they tread on insects.'[4]

For some, this sentiment jarred with the many people that Humphreys sent to the gallows across his time as a prosecutor — including several high-profile cases that helped sour the public mood on capital punishment. Most notable was that of Timothy Evans, a Welsh truck driver found guilty in 1950 of murdering his wife and daughter, based largely on the testimony of their neighbour John Christie. Evans had already met the hangman by the time Christie was exposed as a prolific serial killer whose other victims, hidden and buried around the building and garden he had shared with the Evanses, had been missed by the police investigation.

Speaking through an interpreter, Humphreys regaled the Dalai Lama with stories of the society's progress in England before handing him a copy of *Buddhist Texts Through the Ages* signed by each member of their party. Next, Mrs Carlo Robbins, an older woman who edited the society's newsletter *The Middle Way,* presented a large bouquet of white and yellow flowers.[5] Lastly, a forty-seven-year-old man with a ginger moustache and film camera close to hand stepped forward. He had been designated official photographer for the World Congress, and had already taken hundreds of stills and captured 1,000 feet of colour film on behalf of the London society. He handed over his own copy of *Buddhist Texts Through the Ages* for the Dalai Lama to sign as a souvenir while he soaked up every moment of the exchange to add to his already overflowing fund of astonishing anecdotes.

'I have only two real claims to fame,' Colin Wyatt would later tell a journalist of the experience. 'I am one of the few who has ever played chess with an Eskimo in an igloo, and had a personal interview with the Dalai Lama.'[6]

Around the time of his New Delhi pilgrimage, Colin Wyatt wrote a three-page essay for *United Asia* journal that sought to explain the steady flow of Westerners like himself who were abandoning the Sunday services and automatic Anglicanism of their upbringings in their thousands, years before the Beatles and the summer of love

To Wyatt, there seemed to be a groundswell of disillusionment across the West, where even the man on the street could, on some subconscious level, recognise there was something 'radically wrong' with modern British life.[7] The devastating toll of two world wars, combined with the scientific revolution, had fundamentally shaken their faith in a Christian God and left the masses blind, rudderless, and materialistic. Whether they found numbing escapism by staring up at a cinema screen, or cheering on their favourite sporting team, they would do anything to fill that nameless, aching void.[8]

For Wyatt, Buddhism provided an anchor. But, of course, in light of his earlier history of seeking solace, and of trying to occupy his mind through some outlandish diversions of his own, the piece is revealing in a different way. Wyatt might have been able to look the part of the classic British gentleman, a dazzling specimen of establishment privilege, but this article hinted at a streak of restless, bohemian nonconformity that bristled at the conventions of Western society. Like butterflies in a declining ecosystem, it was as if men such as Wyatt were flagships of a deeper malaise at the root of imperialist hierarchies that, on paper, they were meant to be the greatest beneficiaries of. Perhaps, for all the global conquests and cultural influence, there was an emptiness there that all the collecting in the world couldn't fill.

Wyatt's interest in Buddhism had gradually taken root in the years since he had glimpsed the forest temples and monks of Ceylon in 1937. After returning from his second stint in Australia, he had fallen in with Humphreys and his Buddhist Society, and before long he was serving on its council — he had even founded a small Farnham branch while living with his mother. But Wyatt had spent his adult life pursuing his passions to their extremes, and his high-altitude pilgrimage to Kathmandu and his encounter with the Dalai Lama himself were just another step on his journey. In 1957, he hiked for eighteen days through the Himalayas to reach the Tengboche monastery in the eastern Nepalese region of Khumba, not far from Mount Everest. He posed for a photo with the chief monk and another young, reincarnated lama — Wyatt's artfully dishevelled khaki traveller's outfit, with the cuffs of his trousers fringed with dirt, contrasting sharply with the monks' crisp robes.

'The Explorer made welcome,' read the caption when the photograph was printed in *The Middle Way* in 1957, alongside a lengthy dispatch from Burma (present-day Myanmar), where Wyatt had spent weeks in quiet isolation at the Thathana Yeiktha Meditation Centre, not far from the golden Hewegadon Pagoda he had flown over in December 1946.[9] At Thathana Yeiktha, the goal was ambitious, and the discipline strict: a serious resident would commit to between one and four months' stay, receiving no visitors, no mail, and making no contact with the outside world. From the moment that Colin was woken at 4.00 am by gongs each morning, he would spend hour after unbroken hour in silent pursuit of *Satipatthāna Vipassanā*, or the 'one-pointedness of the mind'. Paying close attention to the rise and fall of the body with each breath, a student would seek to master their mind and physical being in pursuit of *anicca* and *anattā* — what Wyatt described as a sense of 'impermanence', and the erasure of any sense of self or ego.[10] There were moments when the process reminded him of the skiing exercises that people once practised in the old 'Little Switzerland' he had helped set up at Lillywhite's, or the indoor ramp at Earl's Court where he and Mary had posed to announce their engagement. At other times, life at the centre recalled his London years for a different reason — the constant, round-the-clock background noise seemed to rival Piccadilly Circus at peak hour.[11]

By day, he could hear the noise from the main road outside — the market bazaar, the tinny loudspeakers — all vying to drag him out of his contemplative state. Night was hardly any better, accompanied by a gruff chorus of barking and howling ever since the monks had started giving rice to the stray dogs that sidled up, hungry and bedraggled, to the temple. But he persisted, and on his fourth day he willed himself into a kind of trance, and for a moment the former champion skier almost convinced himself that he had achieved a state of *satori* in record time. When he told the Master, however, he received a dressing down for trying to force the process.

The Master's message was simple: the point of meditation was not to 'break through' to reach some clearly conceived goal, but to sit back and surrender oneself to quiet observation and contemplation.[12]

It was a pointed lesson. Decades earlier, Wyatt's impatience on the ski jumps of St Moritz had led to him crashing out, as observers speculated that the ex-Cambridge ace seemed to be losing his touch. Cut off from the outside world at Thathana Yeiktha, there would be no shortcuts through the Tyrolean woods, no Frenchman's fence or national park boundaries he could skirt around with a little creativity, commitment, and smooth-talking charm. There were no forbidden drawers full of rare butterflies — the kind that might ordinarily take several lifetimes to gather, sitting ripe for the taking when nobody seemed to be watching them. Eventually, he found himself entering a state of full *samāadhi* for three or four hours at a time — a conscious mind seemingly untethered from his earthly body and the passage of time.

The Master was right: the long way was the only way, and as Colin later explained to *The Middle Way*'s readers, a student had to treat the experience like boarding a ship with an open-ended ticket, sailing out into endless open ocean, destination unknown. They would have to free their minds from all earthly preoccupations, and liberate themselves from the worries of the present — and the regrets of the past.[13]

The question of past regrets was a loaded one — Wyatt had done plenty of looking back in the years since walking out of the West Ham Magistrates Court in 1947. He had travelled the world as a famous athlete, a middle-of-the-road artist, and a notorious butterfly collector, but as a new decade arrived, he refashioned himself as a travel writer and author. Art remained his great passion, but over the years he strung together a healthy set of bylines and photography credits from the *Alpine Journal* and *Country Life* to Australia's *Walkabout* and *Pix* magazines. After returning to England, he resolved to turn writing, photography, and filmmaking into his main source of income, and with a ready-made back catalogue of photography and published work, it didn't take long for a relatively new London publisher called Thames & Hudson to acquire his debut book, *The Call of the Mountains.*

A large-format compilation of nearly two decades of adventures and photography, it was dedicated to Wyatt's late father, while invoking the 'golden age' of European mountaineering that James William Wyatt had known. Name-checking the deep impression that his father's generation of author-adventurers such as Whymper and Mummery had made on him as a boy, he now sought to write himself into that same canon of alpine literature, and to elevate the landscapes, peoples, and wildlife he had encountered to the same pedestal on which the mountains of Switzerland and Austria had long been held.

Written with the style of a storyteller well practised from yarning around campfires, spending weatherbound days in mountain huts, and taking long hikes with butterfly nets in hand, *The Call of the Mountains* invited the reader to retrace Wyatt's snow-printed footsteps. The book also filled in the gaps since he had left for Sweden in May 1947; in March

1949, he made his way to Morocco, where he invoked clunky Orientalist stereotypes — 'hook-nosed Arabs' and women who 'gazed aslant' from their veils — to describe the market squares of Marrakech, before heading to the mountains, where the sirocco winds swept in from the Sahara bearing desert sand and gales so strong he could barely hold on to his skis.[14] He was back again in April 1950, travelling into what French colonial authorities still considered a *zone d'insécurité* in the hidden valleys where tribesmen continued to hold out in their battle against the French. With special permits from the French army, Wyatt drove south from Casablanca in a small car crammed with skis and pickaxes, joined by his old friend and former housemate Peter Blaxland — the same Blaxland who had testified for him in the Sydney divorce court.

Venturing out from an abandoned French Foreign Legion fort, Wyatt and Blaxland began to cross the m'Goum massif, a triptych of 13,000-foot–high ranges. Wyatt took in the wide, red waters of Lake Izourar and the snow-covered peaks of the Ouaougouzlat Range, while shivering through some of the coldest nights of his life as they summited a series of peaks 12,500 to 13,400 feet high to reach the desert beyond. By the end of the trip, Wyatt had taken to heart the ubiquitous refrain heard among the Berber guides and the villagers they encountered along the way: '*insh'Allah!*' — 'God willing'.

In the book's final third, Wyatt repeatedly quoted his literary hero Lord Byron, the poet and 'mountain lover' whose pining for the solitude of the Alps seemed to mirror the sentiments of Wyatt's *United Asia* article:

> I live not in myself, but I become
> Portion of that around me; and to me
> High mountains are a feeling, but the hum
> Of human cities torture; I can see
> Nothing to loathe in nature, save to be
> A link reluctant in a fleshly chain,
> Class'd among creatures, when the soul can flee,
> And with the sky, the peak, the heaving plain
> Of ocean, or the stars mingle, and not in vain.[15]

Wyatt had already abandoned the 'torture' of human cities by the time *The Call of the Mountains* was published. Writing to Pam Rutherford Darling, a London-based columnist for the Australian *Daily Telegraph,* Wyatt said he had 'just taken a house in the National Park at Banff, the animal sanctuary'.[16] He had visited the Canadian Rockies once before in 1939, on his honeymoon tour with Mary as they made their way to Australia via North America, Hawaii, and New Zealand. Once again, he hadn't come to Canada alone, and as Rutherford Darling would explain to her *Daily Telegraph* readers, in addition to his new house and the 'great success' of his first book, Colin had remarried four years after he and Mary had parted.

'His attractive South American wife Elsa simply cannot get used to seeing elk and moose in her front garden, and once she found a bear sitting on a rubbish heap at the back of the house licking an old jar of honey,' Rutherford Darling wrote, in one of the only times the second Mrs Colin Wyatt—a Colombian photographer named Elsa Maria Herran—would be named in print. Elsa's backyard brush with the black bear would later appear in Wyatt's second book, along with a black-and-white photograph of another occasion in which a bear peered in from the back door of their renovated log cabin.[17]

While *The Call of the Mountains* was driven by his alpine exploits, his ambitious second book, *Going Wild: the autobiography of a bug-hunter,* framed his life through lepidoptery. Dedicated to his mother, the book spanned the entirety of his life to date, opening with a brief account of James William Wyatt's 1881 journey to Australia before revisiting his own childhood illness, his convalescence at Gstaad, and his father's efforts to mould his only son into a first-class mountaineer, skier, and butterfly collector. Published by Hollis & Carter in June 1955, it followed Wyatt from the butterfly fields of Digne and the Dolomites to his months as a camouflage officer in New Guinea. It even touched on his decoy experiments with Athol Waterhouse in 1941—although no mention was made of Waterhouse's presence at the bottom of the sheoak tree.

On its surface, *Going Wild*'s account of his childhood shared many of the same basic tenets as his lawyer Gerald Howard's address at the

West Ham court in May 1947—the 'delicate' only child nudged by his father to begin collecting butterflies, seeding a lifelong passion that would one day overwhelm his sense of reason. In *Going Wild*, however, Howard's story of the 'lonely self-centred boy', carefully calibrated to elicit sympathy in the judge and public, had undergone a dramatic metamorphosis. It was no longer a sad tale of a boy whose only respite from the outside world was collecting; instead, it was the picaresque story of a bold, inquisitive, if clearly eccentric gentleman scientist whose love of butterflies was merely one of the lenses through which he appreciated the world around him. If John Evans had thought that Howard's courtroom play was designed to make Wyatt seem 'almost a hero', a reader of *Going Wild* might be left wanting an autograph.

In 1955, Wyatt embarked on a seven-month journey in the northwest territories of Canada that would form his third and final book, *North of Sixty*. Once again invoking an earlier age of British exploration by the likes of Samuel Hearne, Alexander Mackenzie, and Sir John Franklin, Wyatt would reflect on the history of this seemingly remote and inhospitable place, and the Inuit people who had long thrived there, as it was transformed into a 'New North' by the advent of the Cold War. The book retraced Wyatt's journey across a 'vast white waste' where planes could disappear into fog for days at a time, if they returned at all. Out in the open, Wyatt's nose periodically turned white, his eyelashes froze shut, and his fingers fumbled on the cold metal trigger of his camera when it wasn't jammed up entirely, while the hood of his heavy caribou-skin parka became fringed with solid ice as did the eyes and muzzles of the sleigh-dog teams that carried him from settlement to settlement.[18]

As he travelled, he observed how modernity had impacted the land and its peoples. He heard how the caribou had been hunted to a 'shadow of their former glory', their numbers plummeting from the millions reported by early European explorers to just 300,000 in 1955.[19] As he reflected on the fur industry, Wyatt wrote that while he could understand the killing of an animal out of self-preservation, trapping wild creatures for the vanity of the fashion industry seemed to him a senseless transgression equal to the collectors who had driven New Guinea's birds of paradise to the edge of extinction.[20] He would also comment harshly on the 'patronising' interventions of the Canadian government on the lives and culture of the Inuit people who often hosted him.

For all the social and environmental commentary, *North of Sixty* packed plenty of high-flying adrenaline. In one memorable passage, Wyatt described catching a ride to Bathurst Inlet aboard the *Norseman*, a yellow seaplane whose cabin had already been packed with a full berth of cargo. The pilot had presented an option he hardly believed that Wyatt would entertain: he was welcome to ride along in a three-foot-deep cavity in one of the plane's floats that had apparently been used before in emergencies. Wyatt quickly accepted, although by the time he walked out onto the pontoon to see spectators with cameras lining the beach, he felt like a condemned man taking his final walk out to the scaffold before squeezing himself into place, cross-legged like a 'Yogi'.[21]

'You can't expect luxury, dash it, when you travel Economy Flight,' Wyatt would later tell a newspaper journalist of the experience.[22]

Despite the freezing cold and terrifying transportation, Wyatt often felt entirely at home in the isolation of the Arctic; after an extended period of living in igloos, he was happy with Arctic life, and dreaded the thought of leaving.[23] Perhaps unsurprisingly, when Hodder & Stoughton published *North of Sixty* in 1958, Wyatt declared it his best book yet, and dedicated it to another family member: he and Elsa's three-year-old daughter, 'whose first doll was made by an Eskimo'.

But while his family had grown, in some ways he was once again a lone wanderer; he had separated from Elsa by the time *North of Sixty* was released, and although he generally kept his marriages out of his books, there were moments that revealed the perspective of a middle-aged man whose second marriage had collapsed even faster than his first one had. While observing the matrimonial norms of the Inuit people he visited, he made a curious observation that they seemed to lack the 'licentious immorality' he saw among Westerners, which he believed was evident in the growing prevalence of divorce. This, in turn, Wyatt blamed on a lack of morals, a disregard for 'family responsibilities', and the rising phenomenon of women's liberation.[24] The author photograph on the back of *North of Sixty*'s dust jacket saw the once-dashing ski prodigy, who in the early pages of *The Call of the Mountains* and *Going*

Wild had travelled the world chasing a romanticised vision of adventure, exploration, and butterflies, looking a little more weathered, just shy of fifty years of age. Wyatt still looked striking in tall boots and high-waisted trousers, but his hairline was higher, his face lined, and, despite the seemingly weightless nature of his itinerant lifestyle, he was clearly a man with baggage.

Taken as one body of work, *The Call of the Mountains, Going Wild,* and *North of Sixty* might reasonably leave readers thinking they had been granted an all-access, first-person view of Wyatt's half-century on earth — a life that was, by any account, an extraordinary one. But while Wyatt revealed much in his short but fruitful career as an author, the details and stories he deliberately omitted were often just as revealing. Across these 530 pages, Wyatt walked a seemingly impossible tightrope; in words and pictures, he told the story of his lifetime of butterfly collecting, of the exotic and remote places it would take him, and of the delicate and beautiful creatures that crossed his path and fell into his net. Carefully carved out of those narratives, however, was any mention of his encounters with Norman Riley, the detectives in Farnham, the hearing at West Ham, and the vast shadow it cast over his Australian collection and the seven years he spent in Australia. A single reference to the late 'Dr Waterhouse', described in passing by Wyatt as 'Australia's leading butterfly expert', bore no hint of the many earlier occasions in which he had invoked the old collector's name — or the profound betrayal that ensued.[25]

Historians describe such gaps in an archive as lacunae, and the Wyatt story is full of them. A reader of *Going Wild* would never know that, in between the field trips so lyrically described within its pages, its author had undertaken an unknown number of visits to museums in three Australian cities over the course of nearly a year, quietly, politely, and systematically harvesting the three richest collecting spots in the country. As the curator and chronicler of his own history books, Wyatt had captured his own personal golden age in black and white. But, not unlike the old history books that glorified Australia's great explorers, it was a white-washed edifice, riddled with cracks.

***

There was one more Colin Wyatt adventure that never made it into print. On 19 October 1948, he had found himself back in London, in another courtroom, as a woman named Barbara McKechnie laid out her case against him. Dressed in a white hat and veil and a pussy bow, in lieu of a barrister's wig and gown, McKechnie was no government prosecutor — she wasn't even a lawyer. As she stood before the judge, the self-described freelance journalist was doing the one thing no good lawyer recommends: representing herself in court. Despite her lack of legal qualifications, McKechnie had spent the previous fifteen months 'swotting up' on the law, later telling reporters that she had lived off her savings — 'existing on bread and cabbage' — just to have her day in court.[26]

Over a year earlier, she explained, she had been planning a trip to Norway, across Lapland, when she felt a pang of 'writer's loneliness'. Spotting an article by Colin Wyatt in a copy of a mountaineering journal, she wrote to him with an invitation to discuss the possibility of him joining her. When Wyatt's initial reply seemed receptive, she claimed to have sent him a questionnaire to gauge his character — not a bad idea for a single woman cold-calling male travel companions they found in a magazine. The first few questions, as recited in court, seemed to suggest that she hadn't heard of Wyatt before and was as uncertain of his nationality and character as all those anonymous informants in wartime Australia had been.

'Do you think and feel like the British?' read the first question, followed by 'Do you believe in our general codes of behaviour?'

The final question, however, seemed oddly specific: 'Is there anything in your record you regret, as it is bound to come out?'

In court, McKechnie claimed that before they left on their 'long trip', Wyatt had given the impression he was both an 'expert photographer' and a 'man of complete integrity'.

'This was untrue,' she argued, 'as he was convicted at West Ham court of the theft of 1,600 priceless butterflies.'[27]

When the truth came out after their trip, McKechnie claimed that her onetime companion withheld the photographs he had taken on their adventure — a collection that Wyatt himself valued at £576. This, McKechnie said, had provoked her to sue him for fraud, trespass, and negligence. According to one newspaper report, Wyatt claimed through his lawyer that he had accompanied McKechnie as a partner in a joint 'literary-pictorial venture', not merely a hired hand. At some point in the trip, however, Miss McKechnie had 'made advances to him', advances he 'repulsed'. The case, therefore, was an act of embarrassed retribution.

The judge didn't quite know what to make of the dogged Miss McKechnie, and times appeared visibly annoyed to the point of throwing down his pencil in despair.[28] All the same, he did occasionally concede that she made some good points, and in his ruling declared her to be 'bitter and vindictive' but ultimately truthful. He disregarded Wyatt's alternative story of a spurned woman, and ruled in McKechnie's favour on the count of trespass while dismissing the charges of fraud and negligence. Wyatt was ordered to return the photographs and to pay McKechnie damages of £500, plus two-thirds of her costs. All up, this amounted to at least ten times the penalty that Wyatt had received at West Ham over a year earlier. This unqualified, eccentric, and unrelenting woman had done what police, prosecutors, government, and entomologists in Australia and England could not, and her revenge was tenfold.

After the verdict, a triumphant McKechnie fronted reporters, telling them that, 'The judge was a perfect dear, though I do not know why he thought I was vindictive.'[29]

It appears that McKechnie never published a word in any major outlet, but within three months of the trial began delivering a lecture entitled 'Land of the Midnight Sun' to memorial halls and tennis clubs around Middle England.[30] From the Hinchley Wood Townswomen's Guild to the West End Women's Institute, McKechnie would speak colourfully about the land and its peoples she had encountered — all with the aid of a series of lantern slides.[31]

With or without his photographs, Colin Wyatt made sure that McKechnie was also written out of his many Lapland adventures when they appeared in *The Call of the Mountains* and *Going Wild* years later.

But the case does highlight one cold truth: history has a way of catching up with us. Or, as his old friend Christmas Humphreys wrote in his twelve principles of Buddhism, 'all effects have causes, and man's soul or character is the sum total of his previous thoughts and acts'.[32] You can try to push unpleasant truths out of the frame, but they will always be a part of your story—along with the consequences. According to Humphreys, Buddhism offered a more succinct word for this principle of action and reaction: karma.

CHAPTER TWENTY-FOUR

The Exile

Colin Wyatt was frozen in place, crouched precariously on a steep slope of loose, crumbling scree, using every ounce of strength and concentration to remain perfectly, painstakingly still.[1] He was fifty-four years old, some 3,500 metres above sea level, and close to exhaustion as he clung to the side of the valley, which was almost bare except for a specific breed of prickly alpine flower that crept through the gaps in the red rockface.

As he lay in wait in the summer of 1963, he knew that even the slightest movement of his arm, head, or foot might send his target — so reclusive, so fast, so careful to rarely settle on the ground — sailing back up the cliff face and out of sight. But an even greater challenge, perhaps, was ignoring all the other rare Asiatic butterflies fluttering past — *Parnassius delphius,* or even *Melitae shandura,* named by the late brigadier William Harry Evans in 1924 — that on any other day might have drawn his attention and net. But he had come all this way, to a special and remote part of Afghanistan's Hindu Kush mountains, for a specific purpose: to capture fresh and flawless specimens of *Parnassius autocrator,* a breed so rare that it had taken him years to track it down. It was so elusive that not even the British Natural History Museum's *Parnassius* collection, the one that Norman Riley had suspected him of raiding thirty years earlier, could lay claim to a specimen. On this mission, in July 1963, it was now a case of *Parnassius autocrator* or nothing.

It had taken all his skill and charm to get this far: following a trail of clues that required his best Sherlock Holmes impression, crossing terrain that tested his famous mountaineering skills, and navigating delicate negotiations with the suspicious Afghan authorities who had turned him away in 1937.[2] He knew that only two other collectors before him had caught *P. autocrator* in the wild—a Russian, Andrey Avinoff, in 1914, and a German collector who had roamed these mountains in 1936. But the German had died in World War II, and his *P. autocrator* specimens had long since disappeared into the collectors' market.[3]

As the years passed, Wyatt had almost given up hope; like his earlier attempts in his twenties, the mountains of Asia and the Middle East seemed too far, too expensive for his reach, even before considering the perpetual unrest that saw successive Iron and Bamboo Curtains fall between him and his most coveted prizes.[4] But Wyatt had managed to track down the German's daughter, and after exchanging many letters he had set out in 1960 to retrace the dead man's steps.

It was while riding through the mountains of Badakhshan in north-east Afghanistan, near the Russian Pamir border, in present-day Tajikistan, that he first saw *P. autocrator* for himself. He was half-asleep in the saddle as his horse trundled uphill, when, out of nowhere, a glimpse of something dark and fluttering set him on edge—it was as if he had a sixth sense that had suddenly been stirred. It was *P. autocrator*, a little out of place at only 2,800 metres above sea level, but still unmistakable. By the time the butterfly had settled to sun itself on a rock—dusty grey with two egg-yolk-yellow spots—he knew he was about to join Avinoff and the German as the third collector in history to capture it.

He saw two more, and after deducing they must have been blown down from their preferred altitude by a strong gust of wind, he followed them uphill to a height of around 3,500 metres. This had to be the place, and, sure enough, he spotted four more fluttering by. He managed to bag a handful of both male and female specimens on that trip, but by the time he got back down off the mountain, the majority of them were worn and tattered.[5] Ever since, Wyatt had dreamed of returning to this 'fairytale place', and now, with a Japanese entomologist from the University of Munich named Keiichi Omoto by his side, it was time for round two.

Wyatt and Omoto had set out from Kabul in July 1963, travelling by jeep and horseback with a local university student as their government-appointed interpreter. The trio spent long hours in the saddle navigating narrow, winding paths as the wind lashed their faces. They reached villages of red mudbrick houses ringed with poplar and apricot trees, and led their horses on foot as they waded through snow, passing jagged crests and sheets of ice on either side of the path. Finally, they arrived at the same area that Wyatt had identified years earlier, and, after making their base camp at 2,800 metres, spent a week straight climbing for one or two hours each morning to reach the sweet spot before stumbling back each afternoon after a full day of collecting. By the time they finished their trip, Wyatt and Omoto had lost around ten kilos each. But all that time spent teetering on the side of the mountain had paid off handsomely. The pair had gained something special, and unforgettable: another historic haul of *Parnassius autocrator*.

Upon their return home, Wyatt and Omoto wrote an article about their Afghan adventures for the October 1963 edition of German journal *Zeitschrift der Wiener Entmologischen Gesellschaf.* Ten years later, that article caught the eye of an English entomologist named Phillip Ackery, who on 28 September 1973 wrote a letter addressed to Colin Wyatt at his mother's old house in Farnham.[6] Based in the New Spirit Building at the Natural History Museum, Ackery was of a younger generation than the likes of John Evans and Norman Riley, and had never heard of Wyatt before reading the 1963 paper. In the letter, Ackery explained that he was working on an illustrated guide to Parnassinae, and had read with interest of their hunt for *P. autocrator* and of its passing references to that other species, *P. delphius.* He asked Wyatt if he had observed the larval food plants of the latter on his journey, and whether he might share the information for inclusion in Ackery's paper. It was a perfectly routine request from one scientist to another, part of the collegial exchange of information that kept the scientific world ticking — the kind of request that once perennially occupied Athol Waterhouse's letterbox and pen.

It only took a few days for Wyatt to respond, with a typewritten, two-page letter on 3 October on the same old Cobbetts letterhead he had used in his letter to Ras Wilson back in January 1947. It began politely enough, as Wyatt told the younger scientist that he was delighted to hear that the paper had piqued his interest. Within a few lines, however, his tone began to shift. Wyatt told Ackery that while he might ordinarily be happy to assist, these days he was a widower with a daughter to put through university, who relied on lecture tours and televised travelogue programs to make an income.[7]

Then Wyatt dropped a bombshell: in increasingly spiky language, he began to air a series of accusations that had clearly been waiting for an outlet. He claimed that unnamed authorities at the Natural History Museum had threatened this livelihood — authorities he believed had forwarded 'affidavits' and spread rumours to their museum counterparts in America. These statements, Wyatt insisted, were 'malicious and unfounded', and he had half a mind to sue.

'Marco Polo himself never told of greater wonders than lecturer Colin Wyatt described to an audience of 700 last night at a Mansfield Lions travelogue,' read Ohio's *Mansfield News Journal* in March 1962, after the screening of a documentary dubbed *Nepal: Hidden Kingdom of the Himalayas.*[8]

Spliced together from the reels of footage captured across his trips to Kathmandu, Nepal, and New Delhi in 1956 and 1957, Wyatt had toured his one-man picture show to small-town church halls, high school auditoriums, and local television stations across North America, from the Santa Barbara Women's Club to the Maryland Academy of Science, the Honolulu YMCA to the First Methodist Church of Noblesville. It was not, perhaps, the most prestigious speaking circuit that America had to offer, but from Petoskey, Michigan to Sandusky, Ohio, audiences were entranced as he screened flickering colour footage of Himalayan rhododendron forests in full crimson blossom, ancient Tibetan temples with rows of prayer wheels set spinning by pilgrims, and a seventeen-day trek to the base of Mount Everest.[9] He had other films too — *Hindustan Holiday,* and later, *Iran: Land of the Peacock Throne* — and as the projector churned through each reel, Wyatt would settle into the familiar role of storyteller, narrating each scene from a pre-written script much as Sir Henry Galway once regaled the Public Library in Adelaide with his Benin tales and 'electric light illustrations'.

'Better describe me as an international bum and a jack of all trades,' he told a columnist from the *Honolulu Star-Bulletin,* who presented readers with a pith-helmeted caricature of a 'veddy, veddy British' man who 'looks and sounds like a puka sahib who has played polo in Poona, gone pig-sticking in Peshawar, and exterminated half the jolly old tigers in Travancore'. He was also, the columnist added, 'a master of the understatement'.[10]

It was a cartoonishly inaccurate but nonetheless suggestive cliché. To American audiences, it seemed that Colin Wyatt had become something of an exotic curiosity himself — a road-worn explorer who seemed to have stepped into the modernising 1960s from another era, full of astonishing tales of far-off locations that, in his telling, seemed frozen in time.

At times, the strangeness of his material only added to the sense of novelty — like the footage of an 'Abominable Snowman' scalp in a remote Himalayan monastery. A few years earlier, the famed mountaineer Sir Edmund Hillary had taken an animal expert from the Chicago Zoo to examine a similar series of 'Yeti' relics — scalps, skins, and bones — held in monasteries and homes across Khumjung, Tengboche, Pangboche, and Namche Bazaar.[11] While Hillary's party couldn't explain the sightings of large tracks around the mountains, the organic matter was debunked as belonging to bears or antelopes. Wyatt, however, remained open-minded.

'I believe the snowman does exist,' Wyatt told The *Honolulu Advertiser* in 1959. 'I know something of zoology. The scalp is certainly not a red bear as some say.'[12]

In 1962, he was still 'firmly convinced', although he had no clue as to what it could be, telling the local newspaper in Mansfield, Ohio, that, 'There is too much circumstantial evidence — too many identical reports from places 6,000 miles apart for me to disbelieve.'[13] A less charitable reading might chalk these convictions up to a late-in-life slide into fantasy or hucksterism — somewhere between Dr Robin Tillyard's 'flights of phantasy' in Boston, or the scoundrel John Roach's 'bunyip' skull in Sydney. But Wyatt had, after all, lived through a time when the tracks of the Tasmanian Tiger could still be seen in the snow in remote areas.[14] While on the South Island of New Zealand in 1936, he had encountered a hunter who insisted that he had recently heard the 'mournful cries' of the flightless bird *Notornis,* thought to have been driven out of existence. In *Going Wild,* Wyatt noted that a decade later, in 1948, a live *Notornis* was successfully photographed not far from where the hunter had seen it.[15]

Flashes of cryptozoology notwithstanding, the 1960s were a comparatively grounded decade for Colin Wyatt, a period of endings and beginnings. In March 1961, his second wife, Elsa, died in Canada, leaving Wyatt the sole parent of their seven-year-old daughter, Monica. He eventually brought her back to his mother Margaret's home in Farnham, the same rambling old country house that Detective Sergeant Cameron and Norman Riley had visited all those years earlier. When Margaret Wyatt died the following year at the age of eighty-six, having outlived her husband, James, by two decades, her son decided to lay down roots in Farnham, selling off the log cabin in Banff to give his daughter some stability, even if the English countryside seemed an odd fit for the lifelong traveller.

While his daughter settled into school, Wyatt set his old pith helmet on top of a wardrobe, built a darkroom to develop his photographs, and hung his old paintings of alpine flowers around her bedroom, having all but retired his paintbrush a few years earlier.[16] But there were signs that Cobbetts' new owner was cut from a different cloth from his neighbours.

Over the hedge, a neighbour might have been able to make out distant notes of exotic-sounding Mexican and Brazilian records he had brought back from his travels, or from field recordings he had made himself. Come summertime, they might have peeked through the blinds in disbelief at the sight of Wyatt in flip-flops, with a silk sarong patterned with birds wrapped around his waist, as he headed into town to lodge outlandish requests with the perplexed greengrocer. (In the 1960s, ingredients such as red chilli and 'avocado pears' were a rare sight on

Surrey shopping lists, but Wyatt was an ambitious, experimental cook, inspired to prepare his own twists on the exotic dishes he had sampled abroad.)

The quietude of Farnham life was, occasionally, punctuated by other close shaves. In the early hours of 26 October 1963, Wyatt was driving along the main road between Farnham and London when, at around 1.15 am, he crashed into a well-to-do couple in a Jaguar.[17] According to one eyewitness, his car 'bounced off, went across the road, over the grass verge and disappearing down a bank', while Wyatt himself told police that he had intended to safely overtake the Jaguar when it 'swung out' in front of him, turning right without indicating. When the case reached a Woking courtroom that December, however, the Jaguar's driver insisted that he had his indicator flashing, and his arm signalling out the window, when there was a 'terrific smash'. Wyatt pleaded not guilty to driving in a dangerous manner, and even produced photographs he had taken of the crash site. He told the court he was an 'expert photographer', but was fined £40 and banned from driving for a year anyway.

Within weeks of the verdict, he was off again. Despite their Farnham base, Wyatt made sure his daughter knew there was a bigger world beyond the English countryside, and in January 1964, like the previous year, he returned to St Moritz and then on to France in April. Like his own father, Colin had introduced her to skiing when she was still a toddler in the Banff years, and would take her to St Moritz, a ski school in Europe, and on trips to Spain, France, America, and Mexico. He would also continue to venture out on his own expeditions to collect butterflies and to capture more film for his lectures about Iran, Azerbaijan, or Mexico, returning home to air out his little tent in the backyard, his well-worn travelling clothes still carrying the musk of every sweaty mile.

In October 1970, after her sixteenth birthday, Colin took his daughter on a six-month around-the-world trip. They visited her mother's family in Colombia, and travelled through Peru, the United States, and Canada before making their way to Australia. Despite the explosive aftermath of his original seven years as an Australian, Wyatt spent the trip reconnecting with the Blaxlands and other friends he had made decades earlier. One day, they paid a visit to Sydney Harbour, where the father of one of Monica's old school friends in Farnham was working on an ambitious new building, an opera house right on the waterfront. Her friend's father was an engineer, tasked with designing the glass curtain walls that enclosed the openings of massive concrete shells, recalling the shell middens that dotted the coastline when Joseph Banks first sailed into those waters in 1770.

As they looked out from the Sydney Opera House's unfinished skeleton, and across the city that Wyatt had first visited as a twenty-eight-year-old wanderer, and then again as a newlywed when the world was on the cusp of war, it was clear that a lot of water had passed under the Sydney Harbour Bridge—which had been near-new when he first laid eyes on it.

His former collecting partner Athol Waterhouse had been dead for twenty years, and practically every person involved in the 1947 case had either died or retired. For years afterwards, the museum world had remained on high alert, trying in vain to convince British authorities to help them track down additional missing specimens. In 1951, Dick Pescott wrote to Riley, Walkom, and Hale after hearing that 'our mutual friend' planned to visit Australia under 'an assumed name'.[18] In response, Riley joked, 'You can keep him.'[19] But by 1971, even John Evans had called time on his directorship after nine years, and whereas Colin Wyatt had once been a subject of scandal, a confessed thief whose misdeeds had been splashed across newspapers in every city and town in the country, as he walked around Sydney Harbour he could be mistaken for any tourist showing his daughter the world.

Back in Farnham, Wyatt had even been paid a visit by a familiar woman now in her early fifties. Whatever had happened to their marriage back in 1946, enough time had passed for the former Mary Wyatt to seek out Colin's old photo albums of their Australian years, which she hoped to borrow to give her daughter and son a glimpse of her past life on the far side of the world. Colin obliged, even if for a moment he wondered if he would ever see the photo albums again. To the outside world, Colin Wyatt seemed at peace with his past as the 1960s ended. Then a letter like Ackery's could come along and expose old wounds and resentments that, even after all those years, had never quite healed.

***

As Wyatt tapped out his response in October 1973, he explained to Ackery that, two years earlier, a pair of friends at the Carnegie Museum in Pittsburgh had tipped him off to his apparent blacklisting, telling him that, due to some 'damn bad enemies' he must have made at the British Natural History Museum, the Pittsburgh museum had been banned from hiring him on future lecture tours. Wyatt acknowledged that there were indeed sins in his past — sins that he insisted had been made under extreme emotional and psychological pressure. But, he claimed, he had already made 'full restitution' for those earlier indiscretions, and these additional accusations circulated by the Natural History Museum were false and mistaken.

Wyatt stopped short of specifying what incident these 'false statements' referred to, but there were a few contenders. Wyatt's name had come up again two years after his own trial, when in February 1949 the famous French collector Eugène le Moult discovered 20,000 butterflies missing from his Parisian mansion.[20] The thief clearly knew their way around a butterfly collection — which, in le Moult's case, numbered well over one million. 'They took only the best', the sixty-seven-year-old told reporters, while noting that a layman would have taken months to sift through his thousands of cases.[21] Le Moult suspected an 'inside job' and offered two names to investigators, telling one newspaper that, 'The culprit had pinned ordinary, common butterflies on the pins that formerly impaled the valuable specimens so that I would not notice their disappearance.'[22]

A sweep of local collectors soon identified a mysterious seller who went by the name of 'Peler Eck'.[23] Described as a 'tall, heavyset Dutchman', Eck had sold several hundred stolen butterflies to dealers around the Sorbonne, which he claimed to have caught while serving in the Pacific with the American military — including a one-of-a-kind birdwing, *Ornithoptera rothschildi,* bequeathed to le Moult by Baron Walter de Rothschild.[24] The details of the case raised obvious parallels to the 1947 Wyatt trial. Like a great artist, had Wyatt's widely publicised thefts inspired a school of imitators? Or had he crossed paths with the mysterious 'Eck' during the war, as the butterfly craze gripped servicemen around the Pacific? According to one report, a French detective had even visited England to review the dossier of the Wyatt case — but it seems that nothing ever came of their enquiries.

Much like the coverage of the 'butterfly corporal', Fred Brandt, a few years later, the media relished the now-familiar trope of a villainous butterfly collector — 'Pssst, Bud! Wanna Buy Some Hot Butterflies?' read one headline in New York's *Daily News*.[25] All the same, the reporting that linked Wyatt to this new theft drew on anonymous police gossip that bore little resemblance to original case files — one widely syndicated American article floated a wild theory that investigators suspected Wyatt's Australian thefts of having been coordinated by an unidentified 'master mind', and suggested that 'a unique gang of butterfly burglars is on the job'.[26] It also misquoted Wyatt's trial testimony with the poetic mea culpa: 'Some men would have taken to drink. I took to butterflies.'[27]

Over a decade later, another case mystified Canadian authorities. In February 1962, an estimated 10,000 specimens were found to be missing from Ottawa's Central Experimental Farm, a government research facility with a four-million-strong insect collection. Much like the Australian museums in 1947, the theft had been discovered by chance — in this case, three-and-a-half years after the last comprehensive inventory of its drawers.[28] 'It was a pretty tricky business,' the institute's director told reporters, 'a real sneaky operation.'[29] Local police joked that they were looking for 'a possible Walter Mitty type', but the case would remain unsolved for decades, even as the original tally was eventually revised down to between 400 and 500 — it turned out that most of the 10,000 specimens had been lent to other institutions, apparently with little paperwork.[30]

Whichever case Wyatt was referring to, in his letter to Ackery he claimed that another close friend had confided the real culprit's identity to him years earlier. There was no way to corroborate this story: the friend, a Maryland collector named Frank Chermock, had died in 1967, and despite his outrage at being 'loused' up, Wyatt refused to 'rat', even if it cleared his own name. As a result, Wyatt said, Ackery's colleagues had 'queered [his] pitch' with most American entomologists, and were it not for the lack of hard proof, he would have sued over their whisper campaign.

These were vague but incendiary claims, and when an understandably bewildered Ackery finished reading the letter, he promptly ran its contents up the chain of command to his superiors. The keeper of entomology forwarded him a file of papers written by Norman Riley four decades earlier: a contemporaneous account of the missing *Parnassius* specimens, his quiet confrontation with the young Colin Wyatt, and the specimens' subsequent, mysterious return the very next day. Riley's testimony from April 1930, though legally untested, still seemed plausible, and if there was some other false accusation levelled at Wyatt in affidavits, whether it was a Parisian bait-and-switch, a decade-old Canadian heist, or some other unsolved case, Ackery wasn't told.

Nevertheless, Wyatt maintained his innocence while making a barbed appeal to Ackery's sense of Christian forgiveness. He then made an offer: he would happily help the younger scientist if Ackery first convinced the director of entomology at the Natural History Museum to pen him a personal apology, and write to the head of the Carnegie Museum clearing his name. Upon receipt of carbon copies of the correspondence, Wyatt promised, he would give Ackery all the information he could. But even as he laid out his demands, it was clear that Wyatt knew no letters would be forthcoming—and that he fully expected to never hear from Ackery again.

Years earlier, Wyatt had given yet another newspaper interview to *The Ottawa Citizen*, this time while attending an annual meeting of the Lepidopterists Society in July 1952—hosted in the 'Bughouse' of the same Central Experimental Farm that, within a few years, would be struck by a 'Butterfly Bandit' of its own. In just a few quotes, Wyatt sought to give the reporter a glimpse of the entomological world, a kind of secret society that spanned the globe, with a universal language of knotty Latin nomenclature and the shared tools of a pin, forceps, and net.

'We are a sort of bug lovers' free masonry,' Wyatt explained, as he and four other entomologists smirked and posed for the camera, pointing to a case of clouded yellow butterflies, his tie tucked into his shirt to stop it brushing over the pinned insects.

'Any secret signs?' the reporter asked.

'No and no passwords,' he replied[31]

Wyatt had, for the moment, charmed his way into the heart of North America's butterfly-collecting community, much like he had in Australia during the war. But it wouldn't be long before his past caught up with him again: at an annual meeting of the Lepidopterists Society in 1958, the president made a veiled reference to Wyatt's earlier criminal history in his address. '[We] have all heard tales of a past generation of collectors who lived by the adage that "The best collecting is in someone else's collection"', he said.[32] 'It is not amiss, I trust, to mention that such rugged individualism still survives; in fact some in this room would be surprised at the name of a member of our own generation who was forced only by police action to disgorge thousands of museum specimens, including many butterfly types, looted on two continents.'

Much like his short and barbed correspondence with Ackery two decades later, it was another painful reminder that, in certain powerful corners of the entomological establishment, Colin Wyatt remained an exile, excommunicated and blacklisted. He was marked for life, just as John Evans had predicted, even as an uninitiated scientist such as Ackery recognised the legitimate scientific impact of his work. He finished his letter to Ackery with a bitterly sarcastic sign-off:

> Cordially,
> Colin W. Wyatt.[33]

Two years after his letter to Ackery, and the old resentments it dragged to the surface, Wyatt seemed to be standing on the precipice of something big. After all the lost opportunities and lingering suspicions that dogged him from England to the United States, he appeared optimistic that 1976 was shaping up to be a promising year. There was talk of taking his film-and-lecture travelogue series onto the cruise-ship circuit, and of returning to Switzerland to participate in public health programs half a century after his mother saved his life by taking him to Gstaad.[34]

But, for the most part, his attention was now fixated on Central America, as the erstwhile skier, mountaineer, painter, photographer, and author reinvented himself once again as a roving archaeologist. For well over a decade, he had been travelling on and off to Mexico, visiting Yucatán, Chohulo, El Tajín, Xochicalco, Oaxaca, and Palenque. On trips to Peru, he hiked to Machu Picchu, Puno, Cusco, Pisac, and Ollantaytambo, filling photo albums with studies of market scenes and carved stone monuments.

Years earlier, when recounting his visit to the jungles of Ceylon in *Going Wild*, Wyatt explained how its decaying temples and cities seemed to capture a lost way of life, even as they had lain abandoned and practically undisturbed for a millennia.[35] It would seem he found a similar sense of peace and timeless continuity in Mesoamerica. Now that his daughter had moved out of home to begin studying at university in London, Wyatt even considered moving to Guatemala — he already spoke fluent Spanish, and after a decade in Farnham was no doubt restless to put England, its law courts, and its scientific establishment behind him.

In November 1975, he wrote to his daughter from Guatemala with exciting news: he had planned to keep moving, travelling onto Mexico in December, but an unexpected stroke of luck now forced him to change his plans. Like the archaeologist-spy Sylvanus Morley before him, Wyatt had received a tip-off about a little-known site not far from Uaxactún, which he had become convinced was the location of an ancient, hitherto unexcavated ruin.[36]

'In leaving the ruins to their majestic solitude again, I could not help but wonder when and under what circumstances it would be broken again,' Morley had written nearly six decades earlier as he prepared to leave Uaxactún in May 1916. 'Our trails will soon be overgrown, the traces of our brief sojourn effaced. They will be as before with this one exception — their secret, or better, a fraction of it — will have been given up to the outside world.'[37]

Perhaps Wyatt had something similar in mind as he eagerly reshuffled his itinerary to investigate whatever secrets awaited him in the jungles that Morley and his team of archaeologists and chicleros had once penetrated. Even by 1975, venturing beyond tourist-friendly destinations such as Tikal wasn't easy; by road, it would take what one Associated Press journalist described as 'a kidney-jarring daredevil ride over dirt, mud and rock roads' with little evidence of any civilisation at all.[38] But in his November letter, Wyatt told his daughter that he had managed to secure a seat on a plane — a small service, run once a week by Guatemala's national airline to ferry locals back and forth from Guatemala City to the small, remote airstrip near Uaxactún.

Wyatt posted the letter, and made his way to Flores International Airport on Tuesday 18 November. It was a gloomy day, with rainclouds hanging ominously even at this late stage of the wet season. He settled into his seat on Aviateca TG-AGA all the same — after all, he had seen worse weather and endured much bumpier rides. As the plane prepared for take-off, he was on his way to another adventure, another discovery, maybe even another golden age.

CHAPTER TWENTY-FIVE

The Overture

Aviateca flight TG-AGA had already crashed in the jungle near El Caobo by the time Colin Wyatt's last letter reached his daughter in England. Eventually, what remained of the passenger with the signet ring was finally identified as its author, the Canadian citizen whose name was initially mistranslated as 'Colin Wiatt'.[1] It was that signet ring—the one bearing the family crest of a once-great architectural dynasty, not unlike the ring seen on his hand as it gripped a ski pole on the slope in St Moritz in 1929, while leading a dance partner around a London ballroom in *The Tatler* in 1935, or arm in arm with Mary Scott Barrett on their wedding day in 1939—that helped authorities answer the final riddle of Colin William Fforde Wyatt's long, adventurous, and occasionally inexplicable life, now over at the age of sixty-six.

Even once Wyatt's fate was clear, it remained a complicated case. The Guatemalan authorities had enlisted the Canadian consulate soon after realising that one of their citizens had been on board Aviateca TG-AGA, but tracking down his next of kin proved a tall order. After all, Wyatt hadn't lived in Canada for years, the log cabin address at Banff had been sold a decade earlier, and his estranged wife, Elsa, had predeceased him. When they finally found out about the twenty-one-year-old daughter in England, it turned out that she wasn't living at his listed address in Farnham at all.

Monica Wyatt had been out for the day when authorities finally found out which London university she was studying at and managed to get hold of its registrar. She had been off visiting a sick friend in hospital, and arrived back at her student digs to find the landlady waiting with serious news written all over her ashen face.

'There's someone here to see you,' she said, before asking Monica to follow her to another room, where she was told the news of the plane crash and her father's death.[2]

It was a lot to take in. Along with the shock of her father's death, and the harrowing circumstances of the plane crash, she faced a mess of confronting, convoluted logistics to unravel from opposite sides of the Atlantic Ocean. It was initially unclear who Colin had named as executor of his will and estate, further delaying any attempt to repatriate his body to England. Amid the uncertainty, some friends of his on the ground in Guatemala took the initiative to bury what the authorities were able to recover. Perhaps, on some level, it made sense that his final resting place was not in an Anglican cemetery in some dull English town, but on the distant land he had hoped to make his new home. Later, however, it emerged that, according to his will, Colin had stated that, in the event of his death, he wished to be buried in the presence of a Buddhist monk. But by then it was already too late.

As news of Wyatt's death spread, over one hundred letters of condolence began to arrive at his mother's old address in Farnham, the one that for decades had appeared in Buddhist newsletters and entomological journals seeking exchanges and trades. Some noted that, despite the terror of the plane crash, in some ways Colin had died as he had often lived — at high altitude, seeking out new adventures, hopeful that it might result in the kind of discovery that would deliver the 'ineffable thrills' he had spent his whole life chasing. One friend made the poignant observation that it was a wonder he hadn't already been swallowed up by a crevice while traversing some snowy peak.

The following February, his old friend Christmas Humphreys penned a short tribute in *The Middle Way*. 'Few men knew the world so widely and so well,' Humphreys wrote.[3]

Later, another friend of her father sent a reel of tape containing a recording of the last grand story that Wyatt had sent him — like a precursor to voice memos, the pair had taken to exchanging rambling recordings in the post. The friend felt this final reel captured Wyatt's gifts as a raconteur so perfectly that it had to be preserved. It would join the already deep personal archive at Farnham that now passed into his daughter's care — the paintings, the dozens of old photo albums, the newspaper clippings, the film reels, the thousands of slide negatives. Even James William Wyatt's 1881 Queensland journal, and the Hawaiian-themed menus from the SS *Mariposa* on the final leg of Colin and Mary's honeymoon, had been carefully saved. But, like her father during his life, there were some stories the family archive didn't tell.

In subsequent years, a slow trickle of news articles, blog posts, and academic journals offered a reminder that the late Colin Wyatt had a past — one that jarred with the memory of the responsible, dedicated parent who raised Monica and with the hagiographic condolence letters that had rolled in from around the world.

'He didn't talk about the war, he didn't talk about the theft, about the butterflies, about the marriage,' Monica Wyatt told me in November 2024, at the end of a long day in a quiet corner of England. She is a very private person, and as she tells the story, each detail hangs heavily in the air between us. 'I did pick up on things I shouldn't ask too much about.'

I first reached out to Colin Wyatt's daughter after seeing a comment left on an online entomology forum, where a long discussion thread had raked over her father's life and thefts.

'Please put yourself in my shoes and imagine your children reading about you (unless, of course, you are all saints),' she wrote at the time.[4] He was an 'extraordinary man', she added, 'but as vulnerable as we all are.' The post also mentioned that she planned to prepare an article of her father's life on Wikipedia, the crowd-sourced encyclopaedia.

As part of Wikipedia's open-access model, any edits and changes to an article can be seen by anyone with an internet connection, and for months I had watched a draft entry take shape. From my computer in Australia, I could see its pseudonymous author persist through repeated rejections by volunteer editors, who seemed baffled by the exhaustively detailed work-in-progress. The very first draft omitted any reference to the thefts at all, while subsequent revisions were critiqued for their lack of neutrality and reliance on 'unsourced' material from an unpublished private archive.

At times, the hundreds of edits raised entirely new questions — such as a short-lived reference to a former associate of Wyatt who believed that 'possibly he was bisexual'. Modern labels aren't always a perfect fit for people of the past, but it's a notion that offers a fleeting, poignant context to his at-times enigmatic behaviour: the streak of nonconformity; a tendency to mask his true feelings and intentions; a preference for escaping conventional society for wild solitude; and the string of failed relationships.

Certainly, English and Australian society in the early 20th century had a low tolerance for anyone who appeared to challenge traditional masculinity — one newspaper report on the thefts, for example, opened with the line, 'To rugged Australians the hobby of collecting butterflies seems so very sissy.'[5] A man who quietly went against the heteronormative grain may indeed have faced emotional and psychological pressures that could manifest in unaccountable ways.

On Wikipedia, however, the author dismissed this possibility out of hand before eventually deleting it entirely. Like Wyatt's own writings, seeing this unfolding article could feel like the broader historiographic process rendered in miniature, with all its tensions, competing perspectives, endless revisions, and unknowable gaps and cul-de-sacs as we try to sort myth and memory from reality and truth.

In her original post to the entomology forum, Monica Wyatt also added another bittersweet coda to her father's life story: 'This theft did not deter leading museums beating a path to my door to acquire his collection after his death in an airplane in Guatemala in 1975.'

Growing up, that collection was never far from her view — by the 1960s, Colin Wyatt had almost doubled the 40,000 that had been there when Norman Riley and the detectives appeared on the doorstep in January 1947. After the crash, however, it quickly became clear that something had to be done before they were left to the mercy of museum beetles. Back in 1973, in his letter to Phillip Ackery, Wyatt had offered a clue of his plans for the collection, writing that, according to his will, in the event of his death his collection would be carved up and auctioned off in Europe to support his daughter. (The museum entomologists of Germany, he said, had always remained friendly to him, unlike the 'short-sighted' museums of his country of birth.)[6]

In the months that followed the accident, word quickly spread about the vast Wyatt Collection. As the executors appointed to manage his estate began reaching out to corners of the butterfly-collecting community for advice, his daughter began to receive discreet overtures. Some, she told me, claimed to be serving as intermediaries for the British Museum and the Smithsonian. Despite Colin's efforts to shield her from the uncomfortable aspects of his past, she had gathered that there was bad blood between her father and certain corners of the scientific establishment. But now, it seemed the very establishment that had shunned him in life had no qualms about swooping on the life's work of a man they still considered a thief.

'They had it in for him,' Monica told me. 'Hypocrisy is the word that came to mind ... he paid the price.'

In the end, true to Wyatt's threat, it was the Landessammlungen für Naturkunde museum in Karlsruhe, Germany, that successfully bid for the collection, which by 1975 had reached 90,340 specimens. As one acquaintance, a Czech entomologist named Otakar Kudrna, wrote soon after, Wyatt named sixty-one new species over the course of his life, and while the limits of his taxonomic training all but guaranteed that some would be found to be synonyms of existing species, many were 'likely to survive the test of time and scrutiny of revisors, perhaps because they are from those parts of the world lepidopterists rarely visit'.[7] It was this 'original choice of his collecting ground', Kudrna reflected, that ensured Wyatt would be remembered as a 'gifted and imaginative collector' — and as a 'universal character'. Kurdna also added, however, that 'the very unkind stories spread about him by those who never forgive sinns [sic] of other people, probably because they think that they never sin themselves, were — so far as I am aware — exaggerated and partly untrue.'[8] It was Kudrna, who died in 2021, who supposedly made the observation about Wyatt's sexuality.

Perhaps unsurprisingly, there appears to be no formal record of any attempted acquisition of the Wyatt Collection by the British Natural History Museum in its archives, and the file that contains the final correspondence between Wyatt, Ackery, his superiors at the museum, and Norman Riley's report of the 1930 *Parnassius* incident bears no mention of it. Instead, it concludes with one final addition: an August 1976 article from *The Victorian Entomologist* journal in Australia, in which John Cecil Le Souëf, one of Wyatt's former associates, offered a lengthy reflection on the 'charming companion' he knew—and the strange revelations that followed his return to England.

'As might be imagined, we were "electrified" when we heard the evening news on the 15th February, 1947. So began the story which must surely be the most bizarre event in the modern history of entomology,' Le Souëf wrote.

'Despite this lapse, Wyatt continued with his insect work, writing at least one book, and restricting his comments on collecting in Australia to specimens taken in the wild. From this final note it will be seen that his charm had won him many friends in many parts of the world.'[9]

After sixty-six years spent circling the globe, reaching astonishing peaks and humiliating lows, Wyatt's life of entomology and adventure was over, his archive safe with his daughter, and the tens of thousands of butterflies he collected secure at, of all places, a natural history museum. But, like that of Johnny Hopson, Athol Waterhouse, or any other notable collector, the Wyatt story doesn't quite end there.

EPILOGUE

The Lost Holotypes

The two butterflies lay pinned in front of me, each with dark-brown wings with a long stripe down the middle, a sunset-like gradient of orange fading into amber. To my eyes, one of them appeared slightly larger, while the other looked a little worse for wear. I knew that one was the original flame hairstreak, *Pseudalmenus chlorinda barringtonensis*, that the late Johnny Hopson, the so-called Father of the Tops, had collected in October 1922. I also knew that the other was its doppelgänger, a fake with painted streaks on the pale underside of its dry old wings. But if I was being honest, left to my own devices, I'm not sure I could have said with any certainty which was which — if this was a police line-up, I would have made a terrible witness.

It was September 2024, and, luckily, I wasn't alone. In fact, it appeared to be a point of policy that I didn't stray too far from Russell Cox, a friendly research assistant at the Australian Museum who had buzzed me in at the museum's back gate minutes earlier. I went through the motions of logging my details on a tablet screen, which spat out a sticker with my name and the word 'VISITOR' in bold for all to see. Next, he led me down a series of passages, through a number of locked doors, to end up in a darkened mezzanine with a curved corrugated-iron roof. As I took in the now-familiar sight and smell of wooden entomological cabinets and insecticide, it occurred to me that I wouldn't know how to get out, even if I wanted to.

Cox had has already laid out several trays of specimens ahead of my arrival, from bright-green birdwings to little orange tigers: some so small that the rush of a slammed door might send them flying; some so large that the idea of slipping them into open-topped metal tins, and getting them home intact, seemed physically impossible. Among the butterflies was a little white box with those two possible *P. barringtonensis,* and two newly printed labels telling a small part of a long and complicated story.

Cox explained that the new labels had been left there just a few weeks earlier by Dr Michael F Braby, the entomologist from the Australian National University who had first noticed the fake holotype with the painted streaks years earlier. He had overseen this new setting and the text that accompanied it, seeing it as a new solution to a decades-old problem. Back in 2016, not long after his initial discovery, Braby had travelled to Sydney, to this same collection, to see the painted *P. barringtonensis* with his own eyes. He had also come to view another specimen deep within the Australian Museum's collections, one that also claimed to be *P. barringtonensis*. According to its label, this one had been collected at Barrington Tops in October 1942, and looked a little larger, the markings on its dorsal side a little richer, more natural-looking. Other clues became evident when Braby looked at its pinning under a microscope—and the gaping puncture hole running straight through its mid-section. From Waterhouse's notes, he knew that the Hopson specimen had already been dead at the time of collection, and, like a coroner at a crime scene, he detected clues that this specimen had met a suspiciously similar end.

'When you've got a soft, fresh specimen, it makes a very clean hole, and basically all the "juices of insect" kind of solidify around the pin,' Braby explained when I first spoke to him in January 2024. 'When you've got a dead, dry specimen, it doesn't happen. You're basically punching through very dead, dry cuticle, and you've got to actually glue the pin into place.'[1]

Then there was the time of death: the October 1942 date on its label just didn't add up. Braby knew that, officially, there had been no specimens collected between October 1922 and December 1946, when

Alec Burns visited Barrington Tops just a few weeks before his discovery of the missing butterflies in Melbourne. Burns published the results of his hatched pupa and its true identity as *P. barringtonensis* in October the following year, shortly after returning from his nine days in Adelaide.[2] Any other breakthrough between those dates couldn't have been kept a secret, so Braby concluded that the label in front of him had to be a fabrication, and that he was staring at Hopson's original 1922 holotype, which had sat undetected for over seventy years in an entirely different part of the museum's collection.

'That was the smoking gun,' Braby explained. 'If the labels hadn't been transferred, I wouldn't have been suspicious. But that was the thing that cemented the whole thing.'

There was one other pretty obvious clue: alongside the faked label, Hopson's long-lost holotype bore another tag, a small piece of yellow paper identical to ones attached to thousands of specimens across Sydney, Melbourne, and Adelaide. It was a gift from Alec Burns, Anthony Musgrave, and Norman Tindale all those years ago, which read, 'Passed through C.W. Wyatt Theft Coll. 1946–1947'.

Later, as I flicked through the paper trail of those months in 1947, and then the letters between Athol Waterhouse and George Lyell held in the Melbourne Museum's archives, a picture began to form. Braby wasn't actually the first person to notice that Waterhouse's *P. barringtonensis* had been displaced by the Wyatt affair — Norman Tindale had spotted it in Adelaide, and, later, Athol Waterhouse himself took note as he angrily examined Musgrave's memo from the sorting in Adelaide.

'This is the worst mistake I have found,' Athol Waterhouse wrote to George Lyell in September 1947. '*Pseudo. Chlorinda barrington.* This is surely my type but is assigned to National Museum. Why?'[3]

In February 1948, Walkom sent Waterhouse an update, explaining that the reference to Melbourne was a 'typographic error' and that the *P. barringtonensis* had, in fact, been returned to Sydney. The original, which in the space of a year had travelled from Sydney to London, London to Adelaide, then finally back to Sydney, lay waiting for Waterhouse to restore it to its rightful place. The only conclusion, it seems, is that Waterhouse simply ran out of time to set it right before he died in 1950.

This wasn't a long-neglected secret — it was just a job left half-finished, another entomological cold case set to the longer time scale of a museum collection, just waiting for a worthy successor to finish Waterhouse's work. The fact that it took seventy years was, in the grand scheme of things, not a failure — it was everything going to plan.

'A collection might sit there for fifty years before the next researcher comes and looks at the material,' Braby explained. Sometimes, when he reads Waterhouse's work and views his specimens, it's as if the decades and centuries fall away. 'It's like you're reading in real time,' he said.

It was with this in mind that Braby, with typical humility, put together a fresh set of labels for the painted fake and the true holotype.

'This specimen is almost certainly the true holotype of *Pseudalmenus chlorinda barringtonensis*,' began one label. 'The specimen is part of the C. Wyatt Theft Collection, has a fictitious label, and has been repaired with glue.' The other label, pinned beneath the second, slightly smaller hairstreak, read, 'This specimen is not the holotype … It is a fake, most likely *P. chlorinda chloris* Waterhouse & Lyell, 1914 that has been painted with red paint to resemble *P. chlorinda barringtonensis*. The original labels have been removed from this holotype and placed with this specimen.'

'I was very reluctant to swap the name of the labels over in case I'm wrong,' Braby later explained to me. 'So I think it was important to keep the two specimens together, and have those separate labels. That's my conclusion — in one hundred years' time, someone might have a different conclusion.'

The case of the fake *P. barringtonensis* may have been solved, but it isn't the only Wyatt lead still being chased down decades later. In March 2024, Ken Walker showed me another holotype with a yellow label in the collections of the Melbourne Museum. It was supposed to be a peacock jewel, *Miletus meleagris*, with leopard-like orange spots, each one ringed in shimmering silver-green — but it was an imposter too. While undertaking another routine project of taxonomic revision, a British entomologist named John Tennent and an Australian named Chris J Müller suspected that the *M. meleagris* holotype was actually synonymous with another species, *Hypochrysops euclides*, and due for reclassification.[4] But, like Braby's butterfly in Sydney, upon closer inspection they realised that the holotype in Melbourne wasn't *M. meleagris* or *H. euclides* at all, but *Hypochrysops pythias,* a similar-looking species from New Guinea that had been swapped for the original.

Like art experts detecting a forgery, they determined that the colours of *H. euclides* were paler than *H. pythias*, the splashes of colour on its wings closer to orange than red. Unlike the fake *P. barringtonensis,* however, this one was among the thousands of butterflies returned to Australia after the trial at West Ham — the swap, the scientists deduced, must have happened some time before Wyatt surrendered his collection. The original might still be out there.

The mystery was solved in Munich, Germany, when in 2022 Tennent visited the Zoologische Staatssammlung München to view a series of *Hypochrysops.* The labels bore Wyatt's handwriting, and placed their location as Darnley Island in the Torres Strait Islands, north of mainland Australia. While Wyatt's estate had sold the bulk of his collection to the Landessammlungen für Naturkunde in Karlsruhe after his death, these specimens had apparently been the result of earlier trades and exchanges. Tennent had already spent years retracing Wyatt's labels through museum collections around the world, and in 2014 had seen a similar series in the Carnegie Museum in Pittsburgh — presumably before the alleged 'affidavits' from the British Natural History Museum left Wyatt a virtual pariah in America. Tennent had begun to suspect that none of these labels made sense; no other collector had recorded these species on Darnley Island, and the plant varieties they relied upon didn't even grow there.

Tennent sent photographs to Müller back in Australia, who almost immediately surmised that one of the specimens, labelled *H. euclides* by Wyatt, might be the long-lost Melbourne *M. meleagris.* Much like the dossier that John Evans had compiled in February 1947, the pair concluded that their evidence was 'circumstantial, but compelling'.[5] It was good enough for collections managers in Munich and Melbourne, who decided that the long-lost *M. meleagris* — which, thanks to Tennent and Müller's study, was now re-designated as *H. euclides* anyway — would be repatriated back to Melbourne, nearly eighty years after it originally left Australia aboard the SS *Perim.* It is unlikely to be the last.

As these stories gradually come to light, there have also been timely reminders of lepidoptera's important role in understanding the natural environment. In 2019, scientists watched in horror as years of climate change and drought pushed the once-ubiquitous bogong moths, the same species that Colin Wyatt once saw in abundance, to the brink of extinction with a population collapse of around 99.5 per cent in just a few years.[6] While the moth has gradually recovered, it's one flagship signalling a bigger crisis — one that rarer species, ones with smaller populations and more restricted habitats, might not bounce back from. It's the pointy end of a process that Athol Waterhouse observed with anguish as suburban Sydney gradually swallowed the remnant forest that had once surrounded the house at Killara — a centuries-long downward spiral of environmental degradation, disappearing habitat, and dwindling biodiversity that began around the time that Joseph Banks netted that first common brown. These are the kinds of calamities that make museum collections — those precious biological time capsules — so important.

When I first spoke to Michael Braby, I asked him about the public response when he first went public with his discovery of the painted holotype back in 2019.

'I don't think I got any feedback,' he reflected. 'It's a bit like that in science — you put stuff out there, and unless it's really bad, people don't harass you. I remember my colleagues were quite amazed, but broadly, no, I didn't get a lot of reaction.'[7]

Braby's answer reminds me of my time in the archives, as I read about the outrage that men such as John Evans and Alec Burns felt, not only at the theft itself, but at the apathy of almost every layer of police, government, and the judiciary that touched the case. Like the race to acquire Wyatt's collection in 1976, and Athol Waterhouse's initial response to news of the theft — immediately brainstorming a hit list of specimens he imagined a thief would covet most — it's another moment when I can't help but think that Colin Wyatt had more in common with the 'bug lovers' free masonry' he betrayed than either might like to think. Wyatt appreciated the stakes better than anyone outside the entomological community, and, misguided as he was, actually cared enough to steal them. It partly explains how he was able to pull off the heist—and also the unforgiving backlash that haunted him for the rest of his life.

There is a poignant irony to the fact that when the *M. meleagris* holotype from Munich does eventually fly back to Australia, via London, in the carry-on luggage of an Australian entomologist, it will become a small, moving part in an international circuit of fragile cargo making long overdue homeward journeys from overseas museum collections. If the first two-and-a-half centuries of natural history museums were defined by generations of collectors rounding up and cataloguing the people of the world with the same acquisitive, taxonomical mindset applied to butterflies, plants, and animals, recent decades have seen that process thrown into reverse.

From the Natural History Museum to the Smithsonian, to the museums of Adelaide, Melbourne, and Sydney, there has been a long, slow reckoning of an even greater magnitude than the Wyatt Theft Collection. Over the past five decades, a series of small, hard-fought breakthroughs have led to a tipping point. In 1985, a procession of over 200 people stopped Melbourne traffic as small bundles of ancestral remains wrapped in paperbark and string were brought up from a cold, windowless space deep in the National Museum of Victoria and out into the sunlight. As the procession marched solemnly down Swanston Street, a long banner of the black, yellow, and red Aboriginal flag stretched across both lanes before the ancestors were buried in a special memorial site in Kings Domain.[8]

In 1991, a change in policy at the University of Glasgow saw Poltpalingada Booboorowie finally returned to his family, who were able to lay him to rest nearly one hundred years after his first mockery of a funeral.[9] In 2008, the Smithsonian returned ancestors that had been disturbed from Groote Eylandt, Gunbalanya, Yirrkala, and Milingimbi during the 1948 Australian–American joint expedition to Arnhem Land led by Norman Tindale—just months after he sorted through the recovered butterflies in Adelaide.[10] In April 2024, Edward Charles

Stirling's alma mater, Trinity College, Cambridge, handed back four spears to members of the La Perouse Aboriginal community — the last surviving handful from the spears that Joseph Banks, James Cook, and their men took from a Gweagal house on that formative first day in Kamay in 1770.[11]

'They had *everything* in there,' Ngarrindjeri and Kaurna Elder Major Moogy Sumner once told me of his visits to museums around England over three decades of repatriation work. 'Most of the museums I went to, they had all these big cupboards with these little drawers about *that* wide and about *that* long. And they were all on top one another, from the floor nearly up to the ceiling — you had to get ladders to climb up to see what was in the top shelf.'[12]

These watershed moments, and dozens more like them, have exposed an uncomfortable truth that colonised peoples around the world have known for a long time: beneath the noble and learned veneer of the British Empire lies a dark history, often tucked away in far-flung colonial outposts, whose profits made London the centre of Western civilisation. It was an empire built on an insatiable drive to claim, extract, and accumulate land, resources, people, and profit. Often, these historic fault lines converged in museums, where the material proceeds of empire not only repositioned Great Britain as the centre and curator of the known world, but provided a polite front to an empire that was often anything but civilised. The Age of Enlightenment, it seems, had also spawned one of entitlement.

Shortly after visiting Monica Wyatt, I poked my head into the British Museum, where an exhibition by the Guyanese British artist Hew Locke presented a suite of collection items and his own work that expose this underbelly, from a pile of cowrie shells, to a necklace of glimmering beetles, to the polished brass barrel of a Maxim gun. Throughout the exhibition were little yellow labels featuring a running commentary from Locke that pierced the mythology of empire, from the 'collecting instinct' of Queen Victoria to burned and fractured brass discs looted from Benin in 1897.

'It's almost like a whole civilization was being boxed up and shipped out,' read one of Locke's labels.[13]

Like the yellow labels I had seen in butterfly collections around Australia, Locke's notes offered a stark warning to the viewer. But the story they told was an even bigger one, a story that recast the Western museum as something else entirely: a theft collection, where for centuries 'collector's mania' wasn't a bug in the system. It was a feature.

One day, some years after the case of the missing butterflies reached its unsatisfying conclusion, John Evans and his wife, Faith, found themselves in back in Boston, Massachusetts, the same city he had visited with her father during that strange world tour in the distant past. In a moment of nostalgia, the pair cut a path to Lime Street and the red-brick house where he and Dr Robin Tillyard had spent several long nights in the dark, conversing with 'Walter' and watching as Mina Crandon worked through her well-practised routine—the gravelly voices, the ectoplasm, the 'spirit hand' that was later revealed to be carved out of raw liver. As the Evanses lingered outside, they were surprised by a face peering out of the window—it wasn't a disembodied ghost, but the mildly alarmed current resident.

Evans rang the doorbell and explained why he and Faith were haunting the doorstep. It soon emerged that visitors such as John and Faith Evans weren't uncommon at 10 Lime Street—all those séances had made the address infamous. The new owners explained that they had moved in shortly after the Crandons, and soon discovered a strange legacy: a series of unusually placed electric wiring, bells, and 'all sorts of other devices suggestive of trickery'.

'I assumed at the time that all the phenomena we witnessed were genuine, very largely because I could not understand, any more than I can today, what purpose their production could have served if they were fraudulent,' Evans would later reflect. 'The Crandons were well to do and money did not enter in to their psychic transactions and, while they certainly gained great notoriety which they surely must have found distasteful, they also suffered much loss of reputation.'

Despite the evidence, Evans still couldn't get his head around the how or the why. Eventually, he concluded that, 'nevertheless, I still cannot believe that the Crandons *were* cheats'.[14]

It's a moment that keeps coming back to me as I piece together the story of Colin Wyatt, trying to untangle the same inscrutable, unknowable questions that remain stubbornly pinned in place. Like Alec Burns in September 1947, I'm left wondering, perhaps hoping, that somewhere in Farnham there was a secret codebook that might unravel the final questions about the Wyatt Theft Collection, and perhaps about its creator too.

What satisfaction did he really find in hoarding these butterflies, when, for all the faked labels, he knew that the truth of their origins wasn't a moment of ecstasy out in the field, but a careful, premeditated theft? Had the stress of his failing marriage really sparked his year-long spree, or were there deeper, unnamed disaffections that prompted him to fall back into an old compulsion that Norman Riley had first rumbled in 1930? Did his privileged position in the old imperial hierarchies of class, race, and gender — the celebrated, charming scion of an Establishment dynasty — leave him thinking he might slip through the net once again? Hadn't the ease with which he'd walked in and out of the Australian museums, and later, the West Ham Magistrates Court, proved him right?

I'm reminded of how Ken Walker once described entomological collections as 'postcards to the past', and the bigger notion of museums as places of history and memory. For all their scientific rigour and integrity, museums and their collections are just as often flawed, partial, and tragically human as our own memories. Those postcards are only as useful as the knowledge of the person reading them, and occasionally we encounter something that makes us question whether we really understood the past at all: some wires hidden in a wall; a white-washed portrait; a noble explorer revealed as a bloody invader; a few empty spaces in a drawer full of butterflies; a knock at the door from three men standing outside in the snow.

As historians, we can spend months in collections and archives, we can turn every page and read every letter to try to put ourselves in the room. But, all too often, we're just tourists looking through a window, noses pressed to the glass, trying to make sense of the blurry shapes and muffled voices on the other side. In the final pages of *Going Wild*, as he writes eloquently about how a collection can bring to life cherished memories and offer a 'key to unlock the shutters' of the past, it's as if Colin Wyatt knows this too—even as he draws the blinds over the less flattering parts of own story.

Perhaps the key I'm looking for boarded a plane to Uaxactún in November 1975. Or maybe there was never a secret codebook, and there were things in Colin Wyatt's past, and his heart, that no amount of silent meditation can unlock or reconcile. But even when he's only telling half the story, there are moments when Wyatt reveals more than he realises.

As I pore over his books for the umpteenth time, one detail lodges itself in my mind: Wyatt's seven years in the Australian bush proved so inspiring that the cover of *Going Wild* featured a black-and-white shot of Wyatt looking out from a high rocky outcropping, leaning against a windswept eucalypt. It's only when I buy a copy online of *Going Wild*'s 1959 Spanish edition, retitled *Tierra Salvaje*, with a deliciously pulpy, bright-red cover, that I learn the photograph was taken '*en la cima de Barrington Tops, Nueva Gales del Sur*'—at the summit of Barrington Tops in New South Wales.

Wyatt had indeed visited Barrington Tops, the same 'Nature's Wonderland' that had drawn the likes of Athol Waterhouse, Alec Burns, Anthony Musgrave, and countless others over the years. The very same place where Johnny Hopson had found that first flame hairstreak, *Pseudalmenus chlorinda barringtonensis*, dead in the snow in October 1922. But if Wyatt did visit the Tops, he clearly went home empty-handed, without any of the rare specimens or exciting adventures that might have warranted a mention inside *Going Wild*'s pages. He certainly never managed to achieve what even Waterhouse never could, and become the second man in history to snare that rare flame hairstreak—we'd know about it if he had.

But Wyatt did, it seems, find the next best thing. In the middle chapters of *Going Wild*, he tells the reader about another subspecies of hairstreak, the handsome but rare *Pseudalmenus chlorinda chloris.*[15] First named and described by Waterhouse and Lyell in *The Butterflies of Australia*, Wyatt knew that less than a dozen specimens had been recorded since the book's publication in 1914, and whenever he visited the Blue Mountains he would take a moment to search for it himself. Until one day, while exploring the mountains' red cliffs and fern-filled gullies, he tripped and fell over a creeping vine and into the trunk of a sturdy-looking tree. It was almost branchless, supporting a canopy so high up that it reminded Wyatt of a column in a church.

It was the sight of a small black ant that prompted Wyatt to slip into the familiar mode of a lepidopteran Sherlock Holmes; realising that the tree was a rare species of wattle that hairstreaks loved, he prised off the first loose hunk of bark he could find to reveal three plump black-and-yellow caterpillars. He began searching for similar-looking trees in the area, and eventually returned to Sydney with six fully grown larvae and two pupae of *P. chlorinda chloris*. It was nothing short of a triumph, delivering the kind of ecstasy and ineffable thrill he had spent his whole life pursuing. He took care to tie identifying strips of bark to the most bountiful trees, before returning the following year to add more specimens to his breeding population of rare, silvery hairstreaks.

Wyatt leaves the story there, and it's up to the reader to imagine what became of that healthy supply of *P. chlorinda chloris* from the Blue Mountains, barely distinguishable from its fiery cousin *P. barringtonensis*, were it not for the reddish markings on the underside of their wings. It was a difference so slight that someone with a steady hand, a sound knowledge of butterflies, an eye for detail, and perhaps an intimate understanding of the art of camouflage could make disappear.

In the years before the butterfly heist made him infamous, the art critics in Britain and Australia had often said that Colin Wyatt's work had an emptiness about them; as the writer from *The Scotsman* put it, 'he is wanting in these qualities that come of the painter's sheer delight and absorption in the manipulation of his medium'.[16] But of all the consuming obsessions that had lured him all around the globe, no one could question the delight he found in the world of lepidoptera. And with just a few strokes of his paintbrush, a spare *P. chlorinda chloris* specimen from the Blue Mountains in his pocket, and a few carefully chosen moments left alone among the cabinets of the Australian Museum, Wyatt pulled off a remarkable artistic and scientific legacy.

He left behind a tiny work of art that people would still be talking about nearly eighty years later — a rare butterfly that was truly one of a kind.

Acknowledgements

This book was written on the lands of the Kaurna Miyurna, whose sovereignty was never ceded. I also offer my respect and gratitude to all First Nations communities whose land I travelled across while undertaking research. To explore the history of this continent is to reckon with deep and complex legacies, and I've done my best to tread lightly and with respect.

To my friend Lara Torr, who first told me about Colin Wyatt and set me on a long and winding path: I bought a copy of *Going Wild: the autobiography of a bug-hunter* online that evening, and never looked back.

I started writing this book after receiving a South Australian Literary Fellowship from the State Library of South Australia and Writers SA, and was fortunate to receive a project grant from Arts South Australia to get it over the finish line. I am grateful for this support at a time when funding for writers and our cultural institutions is more essential than ever.

This book paints a complicated picture of museums and their collections. At the same time, it could not have been written without the generous access and assistance given by present-day museum staff around Australia, who welcomed me into their archives and collections, and offered advice, contacts, and encouragement along the way. Thank you to my former colleagues Lea Gardam and Fran Zilio at the South Australian Museum; Dr Shannon Faulkhead, Nik McGrath and Belinda

Borg at Melbourne Museums; Simon Dooley, Vanessa Finney, Heather Bleechmore, and Alison Miller at the Australian Museum in Sydney; and Joanne Smedley and Sarah Kershaw at the Australian War Memorial. I want to especially recognise Nik McGrath and Deidre Coleman for their work transcribing the decades' worth of correspondence between Gustavus Athol Waterhouse and George Lyell held by Museums Victoria.

Thank you to the staff at the State Library of South Australia, the National Library of Australia, the State Library of New South Wales, and State Library Victoria. Particular mention goes to Patrick Bugeja, Mark Gilbert, Chris Read, Lucy Guster, and Geoff Strempel for their support of this project and my first book.

I'm also grateful for the insight, materials, and perspectives shared by a range of entomologists and collection managers, including Michael Braby, Ken Walker, Simon Hinkley, Ben Parslow, Russell Cox, and Matt Shaw. Thank you also to Blanca Huertas and Suzanne Ryder at Britain's Natural History Museum, and Phillip Ackery, Julian Donohue, Christopher Grinter, and Vazrick Nazari.

Thank you to the many people who spoke to me about their families, communities, and personal experiences, including Noah A Enahoro, Jeremy and Helen Evans, Janet McIntosh, Leigh Purcell, Beth Robertson, Simon and Nicholas Scott Barrett, Mark Sutton, Robert Syron, Hendrikus van Leeuwen, and Peter White of Max Dupain Exhibition Photography.

I must also acknowledge Monica Wyatt for the time, material, and perspectives she shared with me over many months of correspondence and a visit to her home. This book draws from a range of published and unpublished photographs, letters, paintings, family albums, and articles that Monica shared with me along with her own memories, which were all enormously useful in trying to understand her father's life. Ultimately, however, Monica would like me to make clear that she in no way endorses or approves of the final book. All the same, I remain deeply grateful for her input, which I know has been challenging at times. Thank you to Frank for the hospitality.

Henry Rosenbloom, Alice Richardson, Tina Gumnior, and the team at Scribe have put a lot of trust and hard work into this book and *Young Rupert*, and I'm grateful for their continued faith.

Thank you to all the friends and colleagues who provided support, advice, and encouragement over the past few years: Jessica Alice, Gemma Beale, Sophie Byrne, Sian Cain, John Carty, Luke Chenoweth, Nici Cumpston, Galen Cuthbertson, John Dexter, Marc Fennell, Will Fisher, Dominic Guerrera, Amy Haring, Steph Harmon, Jenny Hocking, Olivia Huynh, Celina Ribeiro, Tace Kelly, Sean Kelly, Hannah Kent, David Knight, Royce Kurmelovs, Jill Mackenzie, Rick Morton, Patrick Mullins, Saskia Scott, Tory Shepherd, Jeff Sparrow, Sebastian Tonkin, and David Washington.

Thank you to my Marsh and Duff families for their love and support: my parents, Janis and Simon Marsh; Bill and Angela Marsh; Kate Reid; Caitlin Duff; Bing and Miles Rowland; Mairead Duff; Isobel Reid; Christo Reid; Stephen Schuetz and Michael Bowden; and all my nieces and nephews. And Andromeda, for the company.

And most of all to Sia Duff, my best friend, sounding board, literary adviser, and travel companion — I couldn't do any of it without you.

Note on sources

This is a work of non-fiction drawing from a wide range of published and unpublished archival sources, books, articles, photographs, and interviews. The discovery of the National Museum of Victoria's missing butterflies, subsequent revelations in Sydney and Adelaide, and the investigation and prosecution in England are reconstructed from overlapping internal reports and correspondence held in the archives of each institution — Museums Victoria (MVA), the South Australian Museum (SAMA), and the Australian Museum (AMA) — supplemented by contemporary newspaper accounts and material held in the National Archives of Australia (NAA), the State Records of South Australia (SRSA), and Britain's Natural History Museum (BNHM). John Evans's 1990 memoir, *Insect Delight: a life's journey*, was also a key source, and I thank his son Jeremy for permission to use material from the book.

Colin Wyatt's life story and perspective before and after January 1947 is drawn heavily from his own published works, including his three books, *The Call of the Mountains* (Thames & Hudson 1952), *Going Wild: the autobiography of a bug-hunter* (Hollis & Carter 1955), and *North of Sixty* (Hollis & Carter 1957), along with various newspaper and magazine articles, photographs, archival reports, and correspondence. Some of Wyatt's anecdotes omit specific dates and other details, but I've tried to corroborate where possible. I also refer to a range of published and unpublished material held by the Wyatt family that Monica Wyatt shared with me along with her own notes and recollections.

Notes

Prologue: The Fake

1 Gustavus Athol Waterhouse, 'Notes on Australian Lycaenidae, Part VI', *Proceedings of the Linnean Society of New South Wales*, 29 August 1928, p. 412

2 Donald Barr, 'The Land of the Mist: Barrington Tops', *Sydney Mail*, 8 September 1926, p. 13, http://nla.gov.au/nla.news-article166523249; Dulcie Hartley, *Barrington Tops: a vision splendid*, Knight Bros Printery, 1993, p. 17; HJ Carter, 'John Hopson', *The Maitland Weekly Mercury*, 30 June 1928, p. 11, http://nla.gov.au/nla.news-article135366186

3 Gustavus Athol Waterhouse, *What Butterfly Is That?: a guide to the butterflies of Australia*, Angus & Robertson, 1932, p. 267

4 Ibid.

5 Hartley, pp. 17, 28; Carter, 1928

6 Carter, 1928

7 Robert Syron, author's interview, 2024

8 Syron, 2024; 'Conflicts with the Natives', *The Wingham Chronicle and Manning River Observer*, 25 April 1922, p. 22

9 'Trip to the Tops', *Dungog Chronicle*, 13 April 1923, p. 3, http://nla.gov.au/nla.news-article136142032

10 Hartley, p. 17

11 'A Naturalist on the Barrington Tops', *Dungog Chronicle*, 4 May 1923, http://nla.gov.au/nla.news-article136144347

12 Leighton R Taylor, Jr, 'Untaxing Taxonomy', *Museum Talk*, Vol. 48, No. 4, 1973, Santa Barbara Museum of Natural History, p. 61

13 Mary Armati, *E.G. Waterhouse of Eryldene*, Fine Arts Press, 1977, p. 30

14 Anthony Musgrave, 'The Late John Hopson: an appreciation', *The Australian Museum Magazine*, July 1928, p. 247

15 Michael F Braby, author's interview, 2024

16 Ibid.
17 Michael F Braby, *The Complete Field Guide to the Butterflies of Australia*, CSIRO Publishing, 2004, p. 2
18 Michael F Braby and Rod Eastwood, 'Revised taxonomic status of Pseudalmenus barringtonensis Waterhouse, 1928 stat. rev. (Lepidoptera: Lycaenidae): uncovering Australia's greatest taxonomic fraud', *Invertebrate Systematics*, No. 33, May 2019, p. 531
19 Braby, author's interview, 2024
20 Ken Walker, author's interview, 2024

Chapter 1: The Flight

1 'Avión se estrella; mueren 15', *The Miami News*, 19 November 1975, p. 70
2 Connie Coning, 'Guatemala: history, ruins, markets', *Chicago Tribune*, 30 November 1975, p. 88
3 Sylvanus G Morley, *The Archaeological Field Diaries of Sylvanus Griswold Morley, 1914–1916*, Prudence M. Rice and Christopher Ward (eds), accessed online: https://www.mesoweb.com/publications/Morley/Morley_Diaries_1914–1916.pdf, p. 292
4 Charles H. Harriss III and Louis R. Sadler, *The Archaeologist Was a Spy*, University of Mexico Press, 2003, pp. 41–43
5 Colin Wyatt, *Going Wild*, Hollis & Carter, 1955, p. 122
6 Colin Wyatt, *North of Sixty*, Hollis & Carter, 1958, pp. 147–48
7 Monica Wyatt, author's interview, 2024
8 'Survivors in critical condition', *Florida Today*, 21 November 1975, p. 15
9 'Seven survive plane crash', *The Leader-Post*, 21 November 1975, p. 2

Chapter 2: The Fluke

1 'Discovery of butterfly loss was fluke', *The Argus*, 23 May 1947, p. 6, http://nla.gov.au/nla.news-article22428189
2 Walker, author interview, 2024
3 Richard Pescott, *Memorandum for The Chief Librarian & Secretary, Public Library, Museums and National Gallery*, 20 November 1944, Melbourne Museum Archives P.B. 238
4 'Expert Advice on Museum', *The News*, 19 May 1938, p. 17, http://nla.gov.au/nla.news-article137470606
5 'Nature Notes', *Portland Guardian*, 31 August 1944, p. 2, http://nla.gov.au/nla.news-article64390334; Walker, author interview, 2024
6 Richard Pescott, *Memorandum Re: Painting—Entomologist's Room*, 30 September 1944, MVA P.B. 116
7 'Butterfly Chase from Australia to England', *The Herald*, 15 February 1947, p. 1, http://nla.gov.au/nla.news-article245868125

8 Richard Pescott, *Collections of a Century: the history of the first hundred years of the National Museum of Victoria*, National Museum of Victoria, 1954, p. 129
9 Richard Pescott to Chief of Staff of *The Sun*, 29 March 1946, MVA P.B. 325/46
10 Pescott, 1954, p. 139
11 Pescott, 1954, pp. 95–96, 142,
12 Alexander Burns, *Theft of Specimens (Butterflies) from the George Lyell Collection at National Museum, Victoria*, 27 January 1947, MVA 00238, p. 2
13 'Here, There, & Everywhere', *The Sun News-Pictorial*, 12 October 1933, p. 7, http://nla.gov.au/nla.news-article276713633; Pescott, 1954, p. 148
14 Pescott, 1954, p. 148
15 *Victorian Naturalist*, Vol. 3, No. 6, 1994, p. 247; 'Our Butterflies Board with Ants', *The Sun News-Pictorial*, 24 April 1937, p. 44, http://nla.gov.au/nla.news-article277743184
16 Burns, 1947, p. 1
17 Ibid.
18 'Australian Moths', *The Argus*, 25 November 1932, p. 6, http://nla.gov.au/nla.news-article4510703
19 Burns, 1947, p. 2
20 John Clark to Public Services Commissioner, 30 October 1939, MVA 03968, 39/1092
21 Murray S Upton, 'John Clark (1885–1956)', *Australian Dictionary of Biography*, Vol. 3, 1993
22 George Mack to Under Secretary, Department of Chief Secretary, 27 April 1944, MVA 03969
23 'Premier and Mr Cain in Angry Scene', *The Argus*, 7 September 1944, p. 5, http://nla.gov.au/nla.news-article11359994
24 Mack, 27 April 1944
25 Richard Pescott, *Memorandum Re Buildings — Ladder between National Museum and Lending Library, Russell Street Frontage*, 28 August 1944, Melbourne Museum Archives P.B. 46
26 Richard Pescott, *Memorandum Re Mr W Newcombe*, 19 October 1944, MVA P.B. 175; Pescott to Newcombe, 19 October 1944, MVA P.B. 176
27 Richard Pescott, *Memorandum Re Forcing of Case — Australian Section*, 9 November 1944, MVA P.B. 213
28 Ibid.
29 Richard Pescott, *Memorandum Re Iron Door at Top of Stairs Leading to Basement National Museum*, 1 November 1944, MVA P.B. 202
30 Pescott, 20 November 1944
31 Pescott, *Memorandum Re Report on Ethnological Collections of the National Museum*, 20 February 1946, MVA P.B. 167/46

32 Ibid.
33 Richard Pescott, *Memorandum Re Insurance — Theft, Damage,* 20 November 1944, MVA P.B. 243
34 The National Museums of Victoria, *Minutes of Trustees Meeting Held on 18th July, 1946*, p. 3, MVA VOL/299
35 Pescott to Norman Riley, 18 February 1947, AMA 33/1
36 'Butterflies for Museum', *The Herald,* 31 March 1932, p. 18, http://nla.gov.au/nla.news-article242818553
37 'Australian Moths', *The Argus,* 25 November 1932, p. 6, http://nla.gov.au/nla.news-article4510703
38 George Lyell to Daniel Mahony, 21 January 1942, MVA 00021
39 Ernest Pitt to Richard Mahony, 8 September 1939, MVA 00217, 39/195; Chief Architect, Department of Public Works, *Memorandum Re Storage of Government of Documents etc,* 13 January 1942, MVA 00029
40 Chief Architect, Department of Public Works, 13 January 1942; Pescott, p. 146
41 George Lyell to Richard Mahony, 21 January 1942, MVA 00029 42/17
42 'Nature Notes', *Portland Guardian*, 31 August 1944 p. 2, http://nla.gov.au/nla.news-article64390334
43 Richard Pescott, *Theft of Entomological Specimens, National Museum of Victoria 1946/47*, MVA 33/1/42
44 Richard Pescott, *Thefts of Butterflies from Three of the Museums of Australia,* 16 February 1947, AMA, p. 1
45 Burns, 1947, p. 2
46 Ibid.
47 Alexander Burns, 'New Races of Australian Butterflies', *Memoirs of the National Museum of Victoria*, 6 October 1947, p. 98
48 Burns, 1947, p. 1
49 Ibid.

Chapter 3: The Collector

1 Colin Wyatt, 1955, p. 22
2 'Foot-Loose Freelancer Exhibits Painting Here', *The Calgary Herald,* 24 November 1954, p. 29
3 'Bug lovers' Free Masonry', *The Ottawa Citizen*, 5 July 1952, p. 15
4 Ibid., pp. xi–xii
5 Ibid., p. 4
6 Colin Wyatt, 'Unvergeßliche Erlebnisse', *Zeitschrift der Wiener Entomologischen Gesellschaft*, Vol. 68, No. 4, 15 April 1957, p. 4
7 Ibid., pp. 21–23
8 Ibid., p. 22

9 Ibid.
10 Ibid., p. 41
11 'Ants and Butterflies', *The Bulletin*, 7 September 1955, p. 2, http://nla.gov.au/nla.obj-675617625
12 Wyatt, 1958, p. 30
13 'Hitler and Mussolini Meet in Train', *The Sydney Morning Herald*, 19 March 1940, p. 11, http://nla.gov.au/nla.news-article17654494
14 Wyatt, 1955, p. 32
15 Robin Wood, 'From a Musician's Scrap Book', *The Examiner* (Launceston), 10 April 1937, p. 1, http://nla.gov.au/nla.news-article52132829
16 Wyatt, 1955, p. 31
17 Ibid., p. 33
18 Wyatt, 1955, p. 3
19 Sir Robert Baden-Powell, *My Adventures as a Spy*, C. Arthur Pearson, 1915, p. 59
20 Ibid., p. 48
21 Arthur Conan Doyle, *The Hound of the Baskervilles*, Penguin, 1902 (2001 edition), pp. 69–70
22 Baden-Powell, p. 59
23 Waterhouse, 1932, p. 272
24 Gustavus Athol Waterhouse to George Lyell, 20 September 1947, MVA 00369
25 Wyatt, 1955, pp. 102–3
26 *Camp 020 Interim Report on the Case of Fred Hermann Brandt*, 18 January 1945, National Archives (United Kingdom), KV 2/752, item 73a, p. 6
27 Hans Bytinski-Salz and Wilhelm Brandt, 'New Lepidoptera from Iran', *The Entomologist's Record and Journal of Variation*, Vol. 49, No. 5, May 1937, pp. 1, 11, https://www.biodiversitylibrary.org/item/95155#page/82/mode/1up
28 Julian Amery, *Sons of the Eagle*, Macmillan 1948, p. 139
29 Ibid., p. 140
30 Ibid., p. 141
31 Ibid., p. 142
32 *Camp 020 Interim Report on the Case of Fred Hermann Brandt*, January 1945, National Archives (United Kingdom), KV 2/752, item 73a, pp. 3–28
33 Ibid., p. 29
34 Ibid.
35 *Camp 020 Interim Report on the Case of Fred Hermann Brandt*, January 1945, National Archives (United Kingdom), KV 2/752, item 73a, 18 January 1945, p. 1
36 Wyatt, 1955, p. 33

Chapter 4: The Confidants

1 Thomas Ireland, 'The Waterhouse Collections', *The Australian Museum Magazine* Vol. 4 No. 4, October 1930, p. 113
2 Ibid.; Joyce K Allan, 'Shells in the Waterhouse Collection', *The Australian Museum Magazine*, Vol. 5 No. 2, April 1933, p. 39
3 Joyce K Allan, 'Australian Shells: helmet, tun, fig, and egg shells, and the cowries', *The Australian Museum Magazine*, Vol. 6, No. 8, October 1937, p. 285
4 Saidiya Hartman, *Lose Your Mother: a journey along the Atlantic slave route,* Serpent's Tail, 2021, pp. 206, 210
5 Ireland, 1930, p. 113
6 John W Evans, 'Gustavus Athol Waterhouse (1877–1950)', *Australian Dictionary of Biography*, 1990, https://adb.anu.edu.au/biography/waterhouse-gustavus-athol-8992/text15829
7 Gustavus Athol Waterhouse to George Lyell, 19 January 1897, MVA 00373 (Transcribed by Nik McGrath)
8 Graeme Rushworth, *G.A. Waterhouse of Allowrie: Dr Waterhouse's garden*, self-published thesis, 2016, p. 12
9 'Family Notices', *The Age*, 21 December 1893, p. 1, http://nla.gov.au/nla.news-article197181199
10 Waterhouse to Lyell, 3 August 1904, MVA 00373
11 Ibid.; Waterhouse to Lyell, 13 January 1925, MVA 00373; Waterhouse to Lyell, 9 January 1902, MVA 00373; Lyell to Waterhouse, 22 February 1928, MVA 00373
12 Waterhouse to Lyell, 1 December 1913, MVA 00373
13 Waterhouse to Lyell 28 March 1914, MVA 00373
14 Gustavus Athol Waterhouse and George Lyell, *The Butterflies of Australia*, Angus & Robertson, 1914, p. vi
15 Ibid., p. 29
16 Rushworth, pp. 10–11, 15
17 Waterhouse to Lyell, 10 July 1910, MVA 00373
18 Waterhouse to Lyell, 28 May 1913, MVA 00373
19 John W Evans, *The Life and Work of Robin John Tillyard, 1881–1937,* University of Queensland Press, 1963, pp. 9–12
20 Murray S Upton, *A Rich and Diverse Fauna: the history of the Australian national insect collection 1926–1991,* 1997, CSIRO Publishing, p. 11
21 John W Evans, *The Life and Work of Robin John Tillyard, 1881–1937,* University of Queensland Press, 1963, pp. 18–19, 26; Lyell to Waterhouse, 17 August 1928, MVA 00373
22 Waterhouse to Lyell, 14 August 1928, MVA 00373
23 Waterhouse to Lyell, 27 January 1929, MVA 00373

24 Waterhouse to Lyell, 1 April 1929, MVA 00373
25 Robin J Tillyard, 'Science and Psychical Research', *Nature*, Vol. 118, No. 2961, 31 July 1926, p. 147
26 Harry Houdini, *Houdini Exposes the Tricks Used by the Boston Medium 'Margery'*, Adams Press Publishers, 1924, p. 8
27 Lyell to Waterhouse, 17 August 1928, MVA 00373
28 Robin J Tillyard, 'Evidence of Survival of a Human Personality', *Nature*, Vol. 122, No. 3068, 18 August 1928, pp. 243–46
29 Richard Gregory, 'Normal and Supernormal Phenomena', *Nature*, Vol. 122, No. 3068, 18 August 1928, p. 231
30 John W Evans, *Insect Delight: a life's journey,* 1989, Brolga Press, Canberra, p. 43
31 Harry Price, *Fifty Years of Psychical Research: a critical survey,* Longmans, Green and Co., 1939, pp. 153–55
32 Evans, 1962, p. 18, 'Dr. Tillyard in Crash', *The Sydney Morning Herald,* 13 January 1937, p. 14, http://nla.gov.au/nla.news-article17303529
33 'Mr G.A. Waterhouse's experiences', *Daily Telegraph* (Launceston), 18 February 1916, p. 4, http://nla.gov.au/nla.news-article152685335
34 Price, p. 155
35 Upton, p. 25
36 Waterhouse to Lyell, 24 August 1929, MVA 00373
37 Waterhouse to Lyell, 5 October 1928, MVA 00373
38 GJ Waterhouse, *A Brief Account of the Life and Activities of Rev. John Waterhouse,* Epworth, 1937, p. 17
39 Allan, 1937, p. 285
40 Waterhouse to Lyell, 24 August 1929, MVA 00373

Chapter 5: The Cadet

1 Prue Walker, 'Nancy Adams', Australian Museum, 15 November 2018, https://australian.museum/about/history/people/nancy-adams/
2 Anthony Musgrave, 'Vale — Nancy B. Adams', *The Australian Museum Magazine,* Vol. 40, No. 10, 15 June 1955, p. 325
3 Ibid.
4 Walker
5 Roser Docker, 'Harriet and Helena: the Scott sisters', Australian Museum, 22 November 2018, https://australian.museum/learn/collections/museum-archives-library/scott-sisters/harriet-and-helena-the-scott-sisters/
6 *Annual Report of the Trustees for the Year Ended 30th June 1933,* Australian Museum, p. 6
7 Anthony Musgrave, 'The Waterhouse Collections', *The Australian Museum Magazine,* Vol. 4, No. 4, October 1930, p. 113

8 'Museum Party at Barrington', *Maitland Mercury*, 20 February 1946, p. 4, http://nla.gov.au/nla.news-article281217526
9 Waterhouse to Lyell, 12 July 1943, MVA 00373
10 Ibid.
11 Stretton Gustavus John Waterhouse Service Record, NAA B883, NX60288
12 Rushworth, p. 20
13 Musgrave, 1930, p. 112, Rushworth, p. 20
14 Arthur Walkom to the Central Investigation Branch, Sydney, 17 February 1947, AMA 33/1
15 Waterhouse and Lyell, p. 230
16 Walkom to Evans, 24 January 1947

Chapter 6: The Golden Age

1 Monica Wyatt's author interview, 2024
2 Wyatt, 1955, p. 5
3 Ibid.
4 Ibid.
5 Ibid.
6 Matthew J Bruccoli (ed.), *As Ever, Scott Fitz—: letters between F. Scott Fitzgerald & His Literary Agent Harold Ober*, 1919–40, JB Lippincott & Co., 1972, pp. 171–72
7 Jackson R Bryer and Cathy W Barks (eds), *Dear Scott, Dearest Zelda: the love letters of F. Scott and Zelda Fitzgerald*, Bloomsbury, 2003, pp. 87, 99
8 'Ernest Hemingway, February 1927', in Ernest Hemingway Photograph Collection, John F. Kennedy Presidential Library and Museum, Boston
9 Wyatt, 1955, p. 6
10 Ibid.
11 John Martin Robinson, *The Wyatts: an architectural dynasty*, Oxford University Press, 1979, p. ix
12 Ibid., p. 129
13 Ibid., pp. 56, 69
14 Ibid., pp. 77–80
15 Ibid., p. 58
16 EL Strutt, 'In Memoriam: James William Wyatt', *Alpine Journal*, 1940, pp. 118–19
17 Monica Wyatt's author interview, 2024
18 Wyatt, 1955, pp. 10–11
19 Francis Hemming, 'My Highest Catch of Butterfly Species in a Single Day: Digne (France) 6th August 1926', *The Lepidopterists' News*, 1955, pp. 144–45
20 Wyatt, 1955, p. 10

21 Wyatt, 1955, pp. 31–32
22 Colin Wyatt, *The Call of the Mountains*, Thames & Hudson, 1952, p. 7
23 AF Mummery, *My Climbs in the Alps and Caucasus*, Thomas Nelson & Sons 1913, p. 36
24 Ibid., p. 347
25 Pamela Murray, 'Winter-Sports Land', *The Sketch*, 7 January 1931, p. 10
26 Ibid.
27 Ibid.; *The Bystander*, 21 January 1931, p. 98
28 'Rushing Down the Mountain Side at Express Train Speed', *The Oshkosh Northwestern*, 12 February 1929, p. 10; 'Ski-Racing in Switzerland', *The Daily Province*, 26 January 1929, p. 2
29 'Ski-ing: Cambridge Beat Oxford at St Moritz', *The Guardian*, 27 December 1929, p. 4
30 'European Ski Championships', *The Daily Telegraph*, 3 February 1931, p. 17; 'British "Varsity Skiers" Win', *Western Daily Press*, 1 January 1930, p. 6
31 'Of Sunlit Snow and Shining Sands — Inter-Varsity Ski Race', *The Daily Mirror*, 28 December 1928, p. 13
32 'The Talk of London', *The Daily Express*, 5 January 1931, p. 15
33 'Letters of Eve', *The Tatler*, 18 January 1933, p. 88
34 Ibid.
35 Pamela Murray, 'London Asides', *The Sketch*, 2 May 1934, p. 194
36 'And the World Said', *The Tatler*, 22 December 1937, p. 525
37 'Alpine Club Gallery—The Work of Colin Wyatt', *The Daily Telegraph*, 22 November 1932, p. 13
38 'Art in London', *The Scotsman*, 28 November 1934, p. 13
39 'Grubb Group', *The Yorkshire Post*, 13 June 1933, p. 8; 'London Notes and Comment, *Yorkshire Post and Leeds Intelligencer*, 13 January 1933, p. 18
40 'Ski-ing School Attraction of London Season', *The Winnipeg Tribune*, 14 November 1931, p. 40
41 'Why Collide with the Alps? Learn Your Ski-ing in London', *Illustrated Sporting and Dramatic News*, 31 October 1931, p. 25
42 Colin Wyatt, 'The Zillertal Alps', *Alpine Journal*, 1936, p. 68
43 Ibid.
44 Ibid., p. 71
45 'New Use for Troops', *Taranaki Daily News*, 16 October 1936, p. 9

Chapter 7: The Wanderer

1 'The Letters of Letty', *Table Talk*, 13 May 1947, p. 14, http://nla.gov.au/nla.news-article149327575
2 Wyatt, 1955, p. 45
3 Ibid.

4 Ibid., p. 43, Wyatt, 1952, p. 8
5 Nan Bowie, *Mick Bowie: the Hermitage years*, A.H. and A.W. Reed, 1969, p. 53
6 Ibid.
7 *New Zealand Alpine Journal*, 1937, p. 138
8 'George's Column', *The Sun*, 5 September 1946, p. 13, http://nla.gov.au/nla.news-article231587787
9 Wyatt, 1952, pp. 50, 57
10 'Lost on Mountain Side', *The Argus*, 26 March 1913, p. 6, http://nla.gov.au/nla.news-article10773848; 'Lost on Mountain', *The North Western Advocate and the Emu Bay Times*, 28 March 1913, p. 2, http://nla.gov.au/nla.news-article64916075
11 'Mountaineers Missing', *Northern Star*, 26 March 1913, p. 5, http://nla.gov.au/nla.news-article72404175
12 'Disaster In Snow', *The Daily News*, 1 November 1948, p. 1, http://nla.gov.au/nla.news-article80803303
13 'Mount Ruapehu', *Moree Gwydir Examiner and General Advertiser*, 9 November 1931, p. 3, http://nla.gov.au/nla.news-article111701519
14 Ibid., p. 51
15 'Ski Championship Postponed', *The Daily Telegraph*, 26 August 1936, p. 20
16 'Ski-ing in New Zealand', *Morning Bulletin*, 6 October 1936, p. 6, http://nla.gov.au/nla.news-article54978349
17 'Ruapehu Ski Club', *New Zealand Herald*, 31 August 1936, p. 3
18 Ibid.; 'Skiers' Ball', *Evening Post*, 1 September 1936, p. 15; 'Ruapehu Ski Club', *Wanganui Chronicle*, 2 September 1936, p. 2
19 Wyatt, 1955, p. 76
20 *Collage Featuring Drawings of Mountaineering and a Photograph of Robert and Anna Lendenfeld*, Haast family: Collection, Alexander Turnbull Library, Wellington, Ref: 1/2-C-047543-F
21 Bowie, 1969, p. 25
22 Ibid., p. 26
23 Wyatt, 1955, p. 62
24 Ibid., p. 54
25 Wyatt, 1952, p. 62
26 *New Zealand Alpine Journal*, 1937, p. 5
27 Wyatt, 1952, p. 64
28 Wyatt, 'Ski-Mountaineering in New Zealand', *Alpine Journal*, p. 87, Wyatt, 1952, p. 60
29 'And the World Said', *The Tatler*, 22 December 1937, p. 525
30 Ski Council of New South Wales, 'New Zealand Section: Editorial Notes', *The Australian and New Zealand Ski Book*, 1937, p. 151
31 Bowie, p. 53

32 Ski Council of New South Wales, 1937, p. 149
33 JGR Harding, 'Ski Mountaineering is Mountaineering …', *Alpine Journal*, 1998, p. 143
34 JGR Harding, 'Mountaineering Eden: The Southern Alps', *Alpine Journal*, 1991–92, p. 101
35 Wyatt, 1952, pp. 95–96
36 'Ski-Jumping', *The Sydney Morning Herald*, 14 December 1936, p. 13, http://nla.gov.au/nla.news-article17300171, Wyatt, 1955, p. 77
37 Wyatt, 1952, p. 84
38 Wyatt, 1955, p. xi
39 Robert Watson, *Queensland transcontinental railway: field notes and reports, with map showing positions of various camps*, 1883, W.H. Williams, Melbourne, pp. 47, 78
40 Ibid., p. 47
41 Ibid.
42 Ibid., p. 60; 'Overland to Point Parker', *The Brisbane Courier*, 12 May 1881, p. 3, http://nla.gov.au/nla.news-article920664
43 Wyatt, 1955, p. xi
44 Wyatt, 1955, p. 76

Chapter 8: The Flycatchers

1 Joseph Banks, *The Journal of Joseph Banks in the Endeavour*, Vol. 2, Genesis Publications, 1980, p. 276
2 Edward Smith, *The Life of Sir Joseph Banks*, John Lane, The Bodley Head, 1911, p. 6
3 Ibid., p. 7
4 Banks, p. 253
5 Gustavus Athol Waterhouse, 'The Biology and Taxonomy of the Australasian Butterflies', in *Report of the Australasian and New Zealand Association for the Advancement of Science*, Vol. 23, 1937, p. 3
6 Banks, p. 276
7 Ibid., p. 277
8 Grantlee Kieza, *Banks*, HarperCollins, 2021, p. 102
9 Hans Sloane, *A Voyage to the Islands Madera, Barbados, Nieves, S. Christophers and Jamaica*, 1725, p. lvii
10 Charlie Jarvis, Mark Spencer, and Robert Huxley, 'Sloane's Plant Specimens at the Natural History Museum', in Arthur MacGregor, Michael Hunter, and Alison Walker (eds), *From Books to Bezoars: Sir Hans Sloane and his collections*, The British Library, 2012, pp. 137–39
11 *Will of Sir Hans Sloane, Bart, Deceased*, John Virtuoso, London, 1753, p. 28

12 Harold B Carter, *Sir Joseph Banks, 1743–1820*, Natural History Museum, 1988, pp. 27–28
13 Daniel Solander to Carl Linnaeus, 1 December 1768, trans. Edward Duyker and Per Tingbrand, *Daniel Solander: collected correspondence 1753–1782*, Miegunyah Press, 1995, p. 181
14 Solander to Linnaeus, August 1768, ibid., p. 282
15 Kieza, pp. 88–90
16 *Secret Instructions to Lieutenant Cook*, 30 July 1768, https://www.foundingdocs.gov.au/resources/transcripts/nsw1_doc_1768.pdf
17 Joseph Banks, *The Journal of Joseph Banks in the Endeavour*, Vol. 1, Genesis Publications, 1980, p. 300
18 Banks, Vol. 2, 1980, pp. 22, 26
19 Ibid., p. 209
20 Ibid., p. 247
21 Ibid., pp. 248–49
22 Kieza, p. 235
23 Ibid., p. 236
24 Ibid., p. 417
25 Smith, p. 175
26 John E Clark, *Bugs and the Victorians*, Yale University Press, 2009, pp. 20–21
27 Carter, p. 164
28 Deidre Coleman, 'Insect Itineraries: from Sierra Leone, West Africa to Sydney, New South Wales', *Humanities Australia*, 2016, p. 51
29 Deidre Coleman, *Romantic Colonization and British Anti-Slavery*, 2005, Cambridge University Press, p. 29
30 Coleman, 2005, p. 33
31 Ibid., p. 34
32 Smith, p. 178
33 James Gillray *The Great South Sea Caterpillar, Transform'd into a Bath Butterfly*, etching published on 4 July 1795 by Hannah Humphrey
34 Waterhouse, 1937, p. 101
35 Waterhouse and Lyell, 1914, p. 1
36 Waterhouse, 1937, p. 102
37 Ibid.
38 Waterhouse to Lyell, 5 November 1936, MVA 00369
39 Ibid.

Chapter 9: The Scoundrels

1 Vanessa Finney, 'August 23, 1831 — shot with his own gun' (blog entry), *Australian Museum*, 23 August 2013, https://australian.museum/blog-archive/science/august-23-1831-accidentally-shot-with-his-own-gun/

2 Ronald Strahan, *Rare and Curious Specimens: an illustrated history of the Australian Museum, 1827–1979*, Offset Alpine Printing, 1979, p. 12
3 Ibid., p. 8
4 FrederickWatson (ed.), *Historical Records of Australia*, Series 1, Vol. 13, Library Committee of the Commonwealth Parliament, 1920, p. 210
5 Julian Holland, Peter Stanbury, and Julian Holland (eds), *Mr Macleay's Celebrated Cabinet: the history of the Macleays and their museum*, Macleay Museum, 1988, pp. 12, 17
6 Finney
7 Alan EJ Andrews (ed.), *Stapylton: With Major Mitchell's Australian Felix Expedition*, Blubber Head Press, 1986, p. 255
8 Ibid.
9 Ibid., p. 14
10 'Lines', *The Sydney Gazette and New South Wales Advertiser*, 10 March 1836, p. 4, http://nla.gov.au/nla.news-article2203161
11 Andrews, pp. 253–54
12 Ibid., p. 137–38, 222
13 Ibid., p. 114
14 Ibid., p. 200
15 Ibid., p. 222
16 Ibid., pp. 114, 147, 185
17 Ibid., p. 216
18 Ibid.
19 Ibid., p. 222
20 'Examination of John Matthew Richardson, before the Executive Council, 16th December, 1836', *The Sydney Monitor*, 27 January 1937, p. 3, http://nla.gov.au/nla.news-page4259545
21 'Domestic Intelligence', *The Sydney Times*, 14 January 1837, p. 2, http://nla.gov.au/nla.news-article252653407
22 Vivienne Parsons, 'Cunningham, Richard (1793–1835)', *Australian Dictionary of Biography*, National Centre of Biography, Australian National University, 1966, https://adb.anu.edu.au/biography/cunningham-richard-1943/text2329
23 'Major Mitchell's Expedition', *The Colonist*, 2 February 1837, p. 6, http://nla.gov.au/nla.news-page4247370
24 Thomas Mitchell, *Three Expeditions into the Interior of Eastern Australia*, Vol. 2, 1838, T and W Boone, accessed online: https://gutenberg.net.au/ebooks/e00036.html
25 *New South Wales Government Gazette*, 21 January 1837, p. 74, http://nla.gov.au/nla.news-article230669245
26 'Major Mitchell's Expedition', *The Colonist*, 2 February 1837, p. 6, http://nla.

gov.au/nla.news-article31719031
27 *The Sydney Gazette and New South Wales Advertiser*, 31 January 1837, p. 4, http://nla.gov.au/nla.news-article2209109
28 'Government Gazette Notices', *New South Wales Government Gazette*, 21 January, p. 59, http://nla.gov.au/nla.news-article230669245
29 *The Sydney Monitor*, 14 November 1836, p. 3
30 James William Wyatt, *Transcontinental Survey Expedition, Diary*, 1881 (unpublished)
31 Watson, 1883, p. 48
32 Ibid.
33 Andrews (ed), *Stapylton*, pp. 137–38
34 Australian Museum, *A Catalogue of the Specimens of Natural History and Miscellaneous Curiosities Deposited in the Australian Museum*, James Tegg, 1837, p. 5
35 Tom Iredale and GP Whitley, 'John Roach and the Budgerigar', *Australian Museum Magazine*, September 1962, pp. 99–101
36 'Sydney', *Geelong Advertiser*, 5 November 1847, p. 1, http://nla.gov.au/nla.news-article91457746

Chapter 10: The Honeymoon

1 Wyatt, 1952, pp. 85–86
2 Ibid., p. 88
3 Wyatt, 1955, p. 100
4 Ibid., p. 100
5 Ibid.
6 Wyatt, 1955, pp. 102–3
7 Wyatt, 1955, p. 32
8 Ibid., p. 36
9 Ibid., p. 37
10 Wyatt, 1955, pp. 102–3
11 Ibid., 1955, p. 105
12 *The Sketch*, 18 January 1939, p. 103
13 'Ski Champion Will Take Plunge', *Manchester Evening News*, 5 January 1939, p. 12
14 'Wyatt-Scott Barrett', *The Sutton and Cheam Advertiser*, 8 June 1939, p. 6
15 *The Tatler*, 14 June 1939, p. 475
16 'Life of Sydney', *The Daily Telegraph*, 20 December 1939, p. 10, http://nla.gov.au/nla.news-article247826341; 'Jottings of a Lady about Town', *Truth*, 26 May 1940, p. 37; *Truth*, 27 February 1944, p. 25; *The Daily Telegraph*, 18 February 1940, p 35
17 'On The Social Record', *The Australian Women's Weekly*, 14 June 1941, p. 35

18 Strutt, pp. 118–19
19 Mary Wyatt, 'The Threadbo and a Search Party', *Australian Ski Yearbook*, 1942, p. 52
20 Wyatt, 1955, p. 99
21 Ibid., pp. 94–95
22 Wyatt, 1944, p. 113
23 Wyatt, 1955, p. 93

Chapter 11: The Camoufleurs

1 William Dakin, 'Special Camouflage Methods at Bankstown and Aerodrome Laverton', *Professor Dakin's Camouflage Report (draft and notes)*, NAA C1908, Item 4, pp. 318–19
2 *Bankstown [aerodrome] — black & white camouflage photograph* [No. 3 Hideout. South side. Store & dwelling], NAA C1905/T1, Item 19
3 Ann Elias, *Camouflage Australia: art, nature, science and war*, 2011, Sydney University Press, p. 31
4 Colin Wyatt to Margaret Wyatt, 28 July 1942, quoted in *Security Service memo, 16200/239*, 11 August 1942, NAA C123 13956, p. 9
5 Max Dupain, *Max Dupain Diary Notes*, 18 April 1942, National Gallery of Australia MS93 Box 1, Folder 12, pp. 15–16
6 Ibid.
7 Wyatt, 28 July 1942, NAA C123 13956, p. 9
8 Wyatt, 1955, p. xii
9 Dupain, 27 October 1942, p. 25
10 'Dispenses Popular Science to Radio Listeners', *Smiths Weekly*, 30 August 1941, p. 4, http://nla.gov.au/nla.news-article234606404
11 'Canberra Wedding', *The Sydney Morning Herald*, 21 February 1934, p. 7, http://nla.gov.au/nla.news-article17071178; Armati, p. 92
12 Armati, pp. 87–88
13 Ibid.
14 Gerald H Thayer, *Concealing-Coloration in the Animal Kingdom*, Macmillan, 1909, pp. 62, 157, 213, 212
15 Richard Meryman, 'A Painter of Angels Became the Father of Camouflage', *Smithsonian Magazine*, April 1999, pp. 116–28
16 William J Dakin (ed.), *The Art of Camouflage*, 1941, Australasian Medical Publishing, 1941, p. 7
17 William Dakin, *A Short Report of the Work of the Camouflage Section, Department of Home Security, During the Period 1940–1944*, 1944, NAA C1908 2, p. 23
18 William Dakin, *A History of, and Report to the Development of Camouflage Research and Control in Australia During the War 1939/45 and in Particular*

the History of the Camouflage Organisation of the Commonwealth Department of Home Security, NAA C1908, 4, p. 6

19 *The Contemporary Arts Society Annual Exhibition 1940* catalogue, 1940, Powerhouse Museum, Object No 98/189/1-36/2
20 *Third Annual Exhibition of the Contemporary Art Society* catalogue, 1940, Powerhouse Museum Object No. 98/189/1-36/4 1941
21 Robert Emerson Curtis interviewed by Barbara Blackman, November 1986, National Library of Australia, NLA ORAL TRC 2125
22 'Letters', *The Sydney Morning Herald*, 16 October 1940, p. 7, http://nla.gov.au/nla.news-article17711624
23 'Contemporary Art', *The Sydney Morning Herald*, 18 October 1940, p. 5, http://nla.gov.au/nla.news-article27948907
24 'Art's the Thing, But Are These Things Art?', *Daily Mirror*, 9 September 1941, p. 6, http://nla.gov.au/nla.news-article271600700
25 'Pictures that startled Sydney', *The Daily Telegraph*, 21 September 1941, p. 2, http://nla.gov.au/nla.news-article247622204
26 Rex Rienits, 'Are These Things Art?', *Daily Mirror*, 9 September 1941, p. 6 http://nla.gov.au/nla.news-article271601232
27 'Startling Art Exhibition', *The Daily Telegraph*, 9 September 1941, p. 7, http://nla.gov.au/nla.news-article247630067
28 'Paintings of Three Lands', *The Daily Telegraph*, 24 September 1941, p. 7, http://nla.gov.au/nla.news-article247622692
29 'Colin Wyatt's Paintings', *The Sydney Morning Herald*, 24 September 1941, p. 8, http://nla.gov.au/nla.news-article17741040
30 'Australia Calling', *The ABC Weekly*, 9 November 1940, p. 9, http://nla.gov.au/nla.obj-1219672776
31 Dakin, 1942, p. 74
32 Dakin, *History of the Camouflage Organisation of the Commonwealth Department of Home Security*, p. 6
33 Elias, p. 31
34 William Dakin, *A Short Report of the Work of the Camouflage Section, Department of Home Security, During the Period 1940–1944*, NAA C1908 2, p. 40
35 *Wyatt, Colin William Fforde staff file*, Staff Register — Camouflage Section, NAA A691

Chapter 12: The Decoys

1 Wyatt, 1955, p. 123
2 'Paratroop Landing Closes Ring Round Lae', *The Mercury*, 8 September 1943, p. 2, http://nla.gov.au/nla.news-article25978953
3 Colin Wyatt, *Notes on New Guinea*, 1 March 1944, NAA A453, 1943/17/1510

pt 2, p. 4

4 Ibid., p. 2

5 Ibid., p. 3

6 Wyatt, 1955, pp. 122–23

7 Wyatt, 1955, p. 123

8 'Sketches of New Guinea', *The Sydney Morning Herald,* 15 March 1944, p. 10, http://nla.gov.au/nla.news-article17884564

9 Robert Emerson Curtis, *Colin Wyatt* (drawing), 1943, Australian War Memorial ART90428

10 Robert Emerson Curtis, *Goodenough Air Strip, Camoufleur Colin Wyatt* (drawing), 1943, Australian War Memorial ART28167.004

11 R. Emerson Curtis, *Camouflage in New Guinea Area,* 31 August 1943, NAA A453, 1943/17/1510 pt 1, p. 1

12 Ibid., p. 3

13 'Aggrieved over camouflage delay', *The Herald,* 23 December 1941, p. 6, http://nla.gov.au/nla.news-article245355004

14 William J Dakin, *Professor Dakin's Camouflage Report, [draft and notes],* NAA C1908, 5, p. 91

15 Ibid., p. 73

16 William J Dakin, *Professor Dakin's Camouflage Report [draft and notes],* NAA C1908, 4, p. 9

17 Ibid., p. 36

18 Elias, p. 105; William J. Dakin, *Professor Dakin's Camouflage Report [draft and notes],* NAA C1908, 5, p. 48

19 William Dakin, *Emergency Notes on the Concealment and Camouflage of Radio Installations — Specially Issued for RAAF,* June 1943, NAA C1909, 4, p. 14

20 *Wyatt, Colin William Fforde staff file,* Staff Register — Camouflage Section, NAA A691

21 Colin Wyatt, *Notes on New Guinea,* 1 March 1944, NAA A453, 1943/17/1510 Pt 2, 1943, p.1

22 Max Dupain interviewed by Hazel de Berg, 3 November 1975, National Library of Australia Hazel de Berg collection DeB 874

23 Wyatt, 1955, p. 133

24 Ibid., pp. 133, 139

25 Wyatt, 1 March 1944, p. 4

26 William J Dakin, *Professor Dakin's Camouflage Report [original, copy and notes],* NAA C1908, 2, p. 31

27 Dakin, *Professor Dakin's Camouflage Report (draft and notes),* p. 206

28 'Sterilise Unfit', *The Sun,* 18 August 1935, p. 7, http://nla.gov.au/nla.news-article231285130

29 Dakin, *Professor Dakin's Camouflage Report (draft and notes),* p. 206

30 A.J. Belot to M.S. Thomson 25 March 1944, NAA A453, 1943/17/1510, Part 2, p. 163
31 LE Castro to AW Welch, 21 February 1944, NAA A453/17/1510 pt 2, p. 294
32 Robert Emerson Curtis to William J Dakin, 23 March 1943, NAA A453 1943/17/1510 pt 2, p. 144
33 William Dakin to Frederick Shedden, 4 July 1944, NAA A5945, 396/2, p. 22
34 'Sketches of New Guinea', 15 March 1944, p. 10
35 Wyatt, 1955, p. 113
36 Ibid., pp. 113–14
37 Wyatt, 1955, p. 35; Gustavus Athol Waterhouse, 'The Small Cabbage White Butterfly', *The Australian Museum Magazine*, March 1941, p. 255
38 Wyatt, 1955, p. 125
39 Ibid., pp. 124–25
40 John Cecil Le Souëf, 'Death of Colin Wyatt', *The Victorian Entomologist,* August 1976, p. 32
41 Gustavus Athol Waterhouse, 'The Small Cabbage White Butterfly', *The Australian Museum Magazine*, March 1941, p. 255
42 Gustavus Athol Waterhouse, 'Butterflies Attracted by Brilliant Colours', *Australian Museum Magazine*, Vol. 7, No. 9, June 1941, pp. 323–24
43 Ibid., p. 323
44 Wyatt, 1955, p. 125
45 Gustavus Athol Waterhouse, 'Stolen Butterflies', *The Sydney Morning Herald,* 9 September 1947, p. 2

Chapter 13: The Loot

1 Herbert Hale to John Evans, 2 June 1947, SAMA AA 298/08
2 Herbert Hale to Arthur Walkom, 29 January 1947, AMA 33/1, pp. 1–2
3 Herbert Hale, *Report Re Theft of Specimens of Butterflies from the South Australian Museum Collection,* 1947, SAMA AA 298/08, p. 3
4 Hale to Evans, 2 June 1947
5 'Expert Advice on Museum', *The News,* 19 May 1938, p. 17, http://nla.gov.au/nla.news-article137470606
6 Herbert Hale, *Report Re Theft of Specimens*, p. 2
7 Ibid., p. 3
8 Ibid.
9 Norman B Tindale, *Map Showing the Distribution of the Aboriginal Tribes of Australia*, 1940
10 Hale to Walkom, 29 January 1947, p. 1, AMA 33/1
11 'Burglar Alarm Rings, *Chronicle*, 19 July 1934, p. 44, http://nla.gov.au/nla.news-article91066047
12 Herbert Hale, *The First Hundred Years of the South Australian*

Museum 1856–1956, The Museum Board, 1956, p. 73; 'The Robbery from the Adelaide Museum', *Evening Journal*, 27 November 1895, p. 2, http://nla.gov.au/nla.news-article198462654; 'Tried to Break into Museum', *The News*, 2 August 1934, p. 6, http://nla.gov.au/nla.news-article128845525; 'Safeguarding Gold Coins In Adelaide Museum', *Chronicle*, 27 April 1933, p. 29, http://nla.gov.au/nla.news-article90897628

13 'Theft From "Burglar-Proof" Sydney Museum', *Advocate*, 17 August 1935, p. 7, http://nla.gov.au/nla.news-article86542614

14 'Thief Escapes With Museum Gold', *The Daily Telegraph*, 17 August 1935, p. 1, http://nla.gov.au/nla.news-article246605276

15 'ALARM!', *Glen Innes Examiner*, 17 August 1935, p. 1, http://nla.gov.au/nla.news-article184609812; 'Thief Escapes With Museum Gold', 17 August 1935

16 'Theft From "Burglar-Proof" Sydney Museum', 17 August 1935

17 'Police Stop Raid on Museum Relics', *The Daily Telegraph*, 23 March 1934, p. 1, http://nla.gov.au/nla.news-article248961583

18 'Thief Escapes With Museum Gold', 17 August 1935

19 'Robbery at the Museum', *The Age*, 20 August 1886, p. 7, http://nla.gov.au/nla.news-article190847701

20 Ibid.

21 'Robberies from Public Buildings in Sydney and Melbourne', *The Sydney Morning Herald*, 26 August 1886, p. 5, http://nla.gov.au/nla.news-article13642856

22 Ibid.

23 Ibid.; 'Acts of Vandalism', *The Sydney Morning Herald*, 9 October 1886, p. 10, http://nla.gov.au/nla.news-article13616794

24 WD Webster to Edward Charles Stirling, 4 October 1898, SAM Archives, AA309/1/192

25 WD Webster to Edward Charles Stirling, 5 October 1898, SAM Archives AA309/1/195

26 Ibid.

27 'Treasures from Benin', *South Australian Register*, 15 December 1898, p. 5, http://nla.gov.au/nla.news-article56545077

28 'People Talked About', *The Mail*, 2 May 1914, p. 8, http://nla.gov.au/nla.news-page5285942

29 'The Governor on Nigeria', *The Register*, 18 July 1914, p. 10, http://nla.gov.au/nla.news-article56702397

30 Dan Hicks, *The Brutish Museums*, Pluto Press, 2020, p. 66

31 Hicks, p. 89

32 'The Governor on Nigeria', 18 July 1914

33 Hicks, p. 112

34 'The Governor on Nigeria', 18 July 1914
35 Hicks, p. 90
36 Edward Charles Stirling, *Professor Stirling Report on His Visit to Museums in America and Europe 1902*, 5 January 1902, SRSA GRG 19/399/7, p. 6
37 'Odds and Ends', *Evening Journal*, 21 October 1899, p. 5, http://nla.gov.au/nla.news-article207931870
38 'The Governor in Education Square', *The Register*, 9 May 1914, p. 14, http://nla.gov.au/nla.news-article59401138
39 Hale, p. 163
40 'A Greater Museum', *Daily Herald*, 9 December 1915, p. 3, http://nla.gov.au/nla.news-article124895192
41 'The Governor on Nigeria', 18 July 1914

Chapter 14: The Pride of the Empire

1 Superintendent of Cemeteries, *Memo Re Exhumation of Remains of the Aboriginal Tommy Walker, at West Terrace Cemetery*, 11 August 1903, SRSA RG38 57/0000, 000001
2 'Tommy Walker', *The Advertiser*, 18 August 1903, p. 5, http://nla.gov.au/nla.news-article4987131
3 'Aboriginal Philosophy', *Adelaide Observer*, 26 July 1890, p. 26, http://nla.gov.au/nla.news-article159550202
4 'The Late Tommy Walker', *Adelaide Observer*, 17 August 1901, p. 31, http://nla.gov.au/nla.news-article161777705
5 Superintendent of Cemeteries, 11 August 1903
6 *Evidence Taken by the Board of Inquiry into Charges Against Dr W Ramsay Smith*, 1903, SRSA GRG24/67, p. E5
7 Ibid., pp. C9–C10
8 'Tommy Walker', *Chronicle*, 22 August 1903, p. 33, http://nla.gov.au/nla.news-article87885898
9 *Evidence taken by the Board of Inquiry into Charges Against Dr W Ramsay Smith*, 1903, p. E4
10 Ibid.
11 Ibid.
12 Ibid., pp. E2–E3
13 Ibid., p. C5
14 Ibid., p. C4
15 Ibid., p. C5
16 Beth Robertson, 'Edward Stirling: embodiment and beneficiary of slave-ownership', *Australian Journal of Biography and History*, 2022, p. 82
17 'The South Australian Museum', *South Australian Weekly Chronicle*,

2 December 1882, p. 22, http://nla.gov.au/nla.news-article93129897

18 Ibid.

19 'Australian Mammals', *Australian Town and Country Journal*, 9 April 1898, p. 23, http://nla.gov.au/nla.news-article7128506

20 'The New Australian Marsupial Mole — Notoryctes typhlops', *Nature*, 10 September 1891, p. 449, https://www.nature.com/articles/044449a0

21 Ibid.

22 Paul Turnbull, 'A Judicious Collector: Edward Charles Stirling and the Procurement of Aboriginal Bodily Remains in South Australia, c. 1880–1912', *The Body Divided: human beings and human 'material'* in Sarah Ferber and Sally Wilde (ed.), *Modern Medical History*, Ashgate, 2011, p. 115

23 'The Science Congress', *The Advertiser*, 26 September 1893, p. 7

24 University Museum of Archaeology and Ethnology, Cambridge, to Edward Charles Stirling, July 1899, SAMA AA 309/1/209; G Brown Good to Arthur F Cate, 25 April 1895, SAMA AA 309/1/7

25 Franz Boas to Edward Charles Stirling, 15 April 1899, SAMA AA 309/1/210

26 Sir Hans Sloane, *Catalogue of Coralls, Sponges, and some other submarines*, The British Library, Department of Western Manuscripts, MS 3972 C 1–8, p. 277, https://enlightenmentarchitectures.reconstructingsloane.org/cataloguefossils1/index.html#doc=1&page=NHM-UK_L_433034_277

27 Neil Chambers (ed.), *The Letters of Sir Joseph Banks: a selection, 1768–1820*, Imperial College Press, 2000, p. 81

28 Cassandra Pybus, *A Very Secret Trade: the dark story of gentleman collectors in Tasmania*, 2024, Allen & Unwin, p. 79

29 Matthew Fishburn, 'The Field of Golgotha', *Meanjin*, Autumn 2017, https://meanjin.com.au/essays/the-field-of-golgotha/

30 Conan Doyle, 1902, p. 10

31 Ronald Elmslie and Susan Nance, 'Watson, Archibald (1849–1940)', *Australian Dictionary of Biography*, 1990, https://adb.anu.edu.au/biography/watson-archibald-8997/text15839.

32 Paul Turnbull, 'Science National Identity, and Aboriginal Body Snatching', *Working Papers in Australian Studies*, No. 65, 1991, p. 6

33 Paul Turnbull, 'Australian Museums, Aboriginal Skeletal Remains, and the Imagining of Human Evolutionary History, c. 1860–1914', *Museum and Society*, Vol. 13, No. 1, 2015, p. 82

34 'Exploring the Interior', *The West Australian*, 6 April 1909, p. 7, http://nla.gov.au/nla.news-article26224982

35 Ibid.

36 'Mr Hann's Headhunting', *The Argus*, 21 April 1909, p. 8, http://nla.gov.au/nla.news-article10681029

37 'Relics of the Blacks', *Adelaide Observer*, 15 October 1904, p. 34, http://nla.

gov.au/nla.news-article163056012
38 Robertson, p. 109
39 Ibid, p. 103
40 *Evidence taken by the Board of Inquiry into Charges Against Dr W Ramsay Smith*, 1903, p. A2
41 Steve Meacham, 'David Unaipon, the "Australian Leonardo", finally gets his due', *The Guardian*, 6 October 2018, https://www.theguardian.com/books/2018/oct/06/david-unaipon-the-australian-leonardo-finally-gets-his-due
42 Hale, 1956, p. 107
43 'Dr Ramsay Smith's Researches', *The Sydney Morning Herald*, 25 September 1903, p. 6, http://nla.gov.au/nla.news-article14562188
44 'The Late Sir Edward Stirling', *The Register*, 13 September 1922, p. 10, http://nla.gov.au/nla.news-article64133716
45 'Discovery by Young S.A. Scientists will be World Famous', 24 July 1930, p. 56, http://nla.gov.au/nla.news-article164798071
46 Hale, 1956, p. 152
47 Richard Pescott to Detective R Lickley, 11 January 1947, MVA P.B. 30/47
48 Richard Pescott, 17 April 1946, MVA P.B. 395/46
49 'The Chronicle's Examiner', *Launceston Examiner*, 16 April 1842, p. 4, http://nla.gov.au/nla.news-article36248120; William Thorpe, 'The Waterhouse Collections', *The Australian Museum Magazine*, Vol. 4, No. 4, October 1930, p. 114
50 'Our Front Cover', *The Australian Museum Magazine*, Vol. 9, No. 10, January 1949, pp. 322–23
51 Hale to Walkom, 29 January 1947, AMA 33/1
52 Ibid.
53 Herbert Hale, *Report Re Theft of Specimens*, February 1947, SAMA AA 298/08, p. 1
54 Robert Keble to George Mack, 31 January 1947, AMA 33/2
55 Alexander Burns to Richard Pescott, 29 January 1947, MVA 00238
56 Burns to Pescott, 1 February 1947, MVA 00238

Chapter 15: The Homecoming

1 Wyatt, 1955, p. 213
2 'Britain still in grip of snow and ice', *Coventry Evening Telegraph*, 29 January 1947, p. 1; 'Frost breaks 76-year record', *The Daily Telegraph*, 30 January 1947, p. 1; 'Power cuts "Grim" as cold snap holds', *The Bolton News*, 30 January 1947, p. 1
3 'Surrey Shivers in Wintry Week', *The Surrey Advertiser, County Times*, 1 February 1947, p. 5

4 Colin Wyatt to Erasmus 'Ras' Wilson, 28 January 1947, MVA 00238
5 'The Lesser Country Houses of Today', *Country Life*, 16 August 1919, pp. 225–27
6 Wyatt to Wilson, 28 January 1947, MVA 00238
7 Ibid.
8 Ibid.
9 'Wintry week-end in the borough', *The Surrey Mirror and County Post*, 31 January 1947, p. 5
10 Mungo MacCallum, 'National Circus: the Pro-British trend is here', *The Sun*, 19 September 1946, p. 4, http://nla.gov.au/nla.news-article231579425
11 Ibid.
12 'Women's Letters', *The Bulletin*, 27 October 1943, p. 25
13 'On and off Duty', *The Australian Women's Weekly*, 10 February 1945, p. 19, http://nla.gov.au/nla.news-article52258482
14 *Divorce Papers Colin William Fforde Wyatt–Mary Scott Wyatt*, State Records NSW AF00332507, p. 44
15 Ibid., p. 27
16 Ibid., p. 11
17 '… dramas of the courts', *The Daily Telegraph*, 24 November 1946, p. 37, http://nla.gov.au/nla.news-article248364796
18 *Divorce Papers Colin William Fforde Wyatt–Mary Scott Wyatt*, State Records NSW AF00332507, p. 4
19 Ibid., p. 26
20 'World Crackenback Snow', *Walkabout*, Vol. 30, No. 6, 1 June 1964, p. 2, http://nla.gov.au/nla.obj-755781202; 'Social', *Daily Mirror*, 29 July 1941, p. 13, http://nla.gov.au/nla.news-article271563945
21 *Divorce Papers Colin William Fforde Wyatt–Mary Scott Wyatt*, State Records NSW AF00332507, pp. 28–29
22 Helen Ennis, *Olive Cotton: a life in photography*, Fourth Estate, 2019, p. 233
23 Max Dupain, *Max Dupain Diary Notes*, 26 February 1942, National Gallery of Australia MS93 Box 1 Folder 12, p. 7
24 Max Dupain, *Max Dupain Diary Notess*, 17 February 1943, National Gallery of Australia MS93 Box 1 Folder 12, p. 31
25 Max Dupain, *Max Dupain Diary Notes*, 29 March 1943, National Gallery of Australia MS93 Box 1 Folder 12, p. 32
26 *Colin William Fford Wyatt — Application for Passport*, NAA SP42/2, C1946/3825, p. 4
27 'Artist on Top of the World', *PIX*, 4 January 1947, pp. 15–17
28 Wyatt, 1955, p. 175
29 Wyatt to Wilson, 28 January 1947

Chapter 16: The Australian

1 'Frost retains grip in east: Midlands warmer', *Coventry Evening Telegraph*, 25 January 1947, p. 1
2 'Power cuts "Grim" as cold snap holds', 30 January 1947; 'Snow and gales in Britain', *The Daily Telegraph*, 7 January 1947, p. 12; 'Thaw begins', *The Daily Telegra*ph, 1 February 1947, p. 6
3 'Thaw Begins', 1 February 1947; 'Thaw delayed: week-end of fog and gales', *Coventry Evening Telegraph*, 1 February 1947, p. 1
4 'Snowstorm holding up fuel transport', *Liverpool Daily Post*, 7 January 1947, p. 1; 'Frost breaks 76-year record', *The Daily Telegraph*, 30 January 1947, p. 1; 'Big Ben Cold', *The Daily Telegraph*, 29 January 1947, p. 6
5 'Power cuts "Grim" as cold snap holds', 30 January 1947, p. 1
6 Evans, 1989, p. 138–39
7 Ibid.
8 Ibid., p. 123
9 Ibid.
10 Ibid., p. 126
11 Ibid., p. 127
12 'Braved Jungle for Butterflies', *The News*, 4 April 1932, p. 5, http://nla.gov.au/nla.news-article129319740
13 Evans, 1989, p. 123
14 William Harry Evans, *My Knee*, private notebook, date unknown
15 Ibid., p. 127
16 Ibid., p. 1
17 Ibid., p. xi
18 Ibid., p. 7
19 'Spirit Who Whistled "God Save the King"', *The Evening Standard*, Saturday 18 August 1928, p. 10
20 Evans, 1989, p. 46
21 Robin J Tillyard, 'Evidence of Survival of a Human Personality', *Nature*, 18 August 1928, p. 245
22 Evans, 1989, p. 37
23 Ibid., p. 47
24 Ibid., p. 38
25 Ibid., p. 70
26 'Canberra Wedding', *The Sydney Morning Herald*, 21 February 1934, p. 7, http://nla.gov.au/nla.news-article17071178
27 Richard Pescott to John Evans, 24 January 1947, MVA 00238
28 Richard Pescott, *Notes Re Theft of Entomological Specimens, National Museum of Victoria 1946/47*, 23 January 1947, MVA 00238
29 Evans to Pescott, 24 January 1947, MVA 00238

Chapter 17: The Confrontation

1 Evans, 1989, p. 139
2 Walkom to Pescott, 22 January 1947, MVA VOL/355
3 Burns, 1947, p. 2
4 Leslie Mosse-Robinson to Alexander Burns, 15 January 1947, MVA VOL/355
5 Burns, 1947, p. 1
6 Arthur Walkom, *Thefts from Butterfly Collections in Melbourne and Sydney*, 27 February 1947, AMA
7 Pescott to Riley, 18 February 1947
8 'Museum to Recover Stolen Butterflies', *The Sunday Telegraph*, 25 May 1947, p. 1
9 Evans, 1989, p. 128–29
10 John Evans to Richard Pescott, 10 February 1947, AMA 33/2
11 Pescott to Walkom, 26 January 1947 AMA 33/1
12 Pescott to Evans, 28 January 1947, AMA 33/2
13 Evans to Pescott, 29 January 1947, AMA 33/2
14 Ibid.
15 Walkom to Evans, 24 January 1947, AMA 33/1
16 Evans to Pescott, 1 February 1947, AMA 33/2
17 'Obituary: Norman Denbigh Riley (1890–1979)', *Entomologists Record*, 1980, pp. 19–22, https://archive.org/details/biostor-187282/mode/2up
18 Pescott to Secretary, Museums Association of Great Britain, 24 January 1947, MVA 00238
19 Evans to Pescott, 1 February 1947 AMA 33/2
20 Pescott to Evans, 28 January 1947
21 West Ham Magistrates Court transcript, Case: Colin William Wyatt, 21 May 1947, SAMA AA 298/08, p. 2
22 Ibid.
23 Evans to Pescott, 24 January 1947, MVA 00238
24 F Cameron, *Central Officer's Special Report: larceny of butterflies,* 1 April 1947, SAMA AA 298/08, p. 2
25 West Ham Magistrates Court transcript, 21 May 1947
26 Ibid., pp. 2–3
27 Ibid., p. 3
28 Evans to Pescott, 25 January 1947, MVA 00238

Chapter 18: The Dossier

1 *Report on Wyatt, Colin*, Intelligence Section, Eastern Command, 15 January 1942, NAA C123, 13956, p. 26
2 Ibid.

3 'Adventure in Butterfly Hunt', *The Herald*, 19 April 1932, p. 6, http://nla.gov.au/nla.news-article242791951
4 John Evans, 1989, p. 53
5 GA Waterhouse, 'Australian Hesperiidae II: notes and descriptions of new forms', *Proceedings of the Linnean Society of New South Wales*, July 1932, p. 218, https://www.biodiversitylibrary.org/page/34961802#page/260/mode/1up; GA Waterhouse, 'Notes on the Type Specimens of Hesperiidae (Lepidoptera) in the Museums in Australia with Special Reference to Those in the South Australian Museum', *Records of the South Australian Museum*, 1933, p, 49, https://www.biodiversitylibrary.org/page/40996853#page/50/mode/1up
6 *Report on Wyatt, Colin*, 1942
7 Ibid., p. 27
8 Ibid., p. 28
9 *Police Report on Antecedents of Colin WYATT, of "Pomeroy", 14 Macleay Street, Potts Point*, NAA C123, 13956, p. 37
10 'New Use for Troops', *Taranaki Daily News*, 16 October 1936, p. 9
11 Ibid.
12 *Report on Wyatt—Alleged B.B.C. Broadcaster on Ski-ing in Norway and Sweden*, 10 June 1941, NAA C123, 13956, p. 32
13 *Report on Wyatt—Alleged B.B.C. Broadcaster on Sli-ing* [sic] *in Norway and Sweden*, 18 June 1941, NAA C123, 13956, p. 31
14 BH Kirke, *Memoraandum re Colin Wyatt*, Australian Broadcasting Commission, 4 May 1937, NAA SP173/1, p. 4
15 CC Wicks, *Memo re Colin Wyatt—Yodeller and Accordoon Player*, Australian Broadcasting Commission, 16 June 1937, NAA SP173/1, p. 2
16 C Charlton, *Memo re Colin Wyatt, Yodeller*, Australian Broadcasting Commission, 20 May 1937, NAA SP173/1, p. 3
17 AN Finlay, *Memo re Colin Wyatt*, Australian Broadcasting Commission, 0 March 1937, NAA SP173/1, p. 8
18 *Copy of report re Wyatt, Colin*, NAA C123, 13956, pp. 22–23
19 *Memorandum re Scrutiny of Colin Wyatt*, NAA C123, 13956, p. 24
20 Norman D Riley to Gustavus Athol Waterhouse (copy), 13 January 1942, AMA 33/1
21 Norman D Riley to Major EE Austen, *Loss and Recovery of Butterflies Belonging to the Genus Parnassius*, 29 April 1930, BNHM DF/ENT/332/9/6, p. 1
22 'Mr Colin Wyatt's Accident', *The Daily Telegraph* (London), 27 January 1930, p. 10
23 Riley to Austen, 29 April 1930, p. 2
24 Riley to Waterhouse (copy), 13 January 1942

25 Ibid.
26 *Security Service Report re: Colin Wyatt*, 2 July 1942, NAA C123, 13956, p. 10
27 Colin Wyatt to Margaret Wyatt, 28 July 1942, quoted in *Security Service memo, 16200/239*, 11 August 1942, NAA C123 13956, p. 9
28 *Report re: Wyatt Colin*, 31 January 1943, NAA C123 13956, p. 2
29 Riley to Waterhouse, 13 January 1942

Chapter 19: The Evidence

1 Harry Procter, 'Butterfly mystery: police seek help', *The Daily Mail*, 17 February 1947, p. 1
2 Evans to Pescott, 17 February 1947
3 Ibid.
4 Pescott to Riley, 18 February 1947
5 Burns to Lyell, 7 February 1947, MVA 00238, P.B. 114/47
6 Pescott to Evans, 18 February 1947, MVA
7 'Butterfly Chase Traverses World', *The Courier-Mail*, 18 February 1947, p. 5, http://nla.gov.au/nla.news-article49352759
8 '"Butterfly" Case: police say ski champ can help', *The Newcastle Sun*, 17 February 1947, p. 2, http://nla.gov.au/nla.news-article158248530
9 'The Long Arm of Scotland Yard', *Barrier Daily Truth*, 17 February 1947, p. 1, http://nla.gov.au/nla.news-article141115922
10 Ibid.
11 Herbert Hale to Chairman, Museum Board, 12 February 1947, SAMA AA 298/08
12 Colin Wyatt, 'Butterfly Immigrants Overrun Nation', *The ABC Weekly*, 25 January 1947, p, 24, http://nla.gov.au/nla.obj-1323798086
13 Hale, 12 February 1947
14 'No Arrest of Butterfly Theft Suspect Likely', *The Sun News-Pictorial*, 17 February 1947, p. 8
15 Evans to Pescott, 2 February 1947, AMA 33/2
16 Riley to Walkom, 25 February 1947, MVA 00238
17 Mack to Walkom, 5 February 1947, AMA 33/1
18 John Evans, *Butterflies Alleged to Have Been Stolen from Australian Museums* (copy), 17 February 1947, SAMA AA 298/08, p. 1
19 Ibid., p. 2
20 John Evans, *Appendix to Statement of J.W. Evans, to Accompany Exhibit* (copy), 17 February 1947, SAMA AA 298/08, p. 1
21 John Evans, *Butterflies alleged to have been stolen from Australian Museums* (copy), 17 February 1947, SAMA AA 298/08, p. 2
22 *List of Specimens of Australian Butterflies Stolen from Collections of*

National Museum, Melbourne, December 1946, MVA 00238, pp. 6–7
23 Ibid., p. 4
24 Evans to Pescott, 17 February 1947, SAMA AA 298/08, p. 1

Chapter 20: The Plea

1 'Robbed the Blind', *Evening Standard*, 31 January 1931, p. 24
2 'Three Members of Rolling Stones Fined', *Liverpool Echo*, 22 July 1965, p. 3
3 John W Evans to Herbert Hale, 21 May 1947, SAMA AA 298/08
4 Ibid.
5 Evans to Pescott, 17 February 1947, SAMA AA 298/08
6 Herbert Hale, *Report to Chairman and Museum Board*, 12 February 1947, SAMA AA 298/08
7 Evans to Pescott, 14 March 1947, MVA 00238
8 William Harry Evans to Arthur Walkom, 11 June 1947, AMA 33/1
9 West Ham Magistrates Court transcript, Case: Colin William Wyatt, 21 May 1947, SAMA AA 298/08, p. 1
10 Larceny Act, 1916, legislation.gov.uk/ukpga/1916/50/pdfs/ukpga_19160050_en.pdf
11 West Ham Magistrates Court transcript, 21 May 1947, p. 2
12 Ibid., pp. 3–4
13 Ibid., p. 4
14 'Famous Counsel to Defend Ley', *The Daily Telegraph*, 15 February 1947, p. 2
15 'Ley Had Promised To "Befriend Mrs Brook"; Wife Reveals Story', *Barrier Miner*, 26 March 1947, p. 1, http://nla.gov.au/nla.news-article48492946
16 'Chalkpit Murder: Ley insane', *Coventry Evening Telegraph*, 6 May 1947, p. 3
17 West Ham Magistrates Court transcript, 21 May 1947, p. 4
18 Ibid., pp. 4–5
19 Ibid., p. 5
20 Ibid., p. 6
21 John W Evans to Herbert Hale, 21 May 1947, SAMA AA 298/08
22 West Ham Magistrates Court transcript, 21 May 1947, p. 6
23 Evans to Hale, 21 May 1947

Chapter 21: The Superman

1 'The Strange Case of the Stolen Butterflies', *The Sydney Morning Herald*, 6 September 1947, p. 2, http://nla.gov.au/nla.news-article27896277
2 Leigh Purcell, author interview, 2024
3 Musgrave, 1947, p. 1
4 Purcell, author interview, 2024

5 Pescott to Evans, 7 July 1947, MVA 00238, P.B. 754/47
6 Walkom to Pescott, 2 June 1947, MVA 00238
7 Alexander Burns, *Report of Visit to Adelaide to Recover Specimens of Butterflies Stolen from the National Museum, Aug 18 to 28 1947,* August 1947, MVA 00238
8 Wyatt to Le Souëf, August 1946, cited in Peter Andrews, 'Colin Wyatt Going Wild: butterfly collecting in Australia', *The Insect Collectors' Forum*, 30 September 2016
9 Walkom to Pescott, 2 June 1947, MVA 00238
10 Burns, August 1947
11 Riley to Walkom, 19 June 1947, AMA 33/1, p. 2
12 Ibid.
13 Musgrave, 1947, p. 2
14 Tindale to Hale, 15 September 1947, SAMA AA 298/08
15 Burns, 1947, p. 1
16 Ibid., pp. 1–2
17 Evans to Hale, 21 May 1947, SAMA AA 298/08
18 Evans to Hale, 13 June 1947, SAMA AA 298/08
19 Hale to Evans, 24 June 1947, SAMA AA 298/08
20 Burns, August 1947, p. 3
21 Ibid.
22 Tindale to Hale, 15 September 1947, SAMA AA 298/08
23 Musgrave, 1947, p. 2
24 'The Strange Case of the Stolen Butterflies', 6 September 1947
25 Anonymous, *Extract from a Letter Received by A.N. Burns Re G. Purcell,* 15 September 1947, MVA 00238

Chapter 22: The Dirty Work

1 'The Strange Case of the Stolen Butterflies', 6 September 1947
2 Waterhouse, '9 September 1947
3 Ibid.
4 Musgrave, 1947, p. 2
5 Anthony Musgrave to Gustavus Athol Waterhouse, 22 September 1947, AMA 33/2
6 Gustavus Athol Waterhouse, *Re Memoranda 20 to 28 August on Stolen Butterflies*, date unknown, SAMA AA 298/08
7 Pescott to Hale, 10 October 1947, SAMA AA 298/08
8 Ibid.
9 Waterhouse to Lyell, 20 September 1947, MVA 00373
10 Waterhouse to Lyell, 30 September 1947, MVA 00373
11 Ibid.

12 Waterhouse to Lyell, 20 September 1947
13 Lyell to Waterhouse, 29 October 1947, cited in John Tennent, Chris J Muller, Axel Hausmann, and Simon Hinkley, 'From München to Melbourne: repatriation of a butterfly holotype stolen by the infamous Colin Wyatt almost 80 years ago', *The Australian Entomologist*, Vol. 51, No. 1, April 2024, p. 47
14 Rushworth, 2016, p. 33
15 Arthur Walkom, 'Gustavus Athol Waterhouse', *The Australian Museum Magazine*, 15 September 1950, pp. 78–79
16 JC Benson to Richard Pescott, 10 May 1951, cited in Nik McGrath, 'The sting of the final letter' (blog entry), Museums Victoria, https://museumsvictoria.com.au/article/the-sting-of-the-final-letter/
17 'Death Of Noted Naturalist', *The Herald*, 19 May 1951, p. 5, http://nla.gov.au/nla.news-article246265843
18 Ibid.
19 Evans to Walkom, 17 December 1947, AMA 33/2
20 Evans, 1989, p. 173
21 Musgrave, 'Vale—Nancy B. Adams', *The Australian Museum Magazine*, 15 June 1955, p. 325
22 Evans, 1989, p. 171
23 'For the love of Lepidoptera', *Time*, 2 June 1947
24 Evans to Hale, 21 May 1947, SAMA AA 298/08

Chapter 23: The Pilgrim

1 'Dalai Lama, "Living Buddha," Arrives in Indian Capital', *Abilene Reporter-News*, 26 November 1956, p. 5
2 Lowell Thomas Jr, *The Dalai Lama: a biography of the exiled leader of Tibet*, Duell, Sloan and Pearce, 1961, pp.14–16
3 Vincent Mulchrone, 'Crime, punishment, and the gentlest judge of all', *Daily Mail*, 21 January 1976, p. 26
4 Paul Tanfield, 'Gen on Zen', *Daily Mail*, 22 September 1960, p. 20
5 Christmas Humphreys, 'Two International Conferences', *The Middle Way*, Vol. 31, No. 4, February 1957, p. 159
6 William Drury, *Honolulu Star-Bulletin*, 1 January 1960, p. 3
7 Colin Wyatt, 'Buddhism and the West', *United Asia*, date unknown, p. 76
8 Ibid.
9 'The Explorer made welcome. Colin Wyatt with his host, the Lama Tulku of Thyanboche and the Monastery's Chief Monk', *The Middle Way*, Vol. 33, No. 3, November 1958, p. 93
10 Colin Wyatt, 'Satipatthana Meditation Centres in Burma', *The Middle Way*, Vol. 33, No. 3, November 1958, pp. 102–5, 124

11 Ibid., p. 124
12 Ibid., p. 104
13 Ibid., p. 102
14 Wyatt, 1952, pp. 9, 13
15 Ibid., p. 72
16 Pam Rutherford Darling, 'Living in London', *The Daily Telegraph*, 12 April 1953, p. 28, http://nla.gov.au/nla.news-article248855932
17 Wyatt, 1955, pp. 110–11
18 Wyatt, 1958, pp. 38, 86
19 Ibid., p. 95
20 Ibid., p. 99
21 Ibid., pp. 147–48
22 Drury, 1960
23 Wyatt, 1958, pp. 104–5
24 Ibid., pp. 47–48
25 Wyatt, 1955, p. 11
26 'She called Judge a "perfect dear"', *Daily Mail*, 30 October 1948, p. 3
27 'The Lonely Woman Asked Author Round To Talk of Lapland', *Daily Mirror*, 19 October 1948, p. 1
28 'I need five minutes says Portia No 1', *Daily Express*, 29 Octobe 1948, p. 3
29 'She called Judge a "perfect dear"', 30 October 1948
30 'Miss McKechnie's Visit', *Melton Mowbray Times*, 14 January 1949, p. 6
31 'Land of the Midnight Sun', *Esher News and Advertiser*, 4 December 1953, p. 5
32 Christmas Humphreys, *Buddhism* 3rd edition, Pelican Books, 1962, p. 74

Chapter 24: The Exile

1 Colin Wyatt and Kei-ichi Omoto, 'Auf der Jagd nach Parnassius autocrator Avin', *Zeitschrift der Wiener Entomologischen Gesellschaft*, Vol. 48, 1963, pp. 163–70, https://www.zobodat.at/pdf/ZOEV_48_0163-0170.pdf
2 Colin Wyatt, 'Hunting for the Autocrat', *Country Life*, 24 November 1960, pp. 1220–21
3 Ibid.
4 Colin Wyatt, 'Unvergeßliche Erlebnisse', *Zeitschrift der Wiener Entomologischen Gesellschaft*, Vol. 68, No. 4, 15 April 1957, pp. 49–53
5 Wyatt, 24 November 1960
6 Phillip R Ackery to Colin Wyatt, 9 October 1973, BNHM DF/ENT/332/9/6, p. 6
7 Colin Wyatt to Phillip R Ackery, 2 October 1973, BNHM DF/ENT/332/9/6, pp. 7–9
8 Dick Collier, 'Traveler Tells of "Hidden Kingdom"', *Mansfield News-Journal*, 29 March 1962, p. 13

9 'Memorial Hospital Guild Presenting Colin Wyatt's Exciting Film on Nepal', *The Sandusky Register*, 1 March 1962, p. 21
10 William Drury, *Honolulu Star-Bulletin*, 1 January 1960, p. 3
11 Edmund Hillary, *Nothing Venture, Nothing Win*, 1976, Hodder & Stoughton, pp. 236–40
12 'Mountaineer to Show Film of Nepal, Everest', *Honolulu Advertiser*, 31 December 1959, p. 9
13 Collier, 1962, p. 13
14 Wyatt, 1952, p. 95
15 Wyatt, 1955, p. 53
16 Monica Wyatt, author interview, 2024
17 'Canadian banned after collision with Jaguar', *The Advertiser* (Guildford and Godalming), 24 December 1963, p. 7
18 Richard Pescott to Norman D Riley, 14 December 1951, MVA 00238
19 Riley to Pescott, 22 December 1951, MVA 00238
20 Janine Sadoch, 'Paris Cops Hunt Insect Thief; (Wanna Buy a Hot Butterfly?)', *Sunday News*, 13 March 1949, p. 4
21 Stephen White, 'Thieves Pick 20,000 Butterflies Worth $70,000 Out of a Million', *The Boston Globe*, 10 February 1949, p. 17
22 Ibid.
23 Janine Sadoch, 'Psst, Bud! Wanna Buy Some Hot Butterflies?', *Daily News*, 20 March 1949, p. 84; Henry Wales, 'Lepidoptera Mystery Has Paris Aflutter', *Chicago Tribune*, 7 February 1949, p. 1; 'Faits Divers', *Le Monde*, 9 February 1949
24 Henry Wales, '20,000 Choice Butterflies Values at $100,000 Stolen', *Buffalo Courier Express*, 6 February 1949, p. 10
25 Janine Sadoch, 'Psst, Bud! Wanna Buy Some Hot Butterflies?', *Daily News*, 20 March 1949, p. 84; Henry Wales, 'Lepidoptera Mystery Has Paris Aflutter', *Chicago Tribune*, 7 February 1949, p. 1; 'Faits Divers', *Le Monde*, 9 February 1949
26 'Butterfly Burglars', *The Miami Herald*, 8 May 1949, p. 22
27 Ibid.
28 Roberth Fothergill, 'Police Net Out But Still Empty', *Ottawa Journal*, 22 February 1962, p. 1; 'Police Net Out for Bug Bandit', *The Ottawa Citizen*, 24 February 1962, p. 17
29 'Butterflies Stolen', *The Kingston Whig-Standard*, 22 February 1962, p. 30; 'Thief Gets Butterflies', *The Windsor Star*, 22 February 1962, p. 4
30 Robrth Fothergill, 22 February 1962, p. 5; Ian MacLeod, 'Handcuffed: Bizarre cases that baffled the police', *The Ottawa Citizen*, 2 January 1988, p. 80
31 'Bug Lovers' Free Masonry', *The Ottawa Citizen*, 5 July 1952, p. 15

32 Alexander B Klots, 'Thoughts on Museums, Collections and Collectors,' Presidential Address to the Eighth Annual Meeting of the Lepidopterists' Society, *The Lepidopterists' News*, Vol. 12, No. 1, 1958, p. 3
33 Wyatt to Ackery, 2 October 1973, BNHM DF/ENT/332/9/6, pp. 7–9
34 Monica Wyatt, author interview, 2024
35 Wyatt, 1955, p. 101
36 Monica Wyatt, author interview, 2024
37 Morley, p. 292
38 Malcolm N Carter, 'Tourists Discovering Guatemala', *The Register* (Danville), 10 April 1975, p. 4

Chapter 25: The Overture

1 Monica Wyatt, author interview, 2024
2 Ibid.
3 Christmas Humphreys, 'Colin Wyatt', *The Middle Way*, Vol. 1, No. 4, February 1976, p. 193
4 Monica Wyatt, 14 May 2023, The Insect Collectors Forum [https://collector-secret.proboards.com/thread/1241/colin-wyatt-butterfly-collecting-australia?page=2/]]
5 'The Genus Ogyris', *Kojonup Courier*, 24 April 1958, p. 7
6 Wyatt to Ackery, 2 October 1973, BNHM DF/ENT/332/9/6, pp. 7–9
7 Otakar Kudrna, 'An Annotated List of the Butterflies Named by Colin W. Wyatt (Lepidoptera: Papilionoidea, Hesperioidea)', *Bonn zoological Bulletin—früher Bonner Zoologische Beiträge*, 1981, p. 235
8 Kudrna, p. 222
9 Le Souëf, p. 32

Epilogue: The Lost Holotypes

1 Braby, author interview, 2024
2 Burns, 6 October 1947
3 Waterhouse to Lyell, 30 September 1947, MVA 00373
4 John Tennent, Chris J Muller, Axel Hausmann, and Simon Hinkley, 'From München to Melbourne: Repatriation of a butterfly Holotype stolen by the infamous Colin Wyatt almost 80 years ago', *The Australian Entomologist*, Vol. 51, No. 1, April 2024, pp. 43–54
5 Ibid., p. 51
6 Harry Saddler, '"A 99.5% decline": what caused Australia's bogong moth catastrophe?', *The Guardian*, 18 December 2021, https://www.theguardian.com/environment/2021/dec/18/a-995-decline-what-caused-australias-bogong-moth-catastrophe
7 Braby, 2024

8 Shannon Faulkhead and Jim Berg, *The Power and the Passion: our ancestors return home,* Museums Victoria Publishing, 2022, pp. 48–49, 70–71, 73, 77

9 Cressida Fforde, *Collecting the Dead: archaeology and the reburial issue,* Bloomsbury, 2004, p. 126

10 'First Aboriginal remains to be returned from U.S.', *Reuters*, 26 July 2008, https://www.reuters.com/article/world/first-aboriginal-remains-to-be-returned-from-u-sidUSSP219996/

11 Katy Prickett, 'Cambridge college returns 18th Century Aboriginal spears', *BBC News*, 23 April 2024, bbc.com/news/uk-england-cambridgeshire-68875158

12 Major Moogy Sumner, author interview, 2024

13 Hew Locke, *What Have We Here?,* The British Museum, October 2024–February 2025

14 Evans, 1989, p. 44

15 Wyatt, 1952, pp. 85–86

16 'Art in London', *The Scotsman*, 28 November 1934, p. 13

Index